POLEMIC FOR DEMOCRACY

ZANE GUSTAFSON

PUBLISHED BY

Impolitik LLC, Seattle, WA

PRODUCTION TEAM

Trish Beaulieu, Literary Agent, book division manager, and editor;
Nancy Ratkiewich, book production, njr productions;
Zane Gustafson, author photographer;
Julia H. Siltzer, cartoonist.

For general information on other products and services, use polemicfordemocracy@gmail.com.

ISBN: 979-8-9912286-2-6 Paperback
ISBN: 979-8-9912286-1-9 eBook

Printed in the United States of America

10 9 8 7 6 5 4 3 2 1

to Mom and Dad
for the Opportunity

TABLE OF CONTENTS

PREFACE

This book might be too late.

I started writing in February 2023 after years of obsessing over American political dysfunction. And after a year and a half of writing this polemic, my opinion of the state of American democracy and American society is largely unchanged. The structural problems that existed then have only grown more obvious and more intractable.

Three events this past summer epitomize the state of play in American politics:

1. Joe Biden's disastrous debate performance and the Democratic Party's internecine conflict about whether and how to replace him.

2. The Supreme Court's series of rulings which pave the way for further consolidation of power within the Executive Branch.

3. An unsuccessful assassination attempt on Donald Trump making political violence a reality and escalation a real possibility.

In response to the structural forces behind these events, this book makes two arguments. First, it argues a Constitutional Convention is the least violent path available to us. Second, it argues for a specific suite of structural constitutional reforms designed to address our present systemic dysfunction.

Events are moving quickly, and it feels like things are accelerating. The paradigm in which this book was written and published may soon be made irrelevant.

But the questions interrogated here go to the core of what it means to be an American and what it means to be invested in the idea of democratic self-governance.

More than anything else, this is a book of political philosophy and, by definition, imperfect. It is my best attempt at coherent political thought in an era of anything but.

This is my country and yours, and together we shall determine our future.

We truly live in interesting times. The 2024 election is here, and only God could know what may happen next.

Zane Gustafson

October 2024

Seattle, WA

PART ONE

FRAMEWORK

JUSTIFICATION

Our country is sick.

Is anyone in America happy with our political system? Every year, our culture war deepens, and our politics take another turn down the vicious cycle of dysfunction.

The structure of our government is the root cause of our political dysfunction: an unrepresentative Legislature stymied by two-party hyper-partisan gridlock; an Executive, elected by an archaic mechanism, gobbling up the power left in the vacuum of decades of Legislative inaction; and a Judiciary losing credibility with the public due to blatant corruption and its weaponization of its authority by partisan judges for their partisan ends.

Our Constitution is failing us. It's time to change it.

We pride ourselves on being the leader of the democratic world, yet by today's standards America is a deficient democracy. And if democracy means equal representation—one person one vote—we have never been a democracy, and we never will be unless and until we address the fundamental contradictions of our founding documents, the Declaration[1] and Constitution.[2]

In the first, we declare it a self-evident truth that "All [humans] are created equal." But in the second, we undermine our declaration by implementing profoundly undemocratic structures of government. These anti-democratic structures of our government were and are intentional, and have worked and continue to work as intended. The early United States was built on the backs of millions of enslaved people, and slavery as an institution was ended only after four years of the bloody Civil War. Part of the reason slavery lasted as long as it did was due to the power of the undemocratic Senate and an unrepresentative House, which granted additional voting power not just to small states but to the enslavers specifically. Slavery is over, but the Senate endures.

The structure of our Constitution limits our government from upholding our inalienable rights of life, liberty, and the pursuit of happiness: it is failing us on climate and migration, it is failing to defend our human rights, and it is failing us on affordable housing while saddling us with medical and student debt. So, in the language of the Declaration, "whenever any Form of Government becomes destructive of [certain unalienable Rights], it is the Right of the People to alter or to abolish it, and to institute new Government . . . "

We can and should build upon the Framers' Constitution, but only insofar as we deem it worthy, relevant, useful, and fair by our standards today. The Framers brilliantly devised a novel system of government. But they are not gods. Their words are not commandments; their government is imperfect. They themselves knew this. As Thomas Jefferson said,[3] "No society can make a perpetual constitution . . . The constitution and the laws of their predecessors extinguished then in their natural course with those who gave them being . . . If it be enforced longer, it is an act of force, and not of right." To change the Constitution is forever our right.

In this book, I propose structural reforms to the Constitution to implement a government that tries to live up to that self-evident truth that all humans are created equal. I modeled these reforms by redrawing every Congressional district and found that, with a new system, over three-quarters of Americans would get to vote in a competitive Congressional district, far better than the current 10% of Americans who will have the opportunity to vote in a competitive district in 2024. With so many competitive elections, new parties, with new ideas, would gain representation in Congress. The two-party establishment would be forced to adapt or die. And rebalancing the checks between our three branches of government would usher in a new era of American democracy. An era of political stability and less economically disruptive civil strife.

The powers that be will not like these reforms. But after January 6th and with the 2024 election upon us, America's political status quo is untenable. As of December 2023, 72% of Americans[4] were dissatisfied with the working of American democracy! People speak openly of civil war! Disillusionment and cynicism permeate every corner of our politics, and for good reason. I believe the antidote to our political cynicism, if there is any, is a positive and realistic vision of what our government could be.

This book attempts to describe such a vision.

Chapter 2

CYNICISM

Your cynicism regarding the feasibility of actually changing our political system is justified. Your cynicism regarding anyone who purports to have a solution to our problems is also justified, including your cynicism of these very words. I know this because I am you.

My name is Zane. I am from Washington State. I was born in 1992. And over the course of my 32 years I have witnessed our government decline, becoming only more and more dysfunctional.

My earliest political memories are of jokes about the scandalous Clinton impeachment. Then came the 2000 presidential election, in which the winner received fewer votes than the loser. From my childhood perspective, such an outcome was absurd. Ever since, it has been one cataclysmic event after the next: 9/11 and its wars, the Great Recession, the vitriolic 2016 election, and the pandemic.

Around these events, our political discourse moved online to social media and, growing every year more poisonous, split families and ended friendships. With the depth of our political vitriol, has not the past decade felt like a Cold Civil War?

The depth of my cynicism toward the entire American political system cannot be overstated. The people with power—the political, financial, and cultural elite —benefit from the sclerotic status quo. They choose (you choose!) to keep our politics stagnant. With such broken politics, who could blame the **30% of eligible Americans**[5] who chose not to vote in 2018, 2020, or 2022? Our collective political cynicism is like a black hole that absorbs not light but hope, leaving us with only despair.

If you are reading this, it is probably because you are an American and you are fed up with our politics. That is why I am writing this. I have worked in or adjacent to politics for close to a decade, and I am beyond tired. Exhausted. Beaten down by the endless, 24/7 news cycle. And maddened by the regular revelations of more corruption and dysfunction. It is enraging.

Given the choice of the candidates nominated by our two major parties, I understand why some people choose to vote for Robert F. Kennedy, Jr., or not vote at all.

You may be wondering about my political views. At the risk of alienating some readers, I will say that my views on most issues are firmly to the left (at least to the extent that left-right is a useful way to define one's political views). I used to identify as a Democrat but have grown disillusioned by their political ineptitude. I will be voting for whoever the Democrats nominate in 2024, but I am far from happy about it. And while I genuinely believe that Donald Trump is an existential threat to American democracy, his appeal to tens of millions of Americans is understandable. His appeal is a symptom of our systemic dysfunction!

We need new political parties to choose from. But for that, we need a voting system that allows multiple parties to win representation in Congress.

This is where it would be standard to shift to a more hopeful or optimistic tone. Some inspiring rhetoric about how we can fix our problems if we can just come together. Or how simply through voting, we can make the change we want to see. But I am not optimistic, and the extent of my hope is fleeting.

Our system is rigged. Voting is necessary but not sufficient. Our democracy is so gerrymandered and divided against itself that "democracy" feels an inappropriate classification. Anything less than structural change is insufficient, yet structural change is not possible without support from the political elite, the people most incentivized to maintain this damned status quo! The cost of their inaction (your inaction!) could be descent into a Civil War. If we keep on our current path, is that not where we end up?

I say again: **Our country is sick!**

In 2024, all the pieces are in place for political breakdown. Like a runaway train hurtling toward a cliff, the American political system is too large and too cumbersome to change its course. Short of profound constitutional change, I'm not sure how we will make it through the next few years without widespread political violence, whatever that might look like.

Am I overly pessimistic? Perhaps. But America is a tinderbox packed with more guns than people, and 2024 could be the spark that sets it off. Our system forces upon us a binary choice: come November, either Kamala Harris or Donald Trump will win the presidency.

And then, what? If the losing candidate refuses to concede, and the partisan supporters of that candidate refuse to acknowledge the legitimacy of the winner, what happens? Will there be violence? If yes, how much, and of what kind?

I could go on at length about what might happen if the Democrats win and Trump refuses to concede or what might happen if Trump wins and faces mass protests in major cities as he takes office or governs. But it is irrelevant to my purpose here.

The point is this: No matter who wins in 2024, the transfer of power might not be peaceful. In other words, America could find itself in a second Civil War. This time, the battlefield will be both physical and digital; America's most destructive military tactics turned against itself. In such a war, the frontlines of the battlefield could be anywhere, even extending to the screen each of us carries in our pocket.

A second Civil War would bring chaos not just to America but to the world. United, America is the most powerful country in the world. Divided, not so much. Would China use the opportunity of an American Civil War to invade Taiwan? Would Russia escalate its ground war in Ukraine or even threaten other European countries like Poland? What about the Middle East? Could a U.S. Civil War spiral into WWIII? Around the world, everyone is watching us, waiting to see which way the coin flip that is our 2024 election lands. My point here is not to argue about foreign policy but rather that our domestic political situation influences global events, which will, in turn, affect us.

I fear we are trapped in a doom spiral of our own creation. I abhor violence. Yet I observe our ever-escalating political rhetoric, and it feels inevitable that someone, or some group, will resort to political violence. The investigations into the motivations of the gunman who came within two inches of assassinating Donald Trump are so far inconclusive, revealing contradictory evidence as to his political ideology or if he was politically motivated at all. The national dialogue following the assassination attempt was full of violent rhetoric, or excuses, from all sides of the political spectrum. If the gunman had been successful, would there have already been more violence?

Maybe I am overly alarmist. Perhaps the 2024 election and its aftermath will be peaceful, and our normal level of dysfunction will persist.

Does that seem likely to you? If not in 2024, what about 2028, or 2032? One thing is certain: without reform, the structural issues will remain. And the continuation of our status quo is unsustainable!

In the long term, a Constitutional Convention might be the only way to avoid bloodshed. But this is a Hail Mary. The work to call a Convention, and then to write and negotiate a new Constitution that lives up to our supposed ideals, is immense. Constitutional change of this magnitude requires a movement of thousands working to convince a country of millions. And this across every state, across every county, across every acre of America.

In addition to a massive grassroots movement, we need people with real power —political, financial, cultural—to speak up and call for a Convention. We need our politicians at every level to speak up and put their (your!) political capital on the line.

My cynicism tells me this will never happen. I expect nothing from our political establishment. In their (your!) shortsightedness, perhaps they believe it is in their self-interest to maintain the status quo. But the status quo is corrupt, and broken, and held in place by its inertia. In sharing drafts of this polemic with close friends, every person has told me some version of, "It'll never happen." Perhaps you are thinking along these lines, too. Fair point. Your cynicism is justified.

But the danger lies when your cynicism turns to apathy. Too many Americans are so disgusted by our two-party system that they have simply tuned out from politics. Perhaps that is you. But the reality is that politics will impact you no matter how much you ignore it. The corporate oligarchs desire nothing more than to profit off your apathy and your cynicism.

My cynicism tells me to give up hope. But I love my country. I know our politics and politicians can be better, if only they were incentivized to do so. The purpose of this book is to design and describe a system to incentivize better politics. After all, no desired political change is feasible until its idea has been expressed! At the same time, expressing an idea is insufficient to make it reality. Coordinated, democratic action is required to make such change a reality.

Despite my eternal cynicism, I believe in the possibility of constitutional reform. I truly believe a new Constitution and multiparty political system would solve our political dysfunction.

As a final answer in response to my cynicism and yours, an axiom:

Constitutional reform is necessary, therefore it is possible.

## Chapter 3

LET THE GOOD OF THE PEOPLE BE THE SUPREME LAW

In America, we, the people, are sovereign. At least, we should be. As it is now, the superstructure of our political system itself acts as sovereign, resistant to change even when desired by a supermajority of the people.

Our longstanding dysfunction, and our democracy's failure to address our problems, heightens the appeal of a strongman who will use executive authority to break through the existing structure.

But such a path is treacherous. In an impossible best-case scenario, the strongman who dismantles democracy rules for life as a benevolent dictator and solves the nation's problems fairly and quickly. And even then, what happens when the benevolent dictator dies? Would democracy return? Or would another dictator, perhaps this time less than benevolent, take control and usurp sovereignty from us, the people? History returns a clear verdict to these questions: dictatorships are rarely benevolent, and even when the dictator governs well, such a government rarely lasts beyond the dictator's death.

When asked what kind of government the Constitutional Convention of 1787 had created, Benjamin Franklin replied, "A Republic, if you can keep it." [6]

We must find a way to reform our government to make our democratic republic functional and not give in to the temptations offered by the empty rhetoric of the would-be strongmen.

I believe the best way forward and to renew our democracy is through a Second Constitutional Convention.

A. What Is An Ideal Democracy?

"It has been said that democracy is the worst form of government, except for all those other forms that have been tried from time to time." So said **Winston Churchill** [7] in 1947.

I believe representative democracy to be the least imperfect form of government yet created. No form of government can be perfect because every political system ultimately relies on the independent and collective wills of human political actors, with their human virtues and flaws.

(Do not interpret the above as an argument for AI government. That is an entirely different question, and impractical given current technology.)

Democratic government has been historically defined by **political scientists**[8] as a government in which (a) "the Executive is directly or indirectly elected in popular elections and is responsible either directly or indirectly to voters or a legislature," (b) "the Legislature is chosen in free and fair elections," and (c) "a majority of adult men have the right to vote." By this definition, America has been a democracy since its constitutional founding in 1789; by the late 1780s, about 56% of adult men could vote (at best, **about 70% of adult white men**[9] could vote, and free whites were about **80% of the total population**).[10]

I find this definition insufficient. Voting rights being available to only 56% of adult men means only about 28% of the adult population was able to vote! It is oxymoronic to call any government lacking voting rights for women (half the population) or enslaved people (18% of the population in 1790) a democracy.

Over the **course of American history,**[11] more and more people gained the right to vote that they should have had from the very beginning. Starting with land-owning white men in the 1780s, then all white men by about 1830, then all men regardless of race (in theory) following the Civil War, then women's suffrage in 1920, then the Civil Rights movement making voting rights for people of all races a practical reality, and most recently the guarantee of voting rights for all citizens 18 years and older in 1971. Today, 98% of adult citizens are allowed to vote, though many do not exercise their right (about **4.6 million Americans**[12] are disenfranchised due to a felony conviction).

Each step brought us closer to becoming an ideal democracy, which I define as a government in which (a) there is universal suffrage where all adult citizens have equal rights and an equal vote, (b) all citizens are equally represented in the Legislature, chosen in free and fair elections, and (c) the Executive is directly elected by all citizens (presidential system) or indirectly chosen by the elected Legislature (parliamentary system).

But wait, isn't the United States a republic, a system of government in which citizens elect representatives to run the government?

Yes, indeed. The United States is a democratic-republic. That is the etymology of the Democratic-Republican Party of the early 1800s and the Democratic and

Republican parties of today. For the originalists out there, back in those days, the words themselves, "democratic" and "republican," were used interchangeably.

Semantics aside, why did American democracy start out so undemocratic? Perhaps the biggest reason is that the U.S. is one of the oldest democracies in the world. The Framers designed our democracy based on the political theory of the 18th century, before the existence of modern democracy. As great as the achievement of inventing modern democracy was, it is because of how the Framers wrote our Constitution back then that we have a dysfunctional two-party system today.

Political theory has advanced considerably in the last 250 years. Now, there are dozens of examples of democratic governance. In the best cases, countries structure their democracies based on the knowledge of how political parties and voting systems work in practice and to correct for specific defects in their prior systems. For example, Germany and New Zealand both use a form of proportional representation to elect their legislative representatives (Figure 3.1).

Germany's current constitution[13] was established in 1949 after being approved by the Allied Powers, including the United States. Designed to make impossible the rise of an autocratic state, Germany's new constitution instituted a parliamentary democracy. Article 21[14] of Germany's constitution recognized political parties as integral to the functioning of the government and denotes minimum requirements for party behavior, such as to not "seek to undermine or abolish the free democratic basic order." Since 1953,[15] German voters have voted for their preferred candidate to represent their district and, in a separate and simultaneous vote, voted for the political party which they prefer to form the government. The result of this system is that, since 2021, Germany has been governed by a center-left coalition of three parties: the Social Democratic Party, the Greens, and the Free Democratic Party. The Social Democrats are the largest party, with 206 seats, or 28% of the 736-member Bundestag. The center-right Christian Democratic Party is the second largest party, with 197 seats (27%), and is the primary opposition party. Under Angela Merkel's leadership from 2005 to 2021, the CDU was the primary governing party. The CDU was often in coalition with the SDP. Together, they governed from the center. The opposition, in turn, was comprised of smaller parties to both the right and left. Alternative for Germany, a xenophobic and climate-denying right-wing party, and the Left, an anti-capitalist party, are the two smallest parties with representation in the Bundestag. The opposition parties in Germany are not united; each opposition party has its own criticisms of the governing coalition. In total, German voters are currently represented by six parties, each with different and overlapping ideologies and policy prescriptions.

Party Strength Comparison
Lower House of Legislative Branch
2023
Germany
New Zealand
United States
Lower House Party Strengths, governing parties from the bottom, opposition parties from the top
100%
50%
0%
Independent, 1%
The Left, 5%
Alternative for Germany, 11%
Christian Democratic Union, 27%
Free Democratic Party, 13%
Greens, 16%
Social Democratic Party, 28%
Te Pati Maori, 5%
Greens, 12%
Labour, 28%
New Zealand First, 7%
ACT, 9%
National, 40%
Democratic, 49%
Republican, 51%

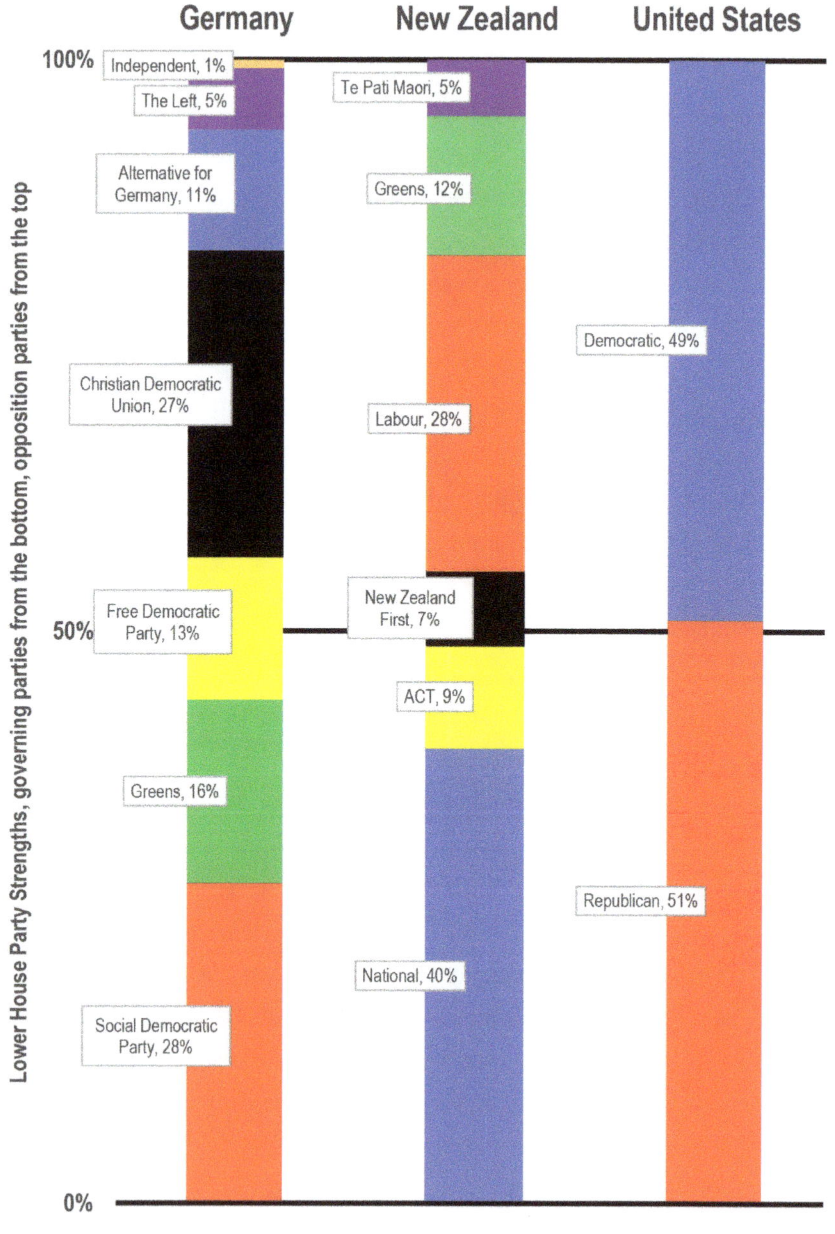

Figure 3.1

Until 1993, New Zealand's electoral system was similar to the United States: each member of the legislature was elected by winning the most votes in a single-member district, also called a first-past-the-post system. The result of this system was two-party domination by the Labour and National parties. In 1984,[16] for example, third parties won a combined 20% of the vote yet won just two seats out of 95. New Zealand voters were fed up and demanded a new electoral system, and eventually implemented **mixed-member proportional representation.**[17] Voters vote once for their preferred local representative and a second time for their preferred political party. The result of this system is that third parties are now a regular part of the New Zealand government. The Labour and National parties remain the dominant political parties in New Zealand, but often neither party wins an outright majority, meaning that a coalition is necessary to create a governing majority. For example, following the 2005 election in which the Labour Party and National Party each received 40% of the vote, the Labour Party formed a governing coalition with support from the Progressives, the Greens, the New Zealand First Party, and United Future. In the November 2023 election, the National Party won 49 seats, or 40% of Parliament. It formed a coalition government with the ACT and New Zealand First parties. Together, the three parties hold 56% of the seats in the New Zealand Parliament. Similar to Germany, there are several opposition parties. Previously the primary governing party, the Labour Party is now the primary opposition party with 34 seats or 28% of Parliament. The other opposition parties are the Greens with 15 seats, and the Indigenous Te Pāti Māori Party with six seats. New Zealand voters like this system: in a **2009 referendum,**[18] 57% of voters voted to retain the current electoral system.

Democratic reform improved the function of government in Germany and New Zealand. In their new constitutions, both countries addressed their most pressing structural issue. For Germany, it was to prevent another authoritarian nightmare. And for New Zealand, it was to break the hold of a sclerotic two-party system.

In the United States today, our two most pressing constitutional needs are to address the dysfunctional two-party system and to prevent authoritarian descent.

I believe a multimember ranked choice voting system would best create the conditions for multiparty democracy while safeguarding against authoritarian descent. I make my case over the course of this book.

However an alternative proposal is made in *Parliamentary America,*[19] by constitutional law professor Maxwell L. Stearns. He argues that a mixed-member proportional system similar to that of Germany and New Zealand, combined with indirect election of the President would be better. I consider Stearns' arguments throughout, as appropriate.

Yet I also believe that the reforms argued for here are imperfect, and that they could be further improved. For example, a key proponent of the multimember ranked choice voting system modeled in Chapters 7 and 8 was political scientist Lee Drutman, who advocated for such a system in his 2020 book *Breaking the Two-Party Doom Loop.*[20] But in September 2023, Drutman published an essay[21] explaining that his views had changed and that he now favors a fusion or open-list proportional representation voting system.

The point here is that the differences between these reforms are minor in comparison to the current structure of America's voting system. From Stearns' mixed-member proportional parliamentary system to my multimember ranked choice voting system modeled after Drutman's 2020 book, to the open-list system that Drutman now prefers, any of them would be preferable to our status quo.

While I attempt in this book to make the strongest possible argument in favor of multimember ranked choice voting, I remain open to being convinced of the merits of another system.

B. Summary Of Proposed Reforms

The following are the reforms proposed in PART TWO of this book:

1. Eliminate the Senate to make the Legislative Branch a unicameral body.
2. Increase the size of Congress to 695 members and require Congress to change its size after each Census depending on the population of the country.
3. Grant statehood to the District of Columbia, Puerto Rico, and the Four Island Territories.
4. Require states with more than one representative to use some form of proportional voting method, specifically proportional ranked choice voting with multimember districts of between three and five members.
5. Eliminate the Electoral College and elect the President by ranked choice popular vote.
6. Lower the threshold for impeaching the President to 60% of Congress.
7. Set a term limit of 21 years for Supreme Court Justices.
8. Create a set schedule for appointments to the Supreme Court.
9. Increase the size of the Supreme Court to 21 Justices.

Combined, these reforms would rebalance the three Branches, increasing the power of the Legislative while reducing the power of the Executive and the Judiciary.

Here is an overview of my rationale, and I go into detail justifying each reform in PART TWO.

Reform 1 will increase the power of the Legislative by removing the internal check, the Senate, on its use of power. In my view, the current structure of the Legislative prevents it from appropriately asserting its power and exercising the will of the people. The Framers intended the Legislative Branch to be the closest to the people, and the most powerful. This reform will accomplish that goal.

The purpose of Reforms 2 and 3 is to ensure universal suffrage and equal representation in Congress.

Reform 4 will make multiple parties electorally viable. While it may be tempting to try to eliminate political parties altogether, political parties are inevitable in democratic government. This is because in a large society, there will always be different factions with different priorities, and they will always find a way to organize. It is impossible to have zero political parties. Having a one-party system is undesirable as well, for obvious reasons. And our two-party system incentivizes conflict and has brought us to the precipice upon which we find ourselves today. In a multiparty system, it is difficult for any single party to win a majority. To govern, parties must form coalitions, and are incentivized to cooperate. At the same time,[22] too many parties can lead to fragmentation and legislative instability. As shown by my state-by-state analysis in Chapter 8, the incentives created by the structure of these proposed reforms will make viable at least 4 political parties.

Reforms 5 and 6 will make the Executive Branch more accountable to the people. First, by ensuring that the person who receives the most votes wins the Presidency. And second, by making it easier for the Legislative to check a rogue or otherwise unfit President.

The three reforms to the Judicial Branch are designed to reduce the political stakes for each individual judicial nomination by limiting the maximum length of time each Justice can serve, increasing the predictability of the appointments, and expanding the Court to dilute the power of each individual Justice.

While these reforms could be implemented one at a time, in a piecemeal fashion, they are intended to be implemented as a complimentary package.

In sum, these reforms would be transformational. If implemented, I believe the new structure of government would create the conditions from which American democracy shall rise to meet head-on the myriad challenges facing our nation in the 21st century, and beyond.

C. How To Call A Second Constitutional Convention

The way to make these reforms a reality is through a Second Constitutional Convention.

One key issue that may arise at a Convention is how to deal with "entrenched clauses." An entrenched clause is a part of a constitution that is more difficult to amend or remove than other parts.[23] For example, Germany's Article 79[24] stipulates that "Amendments . . . to the principles laid down in Articles 1 and 20 shall be inadmissible." Germany's decision to entrench Article 1, its declaration of human rights, and Article 20, its declaration of it being a democratic state deriving its power entirely from the people, was a direct response to the autocratic horror of Nazi Germany.

For the U.S. Constitution, there is an entrenched clause in Article 5 that states, " . . . no State, without its Consent, shall be deprived of its equal Suffrage in the Senate."

How might the delegates of a Second Constitutional Convention deal with this entrenched clause? They could leave it be. Or they could follow the precedent of the First Constitutional Convention. In 1787, the Framers threw out the entire Articles of Confederation and drafted our Constitution from scratch.

If the delegates of a Second Constitutional Convention followed the Framers' precedent, all parts of the Constitution, including its entrenched clause, could be rewritten. Through this, all reforms argued for in this book are possible.

To enact these reforms, a Constitutional Convention is the end goal. Set your cynicism aside! How do we accomplish this goal? What are the necessary steps? What is the best political strategy? What about tactics? What about action?

To begin, the rules for amending our Constitution are denoted in Article 5. Amendments require the approval of 2/3 of both Houses of Congress (67 Senators and 290 Representatives) and become law after ratification by the Legislatures in 3/4 of the States (38 of 50). A Constitutional Convention can be called by the Legislatures of 2/3 of the States (34 of 50).

In short, the State Legislatures are the key. The 7,386 people that comprise the 99 State Houses, Assemblies, Legislatures, and Senates have the power to call a Convention (49 states have bicameral legislatures, while Nebraska has a unicameral legislature). These are the people who must be convinced to call a Convention.

Every State is different, and every legislative body is different, as shown in Table 3.1. The State Houses range in size from 40 representatives (Alaska) to 400 (New Hampshire). And the State Senates range in size from 20 senators (Alaska) to 67 (Minnesota). The Republican Party controls a majority in 28 State Houses and 29 State Senates (Nebraska's unicameral legislature is counted as a Senate).

The Democratic Party controls a majority in 21 State Houses and 20 State Senates. Emblematic of our hyperpartisan time, there are only two states in which one party does not control both legislative chambers: Pennsylvania and Alaska. (The Alaska State Senate is governed by a bipartisan coalition of 9 Democrats and 8 Republicans.)

Because neither party controls enough legislative bodies to call a Convention on its own, the coalition must be bipartisan.

Accordingly, the political strategy to convince each State and each legislative body to call a Convention must be tailored to its specific idiosyncrasies. The strategies that work in my home state of Washington may be wildly different from the strategies that work in New Hampshire or Louisiana. To any activists reading this, I hope you will use your knowledge of your home state's idiosyncrasies to implement the most effective political strategy.

In general, I believe some strategies can be applied to most, if not all, states.

To call a Convention, we will need champions in the State Legislatures. These are people already in office who can introduce legislation, and who can talk to their colleagues. To the State Legislators reading this: this: Use your power! Talk with your colleagues! Use your political capital to call for a Convention!

To assist our champions on the inside, we need a campaign putting pressure on each legislature from the outside, in every state.

Table 3.1: Our 7,386 State Legislators Have the Power to Call a Convention (Color Indicates Majority Party in 2024)

State	House / Assembly	Senate	Total Legislators
Alabama	105	35	140
Alaska	40	20	60
Arizona	60	30	90
Arkansas	100	35	135
California	80	40	120
Colorado	65	35	100
Connecticut	151	36	187
Delaware	41	21	62
Florida	120	40	160
Georgia	180	56	236
Hawaii	51	25	76
Idaho	70	35	105
Illinois	118	59	177
Indiana	100	50	150
Iowa	100	50	150
Kansas	125	40	165
Kentucky	100	38	138
Louisiana	105	39	144
Maine	151	35	186
Maryland	141	47	188
Massachusetts	160	40	200
Michigan	110	38	148
Minnesota	134	67	201
Mississippi	122	52	174
Missouri	163	34	197
Montana	100	50	150
Nebraska	x	49	49
Nevada	42	21	63
New Hampshire	400	24	424
New Jersey	80	40	120
New Mexico	70	42	112
New York	150	63	213
North Carolina	120	50	170
North Dakota	94	47	141
Ohio	99	33	132
Oklahoma	101	48	149
Oregon	60	30	90
Pennsylvania	203	50	253
Rhode Island	75	38	113
South Carolina	124	46	170
South Dakota	70	35	105
Tennessee	99	33	132
Texas	150	31	181
Utah	75	29	104
Vermont	150	30	180
Virginia	100	40	140
Washington	98	49	147
West Virginia	100	34	134
Wisconsin	99	33	132
Wyoming	62	31	93

Likely, we will need wealthy political donors to fund the campaign. It will be difficult to defeat the monied interests defending the broken status quo without having monied interests of our own.

We need to build a massive grassroots movement. To do this, we need to spread the word of constitutional reform, and how a Convention could be the way to fix our broken politics. This means talking to your friends, your family, your neighbors, your colleagues, and anyone who can cast a ballot. We need to build a popular majority, probably a supermajority, in support of a Convention. What if there were a national referendum on constitutional reform, and a clear majority voted in favor of reform? Facing such pressure, our Legislators would have no choice but to call a Convention. And if they do not, we need people to step up and run for office to replace those legislators who remain intransigent in their defense of the sclerotic status quo.

Calling a Convention is a daunting task. It could easily be the work of decades and generations. But political windows can open suddenly. If our political system breaks down in the aftermath of the 2024 election, there could be a once-in-a-generation, once-in-a-century opportunity for transformative political reform. The last time Constitutional reform of this magnitude was passed was during and immediately after the Civil War. The Thirteenth, Fourteenth, and Fifteenth Amendments were passed by the winners of the Civil War and imposed, literally at gunpoint, upon the losers.

The purpose of calling a Convention is to avoid such bloodshed. Further, this is not to say that such horrific violence is or will be necessary for constitutional change; rather, that the window for reform can open suddenly, and will, in all likelihood, not last long. If and when the window for reform happens, it will be important to have the reforms ready to go.

An incomplete list of actions you could personally take to call for a Convention:

- contacting your legislator to ask them to support a Constitutional Convention;
- mailing a physical copy of this book to your legislator;
- talking in person about a Constitutional Convention to your friends and family, classmates and colleagues;
- advocating for a Constitutional Convention on your social media;
- convincing whatever social or political groups you are already a part of to support a Convention;
- organizing with other Americans in support of a Convention;
- marching in the streets, demanding our politicians act; and
- organizing and participating in a general strike.

Yet, still, this seems insufficient.

I can only tell you what I have done, and what I plan to do. To the extent that writing a book counts as action, that is what I have done. I hope to continue working in the democracy reform space in some capacity, but my cynicism means my expectations are low. I hope people read this, and share it, and then use their creativity and energy to further the cause of constitutional reform.

Because successfully calling a Convention, and for it to be successful in creating a more perfect government, would be close to a miracle. The next steps are up to you.

If democratic government is government by the many, democratic action is action by the many.

So, what are you going to do?

We
The
People

PART TWO

PROPOSAL

Chapter 4
SUNSET THE SENATE

Step one in restructuring the Constitution is to eliminate the Senate. This change would unlock an entirely new structure of government that would be more efficient, more democratic, and easier for voters to reasonably assess blame or credit and subsequently cast electoral judgment. All other proposals for reforming the Senate are insufficient.

I am not the first person to make this argument. Representative John Dingell of Michigan, the longest-serving representative in history, argued for abolishing the Senate in a 2018 Atlantic piece[25] published just two months before he passed.

The actual proposal is simple: Abolish the Senate to create a unicameral Legislative Branch. All powers held by the Senate would be vested in the House of Representatives as the sole body of the Legislative Branch. These powers include approving or rejecting judicial appointments made by the executive, investigating potential abuses of power by the executive, negotiating legislation with the executive, overriding executive vetoes, approving treaties with foreign nations, and impeaching the executive or members of the Judiciary.

The intention of this reform is to make possible equal representation for all citizens and increase legislative power through the removal of an unnecessary internal check. Legislative power is already sufficiently checked by the Executive through veto power and the Judiciary through judicial review.

This is the first and most crucial reform because the Senate is the most obstructionist and undemocratic feature remaining in our Constitution. Its constitutional purpose is to be an aristocratic and oligarchic check on, in the Founders' views, the untrustworthy and dangerous whims of the general public. The Senate can block legislation from the House, block Judicial appointments, and block Executive treaty-making. The Senate additionally functions as a check on other checks and balances, such as how throughout all American history it has blocked every attempt by the House to impeach a President. In these ways, the Senate is an unreasonable check.

The Senate's obstructionist power makes it arguably the most powerful body in the constitutional order. In passing legislation, when there is a dispute between the House and the Senate, the Senate almost always gets its way. For example, the final versions of the Affordable Care Act and the Inflation Reduction Act that became law were the Senate's versions. The Senate's absurd filibuster rules allow an obstructionist minority of Senators representing an even smaller minority of voters veto power over most legislation. The Senate's veto power over foreign treaties, executive agency appointments, and judicial appointments can similarly be held by 40 Senators representing potentially as few as 10% of Americans. That is too much power for too small a minority.

(The population of the smallest 20 states is 33,941,368. That is 10.3% of the population of all 50 states, 331,108,434 according to the 2020 Census.)

The issue is not that the Legislative Branch possesses these powers over the Executive and Judicial Branches; it is important for the Legislature to check the Executive and Judiciary. The issue is that the structure of the Senate allows an obstructionist minority to prevent the normal functioning of the other branches of government.

Proponents of the Senate will argue that the Senate balances power appropriately in favor of small states. Supposing this is true, to what extent is equal representation between States more important than equal representation between people? If equal representation between people is more important, as I think most people would agree, should not the House have more authority than the Senate? Yet, the Senate is more powerful. Why should people living in small states get favorable representation compared to people living in larger states? Geographic favoritism makes as much sense as racial or gender favoritism, which is to say it makes no sense at all.

Proponents of the Senate and a bicameral Legislative Branch will argue that the Senate plays an important role in providing stability by ensuring that laws are not changed too quickly or haphazardly. The so-called "cooling saucer" for legislation sent it by the House. But why is this additional check on legislative activity necessary in a system in which legislative authority is checked by both executive approval and judicial review? Is there any function the Senate performs, other than acting as an additional check on the legislative process, that could not be performed by a unicameral legislature? The answer is no. A unicameral House can perform the same checks on the Executive and Judicial Branches as a bicameral legislature: approving or rejecting judicial appointments, investigating potential abuses of power, negotiating on legislation, overriding vetoes, approving treaties with foreign nations, etc.

Proponents of the Senate will argue that its existence is necessary for maintaining federalism and the rights of individual States. I believe this is the strongest argument for maintaining the existence of the Senate, though I do not find it compelling because the Senate is far from the only body that defends the rights of the States. The rights of the States and the structure of federalism would still be defended and maintained by the Judiciary through its interpretation of the 10th Amendment and existing precedent, the exercise of power by the State Legislatures and Governors, and the people of the states through the power of their vote.

Proponents will argue that without the Senate the larger states would be more able to bully the smaller states. In rebuttal, I would note that our politics have not ever been divided along state size. The four largest states, California, Texas, Florida, and New York, have wildly different politics and priorities. California has far more in common with Oregon and Nevada than with Texas or New York; similarly, Texas has far more in common with Louisiana and Oklahoma than with Florida. Congressional decisions about the function of the federal government are determined more by party identity, as are decisions of the various States to either support or oppose the federal government. Further, all States, regardless of size, have an interest in the defense of the rights of the other States because the degradation of one State's rights would set the precedent for the degradation of all other States' rights.

Under various ideas for reform, the Senate would become slightly less obstructionist and slightly more democratic. The most well-known reform would be to **remove the Senate filibuster**,[26] allowing a simple majority (or tie plus the Vice President) to advance all legislation through the Senate. If the filibuster were eliminated, instead of 40 Senators representing as few as 10% of Americans being able to obstruct the other branches, 51 Senators representing as few as 17% of Americans would be required (or 50 Senators representing 16% of Americans plus a sympathetic Vice President). This marginal improvement is far from fair. It is not good enough.

A second idea is to **change Senate apportionment**[27] to correspond to some degree to the state population, as Wharton University Professor Eric Orts argued in 2018. Under his proposal, the Senate would be increased to 110 members (Table 4.1). California, Texas, New York, and Florida would see their representation increase to 12, 9, 6, and 6 members, respectively, while the 26 least populous states would see their Senate representation reduced to 1. The Americans living in the four largest states would have voting power of at least 80% of the national average, far better than their 16%–33% voting power under the current Senate.

Table 4.1: Unequal Representation Would Persist in a Reformed Senate
(Voting Power means the value of each individual's vote compared to the national average)

State	Population (2020 US Census)	Current Senate			Reformed Senate		
		Senators	Pop. Per Senator	Voting Power	Senators	Pop. Per Senator	Voting Power
United States	*331,108,434*	*100*	*3,311,084*	*100.0%*	*110*	*3,010,077*	*100.0%*
California	39,576,757	2	19,788,379	16.7%	12	3,298,063	91.3%
Texas	29,183,290	2	14,591,645	22.7%	9	3,242,588	92.8%
Florida	21,570,527	2	10,785,264	30.7%	6	3,595,088	83.7%
New York	20,215,751	2	10,107,876	32.8%	6	3,369,292	89.3%
Pennsylvania	13,011,844	2	6,505,922	50.9%	4	3,252,961	92.5%
Illinois	12,822,739	2	6,411,370	51.6%	4	3,205,685	93.9%
Ohio	11,808,848	2	5,904,424	56.1%	4	2,952,212	102.0%
Georgia	10,725,274	2	5,362,637	61.7%	3	3,575,091	84.2%
North Carolina	10,453,948	2	5,226,974	63.3%	3	3,484,649	86.4%
Michigan	10,084,442	2	5,042,221	65.7%	3	3,361,481	89.5%
New Jersey	9,294,493	2	4,647,247	71.2%	3	3,098,164	97.2%
Virginia	8,654,542	2	4,327,271	76.5%	3	2,884,847	104.3%
Washington	7,715,946	2	3,857,973	85.8%	2	3,857,973	78.0%
Arizona	7,158,923	2	3,579,462	92.5%	2	3,579,462	84.1%
Massachusetts	7,033,469	2	3,516,735	94.2%	2	3,516,735	85.6%
Tennessee	6,916,897	2	3,458,449	95.7%	2	3,458,449	87.0%
Indiana	6,790,280	2	3,395,140	97.5%	2	3,395,140	88.7%
Maryland	6,185,278	2	3,092,639	107.1%	2	3,092,639	97.3%
Missouri	6,160,281	2	3,080,141	107.5%	2	3,080,141	97.7%
Wisconsin	5,897,473	2	2,948,737	112.3%	2	2,948,737	102.1%
Colorado	5,782,171	2	2,891,086	114.5%	2	2,891,086	104.1%
Minnesota	5,709,752	2	2,854,876	116.0%	2	2,854,876	105.4%
South Carolina	5,124,712	2	2,562,356	129.2%	2	2,562,356	117.5%
Alabama	5,030,053	2	2,515,027	131.7%	2	2,515,027	119.7%
Louisiana	4,661,468	2	2,330,734	142.1%	1	4,661,468	64.6%
Kentucky	4,509,342	2	2,254,671	146.9%	1	4,509,342	66.8%
Oregon	4,241,500	2	2,120,750	156.1%	1	4,241,500	71.0%
Oklahoma	3,963,516	2	1,981,758	167.1%	1	3,963,516	75.9%
Connecticut	3,608,298	2	1,804,149	183.5%	1	3,608,298	83.4%
Utah	3,275,252	2	1,637,626	202.2%	1	3,275,252	91.9%
Iowa	3,192,406	2	1,596,203	207.4%	1	3,192,406	94.3%
Nevada	3,108,462	2	1,554,231	213.0%	1	3,108,462	96.8%
Arkansas	3,013,756	2	1,506,878	219.7%	1	3,013,756	99.9%
Mississippi	2,963,914	2	1,481,957	223.4%	1	2,963,914	101.6%
Kansas	2,940,865	2	1,470,433	225.2%	1	2,940,865	102.4%
New Mexico	2,120,220	2	1,060,110	312.3%	1	2,120,220	142.0%
Nebraska	1,963,333	2	981,667	337.3%	1	1,963,333	153.3%
Idaho	1,841,377	2	920,689	359.6%	1	1,841,377	163.5%
West Virginia	1,795,045	2	897,523	368.9%	1	1,795,045	167.7%
Hawaii	1,460,137	2	730,069	453.5%	1	1,460,137	206.2%
New Hampshire	1,379,089	2	689,545	480.2%	1	1,379,089	218.3%
Maine	1,363,582	2	681,791	485.6%	1	1,363,582	220.7%
Rhode Island	1,098,163	2	549,082	603.0%	1	1,098,163	274.1%
Montana	1,085,407	2	542,704	610.1%	1	1,085,407	277.3%
Delaware	990,837	2	495,419	668.3%	1	990,837	303.8%
South Dakota	887,770	2	443,885	745.9%	1	887,770	339.1%
North Dakota	779,702	2	389,851	849.3%	1	779,702	386.1%
Alaska	736,081	2	368,041	899.7%	1	736,081	408.9%
Vermont	643,503	2	321,752	1029.1%	1	643,503	467.8%
Wyoming	577,719	2	288,860	1146.3%	1	577,719	521.0%

Prof. Orts's proposal would be an improvement but does not go far enough. Reforming the Senate is like rearranging the deck chairs on the Titanic. In this new version, the median state would have one Senator representing three million people. But three states would be significantly less represented, with one Senator representing more than four million people in Louisiana, Kentucky, and Oregon. Those three states, plus Washington and Oklahoma, would have voting power less than 80% of the national average. Conversely, the 11 smallest states would have more than 200% voting power compared to the national average. Only 11 states would have voting power within 5% of the national average. Unequal representation would persist.

A third reform, which could be implemented alongside reapportionment, would be to limit the Senate's power. In Chapter 8 of his 2020 book *Breaking the Two-Party Doom Loop*, political scientist Lee Drutman proposed requiring the Senate to conduct an up-or-down vote on all legislation that receives at least 60% support in the House. The issue with this proposal is that it still allows a majority of Senators who represent a minority of Americans to hold up the function of the Legislative Branch through its veto power over otherwise popular legislation. New York Times columnist Jamelle Bouie proposed[28] stripping the Senate of the power to introduce or veto legislation. In Bouie's proposal, the Senate would have 60 days to act to propose amendments to the House's bill. If it proposed amendments, those amendments would be voted on by a committee of House and Senate members. If it did not act within 60 days, the bill would advance to the President's desk. The Senate would retain its power to approve treaties and to vote on Executive and Judicial nominees. The issue with Bouie's proposal is, again, that a majority of Senators representing a minority of Americans would have the power to hold up the function of both the Executive and Judicial Branches.

To be clear, all these reforms would improve upon the Senate's current form.

But they remain insufficient because they do not mitigate both the Senate's undemocratic nature and its obstructionist power. Its constitutional formation of giving voting power based on land, not people, makes it impossible to democratize. The Senate will always overrepresent some voters and underrepresent others; the Senate will always be unfair. It cannot be sufficiently democratically reformed without becoming something which it is not.

The Senate's function is anti-democratic obstruction. Reform is insufficient. The solution is abolition.

Abolishing the Senate would remove a check on legislative action, effectively making the Legislature more active and, therefore, more powerful. The Legislature, the branch of government closest to the people, was intended to be the most powerful. Removing the Senate as a check on the House would fulfill this intention of the Founders.

Abolishing the Senate would make it easier for the House to check the power of the Executive and the Judiciary through the threat of impeachment. Even if the rules of the House were changed to require a 2/3 majority to impeach and convict the Executive, that supermajority would be easier to reach than the current 2/3 supermajority in the Senate. A group of 34 Senators representing as few as 7.5% of Americans can prevent the Executive from being impeached. In the House, 34% of representatives would represent almost exactly 34% of Americans due to the relatively equal district size in the House.

The Presidency and the House have been controlled by the same party for 14 years since 1981,[29] when President Reagan took office. Depending on your politics, same-party rule could be exciting as more of your policy preferences are enacted, unpleasant as policies you don't like are passed, or a mix. A distinct benefit of more frequent single-party rule is that it is easier for voters to pass judgment on the performance of the party in power. In a divided government, blame and credit are easily distributed and confusing to determine without spending hours upon hours learning about political minutia.

What about the risk of an authoritarian party winning both the Presidency and a majority in Congress? Without the Senate, it would seem that this risk would rise. But because majority control of the Senate can be secured with a miniscule proportion of the national vote, the Senate is potentially the easiest branch of government for an authoritarian party to gain control of. Increasing the size of Congress and implementing a proportional voting system as described in Chapter 6 would make it very difficult for a single party to win an outright majority.

Abolishing the Senate is the most impactful constitutional reform proposed here. On its own, it would make Congress more equal, more effective, and more powerful. A newly unicameral Congress would represent the American people far better than the current, undemocratic bicameral version.

Chapter 5

EQUAL AND UNIVERSAL REPRESENTATION IN AN EXPANDED CONGRESS

If Congress is to be a unicameral body, that single chamber must be as close to a perfect representation of the American people as possible. To make this a reality, we should:

- grant statehood and fair representation for Americans living in Puerto Rico, the District of Columbia, and the Four Island Territories (Guam, U.S. Virgin Islands, American Samoa, and the Northern Mariana Islands).
- expand the House of Representatives from 435 members to 695 members.
- tie future expansion to the cube root of the population taken in each decennial census.

By implementing these proposals, all Americans would have representation in Congress. On average, each member of Congress would go from representing over 750,000 Americans to representing less than 500,000, bringing Congress closer to the will of the people.

These changes, combined with the voting system described in Chapter 6 and modeled in Chapters 7 and 8, would make American democracy very close to ideal.

Prepare yourself for lots of numbers. Specifically, detailed analysis of the state-by-state population data as reported by every U.S. Census[30] going back to 1790.[31]

Each Census table shows the population of every state at each decade in our nation's history. The voting power column on the right side of each Census table shows how fairly or unfairly the people of each state were represented in Congress.

A. Failed Representation, Then And Now

The essential function of the Legislative Branch is to fairly represent the varied groups, interests, and regional cultures that comprise the democratic will of the people.

Congress, composed of the House and the Senate, has historically failed to fairly represent the American people. It continues to fail. As discussed in Chapter 4, the Senate irredeemably distorts representation for people living in different states.

Even the House, as an independent body supposedly designed to represent the will of the people fairly and accurately, has distorted representation. This distortion began with the institution of slavery and the 3/5 Clause, and it has persisted due to difficulties in responding to the growing population disparity between the largest and smallest states.

i. The Antebellum Era: The 3/5 Clause Quantified

From the very beginning, Congress was poorly apportioned. The first census in 1790 tabulated the total population of the new nation to be 3.8 million. At that time, about 18% of the population, nearly 700,000 people, were enslaved. By 1860, at the onset of the Civil War, there were nearly 4 million enslaved people, or 13% of the population. Obviously, enslaved people had no representation. But the perverse apportionment method of the 3/5 Clause also gave additional voting power to their enslavers. Functionally, the 3/5 Clause awarded 23 to 31% more representation to free voters living in slave states compared to free voters living in free states until the Civil War (Table 5.1). In other words, four votes in a slave state were equal to five votes in a free state.

Table 5.1: Free People Living in Slave States Had About 25% More Representative Power Than Free People Living in Free States from 1790-1860)

Year	Free Person Voting Power		
	Slave States	Free States	Slave State Advantage
1790	116.1%	91.0%	27.7%
1800	114.2%	90.4%	26.3%
1810	114.9%	91.4%	25.7%
1820	117.7%	90.4%	30.2%
1830	118.1%	90.4%	30.7%
1840	119.0%	90.7%	31.2%
1850	118.5%	91.2%	29.9%
1860	115.2%	93.9%	22.7%

According to the 1790 Census, more than 10% of the population was enslaved in 7 states. (This includes Vermont and Kentucky, which were admitted as states in 1791 and 1792, respectively.) In 8 states, less than 10% of the population was enslaved. In only 1 state, Massachusetts, all people were free. With the exception of Delaware, which was the least populous state and accordingly difficult to apportion, all of the slave states were overrepresented compared to the eight states in which less than 10% of the population was enslaved. In fact, the states with the greatest proportion of enslaved people were the most overrepresented. South Carolina had the highest proportion of enslaved people, and South Carolina's free population also had the most representation; Virginia had the second highest proportion of enslaved people, and Virginia's free population had the second most representation.

In total, the 1,271,573 free people living in the 7 states where more than 10% of the population was enslaved were represented by 48 members of Congress or 26,491 per representative. Conversely, the 1,927,784 free people living in the eight states where less than 10% of the population was enslaved were represented by 57 members of Congress or 33,821 per representative. The impact of the 3/5 Clause was that the average free person in a slave state had 28% more representation in Congress than the average free person in a free state in 1790.

To put a finer point on it, at the very beginning of our country, the enslavers had more representation than everyone else. They then used their power to keep in place the system that benefitted them, and that forced millions into servitude.

Table 5.2: Free People in Slave States Had Disproportionate Representative Power in 1790 (15 States)

State	Seats	Total Pop.	Free Pop.	Slave Pop.	Percent Slave	Total Pop. Per Rep.	Free Pop. Per Rep.	Voting Power
United States	104	3,893,637	3,199,357	694,280	17.8%	37,439	30,763	100.0%
Slave States	48	1,925,483	1,271,573	653,910	34.0%	40,114	26,491	116.1%
Free States	57	1,968,154	1,927,784	40,370	2.1%	34,529	33,821	91.0%
South Carolina	6	249,073	141,979	107,094	43.0%	41,512	23,663	130.0%
Virginia	19	747,610	454,983	292,627	39.1%	39,348	23,946	128.5%
Georgia	2	82,548	53,284	29,264	35.5%	41,274	26,642	115.5%
Maryland	8	319,728	216,692	103,036	32.2%	39,966	27,087	113.6%
North Carolina	10	393,751	293,179	100,572	25.5%	39,375	29,318	104.9%
Kentucky	2	73,677	61,247	12,430	16.9%	36,839	30,624	100.5%
Delaware	1	59,096	50,209	8,887	15.0%	59,096	50,209	61.3%
New York	10	340,120	318,796	21,324	6.3%	34,012	31,880	96.5%
New Jersey	5	184,139	172,716	11,423	6.2%	36,828	34,543	89.1%
Rhode Island	2	68,825	67,877	948	1.4%	34,413	33,939	90.6%
Connecticut	7	237,946	235,182	2,764	1.2%	33,992	33,597	91.6%
Pennsylvania	13	434,373	430,636	3,737	0.9%	33,413	33,126	92.9%
New Hampshire	4	141,885	141,727	158	0.1%	35,471	35,432	86.8%
Vermont	2	85,539	85,523	16	0.0%	42,770	42,762	71.9%
Massachusetts	14	475,327	475,327	-	0.0%	33,952	33,952	90.6%

By 1800, over 14,000 people lived in the newly created District of Columbia, including over 3,000 enslaved people. None of the people living in D.C. had representation in Congress. Following the 1800 Census, Congress set the ratio for apportionment at 33,000 people per representative.[32] Yet due to the 3/5 Clause, every state with more than 9% of the population enslaved (except Delaware, again) was awarded additional representation (Table 5.3). All of the free states had more than 33,000 people per representative. Excepting Delaware, the slave states ranged from 24,291 people per representative in Virginia to 30,583 people per representative in Tennessee. (I do not include Ohio, which was admitted to the Union in 1802.)

By 1810, the institution of slavery was growing rapidly. In three states, South Carolina, Georgia, and Virginia, enslaved people comprised more than 40% of the total population. Accordingly, the free population in these three states were the most overrepresented people in Congress following the 1810 Census (Table 5.3). The free population in only 1 slave state, Tennessee, was more poorly represented than the free population in the free states. On average, the free population in the slave states had 26% more voting power than the free population in the free states.

Table 5.3: Free People in Slave States Had Disproportionate Representative Power in 1800 (16 States)

State	Seats	Total Pop.	Free Pop.	Slave Pop.	Percent Slave	Total Pop. Per Rep.	Free Pop. Per Rep.	Voting Power
United States	141	5,246,337	4,356,650	889,687	17.0%	37,208	30,898	100.0%
Slave States	65	2,613,051	1,759,175	853,876	32.7%	40,201	27,064	114.2%
Free States	76	2,633,286	2,597,475	35,811	1.4%	34,649	34,177	90.4%
South Carolina	8	345,591	199,440	146,151	42.3%	43,199	24,930	123.9%
Virginia	22	880,200	534,404	345,796	39.3%	40,009	24,291	127.2%
Georgia	4	162,686	103,282	59,404	36.5%	40,672	25,821	119.7%
Maryland	9	341,548	235,913	105,635	30.9%	37,950	26,213	117.9%
North Carolina	12	478,103	344,807	133,296	27.9%	39,842	28,734	107.5%
District of Columbia	-	14,093	10,849	3,244	23.0%	x	x	x
Kentucky	6	220,955	180,612	40,343	18.3%	36,826	30,102	102.6%
Tennessee	3	105,602	91,748	13,854	13.1%	35,201	30,583	101.0%
Delaware	1	64,273	58,120	6,153	9.6%	64,273	58,120	53.2%
New Jersey	6	211,149	198,727	12,422	5.9%	35,192	33,121	93.3%
New York	17	586,761	566,418	20,343	3.5%	34,515	33,319	92.7%
Rhode Island	2	69,122	68,741	381	0.6%	34,561	34,371	89.9%
Connecticut	7	251,002	250,051	951	0.4%	35,857	35,722	86.5%
Pennsylvania	18	602,365	600,659	1,706	0.3%	33,465	33,370	92.6%
New Hampshire	5	183,858	183,850	8	0.0%	36,772	36,770	84.0%
Vermont	4	154,465	154,465	-	0.0%	38,616	38,616	80.0%
Massachusetts	17	574,564	574,564	-	0.0%	33,798	33,798	91.4%

Table 5.4: Free People in Slave States Had Disproportionate Representative Power in 1810 (17 States)

State	Seats	Total Pop.	Free Pop.	Slave Pop.	Percent Slave	Total Pop. Per Rep.	Free Pop. Per Rep.	Voting Power
United States	181	7,060,497	5,926,321	1,134,176	16.1%	39,008	32,742	100.0%
Slave States	76	3,270,477	2,165,559	1,104,918	33.8%	43,033	28,494	114.9%
Free States	105	3,790,020	3,760,762	29,258	0.8%	36,095	35,817	91.4%
South Carolina	9	415,115	218,750	196,365	47.3%	46,124	24,306	134.7%
Georgia	6	252,433	147,215	105,218	41.7%	42,072	24,536	133.4%
Virginia	23	974,622	582,104	392,518	40.3%	42,375	25,309	129.4%
North Carolina	13	555,500	386,676	168,824	30.4%	42,731	29,744	110.1%
Maryland	9	380,546	269,044	111,502	29.3%	42,283	29,894	109.5%
District of Columbia	-	24,023	18,628	5,395	22.5%	x	x	x
Kentucky	10	406,511	325,950	80,561	19.8%	40,651	32,595	100.5%
Tennessee	6	261,727	217,192	44,535	17.0%	43,621	36,199	90.5%
New Jersey	6	245,555	234,704	10,851	4.4%	40,926	39,117	83.7%
Delaware	2	72,674	70,497	2,177	3.0%	36,337	35,249	92.9%
New York	27	959,049	944,032	15,017	1.6%	35,520	34,964	93.6%
Rhode Island	2	77,031	76,923	108	0.1%	38,516	38,462	85.1%
Connecticut	7	262,042	261,732	310	0.1%	37,435	37,390	87.6%
Pennsylvania	23	810,091	809,296	795	0.1%	35,221	35,187	93.1%
New Hampshire	6	214,360	214,360	-	0.0%	35,727	35,727	91.6%
Vermont	6	217,713	217,713	-	0.0%	36,286	36,286	90.2%
Ohio	6	230,760	230,760	-	0.0%	38,460	38,460	85.1%
Massachusetts	20	700,745	700,745	-	0.0%	35,037	35,037	93.4%

The enslaved population almost doubled from 1.1 million people in 1810 to 2 million in 1830. By 1830, more than half the population was enslaved in 2 states, South Carolina and Louisiana. In both 1820 and 1830, South Carolina was the state with the highest percentage of its population enslaved, and also the state which had the greatest representation of its free population (Tables 5.5 and 5.6). Free people in South Carolina had 50% more representation than the free people across the free states. South Carolina had 27,141 free people per representative in 1820 compared to 41,885 free people per representative across all the free states combined. In 1830, South Carolina had one representative for every 29,542 free people, while the free states had one representative for every 49,653 free people. (I count Delaware as a free state due to its enslaved population being significantly less as a proportion of its population than the other states in which slavery was legal.)

Following the 1820 and 1830 censuses, a free person in a slave state had 30% more voting power than a free person in a free state.

Table 5.5: Free People in Slave States Had Disproportionate Representative Power in 1820 (23 States)

State	Seats	Total Pop.	Free Pop.	Slave Pop.	Percent Slave	Total Pop. Per Rep.	Free Pop. Per Rep.	Voting Power
United States	212	9,548,438	8,024,256	1,524,182	16.0%	45,040	37,850	100.0%
Slave States	88	4,332,213	2,830,541	1,501,672	34.7%	49,230	32,165	117.7%
Free States	124	5,216,225	5,193,715	22,510	0.4%	42,066	41,885	90.4%
South Carolina	9	502,741	244,266	258,475	51.4%	55,860	27,141	139.5%
Louisiana	3	153,407	84,343	69,064	45.0%	51,136	28,114	134.6%
Georgia	7	340,989	191,333	149,656	43.9%	48,713	27,333	138.5%
Mississippi	1	75,448	42,634	32,814	43.5%	75,448	42,634	88.8%
Virginia	22	1,065,379	640,226	425,153	39.9%	48,426	29,101	130.1%
Alabama	3	127,901	86,022	41,879	32.7%	42,634	28,674	132.0%
North Carolina	13	638,829	433,812	205,017	32.1%	49,141	33,370	113.4%
Maryland	9	407,350	299,952	107,398	26.4%	45,261	33,328	113.6%
Kentucky	12	564,317	438,585	125,732	22.3%	47,026	36,549	103.6%
District of Columbia	-	33,039	26,662	6,377	19.3%	x	x	x
Tennessee	9	422,813	342,706	80,107	18.9%	46,979	38,078	99.4%
Delaware	1	72,749	68,240	4,509	6.2%	72,749	68,240	55.5%
New Jersey	6	277,575	270,018	7,557	2.7%	46,263	45,003	84.1%
New York	34	1,372,812	1,362,724	10,088	0.7%	40,377	40,080	94.4%
Rhode Island	2	83,059	83,011	48	0.1%	41,530	41,506	91.2%
Connecticut	6	275,202	275,105	97	0.0%	45,867	45,851	82.6%
Pennsylvania	26	1,049,458	1,049,247	211	0.0%	40,364	40,356	93.8%
Illinois	1	55,211	55,211	-	0.0%	55,211	55,211	68.6%
Indiana	3	147,178	147,178	-	0.0%	49,059	49,059	77.2%
Vermont	5	235,764	235,764	-	0.0%	47,153	47,153	80.3%
New Hampshire	6	244,161	244,161	-	0.0%	40,694	40,694	93.0%
Maine	7	298,335	298,335	-	0.0%	42,619	42,619	88.8%
Massachusetts	13	523,287	523,287	-	0.0%	40,253	40,253	94.0%
Ohio	14	581,434	581,434	-	0.0%	41,531	41,531	91.1%

Following the 1840 Census, Congress changed[33] its apportionment formula from the Jefferson method, used since 1792, to the Webster method. (I'm not going to dig into the math here. If you are interested, you can find the information on the U.S. Census website.)[34] The changed formula resulted in the only reduction in the total seats in Congress in American history, from 240 seats in 1830 to 223 seats in 1840. The Webster method was used only once in the 1840 Census. Starting in 1850, Congress used the Hamilton/Vinton method. Regardless of the apportionment formula used, the overrepresentation of free people in slave states remained unchanged.

In 1840 and 1850, a free person in a slave state had 30% more voting power than a free person in a free state, just as they did in 1820 and 1830. The enslaved population had increased by another 1 million people, from 2 million in 1830 to 3.2 million in 1850.

Following the 1840 census, there were 2 states that bucked the trend (Table 5.7). Arkansas was the only slave state whose free population was underrepresented compared to the average free state, and Rhode Island was the only free state whose

Table 5.6: Free People in Slave States Had Disproportionate Representative Power in 1830 (24 States)

State	Seats	Total Pop.	Free Pop.	Slave Pop.	Percent Slave	Total Pop. Per Rep.	Free Pop. Per Rep.	Voting Power
United States	240	12,763,945	10,775,012	1,988,933	15.6%	53,183	44,896	100.0%
Slave States	98	5,706,437	3,724,331	1,982,106	34.7%	58,229	38,003	118.1%
Free States	142	7,057,508	7,050,681	6,827	0.1%	49,701	49,653	90.4%
South Carolina	9	581,185	265,784	315,401	54.3%	64,576	29,532	152.0%
Louisiana	3	215,739	106,151	109,588	50.8%	71,913	35,384	126.9%
Mississippi	2	136,621	70,962	65,659	48.1%	68,311	35,481	126.5%
Georgia	9	516,823	299,292	217,531	42.1%	57,425	33,255	135.0%
Virginia	21	1,211,405	741,648	469,757	38.8%	57,686	35,317	127.1%
Alabama	5	309,527	191,978	117,549	38.0%	61,905	38,396	116.9%
North Carolina	13	737,987	492,386	245,601	33.3%	56,768	37,876	118.5%
Kentucky	13	687,917	522,704	165,213	24.0%	52,917	40,208	111.7%
Maryland	8	447,040	344,046	102,994	23.0%	55,880	43,006	104.4%
Tennessee	13	681,904	540,301	141,603	20.8%	52,454	41,562	108.0%
Missouri	2	140,455	115,364	25,091	17.9%	70,228	57,682	77.8%
District of Columbia	-	39,834	33,715	6,119	15.4%	x	x	x
Delaware	1	76,748	73,456	3,292	4.3%	76,748	73,456	61.1%
New Jersey	6	320,823	318,569	2,254	0.7%	53,471	53,095	84.6%
Illinois	3	157,445	156,698	747	0.5%	52,482	52,233	86.0%
Pennsylvania	28	1,348,233	1,347,830	403	0.0%	48,151	48,137	93.3%
Rhode Island	2	97,199	97,182	17	0.0%	48,600	48,591	92.4%
Connecticut	6	297,675	297,651	24	0.0%	49,613	49,609	90.5%
New York	40	1,918,608	1,918,533	75	0.0%	47,965	47,963	93.6%
New Hampshire	5	269,328	269,325	3	0.0%	53,866	53,865	83.3%
Indiana	7	343,031	343,028	3	0.0%	49,004	49,004	91.6%
Ohio	19	937,903	937,897	6	0.0%	49,363	49,363	91.0%
Maine	8	399,455	399,453	2	0.0%	49,932	49,932	89.9%
Massachusetts	12	610,408	610,407	1	0.0%	50,867	50,867	88.3%
Vermont	5	280,652	280,652	-	0.0%	56,130	56,130	80.0%

free population had equal representation compared to the average slave state. These 2 states were outliers due to their small populations. Arkansas was the second least populous state, and Rhode Island was the third least populous state. Small states often are the worst or best represented because the addition or subtraction of a single representative drastically changes the small state's representative power.

Table 5.7 Free People in Slave States Had Disproportionate Representative Power in 1840 (26 States)

State	Seats	Total Pop.	Free Pop.	Slave Pop.	Percent Slave	Total Pop. Per Rep.	Free Pop. Per Rep.	Voting Power
United States	223	16,934,810	14,473,099	2,461,711	14.5%	75,941	64,902	100.0%
Slave States	87	7,201,860	4,743,856	2,458,004	34.1%	82,780	54,527	119.0%
Free States	136	9,732,950	9,729,243	3,707	0.0%	71,566	71,539	90.7%
South Carolina	7	594,398	267,360	327,038	55.0%	84,914	38,194	169.9%
Mississippi	4	375,651	180,440	195,211	52.0%	93,913	45,110	143.9%
Louisiana	4	352,411	183,959	168,452	47.8%	88,103	45,990	141.1%
Alabama	7	590,756	337,224	253,532	42.9%	84,394	48,175	134.7%
Georgia	8	691,392	410,448	280,944	40.6%	86,424	51,306	126.5%
Virginia	15	1,239,797	790,710	449,087	36.2%	82,653	52,714	123.1%
North Carolina	9	753,419	507,602	245,817	32.6%	83,713	56,400	115.1%
Kentucky	10	779,828	597,570	182,258	23.4%	77,983	59,757	108.6%
Tennessee	11	829,210	646,151	183,059	22.1%	75,383	58,741	110.5%
Arkansas	1	97,574	77,639	19,935	20.4%	97,574	77,639	83.6%
Maryland	6	470,010	380,273	89,737	19.1%	78,335	63,379	102.4%
Missouri	5	383,702	325,462	58,240	15.2%	76,740	65,092	99.7%
District of Columbia	-	43,712	39,018	4,694	10.7%	x	x	x
Delaware	1	78,085	75,480	2,605	3.3%	78,085	75,480	86.0%
New Jersey	5	373,306	372,632	674	0.2%	74,661	74,526	87.1%
Illinois	7	476,183	475,852	331	0.1%	68,026	67,979	95.5%
Connecticut	4	309,978	309,961	17	0.0%	77,495	77,490	83.8%
Rhode Island	2	108,830	108,825	5	0.0%	54,415	54,413	119.3%
Pennsylvania	24	1,724,033	1,723,969	64	0.0%	71,835	71,832	90.4%
Indiana	10	685,866	685,863	3	0.0%	68,587	68,586	94.6%
New Hampshire	4	284,574	284,573	1	0.0%	71,144	71,143	91.2%
Ohio	21	1,519,467	1,519,464	3	0.0%	72,356	72,355	89.7%
New York	34	2,428,921	2,428,917	4	0.0%	71,439	71,439	90.8%
Michigan	3	212,267	212,267	-	0.0%	70,756	70,756	91.7%
Vermont	4	291,948	291,948	-	0.0%	72,987	72,987	88.9%
Maine	7	501,793	501,793	-	0.0%	71,685	71,685	90.5%
Massachusetts	10	737,699	737,699	-	0.0%	73,770	73,770	88.0%

The same phenomenon of small states being outliers with representative power continued in 1850 (Table 5.8). Following the 1850 census, every single slave state's free population was better represented than every free state's free population, except for California and Rhode Island. South Carolina's free population remained the most overrepresented people, with 47,254 free people per representative, having almost double the voting power of free people living in free states, who only received one representative for every 93,268 free people.

Table 5.8: Free People in Slave States Had Disproportionate Representative Power in 1850 (31 States)

State	Seats	Total Pop.	Free Pop.	Slave Pop.	Percent Slave	Total Pop. Per Rep.	Free Pop. Per Rep.	Voting Power
United States	234	23,099,578	19,913,291	3,186,287	13.8%	98,716	85,100	100.0%
Slave States	89	9,573,124	6,389,363	3,183,761	33.3%	107,563	71,791	118.5%
Free States	145	13,526,454	13,523,928	2,526	0.0%	93,286	93,268	91.2%
South Carolina	6	668,507	283,523	384,984	57.6%	111,418	47,254	180.1%
Mississippi	5	606,526	296,648	309,878	51.1%	121,305	59,330	143.4%
Louisiana	4	517,762	272,953	244,809	47.3%	129,441	68,238	124.7%
Florida	1	87,445	48,135	39,310	45.0%	87,445	48,135	176.8%
Georgia	8	906,185	524,503	381,682	42.1%	113,273	65,563	129.8%
Alabama	7	771,623	446,779	324,844	42.1%	110,232	63,826	133.3%
Virginia	13	1,421,661	949,133	472,528	33.2%	109,359	73,010	116.6%
North Carolina	8	869,039	580,491	288,548	33.2%	108,630	72,561	117.3%
Texas	2	212,592	154,431	58,161	27.4%	106,296	77,216	110.2%
Tennessee	10	1,002,717	763,258	239,459	23.9%	100,272	76,326	111.5%
Arkansas	2	209,897	162,797	47,100	22.4%	104,949	81,399	104.5%
Kentucky	10	982,405	771,424	210,981	21.5%	98,241	77,142	110.3%
Maryland	6	583,034	492,666	90,368	15.5%	97,172	82,111	103.6%
Missouri	7	682,044	594,622	87,422	12.8%	97,435	84,946	100.2%
District of Columbia	-	51,687	48,000	3,687	7.1%	x	x	x
Delaware	1	91,532	89,242	2,290	2.5%	91,532	89,242	95.4%
New Jersey	5	489,555	489,319	236	0.0%	97,911	97,864	87.0%
California	2	92,597	92,597	-	0.0%	46,299	46,299	183.8%
Rhode Island	2	147,545	147,545	-	0.0%	73,773	73,773	115.4%
Iowa	2	192,214	192,214	-	0.0%	96,107	96,107	88.5%
Wisconsin	3	305,391	305,391	-	0.0%	101,797	101,797	83.6%
Vermont	3	314,120	314,120	-	0.0%	104,707	104,707	81.3%
New Hampshire	3	317,976	317,976	-	0.0%	105,992	105,992	80.3%
Connecticut	4	370,792	370,792	-	0.0%	92,698	92,698	91.8%
Michigan	4	397,654	397,654	-	0.0%	99,414	99,414	85.6%
Maine	6	583,169	583,169	-	0.0%	97,195	97,195	87.6%
Illinois	9	851,470	851,470	-	0.0%	94,608	94,608	89.9%
Indiana	11	988,416	988,416	-	0.0%	89,856	89,856	94.7%
Massachusetts	11	994,514	994,514	-	0.0%	90,410	90,410	94.1%
Ohio	21	1,980,329	1,980,329	-	0.0%	94,301	94,301	90.2%
Pennsylvania	25	2,311,786	2,311,786	-	0.0%	92,471	92,471	92.0%
New York	33	3,097,394	3,097,394	-	0.0%	93,860	93,860	90.7%

By 1860, on the eve of the Civil War, the 8.2 million free people living in slave states were represented by 84 representatives in Congress, or one representative for every 98,229 people (Table 5.9). Compare this to how the 18.9 million free people living in the free states were represented by 156 representatives in Congress, or one representative for every 121,224 people. Free people in slave states had 23% more voting power than free people in free states.

The 6 states in which enslaved people made up more than 40% of the population, South Carolina, Mississippi, Louisiana, Alabama, Florida, and Georgia, were 6 of the 9 most overrepresented states. The other 3 states? Tiny Rhode Island and newly admitted Minnesota and Oregon.

Table 5.9: Free People in Slave States Had Disproportionate Representative Power in 1860 (33 States)

State	Seats	Total Pop.	Free Pop.	Slave Pop.	Percent Slave	Total Pop. Per Rep.	Free Pop. Per Rep.	Voting Power
United States	240	31,115,920	27,162,206	3,953,714	12.7%	129,650	113,176	100.0%
Slave States	84	12,203,157	8,251,259	3,951,898	32.4%	145,276	98,229	115.2%
Free States	179	22,012,588	21,579,984	432,604	2.0%	122,975	120,559	93.9%
South Carolina	4	703,708	301,302	402,406	57.2%	175,927	75,326	150.2%
Mississippi	5	791,305	354,674	436,631	55.2%	158,261	70,935	159.5%
Louisiana	5	708,002	376,276	331,726	46.9%	141,600	75,255	150.4%
Alabama	6	964,201	529,121	435,080	45.1%	160,700	88,187	128.3%
Florida	1	140,424	78,679	61,745	44.0%	140,424	78,679	143.8%
Georgia	7	1,057,286	595,088	462,198	43.7%	151,041	85,013	133.1%
North Carolina	7	992,622	661,563	331,059	33.4%	141,803	94,509	119.8%
Virginia	11	1,596,318	1,105,453	490,865	30.7%	145,120	100,496	112.6%
Texas	4	604,215	421,649	182,566	30.2%	151,054	105,412	107.4%
Arkansas	3	435,450	324,335	111,115	25.5%	145,150	108,112	104.7%
Tennessee	8	1,109,801	834,082	275,719	24.8%	138,725	104,260	108.6%
Kentucky	9	1,155,684	930,201	225,483	19.5%	128,409	103,356	109.5%
Maryland	5	687,049	599,860	87,189	12.7%	137,410	119,972	94.3%
Missouri	9	1,182,012	1,067,081	114,931	9.7%	131,335	118,565	95.5%
District of Columbia	-	75,080	71,895	3,185	4.2%	x	x	x
Delaware	1	112,216	110,418	1,798	1.6%	112,216	110,418	102.5%
New Jersey	5	672,035	672,017	18	0.0%	134,407	134,403	84.2%
Oregon	1	52,465	52,465	-	0.0%	52,465	52,465	215.7%
Minnesota	2	172,023	172,023	-	0.0%	86,012	86,012	131.6%
Rhode Island	2	174,620	174,620	-	0.0%	87,310	87,310	129.6%
Vermont	3	315,098	315,098	-	0.0%	105,033	105,033	107.8%
New Hampshire	3	326,073	326,073	-	0.0%	108,691	108,691	104.1%
California	3	379,994	379,994	-	0.0%	126,665	126,665	89.4%
Connecticut	4	460,147	460,147	-	0.0%	115,037	115,037	98.4%
Maine	5	628,279	628,279	-	0.0%	125,656	125,656	90.1%
Iowa	6	674,913	674,913	-	0.0%	112,486	112,486	100.6%
Michigan	6	749,113	749,113	-	0.0%	124,852	124,852	90.6%
Wisconsin	6	775,881	775,881	-	0.0%	129,314	129,314	87.5%
Massachusetts	10	1,231,066	1,231,066	-	0.0%	123,107	123,107	91.9%
Indiana	11	1,350,428	1,350,428	-	0.0%	122,766	122,766	92.2%
Illinois	14	1,711,951	1,711,951	-	0.0%	122,282	122,282	92.6%
Ohio	19	2,339,511	2,339,511	-	0.0%	123,132	123,132	91.9%
Pennsylvania	24	2,906,215	2,906,215	-	0.0%	121,092	121,092	93.5%
New York	31	3,880,735	3,880,735	-	0.0%	125,185	125,185	90.4%

The Civil War was fought from 1861–1865 over the issue of slavery (or, if you like, a state's right to allow some people in the state to enslave others). High-end estimates put the death toll from 4 years of Civil War at over 1 million Americans.

ii. Rapid and Unequal Expansion, 1870–1920

Over the half-century following the Civil War, the United States expanded rapidly. The population more than tripled from 31 million in 1860 to 106 million in 1920 as the number of states increased from 33 to 48. To accommodate this growth, Congress passed legislation that increased its size from 240 members in 1860 to the modern 435 by 1920. And, crucially, the 19th Amendment passed in 1920 to guarantee the right to vote for women. Though, functionally, it only guaranteed the right to vote to white women until the passage of the Voting Rights Act of 1965.

The settling (colonization) of western states put added emphasis on the lack of representation for Native Americans. The history of forced migration, broken treaties, and, yes, the genocide of Indigenous peoples is, along with slavery, the gravest of our national sins. The westward expansion of the United States, the idea of manifest destiny, reached its conclusion by the early 1900s. Voting rights for Native Americans were piecemeal until the passage of the **Indian Citizenship Act of 1924,**[35] which finally became nationally enforced with the passage of the Voting Rights Act of 1965.

Newly admitted western states often had very small populations. The people in such states, like Nevada, Wyoming, and Montana, enjoyed additional voting power not just in the Senate but also the House. The residents of other newly admitted small states, such as Colorado, were severely underrepresented in the House due to the mathematical difficulties of assigning appropriate representation across states of increasingly disparate size.

Table 5.10: Maximum Historic Representation Inequality Between States

Census Year	National Average	Most Overrepresented			Most Underrepresented			Maximum Inequality Ratio
		State	Pop. Per Rep.	Voting Power	State	Pop. Per Rep.	Voting Power	
1790	30,763	South Carolina	23,663	130.0%	Delaware	50,209	61.3%	2.1
1800	30,898	Virginia	24,291	127.2%	Delaware	58,120	53.2%	2.4
1810	32,742	South Carolina	24,306	134.7%	New Jersey	39,117	83.7%	1.6
1820	37,850	South Carolina	27,141	139.5%	Delaware	68,240	55.5%	2.5
1830	44,896	South Carolina	29,532	152.0%	Delaware	73,456	61.1%	2.5
1840	64,902	South Carolina	38,194	169.9%	Arkansas	77,639	83.6%	2.0
1850	85,100	California	46,299	183.8%	New Hampshire	105,992	80.3%	2.3
1860	113,176	Oregon	52,465	215.7%	New Jersey	134,403	84.2%	2.6
1870	130,526	Nevada	42,491	308.2%	West Virginia	147,338	88.9%	3.5
1880	151,912	Nevada	62,266	244.9%	Colorado	194,327	78.5%	3.1
1890	173,878	Nevada	45,761	381.4%	Colorado	206,099	84.7%	4.5
1900	192,760	Nevada	42,335	458.2%	Utah	276,749	70.1%	6.5
1910	210,328	Nevada	80,293	262.9%	Washington	228,027	92.6%	2.8
1920	241,864	Nevada	75,820	320.3%	New Mexico	353,428	68.7%	4.7

During this period of rapid expansion, representative inequality between the most and least represented states was high (Table 5.10). The Maximum Inequality Ratio (defined as the population per representative of the most underrepresented state divided by the population per representative of the most overrepresented state) between the most overrepresented and most underrepresented states ranged from 2.8 to 6.5. For example, in 1900, voters in Nevada enjoyed 6.5 times the voting power as voters in Utah; one vote in Nevada was equal to 6.5 votes in Utah.

Tables 5.11 through 5.16 demonstrate that the very smallest states usually were overrepresented, while the medium small states were more often underrepresented

In assigning representation to states with inequal populations, there will always be some degree of inequality. What is an acceptable inequality ratio for representation between states? How equal is equal enough? I suggest an answer this question in part C of this chapter. But first, an analysis of the census data from 1870 to 1920.

During the short lived Reconstruction following the Civil War, American democracy was genuinely multiracial. In 1867, at least 85% of Black men were registered to vote in former slave states like Alabama, Florida, Georgia, Louisiana, North Carolina, and South Carolina.[36] Voting rights led to electoral victory: more than 600 Black Americans were elected to state legislatures, and in 1872 the state legislatures in Mississippi and South Carolina elected Black Speakers of the House.[37]

But it did not last. In an unrelenting campaign of terror, white supremacists murdured nearly 2,000 Black Americans in the decade after the Civil War. While the federal government under the administration of President Ulysses S. Grant successfully intervened

Table 5.11: Representation in 1870 (37 States)

States	Seats	Population	Pop. Per Rep.	Voting Power
United States	292	38,245,341	130,977	100.0%
Nevada	1	42,491	42,491	308.2%
Oregon	1	90,923	90,923	144.1%
Nebraska	1	122,993	122,993	106.5%
Delaware	1	125,015	125,015	104.8%
District of Columbia	-	131,700	x	x
Florida	2	187,748	93,874	139.5%
Rhode Island	2	217,353	108,677	120.5%
New Hampshire	3	318,300	106,100	123.4%
Vermont	3	330,551	110,184	118.9%
Kansas	3	364,399	121,466	107.8%
Minnesota	3	439,706	146,569	89.4%
West Virginia	3	442,014	147,338	88.9%
Arkansas	4	484,471	121,118	108.1%
Connecticut	4	537,454	134,364	97.5%
California	4	560,247	140,062	93.5%
Maine	5	626,915	125,383	104.5%
South Carolina	5	703,606	140,721	93.1%
Louisiana	6	726,915	121,153	108.1%
Maryland	6	780,894	130,149	100.6%
Texas	6	818,579	136,430	96.0%
Mississippi	6	827,922	137,987	94.9%
New Jersey	7	906,096	129,442	101.2%
Alabama	8	996,992	124,624	105.1%
Wisconsin	8	1,054,670	131,834	99.4%
North Carolina	8	1,071,361	133,920	97.8%
Michigan	9	1,184,059	131,562	99.6%
Georgia	9	1,184,109	131,568	99.6%
Iowa	9	1,194,020	132,669	98.7%
Virginia	9	1,225,163	136,129	96.2%
Tennessee	10	1,258,520	125,852	104.1%
Kentucky	10	1,321,011	132,101	99.1%
Massachusetts	11	1,457,351	132,486	98.9%
Indiana	13	1,680,637	129,280	101.3%
Missouri	13	1,721,295	132,407	98.9%
Illinois	19	2,539,891	133,678	98.0%
Ohio	20	2,665,260	133,263	98.3%
Pennsylvania	27	3,521,951	130,443	100.4%
New York	33	4,382,759	132,811	98.6%

to enforce safe, democratic elections in 1872, Reconstruction ended following a negotiated agreement to resolve the disputed 1876 presidential election. White supremacists drove Black Americans out of politics by force, and once they had regained control of the legislatures, they started passing laws to entrench their power.[38] (See Chapter 3 of *Tyranny of the Minority* by historians Steven Levitsky and Daniel Ziblatt for a more detailed look at this time period.)

Starting in the 1880s and accelerating in the 1890s and early 1900s, formerly Confederate states implemented what would be known as Jim Crow laws. These laws were effective: voter turnout among Black Americans went from 61% in 1880 to 2% in 1912.[39] Jim Crow lasted until the Civil Rights movement of the 1950s and 1960s.

During Jim Crow, Black Americans were counted as 1 person for apportionment, yet their disenfranchisement in the South was practically as complete as it was during slavery. The effect of such laws on voting power for southern Whites was likely even greater than the effect of the 3/5 Clause as discussed in the previous section. However, my data analysis for 1870–1920 does not take racial discrimination into account. Here, my focus is on the representative discrepancy between states independent of voter suppression of Black Americans.

Even without accounting for racial discrimination, there was significant representative inequality between

Table 5.12: Representation in 1880 (38 States)

States	Seats	Population	Pop. Per Rep.	Voting Power
United States	325	49,549,014	152,459	100.0%
Nevada	1	62,266	62,266	244.9%
Delaware	1	146,608	146,608	104.0%
Oregon	1	174,768	174,768	87.2%
District of Columbia	-	177,624	x	x
Colorado	1	194,327	194,327	78.5%
Florida	2	269,493	134,747	113.1%
Rhode Island	2	276,531	138,266	110.3%
Vermont	2	332,286	166,143	91.8%
New Hampshire	2	346,991	173,496	87.9%
Nebraska	3	452,402	150,801	101.1%
West Virginia	4	618,457	154,614	98.6%
Connecticut	4	622,700	155,675	97.9%
Maine	4	648,936	162,234	94.0%
Minnesota	5	780,773	156,155	97.6%
Arkansas	5	802,525	160,505	95.0%
California	6	864,694	144,116	105.8%
Louisiana	6	939,946	156,658	97.3%
Maryland	6	934,943	155,824	97.8%
South Carolina	7	995,577	142,225	107.2%
Kansas	7	996,096	142,299	107.1%
New Jersey	7	1,131,116	161,588	94.4%
Mississippi	7	1,131,597	161,657	94.3%
Alabama	8	1,262,505	157,813	96.6%
Wisconsin	9	1,315,497	146,166	104.3%
North Carolina	9	1,399,750	155,528	98.0%
Virginia	10	1,512,565	151,257	100.8%
Georgia	10	1,542,180	154,218	98.9%
Tennessee	10	1,542,359	154,236	98.8%
Texas	11	1,591,749	144,704	105.4%
Iowa	11	1,624,615	147,692	103.2%
Michigan	11	1,636,987	148,817	102.4%
Kentucky	11	1,648,690	149,881	101.7%
Massachusetts	12	1,783,085	148,590	102.6%
Indiana	13	1,978,301	152,177	100.2%
Missouri	14	2,168,380	154,884	98.4%
Illinois	20	3,077,871	153,894	99.1%
Ohio	21	3,198,062	152,289	100.1%
Pennsylvania	28	4,282,891	152,960	99.7%
New York	34	5,082,871	149,496	102.0%

people living in different states. Additionally, Americans living in the District of Columbia continued to be denied representation in Congress.

As shown in Table 5.11, in 1870, Americans living in the smallest states were overrepresented compared to the national average, while Americans living in certain medium-small states were underrepresented. The 5 most overrepresented states were all among the 7 smallest states; the 5 most underrepresented states ranked between 18th and 27th most populous of the 37 states. At the most extreme, Americans voting in Nevada, the smallest state with less than 43,000 residents, enjoyed 3.5 times the voting power as Americans voting in West Virginia.

Americans living in the largest states had voting power within 5% of the national average. This makes sense because, since larger states have greater numbers of representatives, the addition or subtraction of a single representative does not affect the population per representative as dramatically as adding a second representative to a small state. For example, Florida with its two representatives was the third most overrepresented state in 1870. But if Florida had only one representative, its population per representative would have doubled, and it would have become by far the

Table 5.13: Representation in 1890 (44 States)

States	Seats	Population	Pop. Per Rep.	Voting Power
United States	*356*	*62,130,798*	*174,525*	*100.0%*
Nevada	1	45,761	45,761	381.4%
Wyoming	1	60,705	60,705	287.5%
Idaho	1	84,385	84,385	206.8%
Montana	1	132,159	132,159	132.1%
Delaware	1	168,493	168,493	103.6%
North Dakota	1	182,719	182,719	95.5%
District of Columbia	-	230,392	x	x
Oregon	2	313,767	156,884	111.2%
South Dakota	2	328,808	164,404	106.2%
Vermont	2	332,422	166,211	105.0%
Rhode Island	2	345,506	172,753	101.0%
Washington	2	349,390	174,695	99.9%
New Hampshire	2	376,530	188,265	92.7%
Florida	2	391,422	195,711	89.2%
Colorado	2	412,198	206,099	84.7%
Maine	4	661,086	165,272	105.6%
Connecticut	4	746,258	186,565	93.5%
West Virginia	4	762,794	190,699	91.5%
Maryland	6	1,042,390	173,732	100.5%
Nebraska	6	1,058,910	176,485	98.9%
Louisiana	6	1,118,587	186,431	93.6%
Arkansas	6	1,128,179	188,030	92.8%
South Carolina	7	1,151,149	164,450	106.1%
California	7	1,208,130	172,590	101.1%
Mississippi	7	1,289,600	184,229	94.7%
Minnesota	7	1,301,826	185,975	93.8%
Kansas	8	1,427,096	178,387	97.8%
New Jersey	8	1,444,933	180,617	96.6%
Alabama	9	1,513,017	168,113	103.8%
North Carolina	9	1,617,947	179,772	97.1%
Virginia	10	1,655,980	165,598	105.4%
Wisconsin	10	1,686,880	168,688	103.5%
Tennessee	10	1,767,518	176,752	98.7%
Georgia	11	1,837,353	167,032	104.5%
Kentucky	11	1,858,635	168,967	103.3%
Iowa	11	1,911,896	173,809	100.4%
Michigan	12	2,093,889	174,491	100.0%
Indiana	13	2,192,404	168,646	103.5%
Texas	13	2,235,523	171,963	101.5%
Massachusetts	13	2,238,943	172,226	101.3%
Missouri	15	2,670,184	178,012	98.0%
Ohio	21	3,672,816	174,896	99.8%
Illinois	22	3,826,351	173,925	100.3%
Pennsylvania	30	5,258,014	175,267	99.6%
New York	34	5,997,853	176,407	98.9%

Table 5.14: Representation in 1900 (45 States)

States	Seats	Population	Pop. Per Rep.	Voting Power
United States	386	74,883,948	194,000	100.0%
Nevada	1	42,335	42,335	458.2%
Wyoming	1	92,531	92,531	209.7%
Idaho	1	161,772	161,772	119.9%
Delaware	1	184,735	184,735	105.0%
Montana	1	243,329	243,329	79.7%
Utah	1	276,749	276,749	70.1%
District of Columbia	-	278,718	x	x
North Dakota	2	319,146	159,573	121.6%
Vermont	2	343,641	171,821	112.9%
South Dakota	2	401,570	200,785	96.6%
New Hampshire	2	411,588	205,794	94.3%
Oregon	2	413,536	206,768	93.8%
Rhode Island	2	428,556	214,278	90.5%
Washington	3	518,103	172,701	112.3%
Florida	3	528,542	176,181	110.1%
Colorado	3	539,700	179,900	107.8%
Maine	4	691,466	172,867	112.2%
Connecticut	5	908,420	181,684	106.8%
West Virginia	5	958,800	191,760	101.2%
Nebraska	6	1,066,300	177,717	109.2%
Maryland	6	1,188,044	198,007	98.0%
Arkansas	7	1,311,564	187,366	103.5%
South Carolina	7	1,340,316	191,474	101.3%
Louisiana	7	1,381,625	197,375	98.3%
Kansas	8	1,470,495	183,812	105.5%
California	8	1,485,053	185,632	104.5%
Mississippi	8	1,551,270	193,909	100.0%
Minnesota	9	1,751,394	194,599	99.7%
Alabama	9	1,828,697	203,189	95.5%
Virginia	10	1,854,184	185,418	104.6%
New Jersey	10	1,883,669	188,367	103.0%
North Carolina	10	1,893,810	189,381	102.4%
Tennessee	10	2,020,616	202,062	96.0%
Wisconsin	11	2,069,042	188,095	103.1%
Kentucky	11	2,147,174	195,198	99.4%
Georgia	11	2,216,331	201,485	96.3%
Iowa	11	2,231,858	202,896	95.6%
Michigan	12	2,420,982	201,749	96.2%
Indiana	13	2,516,462	193,574	100.2%
Massachusetts	14	2,805,346	200,382	96.8%
Texas	16	3,048,710	190,544	101.8%
Missouri	16	3,106,665	194,167	99.9%
Ohio	21	4,157,545	197,978	98.0%
Illinois	25	4,821,550	192,862	100.6%
Pennsylvania	32	6,302,115	196,941	98.5%
New York	37	7,269,894	196,484	98.7%

most underrepresented state, with voting power of just 68.8% of the national average.

As the least populous state, Nevada continued to be the most overrepresented state in 1880. But the most underrepresented states changed completely, showing how apportionment could have somewhat unpredictable results.

Across the decades, smaller states were more likely to be over- or underrepresented. In 1880, 7 of the 8 least populous states were among the 5 most over- or underrepresented states. Only Delaware was appropriately represented, which was due to the fortunate coincidence that Delaware's population was almost exactly equivalent to the national average population per representative. For the other 7 smallest states, whether they were over- or underrepresented came down to luck.

In 1890, the 4 smallest states were the 4 most overrepresented states, all having more than 130% voting power. Three states (Nevada, Wyoming, Idaho) were so small that they had more than 200% voting power: each vote cast effectively counted as two compared to the rest of the nation.

The 1900 Census is the most extreme example of the representative variability of small states.

Among the 5 most underrepresented and 5 most overrepresented states were 10 of the smallest 12 states.

The 1890 and 1900 Censuses demonstrate the representative variability of this period. In 1890, there were 9 states with less than 95% voting power and 10 states with greater than 105% voting power. Contrast that with 1900, when there were just 5 states with less than 95% voting power and 13 states with greater than 105% voting power. In 1890, most of the small to mid-size states from New Hampshire to Minnesota were underrepresented; in 1900, most of the small to mid-size states from New Hampshire to Nebraska were overrepresented. Rapidly changing state populations made these variable swings in representative power a normal part of American democracy.

The story of the 1910 and 1920 Censuses is one of petty partisanship. Reapportionment following the 1910 Census proceeded as normal, with the same issues of variable representation as in the Censuses from 1870–1900. The 5 most overrepresented states in 1910 were among the smallest 9 states, while the 5 most underrepresented states were small to mid-size states.

But the Census in 1920 tells a different story. While the most overrepresented states in 1920

Table 5.15: Representation in 1910 (46 States)

States	Seats	Population	Pop. Per Rep.	Voting Power
United States	433	91,403,186	211,093	100.0%
Nevada	1	80,293	80,293	262.9%
Wyoming	1	144,658	144,658	145.9%
Delaware	1	202,322	202,322	104.3%
Idaho	2	323,440	161,720	130.5%
District of Columbia	-	331,069	x	x
Vermont	2	355,956	177,978	118.6%
Montana	2	366,338	183,169	115.2%
Utah	2	371,864	185,932	113.5%
New Hampshire	2	430,572	215,286	98.1%
Rhode Island	3	542,610	180,870	116.7%
North Dakota	3	574,403	191,468	110.2%
South Dakota	3	575,676	191,892	110.0%
Oregon	3	672,765	224,255	94.1%
Maine	4	742,371	185,593	113.7%
Florida	4	752,619	188,155	112.2%
Colorado	4	798,572	199,643	105.7%
Connecticut	5	1,114,756	222,951	94.7%
Washington	5	1,140,134	228,027	92.6%
Nebraska	6	1,192,214	198,702	106.2%
West Virginia	6	1,221,119	203,520	103.7%
Maryland	6	1,295,346	215,891	97.8%
South Carolina	7	1,515,400	216,486	97.5%
Arkansas	7	1,574,449	224,921	93.9%
Louisiana	8	1,656,388	207,049	102.0%
Oklahoma	8	1,657,155	207,144	101.9%
Kansas	8	1,690,949	211,369	99.9%
Mississippi	8	1,797,114	224,639	94.0%
Virginia	10	2,061,612	206,161	102.4%
Minnesota	10	2,074,376	207,438	101.8%
Alabama	10	2,138,093	213,809	98.7%
Tennessee	10	2,184,789	218,479	96.6%
North Carolina	10	2,206,287	220,629	95.7%
Iowa	11	2,224,771	202,252	104.4%
Kentucky	11	2,289,905	208,173	101.4%
Wisconsin	11	2,332,853	212,078	99.5%
California	11	2,376,561	216,051	97.7%
New Jersey	12	2,537,167	211,431	99.8%
Georgia	12	2,609,121	217,427	97.1%
Indiana	13	2,700,876	207,760	101.6%
Michigan	13	2,810,173	216,167	97.7%
Missouri	16	3,293,335	205,833	102.6%
Massachusetts	16	3,366,416	210,401	100.3%
Texas	18	3,896,542	216,475	97.5%
Ohio	22	4,767,121	216,687	97.4%
Illinois	27	5,638,591	208,837	101.1%
Pennsylvania	36	7,665,111	212,920	99.1%
New York	43	9,108,934	211,836	99.6%

Table 5.16: Representation in 1920 (48 States)

States	Seats	Population	Pop. Per Rep.	Voting Power
United States	435	105,648,300	242,870	100.0%
Nevada	1	75,820	75,820	320.3%
Wyoming	1	193,487	193,487	125.5%
Delaware	1	223,003	223,003	108.9%
Arizona	1	309,495	309,495	78.5%
New Mexico	1	353,428	353,428	68.7%
Vermont	2	352,428	176,214	137.8%
Idaho	2	430,442	215,221	112.8%
District of Columbia	-	437,571	x	x
New Hampshire	2	443,083	221,542	109.6%
Utah	2	448,388	224,194	108.3%
Montana	2	541,511	270,756	89.7%
Rhode Island	3	604,397	201,466	120.6%
South Dakota	3	631,239	210,413	115.4%
North Dakota	3	643,953	214,651	113.1%
Oregon	3	783,389	261,130	93.0%
Maine	4	768,014	192,004	126.5%
Colorado	4	939,161	234,790	103.4%
Florida	4	968,470	242,118	100.3%
Nebraska	6	1,296,372	216,062	112.4%
Washington	5	1,354,596	270,919	89.6%
Connecticut	5	1,380,631	276,126	88.0%
Maryland	6	1,449,661	241,610	100.5%
West Virginia	6	1,463,701	243,950	99.6%
South Carolina	7	1,683,724	240,532	101.0%
Arkansas	7	1,752,204	250,315	97.0%
Kansas	8	1,769,257	221,157	109.8%
Mississippi	8	1,790,618	223,827	108.5%
Louisiana	8	1,798,509	224,814	108.0%
Oklahoma	8	2,028,283	253,535	95.8%
Virginia	10	2,309,187	230,919	105.2%
Tennessee	10	2,337,885	233,789	103.9%
Alabama	10	2,348,174	234,817	103.4%
Minnesota	10	2,385,656	238,566	101.8%
Iowa	11	2,404,021	218,547	111.1%
Kentucky	11	2,416,630	219,694	110.5%
North Carolina	10	2,559,123	255,912	94.9%
Wisconsin	11	2,631,305	239,210	101.5%
Georgia	12	2,895,832	241,319	100.6%
New Jersey	12	3,155,900	262,992	92.3%
Indiana	13	2,930,390	225,415	107.7%
Missouri	16	3,404,055	212,753	114.2%
California	11	3,426,031	311,457	78.0%
Michigan	13	3,668,412	282,186	86.1%
Massachusetts	16	3,852,356	240,772	100.9%
Texas	18	4,663,228	259,068	93.7%
Ohio	22	5,759,394	261,791	92.8%
Illinois	27	6,485,280	240,196	101.1%
Pennsylvania	36	8,720,017	242,223	100.3%
New York	43	10,380,589	241,409	100.6%

followed the trend of previous censuses, suddenly California and Michigan, 2 of the most populous 10 states, were among the top 5 most underrepresented! What happened? Did the apportionment formula change? The answer is that politics happened.

The 1920 Census revealed a major shift of the population from rural to urban areas, in large part due to massive waves of immigration from Europe following WWI. Under the reapportionment rules, power in Congress would have shifted from the South to the Northeast. Representatives from rural farm states and representatives from the South did not like this.[40] Congress ultimately could not agree on what size it should be, because each size of Congress would have favored some states over others. The end result of this was that the 1920 Census is the only Census in U.S. history after which there was no reapportionment. Despite their sometimes drastically different populations, states kept the same number of representatives that they were assigned following the 1910 Census. For example, California and Michigan experienced massive population growth between 1910 and 1920. California grew from 2.4 million people in 1910 to 3.4 million in 1920; Michigan grew from 2.8 million in 1910 to 3.7 million in 1920. Yet both states kept the same number of representatives they had been apportioned in 1910.

The only thing Congress could agree to was to add one representative for each of the 2 new states, Arizona and New Mexico. The addition of these 2 representatives brought the total size of Congress from 433 in 1910 to 435 in 1920.

The congressional deadlock regarding apportionment following the 1920 Census is a cautionary tale. It shows that we should not leave reapportionment up to each Congress, and that there should be a set of rules that ensure the politics of the moment do not result in a decade of malapportionment. Congress at the time recognized this, and passed a reapportionment bill in 1929 that, among other things, set the size of Congress to 435 members, which has persisted to this day. The resulting modern era of apportionment, beginning in 1930, is the best and fairest method of apportionment in our history. Yet, it still can be improved.

iii. Consistently Inconsistent Representation in the Modern Era

The modern era began with the 1929 Reapportionment and Census Act and the 1941 Act Setting the Apportionment Method for Future Censuses. These two laws[41] determine how Congress is apportioned to this day. Hawaii and Alaska were added as states in 1959, making the 1960 Census the first Census to include today's 50 states, and the Voting Rights Act of 1965 ended nearly a century of Jim Crow discrimination. By the 1970 Census, the United States had a population of 203 milion and was fully democratic, with voting rights for all adults regardless of race or sex.

In our modern era, we are as close as we ever have come to realizing equal representation. A big part of the reason is the modern formula for determining how many seats each state receives in reapportionment. This **Method of Equal Proportions**[42] automatically assigns one seat to each state. Additional seats are assigned to states in order of their Priority Value (PV), calculated based on each state's population. The formula used is as follows:

$$\textbf{PVn = State Population} / \sqrt{(n(n\text{-}1))}\textbf{, where n is the number of seats}$$
$$\textbf{the state would have if it received another seat.}$$

An example would be helpful. Today, California is the most populous state with a 2020 population of 39,576,757. California received its first seat based on its existence as a state. California is assigned a Priority Value of 27,984,993 for its second seat (the math: PV2 = 39,576,757 / $\sqrt{2}$(2-1); PV2 = 39,576,757 / $\sqrt{2}$; PV2 = 39,576,757 / 1.41;

PV2 = 27,984,993). Because California is the most populous state, it makes sense that California would be awarded the first additional seat in Congress; if Congress had just 51 seats, every state would receive 1 seat except California which would receive two. Texas, as the second most populous state, would receive the 52nd seat. While Florida is the third most populous state, it would not receive the 53rd seat. The Priority Value formula would instead award California a third seat (PV3$_{CA}$ 16,157,143) before Florida would receive its second seat (PV2$_{FL}$ 15,252,666). And so on and so forth the seats are awarded to all states according to their Priority Value. In today's 435-seat Congress, based on the 2020 Census, the state that received the 435th seat, or the 385th highest Priority Value, was Minnesota with its 8th seat with a Priority Value of 762,998. If Congress had one more member, the next state to receive another seat would be New York with its 27th seat with a Priority Value of 762,994. Using this formula, Congress would need to reach 811 members before Wyoming, the smallest state, would be awarded a 2nd seat.

The Priority Value system is how one state can go from being overrepresented in one census to being underrepresented in the next. For example, Montana in 2020 became the most overrepresented state after three decades of being the most underrepresented state (Table 5.17). The reason for the change was that Montana's population in 2020 increased such that its Priority Value for a 2nd seat was high enough for Montana to be awarded the 434th seat in Congress. If Montana's 2020 population had been just a little bit lower, Montana would have remained the most populous 1-seat state as opposed to becoming the least populous 2-seat state.

This apportionment formula and Priority Value system works better than any prior system. The inequality ratio between the most over- and the most underrepresented states declined from 4.6 in 1930 to less than 2 in every census since 1980. This is a

Table 5.17: Maximum Representation Inequality Between States in the Modern Era

Census Year	National Average	Most Overrepresented			Most Underrepresented			Maximum Inequality Ratio
		State	Pop. Per Rep.	Voting Power	State	Pop. Per Rep.	Voting Power	
1930	280,675	Nevada	86,390	324.9%	New Mexico	395,982	70.9%	4.6
1940	301,164	Nevada	110,247	273.2%	Vermont	359,231	83.8%	3.3
1950	344,587	Nevada	160,083	215.3%	Rhode Island	395,948	87.0%	2.5
1960	410,481	Alaska	226,167	181.5%	Maine	484,633	84.7%	2.1
1970	469,088	Alaska	304,067	154.3%	North Dakota	624,181	75.2%	2.1
1980	519,235	Montana	393,345	132.0%	South Dakota	690,178	75.2%	1.8
1990	572,466	Wyoming	455,975	125.5%	Montana	803,655	71.2%	1.8
2000	646,952	Wyoming	495,304	130.6%	Montana	905,316	71.5%	1.8
2010	710,767	Rhode Island	527,624	134.7%	Montana	994,416	71.5%	1.9
2020	761,169	Montana	542,704	140.3%	Delaware	990,837	76.8%	1.8

huge improvement. In the modern era, representation between the states has reached its historic best.

But we can do better. The inequality of representation is still too high!

In the current system, as the Montana example suggests, apportionment is a representation lottery for residents of small states. Going back to 1980, Montana has either been the most over- or the most underrepresented state in the country. While voting power is consistent for medium and large states, it is highly variable for the smaller states (Table 5.18). Delaware's voting power has been below 90% since 1970! At the other extreme, Wyoming has had voting power above 110% going back to 1930, a full century by the time the next reapportionment happens in 2030.

The top 20 most populous states almost always have voting power between 95% and 105% of the national average. Medium-sized states, from about 21st in population to 40th, usually have voting power within 90%–110% of the national average. Typically, it is only the smallest states that have outlier voting power, defined as voting power less than 85% or more than 120%. Arizona is an example of a state that had outlier voting power as a small state in 1930 and 1940. Then, as Arizona grew larger, its voting power became more consistent.

In response to the counterargument that over enough time the representation for small states will balance out: the data does not support this argument. The examples of Delaware, Wyoming, and South Dakota show that states do not necessarily balance out their representation over time. Further, it is impossible to predict the future of representation because it is impossible to predict the future population of the states, not just the population of the small states but also the population of the large states, all the information which would be necessary to be able to predict apportionment and voting power.

In a representative democracy, how equal is equal enough?

Morally, our goal should be to have precisely equal representation; functionally, we should find a way to reduce representation inequality as much as possible. The current system has reduced representation inequality to a consistent ratio of 1.8 between the most extreme states. Another benchmark could be the number of states, and the number of people, that possess voting power within 5% or 10% of the national average. If all states had voting power within 10% of the national average, the inequality ratio between the most extreme states would be about 1.2; if all states had voting power within 5% of the national average, the inequality ratio between the most extreme states would be about 1.1.

Table 5.18: Smaller States Have Had Inconsistent Voting Power for the Past 10 Censuses
(Ordered by Average Population Rank)

Rank	State	1930	1940	1950	1960	1970	1980	1990	2000	2010	2020
50	Alaska	x	x	x	181.5%	154.3%	129.7%	103.7%	102.9%	98.5%	103.4%
49	Wyoming	125.5%	120.1%	118.6%	124.4%	139.7%	110.3%	125.5%	130.6%	125.1%	131.8%
48	Vermont	78.0%	83.8%	91.2%	105.3%	104.6%	101.5%	101.3%	106.1%	112.8%	118.3%
47	Delaware	117.7%	113.0%	108.3%	92.0%	85.0%	87.2%	85.6%	82.4%	78.9%	76.8%
46	North Dakota	83.4%	93.8%	111.2%	129.8%	75.2%	79.6%	89.3%	100.5%	105.2%	97.6%
45	South Dakota	83.4%	93.7%	105.6%	120.6%	139.4%	75.2%	81.8%	85.5%	86.7%	85.7%
44	Montana	107.0%	107.7%	116.6%	121.7%	133.7%	132.0%	71.2%	71.5%	71.5%	140.3%
43	Nevada	324.9%	273.2%	215.3%	143.9%	95.3%	129.9%	94.9%	96.9%	104.9%	97.9%
42	New Hampshire	120.6%	122.5%	129.2%	135.3%	125.7%	112.8%	102.8%	104.5%	107.6%	110.4%
41	Idaho	127.1%	114.8%	117.1%	123.0%	130.3%	110.0%	113.1%	99.7%	90.3%	82.7%
40	Hawai'i	x	x	x	129.7%	119.5%	107.6%	102.7%	106.4%	104.0%	104.3%
39	Rhode Island	81.7%	84.4%	87.0%	95.5%	98.0%	109.6%	113.8%	123.3%	134.7%	138.6%
38	New Mexico	70.9%	113.3%	101.2%	86.3%	91.4%	119.8%	112.9%	106.4%	103.1%	107.7%
37	Maine	105.6%	106.6%	113.1%	84.7%	93.2%	92.3%	92.8%	101.3%	106.6%	111.6%
36	Utah	111.0%	109.5%	100.0%	92.2%	87.9%	106.6%	99.4%	86.8%	102.6%	93.0%
35	Nebraska	102.1%	91.6%	104.0%	87.3%	94.0%	99.2%	108.4%	113.1%	116.4%	116.3%
34	West Virginia	97.4%	95.0%	103.1%	110.3%	106.4%	106.5%	95.3%	107.0%	114.7%	84.8%
33	Arkansas	105.9%	108.1%	108.3%	91.9%	96.6%	90.9%	96.9%	96.6%	97.2%	101.0%
32	Kansas	104.5%	100.3%	108.5%	94.2%	103.5%	109.9%	92.1%	96.1%	99.3%	103.5%
31	Oregon	88.6%	110.6%	90.6%	92.8%	88.9%	98.6%	100.3%	94.3%	92.3%	107.7%
30	Arizona	72.1%	120.6%	91.9%	94.6%	105.0%	95.5%	93.4%	100.7%	99.8%	95.7%
29	Mississippi	97.8%	96.5%	94.9%	94.2%	105.0%	103.0%	110.7%	90.7%	95.5%	102.7%
28	Colorado	108.5%	107.2%	104.0%	93.6%	105.3%	107.8%	103.8%	105.0%	98.6%	105.3%
27	Connecticut	104.8%	105.7%	103.0%	97.1%	92.3%	100.3%	104.2%	94.9%	99.2%	105.5%
26	Oklahoma	106.0%	103.1%	92.6%	105.8%	108.9%	103.0%	108.8%	93.5%	94.4%	96.0%
25	Iowa	102.3%	94.9%	105.2%	104.2%	98.9%	106.9%	102.7%	110.3%	93.1%	95.4%
24	South Carolina	96.9%	95.1%	97.7%	103.4%	107.5%	99.9%	98.0%	96.4%	107.1%	104.0%
23	Kentucky	96.6%	95.3%	93.6%	94.6%	101.1%	99.3%	92.9%	95.9%	98.0%	101.3%
22	Louisiana	106.8%	101.9%	102.7%	100.8%	102.2%	98.8%	94.6%	101.1%	93.6%	98.0%
21	Maryland	103.2%	99.2%	102.9%	105.9%	94.9%	98.5%	95.4%	97.5%	98.2%	98.4%
20	Washington	108.5%	104.1%	101.4%	100.7%	95.4%	100.6%	105.4%	98.5%	105.2%	98.6%
19	Alabama	95.5%	95.7%	101.3%	100.5%	94.5%	93.4%	98.6%	101.5%	103.6%	105.9%
18	Minnesota	99.0%	97.1%	104.0%	96.2%	97.9%	101.9%	104.4%	105.1%	107.0%	106.6%
17	Tennessee	96.5%	103.3%	94.2%	103.6%	94.7%	101.8%	105.2%	102.1%	100.3%	99.0%
16	Wisconsin	95.7%	96.0%	100.3%	103.9%	94.9%	99.3%	105.0%	96.4%	99.8%	103.3%
15	Virginia	104.3%	101.2%	103.8%	103.5%	100.0%	97.1%	101.3%	100.2%	97.3%	96.7%
14	Missouri	100.5%	103.4%	95.8%	95.0%	99.4%	95.0%	100.3%	103.9%	94.6%	98.8%
13	Indiana	104.0%	96.6%	96.3%	96.8%	98.7%	94.6%	102.9%	95.6%	98.4%	100.9%
12	Georgia	96.5%	96.4%	100.0%	104.1%	101.4%	95.0%	96.8%	102.5%	102.3%	99.4%
11	Florida	95.6%	95.2%	99.5%	99.5%	102.6%	101.3%	101.3%	100.9%	101.5%	98.8%
10	Massachusetts	99.1%	97.7%	102.9%	95.7%	98.3%	99.6%	95.0%	101.8%	97.5%	97.4%
9	North Carolina	97.5%	101.2%	101.8%	99.1%	100.7%	97.2%	103.2%	104.2%	96.6%	101.9%
8	New Jersey	97.2%	101.3%	99.8%	101.5%	97.6%	98.7%	96.0%	99.8%	96.8%	98.3%
7	Michigan	98.5%	97.4%	97.3%	99.7%	99.7%	100.9%	98.2%	97.5%	100.4%	98.1%
6	Ohio	101.3%	100.3%	99.7%	101.5%	100.5%	101.0%	99.9%	102.4%	98.3%	96.7%
5	Illinois	99.3%	99.2%	98.9%	97.7%	100.7%	100.0%	99.8%	98.8%	99.5%	100.9%
4	Pennsylvania	99.1%	100.4%	98.5%	97.9%	98.7%	100.6%	100.8%	99.9%	100.5%	99.4%
3	Texas	101.2%	98.6%	98.3%	98.6%	99.6%	98.5%	100.7%	99.0%	101.3%	99.1%
2	California	99.0%	100.3%	97.7%	99.2%	100.4%	98.7%	99.8%	101.1%	100.9%	100.0%
1	New York	100.3%	100.5%	99.9%	100.3%	99.8%	100.6%	98.3%	98.7%	98.8%	97.9%

As a general principle, I believe all people across all states should have voting power within 10% of the average voting power, and the goal should be for all people to have voting power within 5% of the national average. These numbers are admittedly arbitrary, yet they feel reasonable.

Under the current system, the overwhelming majority of Americans have voting power within these margins (Tables 5.19 and 5.20). More than 94% of Americans have had voting power within 10% of the national average in every census since 1930. On average, after each reapportionment, there are 20 states whose population has voting power more than 5% above or below the national average, including 10 states whose population has voting power more than 10% above or below the national average. These states with disproportionate voting power are almost always from among the smaller states *(See Tables 21–30, page 199).*

Table 5.19 The Overwhelming Majority of Americans Live in States With Voting Power Close to the National Average, 1930–1970)

Census Year	1930	1940	1950	1960	1970
Total Population	122,093,455	131,006,184	149,895,183	178,559,219	204,053,325
Average Population per Representative	280,675	301,164	344,587	410,481	469,088
# States Voting Power Within 5% of Average	28	28	28	25	27
# States Voting Power Outside 5% of Average	20	20	20	25	23
Pop. With Voting Power Within 5% of Average	105,755,619	114,291,038	124,702,190	147,469,310	163,821,823
Pop. With Voting Power Outside 5% of Average	16,337,836	16,715,146	25,192,993	31,089,909	40,231,502
% of Pop. With Voting Power Within 5% of Avg.	86.6%	87.2%	83.2%	82.6%	80.3%
% of Pop. With Voting Power Outside 5% of Avg.	13.4%	12.8%	16.8%	17.4%	19.7%
# States Voting Power Within 10% of Average	35	38	40	37	39
# States Voting Power Outside 10% of Average	13	10	8	13	11
Pop. With Voting Power Within 10% of Average	116,003,297	126,168,953	145,406,362	168,631,058	195,432,884
Pop. With Voting Power Outside 10% of Average	6,090,158	4,837,231	4,488,821	9,928,161	8,620,441
% of Pop. With Voting Power Within 10% of Avg.	95.0%	96.3%	97.0%	94.4%	95.8%
% of Pop. With Voting Power Outside 10% of Avg.	5.0%	3.7%	3.0%	5.6%	4.2%

Table 5.20: The Overwhelming Majority of Americans Live in States With Voting Power
Close to the National Average, 1980–2020)

Census Year	1980	1990	2000	2010	2020
Total Population	225,867,174	249,022,783	281,424,177	309,183,463	331,108,434
Average Population per Representative	519,235	572,466	646,952	710,767	761,169
# States Voting Power Within 5% of Average	29	29	32	30	32
# States Voting Power Outside 5% of Average	21	21	18	20	18
Pop. With Voting Power Within 5% of Average	192,028,715	197,624,158	242,697,141	257,672,024	287,715,363
Pop. With Voting Power Outside 5% of Average	33,838,459	51,398,625	38,727,036	51,511,439	43,393,071
% of Pop. With Voting Power Within 5% of Avg.	85.0%	79.4%	86.2%	83.3%	86.9%
% of Pop. With Voting Power Outside 5% of Avg.	15.0%	20.6%	13.8%	16.7%	13.1%
# States Voting Power Within 10% of Average	40	41	42	42	39
# States Voting Power Outside 10% of Average	10	9	8	8	11
Pop. With Voting Power Within 10% of Average	218,307,392	239,626,902	270,547,947	300,522,885	317,482,609
Pop. With Voting Power Outside 10% of Average	7,559,782	9,395,881	10,876,230	8,660,578	13,625,825
% of Pop. With Voting Power Within 10% of Avg.	96.7%	96.2%	96.1%	97.2%	95.9%
% of Pop. With Voting Power Outside 10% of Avg.	3.3%	3.8%	3.9%	2.8%	4.1%

To make representation both more consistent and more equal, the solution is simple: increase the size of Congress. As I will show in part C of this chapter, increasing the size of Congress lowers the Maximum Inequality Ratio and increases the proportion of Americans that have between 95% and 105% voting power.

B. Add Three States to the Union for Universal Suffrage

Currently, over 4 million Americans living in Puerto Rico, the District of Columbia, and the 4 island territories are deprived of their right to representation in Congress. Denying statehood, and through statehood the denial of representation in Congress, to D.C., Puerto Rico, and the U.S. territories is wrong. No taxation without representation, right?

At the same time that we expand the number of Representatives in Congress, we should expand the Union to incorporate 3 new states: Puerto Rico; the District of Columbia; and the Four Territories of Guam, the U.S. Virgin Islands, American Samoa, and the Northern Mariana Islands (Table 5.31).

In an expanded Congress, there would be representation for all 335 million Americans across 53 states.

Extending statehood to Puerto Rico and the District of Columbia is a no-brainer. Nearly 3.3 million people live in Puerto Rico. If Puerto Rico were a state, it would be the 30th most populous state, just ahead of Utah, Iowa, Nevada, Arkansas, and Mississippi. Puerto Rico's internal politics are largely defined by the issue of statehood, and a referendum on the issue in 2020 **resulted**[43] in 52% voting in favor of statehood. Whatever the people of Puerto Rico want regarding statehood, they should be allowed to do.

Table 5.31 Americans Without Representation in Congress

Non-State	2020 Population	Would Be State Rank
Puerto Rico	3,285,874	30/53
District of Colombia	689,545	50/53
Four Territories	338,021	53/53
Guam	153,836	x
US Virgin Islands	87,146	x
American Samoa	49,710	x
Northern Mariana Islands	47,329	x

Similarly, there are two existing states with smaller populations than the nearly 700,000 people of the District: Vermont and Wyoming. In a 2016 referendum, 79% of voters in D.C. **supported statehood.**[44] Because the people of D.C. overwhelmingly want to be a state, D.C. should be a state. A bill granting D.C. statehood **passed the House**[45] in 2021 but failed to garner support from Republicans in the Senate. Absent any good faith arguments against D.C. statehood, the real reason for the Senate's decision to block passage is partisanship. Republicans do not want to grant statehood to D.C. because the new state would almost certainly elect Democrats. Yet another instance of the Senate's obstructive and anti-democratic function.

The case for statehood of the four island territories is weaker compared to that of Puerto Rico or D.C. due to the small population of each territory. The largest of the Four Territories is Guam with a population of 153,836. This is hardly more than 1/4 the population of Wyoming. The least populous of the four territories is the Northern Mariana Islands, with a population of 47,329, less than 10% of the population of Wyoming! If the Northern Mariana Islands were awarded one seat in Congress, they would have 16 times the voting power as the average American! Other than the moral argument for universal suffrage, there is little reason for the Northern Mariana Islands to merit statehood. But the moral argument compels a creative solution. The combined population of Guam, the U.S. Virgin Islands, American Samoa, and the Northern Mariana Islands is 338,021, just a little more than half the population of Wyoming. If the Four Territories were awarded 1 Representative in Congress, they would be the most overrepresented state in the Union, with 225% voting power compared to the average American. This is high, but it is far below the historic high of 458%

Table 5.32: Adding Three States to a 435-Seat Congress

Pop. Rank	State	2020 Population	Current Congress			Universal Representation		
			Seats	Pop. Per Rep.	Voting Power	Seats	Pop. Per Rep.	Voting Power
	United States	*335,421,874*	*435*	*761,169*	*100.0%*	*435*	*771,085*	*100.0%*
53	Four Territories	338,021	x	x	x	1	338,021	228.1%
52	Wyoming	577,719	1	577,719	131.8%	1	577,719	133.5%
51	Vermont	643,503	1	643,503	118.3%	1	643,503	119.8%
50	District of Columbia	689,545	x	x	x	1	689,545	111.8%
49	Alaska	736,081	1	736,081	103.4%	1	736,081	104.8%
48	North Dakota	779,702	1	779,702	97.6%	1	779,702	98.9%
47	South Dakota	887,770	1	887,770	85.7%	1	887,770	86.9%
46	Delaware	990,837	1	990,837	76.8%	1	990,837	77.8%
45	Montana	1,085,407	2	542,704	140.3%	1	1,085,407	71.0%
44	Rhode Island	1,098,163	2	549,082	138.6%	2	549,082	140.4%
43	Maine	1,363,582	2	681,791	111.6%	2	681,791	113.1%
42	New Hampshire	1,379,089	2	689,545	110.4%	2	689,545	111.8%
41	Hawai'i	1,460,137	2	730,069	104.3%	2	730,069	105.6%
40	West Virginia	1,795,045	2	897,523	84.8%	2	897,523	85.9%
39	Idaho	1,841,377	2	920,689	82.7%	2	920,689	83.8%
38	Nebraska	1,963,333	3	654,444	116.3%	3	654,444	117.8%
37	New Mexico	2,120,220	3	706,740	107.7%	3	706,740	109.1%
36	Kansas	2,940,865	4	735,216	103.5%	4	735,216	104.9%
35	Mississippi	2,963,914	4	740,979	102.7%	4	740,979	104.1%
34	Arkansas	3,013,756	4	753,439	101.0%	4	753,439	102.3%
33	Nevada	3,108,462	4	777,116	97.9%	4	777,116	99.2%
32	Iowa	3,192,406	4	798,102	95.4%	4	798,102	96.6%
31	Utah	3,275,252	4	818,813	93.0%	4	818,813	94.2%
30	Puerto Rico	3,285,874	x	x	x	4	821,469	93.9%
29	Connecticut	3,608,298	5	721,660	105.5%	5	721,660	106.8%
28	Oklahoma	3,963,516	5	792,703	96.0%	5	792,703	97.3%
27	Oregon	4,241,500	6	706,917	107.7%	5	848,300	90.9%
26	Kentucky	4,509,342	6	751,557	101.3%	6	751,557	102.6%
25	Louisiana	4,661,468	6	776,911	98.0%	6	776,911	99.3%
24	Alabama	5,030,053	7	718,579	105.9%	7	718,579	107.3%
23	South Carolina	5,124,712	7	732,102	104.0%	7	732,102	105.3%
22	Minnesota	5,709,752	8	713,719	106.6%	7	815,679	94.5%
21	Colorado	5,782,171	8	722,771	105.3%	7	826,024	93.3%
20	Wisconsin	5,897,473	8	737,184	103.3%	8	737,184	104.6%
19	Missouri	6,160,281	8	770,035	98.8%	8	770,035	100.1%
18	Maryland	6,185,278	8	773,160	98.4%	8	773,160	99.7%
17	Indiana	6,790,280	9	754,476	100.9%	9	754,476	102.2%
16	Tennessee	6,916,897	9	768,544	99.0%	9	768,544	100.3%
15	Massachusetts	7,033,469	9	781,497	97.4%	9	781,497	98.7%
14	Arizona	7,158,923	9	795,436	95.7%	9	795,436	96.9%
13	Washington	7,715,946	10	771,595	98.6%	10	771,595	99.9%
12	Virginia	8,654,542	11	786,777	96.7%	11	786,777	98.0%
11	New Jersey	9,294,493	12	774,541	98.3%	12	774,541	99.6%
10	Michigan	10,084,442	13	775,726	98.1%	13	775,726	99.4%
9	North Carolina	10,453,948	14	746,711	101.9%	13	804,150	95.9%
8	Georgia	10,725,274	14	766,091	99.4%	14	766,091	100.7%
7	Ohio	11,808,848	15	787,257	96.7%	15	787,257	97.9%
6	Illinois	12,822,739	17	754,279	100.9%	17	754,279	102.2%
5	Pennsylvania	13,011,844	17	765,403	99.4%	17	765,403	100.7%
4	New York	20,215,751	26	777,529	97.9%	26	777,529	99.2%
3	Florida	21,570,527	28	770,376	98.8%	28	770,376	100.1%
2	Texas	29,183,290	38	767,981	99.1%	38	767,981	100.4%
1	California	39,576,757	52	761,091	100.0%	51	776,015	99.4%

voting power for voters in Nevada following the 1900 Census. In my view, the combined population of the Four Territories is high enough to merit statehood.

If statehood were offered to the Four Territories on the condition that they share a single representative, would the people assent? I have no idea. But the decision to become a state should be made democratically by the people of Guam, the U.S. Virgin Islands, American Samoa, and the Northern Mariana Islands. If they agreed, it would require inter-territorial cooperation to determine the logistics. Perhaps they would remain completely independent except for their shared Representative? Again, I have no idea, and such questions should be resolved by the people of the Four Territories.

According to the Priority Value formula, Puerto Rico would receive 4 Representatives while D.C. and the Four Territories would each receive 1 Representative.

Adding three states without increasing the size of Congress would necessarily reduce the number of representatives for some states (Table 5.32). Montana, Oregon, Minnesota, Colorado, North Carolina, and California would each lose 1 Representative to make room for the combined 6 Representatives of the 3 newly admitted states. The impact of losing a representative would be felt most acutely by the smaller states. Montana would go from the most overrepresented state with 140% voting power to the most underrepresented state with 71% voting power. By contrast, in losing 1 Representative California's voting power would change only slightly, from 100% to 99.4%.

Instead of cramming three more states into the same 435-seat Congress, we should also expand the number of representatives in Congress. But by how much? In the next section, I make the case to expand Congress to 695 members.

C. How Big Should Congress Be Now, And In The Future?

Note: All tables in this section assume there are 53 States, as described in the previous section. I use the Priority Value method to assign the appropriate number of seats to each state depending on the size of Congress.

In an ideal democracy, every person would have exactly equal representation in Congress. That is impossible if we are to remain divided into states, which then are apportioned representation based on state populations. Instead, our goal should be to (a) minimize the inequality ratio between the most over- and under-represented states and (b) maximize the population within 5% of average national representation so that the inequality ratio between most citizens is no more than 1.1.

As shown in Figure 5.1, the larger the Congress, the more equal representation becomes across the states. In our current Congress, based off the 2020 Census, 288 million Americans (87% of the population) across 32 states have voting power within 5% of the national average. Only 4% of Americans, 13.6 million people across 11 states, have voting power greater or less than 10% of the national average. All 11 outlier states are among the smallest states; the largest outlying state is Nebraska, the 37th most populous state.

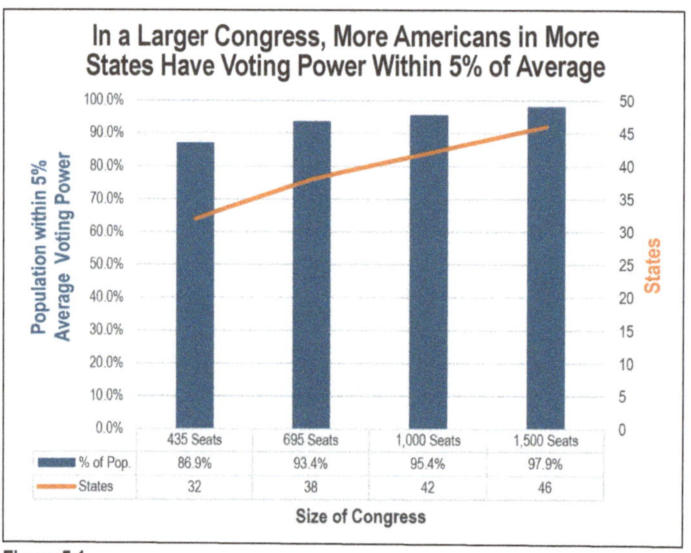

	435 Seats	695 Seats	1,000 Seats	1,500 Seats
% of Pop.	86.9%	93.4%	95.4%	97.9%
States	32	38	42	46

Figure 5.1

A larger Congress reduces the number of outlying states and increases the number of Americans with voting power within 5 or 10% of the national average. In a 1,500-member Congress, 98% of Americans living in 46 states would have voting power within 5% of the national average, and 99.5% of Americans living in 50 states would have voting power within 10% of the national average (the three outlier states would be the Four Territories, Wyoming, and North Dakota).

Interestingly, the Maximum Inequality Ratio for a 1,500-member Congress is higher than for a 1,000-member Congress (Table 5.33). This is due to the difficulty of apportioning the smallest state, the Four Territories. By the Priority Value method, the Four Territories would be assigned the 1,406th seat in Congress. In a Congress around the size of when the smallest state would receive its second seat, the Maximum Inequality Ratio will be high because that smallest state would either be highly under- or overrepresented Additionally, the population of the Four Territories is almost exactly 1/1000th of the total population of the United States, meaning that the Four

Territories are almost perfectly represented by 1 representative in a 1,000-member Congress. In effect, states that are apportioned in 1 or 2 states remain in a lottery. Once Congress is large enough that every state receives 2 or 3 seats, the representation variability decreases.

Table 5.33: Representation Between States is More Equal
With a Larger Congress

Size of Congress	435	695	1,000	1,500
Total Population	331,108,434	335,421,874	335,421,874	335,421,874
States	50	53	53	53
Average Population per Representative	761,169	482,621	335,422	223,615
Maximum Inequality Ratio	1.8	1.9	1.3	1.5
# States Voting Power Within 5% of Average	32	38	42	46
# States Voting Power Outside 5% of Average	18	15	11	7
Pop. With Voting Power Within 5% of Average	287,715,363	313,397,950	319,847,847	328,419,157
Pop. With Voting Power Outside 5% of Average	43,393,071	22,023,924	15,574,027	7,002,717
% of Pop. With Voting Power Within 5% of Avg.	86.9%	93.4%	95.4%	97.9%
% of Pop. With Voting Power Outside 5% of Avg.	13.1%	6.6%	4.6%	2.1%
# States Voting Power Within 10% of Average	39	45	50	50
# States Voting Power Outside 10% of Average	11	8	3	3
Pop. With Voting Power Within 10% of Average	317,482,609	329,473,733	333,176,683	333,726,432
Pop. With Voting Power Outside 10% of Average	13,625,825	5,948,141	2,245,191	1,695,442
% of Pop. With Voting Power Within 10% of Avg.	95.9%	98.2%	99.3%	99.5%
% of Pop. With Voting Power Outside 10% of Avg.	4.1%	1.8%	0.7%	0.5%

But we cannot increase the size of Congress indefinitely. By definition, representative democracy must have representatives; all 335 million Americans should not be asked to vote on every proposal.

At what point would Congress be too big?

The highest proposed size of Congress comes from Thirty-Thousand.org,[46] which advocates for increasing the size of the House to between 6,623 and 11,036 Representatives. With that massive a House, there would be 1 Representative for every 30,000 to 50,000 Americans. Representation across the states would be very close to equal, as even the smallest state would have at least 7 or 8 Representatives. (That is an educated guess based off Tables 5.34 and 5.35. I did not model a 10,000-seat Congress.)

Table 5.34: Representation Between States is More Equal With a Larger Congress

State	2020 Population	Current Congress			Proposed Congress		
		Seats	Pop. Per Rep.	Voting Power	Seats	Pop. Per Rep.	Voting Power
United States	*335,421,874*	*435*	*761,169*	*100.0%*	*695*	*482,621*	*100.0%*
Four Territories	338,021	x	x	x	1	338,021	142.8%
Wyoming	577,719	1	577,719	131.8%	1	577,719	83.5%
Vermont	643,503	1	643,503	118.3%	1	643,503	75.0%
District of Columbia	689,545	x	x	x	2	344,773	140.0%
Alaska	736,081	1	736,081	103.4%	2	368,041	131.1%
North Dakota	779,702	1	779,702	97.6%	2	389,851	123.8%
South Dakota	887,770	1	887,770	85.7%	2	443,885	108.7%
Delaware	990,837	1	990,837	76.8%	2	495,419	97.4%
Montana	1,085,407	2	542,704	140.3%	2	542,704	88.9%
Rhode Island	1,098,163	2	549,082	138.6%	2	549,082	87.9%
Maine	1,363,582	2	681,791	111.6%	3	454,527	106.2%
New Hampshire	1,379,089	2	689,545	110.4%	3	459,696	105.0%
Hawai'i	1,460,137	2	730,069	104.3%	3	486,712	99.2%
West Virginia	1,795,045	2	897,523	84.8%	4	448,761	107.5%
Idaho	1,841,377	2	920,689	82.7%	4	460,344	104.8%
Nebraska	1,963,333	3	654,444	116.3%	4	490,833	98.3%
New Mexico	2,120,220	3	706,740	107.7%	4	530,055	91.1%
Kansas	2,940,865	4	735,216	103.5%	6	490,144	98.5%
Mississippi	2,963,914	4	740,979	102.7%	6	493,986	97.7%
Arkansas	3,013,756	4	753,439	101.0%	6	502,293	96.1%
Nevada	3,108,462	4	777,116	97.9%	6	518,077	93.2%
Iowa	3,192,406	4	798,102	95.4%	7	456,058	105.8%
Utah	3,275,252	4	818,813	93.0%	7	467,893	103.1%
Puerto Rico	3,285,874	x	x	x	7	469,411	102.8%
Connecticut	3,608,298	5	721,660	105.5%	7	515,471	93.6%
Oklahoma	3,963,516	5	792,703	96.0%	8	495,440	97.4%
Oregon	4,241,500	6	706,917	107.7%	9	471,278	102.4%
Kentucky	4,509,342	6	751,557	101.3%	9	501,038	96.3%
Louisiana	4,661,468	6	776,911	98.0%	10	466,147	103.5%
Alabama	5,030,053	7	718,579	105.9%	10	503,005	95.9%
South Carolina	5,124,712	7	732,102	104.0%	11	465,883	103.6%
Minnesota	5,709,752	8	713,719	106.6%	12	475,813	101.4%
Colorado	5,782,171	8	722,771	105.3%	12	481,848	100.2%
Wisconsin	5,897,473	8	737,184	103.3%	12	491,456	98.2%
Missouri	6,160,281	8	770,035	98.8%	13	473,868	101.8%
Maryland	6,185,278	8	773,160	98.4%	13	475,791	101.4%
Indiana	6,790,280	9	754,476	100.9%	14	485,020	99.5%
Tennessee	6,916,897	9	768,544	99.0%	14	494,064	97.7%
Massachusetts	7,033,469	9	781,497	97.4%	15	468,898	102.9%
Arizona	7,158,923	9	795,436	95.7%	15	477,262	101.1%
Washington	7,715,946	10	771,595	98.6%	16	482,247	100.1%
Virginia	8,654,542	11	786,777	96.7%	18	480,808	100.4%
New Jersey	9,294,493	12	774,541	98.3%	19	489,184	98.7%
Michigan	10,084,442	13	775,726	98.1%	21	480,212	100.5%
North Carolina	10,453,948	14	746,711	101.9%	22	475,179	101.6%
Georgia	10,725,274	14	766,091	99.4%	22	487,512	99.0%
Ohio	11,808,848	15	787,257	96.7%	24	492,035	98.1%
Illinois	12,822,739	17	754,279	100.9%	26	493,182	97.9%
Pennsylvania	13,011,844	17	765,403	99.4%	27	481,920	100.1%
New York	20,215,751	26	777,529	97.9%	42	481,327	100.3%
Florida	21,570,527	28	770,376	98.8%	45	479,345	100.7%
Texas	29,183,290	38	767,981	99.1%	60	486,388	99.2%
California	39,576,757	52	761,091	100.0%	82	482,643	100.0%

That would be similar to the population per representative of the United States from 1790–1830. Thirty-Thousand bases much of their argument on a proposed but never ratified amendment during the passage of the Bill of Rights, which would have limited the number of people per representative to 50,000. But I find an argument based on the deification of the Founders unpersuasive: the Founders never could have imagined a united country of more than 330,000,000 Americans. And if they had, would they really have wanted Congress to have more than 6,000 members? A Congress with 6,000 members would have been the 10th largest city[47] in 1790 America!

Reasonable people can disagree about the optimal size of Congress. In *Parliamentary America,* Stearns proposes doubling the size of Congress to 870. Half of the Congress would be elected in the same way it is now, while the other half would be elected in a party list vote similar to those in New Zealand and Germany (more on this in Chapter 6). Stearns chooses this number to make increasing the size of Congress more politically palatable to incumbents in the existing 435 single-member districts.

Yet choosing any specific number of representatives feels arbitrary because, at the end of the day, it is. We make the rules up as we go. Lacking a human authority to whom we might appeal, let us appeal to math: Congress should be the size of the cube root of America's total population. For 2020, that would mean a Congress of 695 members representing 335 million Americans, for a national average of 482,397 people per representative. (The cube root of 335 million is 695 because 695 times 695 times 695, or 695^3, is 335.7 million.)

Why the cube root? First described by political scientist Rein Taagepera in the 1970s, the cube root function is the **strongest empirical relationship**[48] between the size of a population and the size of its legislature. Or, as Professor Emeritus Matthew Shugart of UC Davis put it, "A nation's assembly tends to be about the cube root of its population."

This holds true for the United States, too. In Figure 5.2 (pg. 58), the orange line shows the historic size of Congress. From 1790 until 1910, under its varying apportionment methods, Congress was close to the size of the cube root of the total population. (This includes enslaved people, who did not have representation.) It was only when Congress stopped increasing its size despite a booming population that Congress deviated substantially from the cube root function.

Increasing Congress to 695 members would restore its historic relationship with the total population of the country.

Table 5.35: Representation Between States is More Equal With a Larger Congress

State	2020 Population	1,000 Seat Congress			1,500 Seat Congress		
		Seats	Pop. Per Rep.	Voting Power	Seats	Pop. Per Rep.	Voting Power
United States	*335,421,874*	*1,000*	*335,422*	*100.0%*	*1,500*	*223,615*	*100.0%*
Four Territories	338,021	1	338,021	99.2%	2	169,011	132.3%
Wyoming	577,719	2	288,860	116.1%	3	192,573	116.1%
Vermont	643,503	2	321,752	104.2%	3	214,501	104.2%
District of Columbia	689,545	2	344,773	97.3%	3	229,848	97.3%
Alaska	736,081	2	368,041	91.1%	3	245,360	91.1%
North Dakota	779,702	2	389,851	86.0%	4	194,926	114.7%
South Dakota	887,770	3	295,923	113.3%	4	221,943	100.8%
Delaware	990,837	3	330,279	101.6%	4	247,709	90.3%
Montana	1,085,407	3	361,802	92.7%	5	217,081	103.0%
Rhode Island	1,098,163	3	366,054	91.6%	5	219,633	101.8%
Maine	1,363,582	4	340,896	98.4%	6	227,264	98.4%
New Hampshire	1,379,089	4	344,772	97.3%	6	229,848	97.3%
Hawai'i	1,460,137	4	365,034	91.9%	7	208,591	107.2%
West Virginia	1,795,045	5	359,009	93.4%	8	224,381	99.7%
Idaho	1,841,377	6	306,896	109.3%	8	230,172	97.2%
Nebraska	1,963,333	6	327,222	102.5%	9	218,148	102.5%
New Mexico	2,120,220	6	353,370	94.9%	9	235,580	94.9%
Kansas	2,940,865	9	326,763	102.6%	13	226,220	98.8%
Mississippi	2,963,914	9	329,324	101.9%	13	227,993	98.1%
Arkansas	3,013,756	9	334,862	100.2%	13	231,827	96.5%
Nevada	3,108,462	9	345,385	97.1%	14	222,033	100.7%
Iowa	3,192,406	10	319,241	105.1%	14	228,029	98.1%
Utah	3,275,252	10	327,525	102.4%	15	218,350	102.4%
Puerto Rico	3,285,874	10	328,587	102.1%	15	219,058	102.1%
Connecticut	3,608,298	11	328,027	102.3%	16	225,519	99.2%
Oklahoma	3,963,516	12	330,293	101.6%	18	220,195	101.6%
Oregon	4,241,500	13	326,269	102.8%	19	223,237	100.2%
Kentucky	4,509,342	13	346,872	96.7%	20	225,467	99.2%
Louisiana	4,661,468	14	332,962	100.7%	21	221,975	100.7%
Alabama	5,030,053	15	335,337	100.0%	22	228,639	97.8%
South Carolina	5,124,712	15	341,647	98.2%	23	222,814	100.4%
Minnesota	5,709,752	17	335,868	99.9%	26	219,606	101.8%
Colorado	5,782,171	17	340,128	98.6%	26	222,391	100.6%
Wisconsin	5,897,473	18	327,637	102.4%	26	226,826	98.6%
Missouri	6,160,281	18	342,238	98.0%	28	220,010	101.6%
Maryland	6,185,278	19	325,541	103.0%	28	220,903	101.2%
Indiana	6,790,280	20	339,514	98.8%	30	226,343	98.8%
Tennessee	6,916,897	21	329,376	101.8%	31	223,126	100.2%
Massachusetts	7,033,469	21	334,927	100.1%	31	226,886	98.6%
Arizona	7,158,923	21	340,901	98.4%	32	223,716	100.0%
Washington	7,715,946	23	335,476	100.0%	35	220,456	101.4%
Virginia	8,654,542	26	332,867	100.8%	39	221,911	100.8%
New Jersey	9,294,493	28	331,946	101.0%	42	221,297	101.0%
Michigan	10,084,442	30	336,148	99.8%	45	224,099	99.8%
North Carolina	10,453,948	31	337,224	99.5%	47	222,424	100.5%
Georgia	10,725,274	32	335,165	100.1%	48	223,443	100.1%
Ohio	11,808,848	35	337,396	99.4%	53	222,808	100.4%
Illinois	12,822,739	38	337,441	99.4%	57	224,960	99.4%
Pennsylvania	13,011,844	39	333,637	100.5%	58	224,342	99.7%
New York	20,215,751	60	336,929	99.6%	90	224,619	99.6%
Florida	21,570,527	64	337,039	99.5%	96	224,693	99.5%
Texas	29,183,290	87	335,440	100.0%	130	224,487	99.6%
California	39,576,757	118	335,396	100.0%	177	223,597	100.0%

Tying Congress's size to the cube root of the population would provide for stability going forward. Automatically adjusting the size of Congress to be the cube root of the population after each Census will remove the possibility of political manipulation of the size of Congress for partisan gain, as happened in 1920.

As the population of the country grows, so too would Congress. As shown in Table 5.36, Congress would increase by just a few seats for every 10 million more Americans: from 695 representatives for 335 million Americans to 705 representatives for 350 million Americans, to 737 representatives for 400 million Americans. As the population balloons, the number of seats added slows down. If the population increased from 400 million to 500 million, Congress would increase by 57 seats. From 500 million to 600 million, Congress would increase by only 49 seats. With the Cube Root rule, Congress would reach 1,000 seats when the total population of the country reached 1 billion.

The number of people represented by each member of Congress would steadily increase, as well. Under a Cube Root Congress, the average number of people represented by each member would be the square of the total size of Congress. Mathematically, this results in a function in which the size of Congress is x, the number of people represented by each member of Congress is x^2, and the total population of the country is x^3. The italicized rows demonstrate this function for when Congress would have 700, 800, 900, or 1,000 members.

Putting the theory into practice, how many Americans might there be in 2050 or 2100? Through immigration and longer life spans, and despite declining birth rates, our country will continue to grow. Since 1980, the population of the U.S. has increased by about 10% per decade (Figure 5.3). If the United States continued to grow at 10% per decade, there would be 491 million Americans in 2050 and 719 million in 2100 (Table 5.37). If Congress stayed capped at 435 members, a population of 700 million would mean the average member would represent over 1.6 million Americans. But by tying the size of Congress to the Cube Root, by the time America reached 719 million people, Congress would increase to 896 members, or one member per 802,000 Americans.

Table 5.36: The Cube Root is Predictable for Future Growth

Size of Congress	Pop. per Rep.	Population
695	482,397	335,047,628
698	487,139	340,000,000
700	*490,000*	*343,000,000*
705	496,644	350,000,000
711	506,060	360,000,000
718	515,388	370,000,000
724	524,633	380,000,000
731	533,797	390,000,000
737	542,884	400,000,000
794	629,961	500,000,000
800	*640,000*	*512,000,000*
843	711,379	600,000,000
888	788,374	700,000,000
900	*810,000*	*729,000,000*
928	861,774	800,000,000
965	932,170	900,000,000
1000	*1,000,000*	*1,000,000,000*

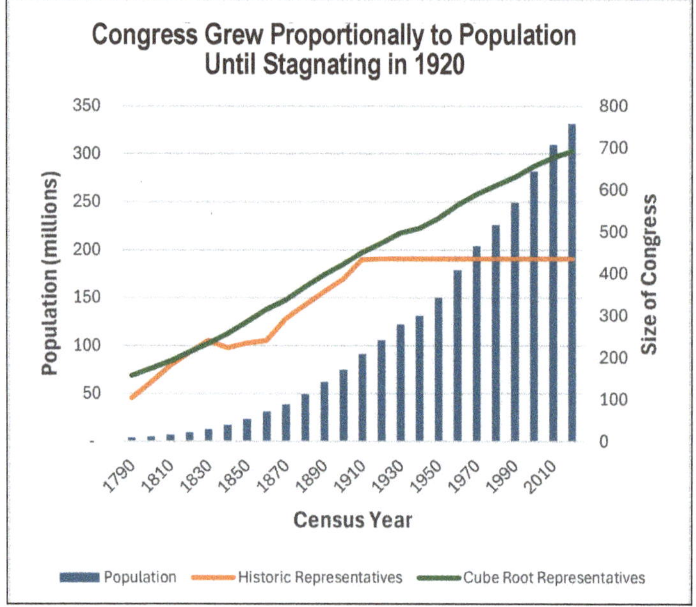

Figure 5.2

Sustained 10% growth per decade may be too aggressive. But even at a lower growth rate of 5% per decade the United States would reach a population of 496 million by 2100. The high end of the **official U.S. Census Bureau population projection**[49] would see the population reach 435 million by 2100.

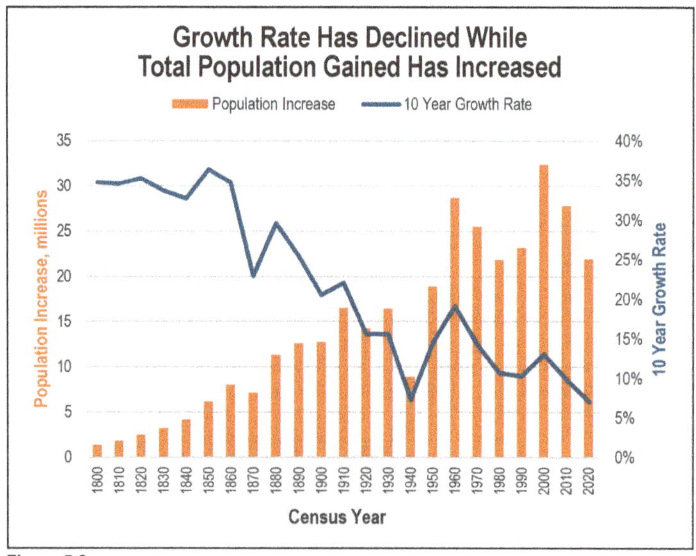

Figure 5.3

However quickly or slowly our population might change, the mathematical simplicity of setting the size of Congress as the cube root of the population would allow Congress to adjust its size accordingly, and without partisan interference.

What do you think? Is the Cube Root the right way to determine how large Congress will be? If not, is there a better option? These questions may have no correct answer. I have made the case for using the Cube Root as a less arbitrary, somewhat objective answer. At the very least, this would be a better way to apportion Congress than leaving it at its current, stagnant 435-members.

Table 5.37: Future Representation in a Cube Root Congress

Census	US Census High Immigration Scenario		5% Growth per Decade		10% Growth per Decade	
	Projected Population	Size of Congress	Projected Population	Size of Congress	Projected Population	Size of Congress
2020	335,421,874	695	335,421,874	695	335,421,874	695
2030	351,302,667	706	352,192,968	706	368,964,061	717
2040	369,865,148	718	369,802,616	718	405,860,468	740
2050	384,053,580	727	388,292,747	730	446,446,514	764
2060	396,953,837	735	407,707,384	742	491,091,166	789
2070	410,208,842	743	428,092,753	754	540,200,282	815
2080	421,213,182	750	449,497,391	766	594,220,311	841
2090	429,130,245	754	471,972,261	779	653,642,342	868
2100	435,346,449	758	495,570,874	791	719,006,576	896

Chapter 6

END THE TWO-PARTY SYSTEM THROUGH PROPORTIONAL RANKED CHOICE VOTING

W e need electorally plausible alternatives to the two major parties. In every presidential election since 2000, more than 1 million Americans voted for a third-party candidate despite the knowledge that those third-party candidates had effectively a zero percent chance of victory. Millions more have simply chosen not to vote.

This voting outcome is unsurprising given that **28% of Americans**[50] hold unfavorable views of both major parties, and **37% of Americans**[51] wish there were more parties to choose from, according to 2023 surveys by Pew Research Center.

If an alternative party had a truly viable chance for electoral victory, would you vote for one? I know I would.

In my opinion, Proportional Ranked Choice Voting (abbreviated as P-RCV, also called Single Transferable Vote) is the best electoral system to adopt because it provides an opportunity for alternative parties while requiring all elected candidates to face the voters as individuals, not just as representatives of a party. Within 10 years of adopting a P-RCV system, I believe the two-party system as we know it would end and that we would have a true multiparty democracy.

This kind of multi-winner ranked choice voting system was supported by political scientist Lee Drutman, author of *Breaking the Two-Party Doom Loop*. I used his work as the jumping off point for imagining a true multiparty democracy in Chapters 6.D and 11. (Drutman's views have **since changed**;[52] he now favors a fusion or open-list proportional representation voting system.) This electoral system is also supported by the nonpartisan group **FairVote**[53] and is in use in **several localities**[54] across the country, including Cambridge, MA; Arden, DE; Arlington County, VA; Minneapolis, MN; and Albany, CA.

There are other voting systems that would also be an improvement over our current system, such as the mixed-member proportional system used by Germany and New Zealand briefly discussed in Chapter 3.A.

Law professor Maxwell L. Stearns advocates for a mixed-member proportional parliamentary system similar to those of Germany and New Zealand in his 2024 book *Parliamentary America.* To be sure, Stearns' system would be better than our current system. In fact, many of his arguments regarding the benefits of a multiparty system are similar to those articulated here.

In Stearns' preferred system, half of the seats in Congress would be determined by elections in single-member districts (the same system we have now). The other half of the seats would be determined by a proportional method, where voters select their preferred political party and seats are apportioned according to the results. Stearns argues that in such a system, alternative parties would win representation and a multiparty democracy would result. This logic is sound.

However, I prefer P-RCV because I prefer a system in which all members of Congress are directly responsible to voters. I don't like the prospect of party bosses deciding who will be in office after the election.

The biggest difference between P-RCV and Stearns' system is that in the parliamentary system, the President would be elected by the new Congress instead of directly by the voters. Stearns argues that the practice of electing the President directly by the voters, even by RCV, inevitably results in American politics being divided into a pro-President and anti-President coaltion. This argument is sound; the Presidency is the most powerful axis around which our politics is defined. This is an extremely important point. However, I am not persuaded that a parliamentary system will fix this problem. If Stearns is right, maybe no voting system can break the two-party system. In the end, I weigh the possibility of reducing the temptation of two-party factionalism against my desire to vote directly for the highest office in the land. I am open to changing my mind on this, but currently prefer electing the President through RCV, discussed in depth in Chapter 10.

What is clear is that there is no perfect system. Just as there are issues with the parliamentary system advocated for by Stearns, there are issues with the P-RCV system advocated here. Yet both systems would be an improvement over our current system.

From a political strategy perspective, advocates for democratic reform need to come together on a unified proposal. We need to both get the reform right and not let the perfect be the enemy of the good. Stearns makes a persuasive argument for a parliamentary system, and I hope that in this book, I have made a persuasive argument for P-RCV. Ultimately, both Stearns and I are in complete agreement that the current two-party system is unsustainable and that a multiparty democracy is the solution. We merely differ on how to get there.

A. How Ranked Choice Voting Works

The way it works is this:

1. When you fill out your ballot, you rank the candidates according to your preference. All first-choice votes are counted, and if a candidate receives a majority of first-choice votes, they are elected.

2. If no candidate receives a majority of first-choice votes, the candidate who received the fewest first-place votes is eliminated. All first-choice ballots cast for the last-place candidate are counted instead for their next choice. Ballots that ranked only a candidate who has been eliminated are exhausted and removed from subsequent rounds of tabulation.

3. If you had ranked the losing candidate first, your vote is transferred to your second-ranked candidate. The votes are recounted, and the process repeated until a candidate receives a majority of non-exhausted votes.

The winning candidate in a Ranked Choice election is required to receive a majority of votes in the final round.

Alaska's 2022 Congressional race shows how RCV works in practice, as the winning candidate, Mary Peltola, received a majority of votes over three rounds of ranked choice counting (Figure 6.1). In Round 1, Peltola received 128,755 first-choice votes (48.7%),

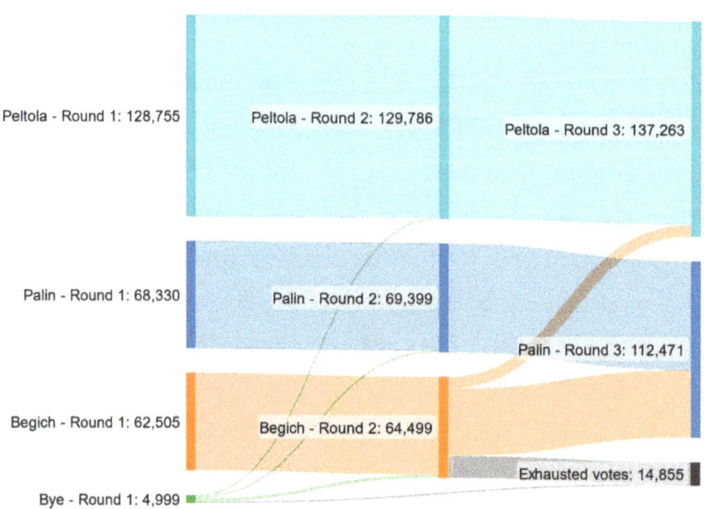

Figure 6.1: Data from **Alaska Division of Elections**.[55] Made with SankeyMATIC

almost a majority. Chris Bye, the fourth-place candidate, received 4,999 first-choice votes (1.9%) and was eliminated. In Round 2, Bye's voters had their votes counted instead for their second-choice candidate; ballots not marked with a second-choice candidate were "exhausted," meaning removed from subsequent rounds. Some of Bye's voters ranked Peltola second, increasing her total in Round 2 to 129,786 votes (49.2%). The third-place candidate, Nick Begich, received 64,699 votes (24.5%) in Round 2 and was eliminated. Round 3 proved decisive. While the majority of Begich's voters preferred the second-place candidate, Sarah Palin, 7,477 voters ranked Peltola as their second choice to push her total to 137,263 votes (55%), securing Peltola a majority and a seat in Congress.

A fair criticism,[56] also made by Stearns in *Parliamentary America,* of the Alaska election is that RCV in this instance did not award victory to the Condorcet winner. The Condorcet winner is the candidate who would beat all the other candidates in a head-to-head matchup. In this example, Begich would have beaten both Peltola and Palin in a head-to-head matchup. But, because he came in third place, he was eliminated before the final round.

I still find RCV compelling despite this criticism. In the case of Begich, while he was the Condorcet winner, he was unable to inspire enough support from voters to rank him first. In this way, RCV still rewards politicians who can inspire passionate support. RCV rewards politicians who can appeal to a broad swath of the electorate while simultaneously inspiring the necessary support to make it to the final round of voting.

B. How Multimember Districts Work

Multimember districts are districts in which multiple candidates are elected to represent the same set of voters.

There are several different ways elections in multimember districts can be run. For example, my home state, Washington, uses multimember districts to elect its legislature. Each of the 49 legislative districts elects 2 Representatives and 1 Senator. Each voter casts a ballot for all three positions: once for Senator, once for Representative Position 1, and once for Representative Position 2. The three winning candidates all represent the same voters. However, they are currently elected in separate elections. In a multimember Washington legislative district with 55% Democrats and 45% Republicans, Democrats would be favored to win all 3 seats because each race would pit 1 Democrat against 1 Republican. Even though Republicans make up nearly half of voters, they win zero representation.

Table 6.1: Multimember District
Electoral Thresholds, Droop Quota

District Size	1 Winner
1 Member	50.1%
2 Members	33.4%
3 Members	25.1%
4 Members	20.1%
5 Members	16.7%

A different way of running elections in multimember districts is with a proportional electoral system using ranked choice voting, also known as a single-transferable vote. In the example above of a 3-seat Washington legislative district with 55% Democrats and 45% Republicans, such a system would elect 2 Democrats and 1 Republican. This outcome better represents the interests of the entire district. It is fair. But how does it work from the perspective of the voter?

Reimagine the ranked choice Alaska election won by Peltola. The only change now is that instead of 1 winner, there will be 3. As before, each Alaska voter would cast a ballot with their first, second, and third choices or however many candidates they wanted to rank. This time, instead of a candidate needing 50% of the vote to win, a candidate would need just 25% (Table 6.1). The 25% electoral threshold is calculated using the Droop Quota, which is the threshold that three candidates can beat, but not four. If three candidates have more than 25% of the vote, no other candidate can reach 25%.

The Droop Quota is calculated by dividing 100% by the number of available seats plus 1. In the case of this hypothetical three-member district, the calculation would be 100% divided by 4 (100%/(3 seats + 1) = 25%) for a 25% electoral threshold. Each candidate, regardless of party, who receives 25% of the vote is a winner.

Figure 6.2 shows how the Alaska election would have played out under this system. Just as before, in the first round, all the first-rank votes are counted. Peltola received 48.7% of the vote in the first round and is declared the first winner. Palin received 25.8% of the vote and is declared the second winner. Begich received 23.6% of the vote, not quite enough to win in the first round.

However, the counting in the second round now proceeds a little differently. Before eliminating Bye, the fourth-place candidate, the surplus votes from the winners are distributed among the remaining candidates. Surplus votes are any votes not needed to declare the candidate a winner. In the first round, Peltola received 128,755 votes, well over the 25% threshold of 66,148 votes. Peltola's surplus 62,607 votes will be distributed among the over candidates according to the proportion of all Peltola voter's second-choice option. (Alaska's RCV Detailed Report on this election does not include data on who the second-choice candidate was for Peltola voters.) Let's say 40% of all Peltola voters ranked Palin second, 40% ranked Begich second, and 20% ranked Bye second. The surplus votes are distributed among the other candidates:

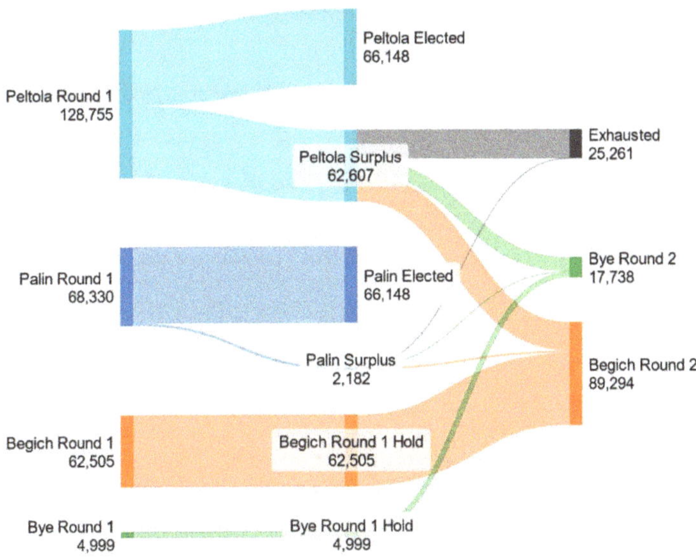

Figure 6.2: Made with SankeyMATIC

Begich receives 25,043 votes (40% of 62,607) and Bye receives 12,521 votes (20% of 62,607). Palin's surplus 2,182 votes are distributed in a similar way, with 80% of Palin voters ranking Begich second, 10% ranking Peltola second, and 10% ranking Bye second. The second-choice votes for Peltola and Palin are exhausted or could be surplus and recounted with their third choice if another round is necessary. Following this recount, Begich receives 89,294 votes and wins the third seat after crossing the 66,148 vote electoral threshold.

In this example, Alaska would elect 2 Republicans and 1 Democrat. The Democrat was the most popular individual candidate, but more Alaskans voted for Republicans overall. With this proportional multimember district system, Alaska's Republican majority and Democratic minority would both be represented.

If Alaska's election were run again with 3 seats available, the Democratic Party would likely put 2 or 3 candidates on the ballot. Democratic voters could vote for their preferred Democrat and rank the other Democrat second, and then rank a Republican third. In this way, the Democratic Party could compete for a second of 3 seats. For a party to win 2 seats in a three-member district, the combined votes for the party's candidates would need to win 50% of the vote.

C. How Alternative Parties Can Realistically Compete

By reducing the electoral threshold from the current 50% to as low as 17%, alternative parties will have a real chance of victory. In a five-member district, all a candidate or party needs is 17% of the vote!

Table 6.2 describes the vote share a party must earn in order to win one or more seats in a multimember district, using the Droop Quota. There are three primary implications. First, in a two-party system, the parties would compete at each vote share threshold. Currently the parties only compete in districts in which there is a near 50/50 split. In a five-member district, parties would compete at the 50/50 threshold, at the two 33/67 thresholds, and at the two 17/83 thresholds. Each seat is equally valuable whether the party earns 17%, 33%, 50%, 67%, or 83% of the vote. Parties would compete in districts in which they have large majorities and in districts in which they are heavily outnumbered.

Table 6.2: Electoral Thresholds For A Single Party To Have Multiple Winners, Droop Quota

District Size	1 Winner	2 Winners	3 Winners	4 Winners	5 Winners
1 Member	50.1%	x	x	x	x
2 Members	33.4%	66.7%	x	x	x
3 Members	25.1%	50.1%	75.1%	x	x
4 Members	20.1%	40.1%	60.1%	80.1%	x
5 Members	16.7%	33.4%	50.1%	66.7%	83.4%

Second, gerrymandering becomes much, much harder. A classic gerrymandering tactic is to pack a large majority of the opposing party's voters into one district. In a single-member district, one party could have as large as a 70% or 80% majority. However, all the votes beyond 50% are essentially wasted votes; they are votes that do not help the party gain a larger majority. Simultaneously, a 40% or 45% minority wins zero representation. Single-member districts punish parties for successfully winning enough support to create a large majority or a large minority in a given district.

Instead, multimember districts reward parties for winning more votes, period, including when parties have a large majority or a small minority of support. In a five-member district, the majority party is rewarded with an additional seat if it can win 67% of the vote. At the same time, the minority party is rewarded with an equally valuable seat if it can win 33% of the vote and thwart the majority party.

In this way, as the majority party is rewarded for running up the score in each district, the minority parties are equally rewarded for winning 20%, or 25%, or 40% of the vote. Larger districts increase the possibility of competition between the parties. The two major parties must adapt their strategies to the new system, or risk irrelevancy as new parties emerge.

Third, larger districts make smaller parties much more viable. In a five-member district, a party must only receive 16.7%, or 1/6, of the vote to earn a seat. And due to the fractional vote transfer, voters would be able to vote for a third-party with the knowledge that, if the third-party failed to earn one seat, their vote would go to their preferred major party and would still have an impact on the overall electoral outcome in their district.

While competition between the two major parties is not guaranteed, multimember districts can remain competitive within parties. For example, a four-member district split 50/50 between Democrats and Republicans will almost certainly see each party cross the 40% threshold to elect 2 candidates each. With 2 seats virtually guaranteed for each party, it follows that there will be fierce primary competition to be one of the two favorites among each party's voters.

One way primaries could work is for each party to nominate a number of candidates equal to the size of the district. Sticking with the evenly split four-member district example, the Republican Party would hold a primary to choose its top four candidates using RCV. The Democrats would do the same.

Alternative parties could choose to nominate just one candidate to attempt to draw votes away from the major parties and give their candidate the best shot possible. For example, in a five-member district, the electoral threshold is 16.7%. A Progressive Party could nominate 1 candidate and then implement a strategy of persuading left-wing voters to rank their candidate first, followed by a Democratic candidate second. Thanks to ranked choice voting, left-wing voters could feel confident that their vote would not be wasted on an unelectable alternative party: if the Progressive candidate failed to surpass the 16.7% threshold, those votes would be redistributed to the Democratic Party and help the Democratic Party win against the Republican Party.

In *Parliamentary America*, Stearns argues that multimember districts do not ensure electoral success for smaller parties. This is true, and rather beside the point. No party should be guaranteed electoral success unless it can demonstrate that it has the support of the people. A 17% electoral threshold is a low bar. And the bar could be lowered further by implementing six- or seven-member districts. Stearns also claims that the dominant parties will engage in strategies like bloc voting to win multiple seats. My response: they can try. I find it highly unlikely that the dominant parties will be able to consistently win the 60.1% of the vote necessary to win 3 seats in a four-member district, or 66.7% of the vote needed to win 4 seats in a five-member district. As I will show in detailed analysis of every state in Chapter 8, bloc voting strategies are rendered less effective due to the larger and more diverse populations within each district.

Both major parties are strife with division. They are too large and represent too many varied interests to remain unified except in opposition to each other. With a believable electoral victory in sight, it is easy to imagine Libertarians getting elected in Texas and Progressives getting elected in New York. Alternative parties might get their start in the big states, but, as I will show in Chapter 8, a P-RCV system would quickly make alternative parties viable all over the country.

D. Ten Years Later: A True Multiparty Democracy

Imagine these changes are implemented in 2025, and the first elections under the new system take place in 2026. In the first few years, the two parties remain dominant, but soon enough, factions break off, and new parties emerge. For example, in the final chapter of his 2020 book Breaking the Two-Party Doom Loop, political scientist Lee Drutman imagines a multiparty system with the following major parties:

- **The Social Democrats,** a left-wing party emphasizing an expansive social welfare state;
- **The New Democrats,** a center-left party emphasizing big government investments in transformative environmental technology;
- **The Reform Conservatives,** a center-right party emphasizing growth and investment through tax benefits for families and community-based nonprofit organizations;
- **The Christian Republicans,** a conservative party emphasizing the role of faith and free markets;
- **America First,** a party emphasizing right wing culture-war policies.

In Drutman's hypothetical, following the 2026 elections, a governing coalition of the Social Democrats, New Democrats, and Reform Conservatives emerges after the three parties together win 55% of seats in Congress (Table 6.3). Then, in 2030, after a session in which the coalition passed several popular and impactful pieces of legislation, Drutman postulates the three governing parties to win a combined 77% of seats in Congress. But this time, the Reform Conservatives would be the lead coalition partner.

Note: Drutman does not postulate the Centrist-Independent and Libertarian vote share for the 2030 elections. Because Drutman postulates the major five parties

Table 6.3: Drutman's Hypothetical Multiparty System

Party	2026 Results	2030 Results
Social Democrats	24%	26%
New Democrats	18%	22%
Reform Conservatives	13%	29%
America First	22%	10%
Christian Republicans	18%	8%
Centrist-Independents	3%	3%
Libertarians	2%	2%

to win a combined 95% of the vote, I kept the two minor parties at the same vote share as he postulated for 2026.

Drutman's is one hypothetical, as reasonable and aspirational as any attempt to predict the future could be in our uncertain time.

Pushing the time horizon out another four years to 2034, how might the political scene continue to change? What if, in addition to the five parties Drutman postulates, there were three more? Perhaps:

- **The Libertarian Party,** a party opposed to big government, and emphasizing personal freedoms such as property rights and gun rights;
- **The Justice Party,** a party emphasizing social progress for people of color, and accommodating of differing economic and faith perspectives; or
- **The Greens,** a party emphasizing state takeover of fossil fuel industries to rapidly decarbonize.

These parties would represent some of the fringe views in American politics. Yet, such fringe political parties are plausible in such a large and diverse country as ours. Each party could easily capture 3% of the vote and may draw support from a portion of the millions of voting eligible Americans so disgusted and disaffected with the two-party system that they choose to not vote. Could each of these parties succeed in winning 17% of the vote in a few five-member districts? Probably yes, because their supporters would see a viable path for victory, and, if not victory, they would see a vote for their second option potentially make a difference in the final tally. For example, a Libertarian Party might be more popular in Mountain West states like Idaho and Montana, while a Justice Party might be more popular in the South.

(Personally, if my options were among these 8 parties, I would probably strategically vote and rank my ballot Greens > Social Democrats > Libertarians or New Democrats > Reform Conservatives. Addressing climate change is my number one issue, but by ranking the SD, L, ND, and RC parties as alternatives, my vote would still be impactful even if my preferred party lost.)

Continuing from Drutman's hypothetical 2030 election results, and including the Libertarian, Justice, and Green parties, the national vote share could look something like Table 6.4. Perhaps, the coalition of

Table 6.4: My Hypothetical Multiparty System

Party	2034 Results
Social Democrats	24%
New Democrats	15%
Reform Conservatives	25%
America First	15%
Christian Republicans	9%
Centrist-Independents	3%
Libertarians	3%
Justice	3%
Greens	3%

Reform Conservatives, New Democrats, and Social Democrats would continue to govern.

If you think my hypothetical overstates the strength of one party or another, let's test it out by implementing the system and seeing which political party, which set of ideas, is the most popular. Let's have that debate. It would be much more productive than what we are doing now.

Chapters 7 and 8 show how a multiparty system might be formed, starting with four parties. Refer to the multiparty color-coded legend to view the projected outcomes in each electoral district, indicated by the boxes below each district number. For instance, in district TX-2, the projection shows two Republicans, one Libertarian, and one Democrat winning seats, with one competitive seat between Republicans and Libertarians.

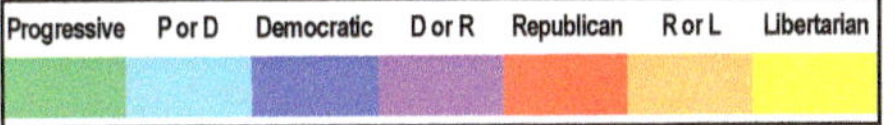

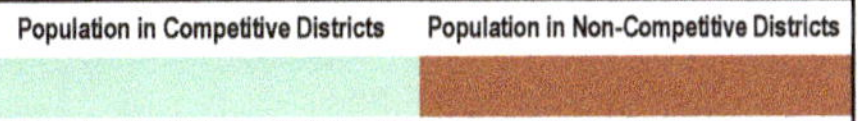

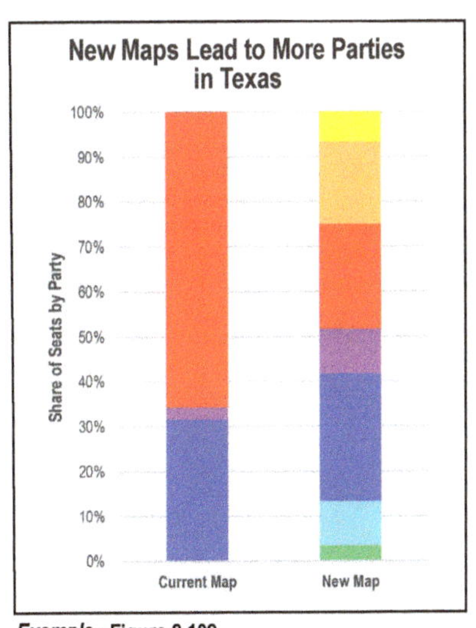

Example - Figure 8.109

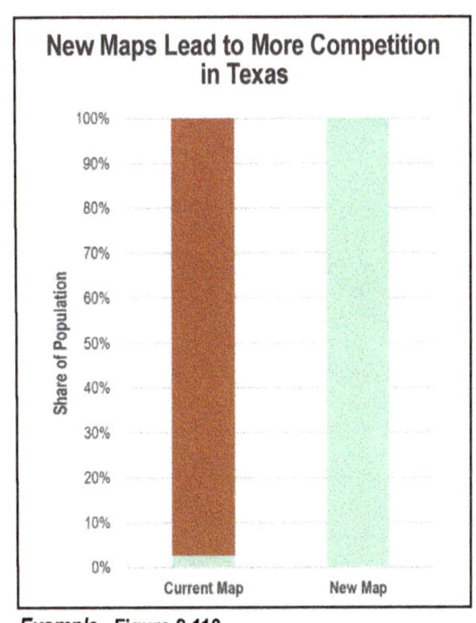

Example - Figure 8.110

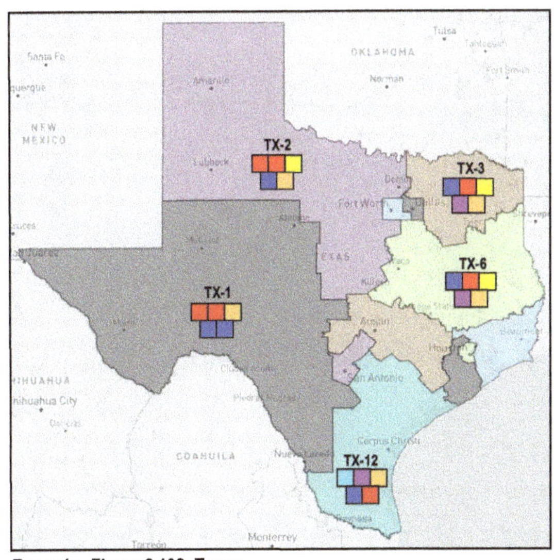

Example - Figure 8.108: Texas

NOTE: The district's background color is for geographic boundary only. The colored boxes reflect the electoral projections. For example, while the geography of TX-2 is purple, the boxes beneath the TX-2 label show how many seats each party is projected to win.

Chapter 7
THE NEW MAPS: NATIONAL ANALYSIS

The United States is a giant country, in both population and geography.

Currently, our country is divided into 435 single-member Congressional districts with an average population of just over 750,000.

A 695-member unicameral Congress elected by ranked choice voting across 164 multimember districts could look like this (Figure 7.1):

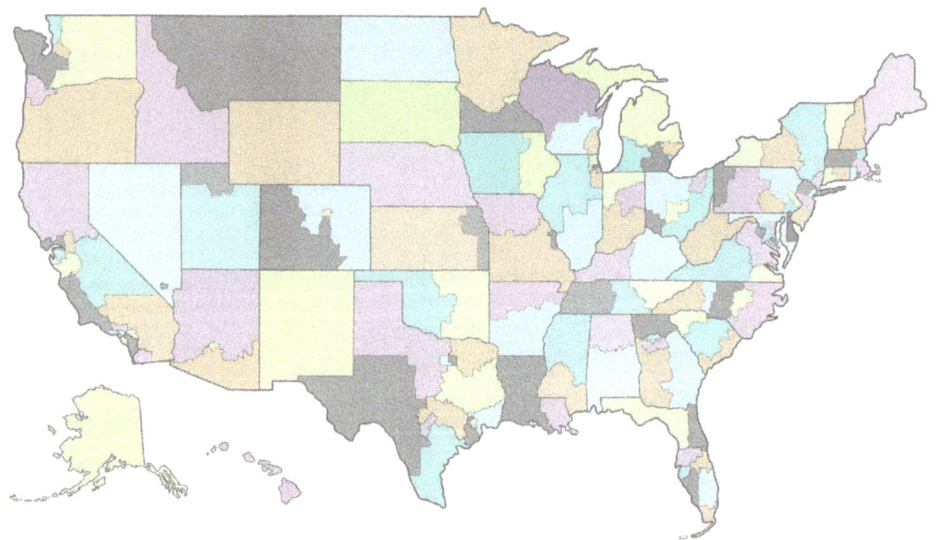

Figure 7.1

The transition from the current two-party system to a true multiparty system would not happen overnight. If, overnight, we started electing Congress with Proportional Ranked Choice Voting, I believe that while two parties would remain dominant at first, each party would face immediate competition from its flank. So deep is our collective dissatisfaction with the two parties that if there were an electoral system that made alternative parties viable, I believe 40% of the people who vote for Democrats would consider voting for a left-wing alternative (I am part of that 40%), and that 40% of the people who vote for Republicans would consider voting for a right-wing alternative.

Also, while many voters may prefer instead an alternative centrist party, or some other party, I do not model that here.

With a Proportional Ranked Choice Voting system, we could immediately have a four-party system (Figures 7.2 and 7.3). Competition would be between Republicans and Democrats (purple), Democrats and Progressives (teal), and Republicans and Libertarians (orange). The data I used to estimate the outcome for each district is based on an aggregate of statewide elections from 2016–2020. Politics changes quickly, so the data is already out of date, but it's close enough to current to provide an estimate for how we might begin to break the two-party system. My analytic methodology is explained in detail in part B of this chapter.

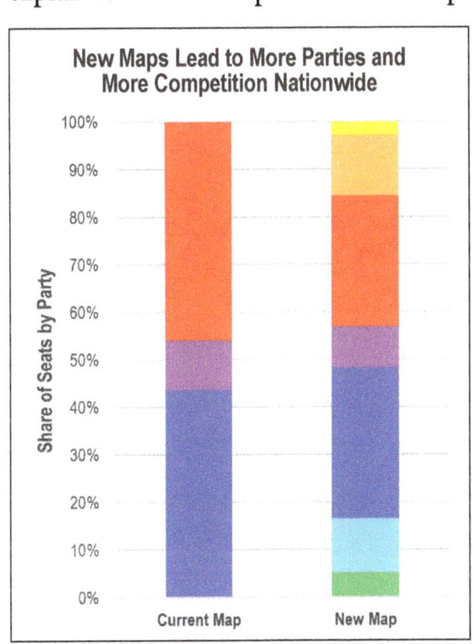

Figure 7.2

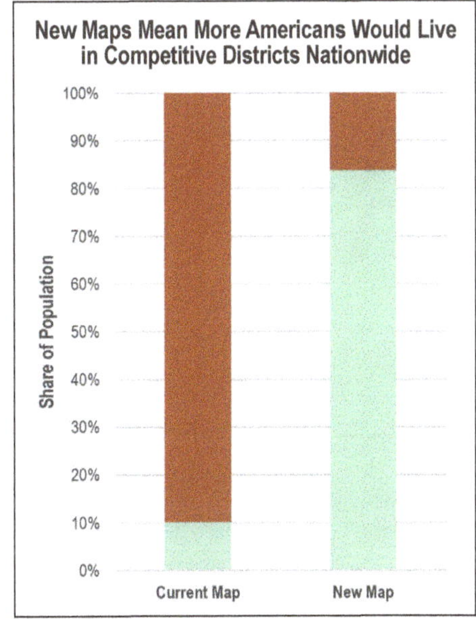

Figure 7.3

Likely, no party would win the 348 seats required for an outright majority (Table 7.1). Consider how a Democratic Party focused on moving to the right to persuade conservative voters could lose as many seats to a Progressive Party from the left as it might gain from a Republican Party to the right. A new party from the left could win up to 115 seats, and a new party from the right could win

Table 7.1: Summary of Projected Outcomes

	Current Maps	New Maps
Total Seats	435	695
Competitive Seats	45	227
Democratic Seats	190	221
Republican Seats	200	192
Progressive Seats	0	36
Libertarian Seats	0	19
D-R Competitive Seats	45	59
P-D Competitive Seats	0	79
R-L Competitive Seats	0	89
Total Districts	435	164
Competitive Districts	45	133
Pop. In Comp. Districts	34 million	281 million

Table 7.2: Multimember Districts Would Mean More Americans Would Live in Competitive Districts

State	Total Population	New Maps Comp. Pop.	Current Maps Comp. Pop.	Comp. Pop. Difference
USA	335,047,628	280,587,404	34,111,110	246,476,294
California	39,523,437	35,185,089	4,566,549	30,618,540
Texas	29,145,505	29,145,505	767,981	28,377,524
Florida	21,538,187	21,538,187	770,376	20,767,811
New York	20,201,249	18,277,338	4,665,173	13,612,165
Pennsylvania	13,002,700	8,668,654	2,296,208	6,372,446
Illinois	12,809,545	10,839,990	754,279	10,085,711
Ohio	11,799,448	6,883,028	2,361,770	4,521,258
Georgia	10,711,908	6,330,172	-	6,330,172
North Carolina	10,439,388	10,439,388	2,986,842	7,452,546
Michigan	10,077,331	8,157,434	1,551,453	6,605,981
New Jersey	9,283,016	9,283,016	774,541	8,508,475
Virginia	8,631,393	8,631,393	786,777	7,844,616
Washington	7,705,281	3,852,751	771,595	3,081,156
Arizona	7,151,502	4,768,104	1,590,872	3,177,232
Massachusetts	7,029,917	7,029,917	-	7,029,917
Tennessee	6,910,840	4,936,135	-	4,936,135
Indiana	6,785,528	6,785,528	754,476	6,031,052
Maryland	6,175,403	4,275,978	-	4,275,978
Missouri	6,154,913	6,154,913	-	6,154,913
Wisconsin	5,893,718	5,893,718	-	5,893,718
Colorado	5,773,714	3,849,470	1,445,543	2,403,927
Minnesota	5,706,494	3,804,316	-	3,804,316
South Carolina	5,118,425	3,257,171	-	3,257,171
Alabama	5,024,279	5,024,279	-	5,024,279
Louisiana	4,657,757	4,657,757	776,911	3,880,846
Kentucky	4,505,836	2,503,441	-	2,503,441
Oregon	4,237,256	2,353,877	1,413,833	940,044
Oklahoma	3,959,353	3,959,353	-	3,959,353
Connecticut	3,605,944	2,060,379	721,660	1,338,719
Puerto Rico	3,285,874	3,285,874	x	3,285,874
Utah	3,271,616	3,271,616	-	3,271,616
Iowa	3,190,369	3,190,369	798,102	2,392,268
Nevada	3,104,614	3,104,614	777,116	2,327,499
Arkansas	3,011,524	3,011,524	-	3,011,524
Mississippi	2,961,279	2,961,279	-	2,961,279
Kansas	2,937,880	2,937,880	-	2,937,880
New Mexico	2,117,522	2,117,522	706,740	1,410,782
Nebraska	1,961,504	1,961,504	654,444	1,307,060
Idaho	1,839,106	-	-	-
West Virginia	1,793,716	-	-	-
Hawaii	1,455,271	1,455,271	-	1,455,271
New Hampshire	1,377,529	1,377,529	-	1,377,529
Maine	1,362,359	1,362,359	681,791	680,568
Rhode Island	1,097,379	-	-	-
Montana	1,084,225	-	-	-
Delaware	989,948	-	-	-
South Dakota	886,667	886,667	-	886,667
North Dakota	779,094	779,094	-	779,094
Alaska	733,391	-	736,081	(736,081)
District of Columbia	689,545	-	x	-
Vermont	643,077	-	-	-
Wyoming	576,851	-	-	-
Four Territories	338,021	338,021	x	338,021

up to 108 seats (assuming a roughly 60–40 split in favor of the established party among voters who voted that party, and that each established party had only 1 splinter party). Alternative parties would be competitive in 45 states; all 8 states lacking alternative party competition are small, single-district states (Maine, Rhode Island, Montana, Delaware, Alaska, Vermont, Wyoming, Four Territories). Only 1 state, Alaska, would see fewer people living in competitive districts. In Alaska, both Democrats and Republicans would win 1 seat, and Alaska's idiosyncratic politics could result in unforeseen competitiveness.

I define a competitive district as a district in which the electoral outcome of at least one seat is uncertain. About 10% of Americans, 34 million people, live in a competitive congressional district for the 2024 elections, according to the Cook Political Report as of 9/7/2023. According to my model, with these new maps more than 75% of Americans, 281 million people, would live in a competitive district, and 43 of the 53 states would feature competitive districts (Table 7.2). Alternative parties could compete for 223 seats, about 30% of Congress.

To make these projections, I drew new multimember districts for every state and analyzed the partisan makeup of each state to estimate the electoral outcome. These maps are the opposite of gerrymandered. I actively worked to counter my implicit urban and liberal biases and tried to draw districts to favor more rural and conservative populations. I discuss this in detail in part A of this chapter.

These maps and this analysis show what elections might look like immediately following the implementation of P-RCV. After several election cycles, there would likely be more parties as the existing Democratic and Republican coalitions fracture, as described in Chapter 6.D.

Because no party would be likely to win a majority, to be elected Speaker of the House a legislator would almost certainly be required to form a coalition government, as in other multiparty democracies. Congress would be forever changed.

A. How I Ungerrymandered The Map

This is my explanation of how I drew the maps. My goal with this explanation is to convince you that I have done everything possible to avoid subconscious bias resulting in unintentional gerrymandering. You can see every map for free here at **Dave's Redistricting.**[57]

To start, I threw out the existing Congressional district map. The existing map is 435 single-member districts, gerrymandered all over the place. The new map would have 695 representatives across some number of multimember districts.

Table 7.3: How Many Districts Should Each State Have Given the Size of it's Delegation?

Seats	Districts	Members Per District	Alternate District Sizes
3	1	3	X
4	1	4	X
5	1	5	X
6	2	3,3	6
7	2	3,4	7
8	2	4,4	X
9	2	4,5	X
10	2	5,5	X
11	3	3,4,4	5,6
12	3	4,4,4	6,6
13	3	4,4,5	6,7
14	3	4,5,5	7,7
15	3	5,5,5	X
16	4	4,4,4,4	5,5,6
17	4	4,4,4,5	5,6,6
18	4	4,4,5,5	6,6,6
19	4	4,5,5,5	X
20	4	5,5,5,5	X
21	5	4,4,4,4,5	5,5,5,6
22	5	4,4,4,5,5	5,5,6,6
23	5	4,4,5,5,5	5,6,6,6
24	5	4,5,5,5,5	6,6,6,6
25	5	5,5,5,5,5	X
26	6	4,4,4,4,5,5	5,5,5,5,6
27	6	4,4,4,4,5,5	5,5,5,6,6
28	6	4,4,5,5,5,5	5,5,6,6,6
29	6	4,5,5,5,5,5	5,6,6,6,6
30	6	5,5,5,5,5,5	6,6,6,6,6
42	9	4,4,4,5,5,5,5,5,5	6,6,6,6,6,6,6
45	9	5,5,5,5,5,5,5,5,5	5,5,5,6,6,6,6,6
60	12	5,5,5,5,5,5,5,5,5,5,5,5	6,6,6,6,6,6,6,6,6,6
60	12		5,5,5,5,5,5,6,6,6,6,6,6
82	17	4,4,4,5,5,5,5,5,5,5,5,5,5,5,5,5,5	5,5,5,5,5,5,5,5,5,5,5,5,5,5,6,6
82	17		5,5,5,5,5,5,5,5,6,6,6,6,6,6
82	17		5,5,6,6,6,6,6,6,6,6,6,6,6

I first determined the size and number of districts for each state's apportioned representatives (Table 7.3). Except for the smallest states which are assigned a single district of just 1 or 2 representatives, each district would have between three and five members, with a top preference of five members per district, followed by four members per district, followed by three members per district. I prioritized maximizing the number of of five-member districts as I believe that is the best electoral threshold to allow alternative parties to win while simultaneously requiring winning candidates to have reasonably widespread support. I experimented with the possibility of districts of six or seven members, but decided against that as such districts would have too low an electoral threshold (to be explored in Chapter 8.B.iv).

Moving from theory to practice, I determined how many districts each state would have (Table 7.4).

As discussed in Chapter 5.C., there would be an average of 482,621 people represented by each member of Congress. When drawing multimember

Table 7.4: Seats and Districts By State

State	Population	Seats	Districts	Pop. Per Seat	Voting Power
Alabama	5,024,279	10	2	502,428	96.1%
Alaska	733,391	2	1	366,696	131.6%
Arizona	7,151,502	15	3	476,767	101.2%
Arkansas	3,011,524	6	2	501,921	96.2%
California	39,523,437	82	17	481,993	100.1%
Colorado	5,773,714	12	3	481,143	100.3%
Connecticut	3,605,944	7	2	515,135	93.7%
Delaware	989,948	2	1	494,974	97.5%
District of Columbia	689,545	2	1	344,773	140.0%
Florida	21,538,187	45	9	478,626	100.8%
Four Territories	338,021	1	1	338,021	142.8%
Georgia	10,711,908	22	5	486,905	99.1%
Hawaii	1,455,271	3	1	485,090	99.5%
Idaho	1,839,106	4	1	459,777	105.0%
Illinois	12,809,545	26	6	492,675	98.0%
Indiana	6,785,528	14	3	484,681	99.6%
Iowa	3,190,369	7	2	455,767	105.9%
Kansas	2,937,880	6	2	489,647	98.6%
Kentucky	4,505,836	9	2	500,648	96.4%
Louisiana	4,657,757	10	2	465,776	103.6%
Maine	1,362,359	3	1	454,120	106.3%
Maryland	6,175,403	13	3	475,031	101.6%
Massachusetts	7,029,917	15	3	468,661	103.0%
Michigan	10,077,331	21	5	479,873	100.6%
Minnesota	5,706,494	12	3	475,541	101.5%
Mississippi	2,961,279	6	2	493,547	97.8%
Missouri	6,154,913	13	3	473,455	101.9%
Montana	1,084,225	2	1	542,113	89.0%
Nebraska	1,961,504	4	1	490,376	98.4%
Nevada	3,104,614	6	2	517,436	93.3%
New Hampshire	1,377,529	3	1	459,176	105.1%
New Jersey	9,283,016	19	4	488,580	98.8%
New Mexico	2,117,522	4	1	529,381	91.2%
New York	20,201,249	42	9	480,982	100.3%
North Carolina	10,439,388	22	5	474,518	101.7%
North Dakota	779,094	2	1	389,547	123.9%
Ohio	11,799,448	24	5	491,644	98.2%
Oklahoma	3,959,353	8	2	494,919	97.5%
Oregon	4,237,256	9	2	470,806	102.5%
Pennsylvania	13,002,700	27	6	481,581	100.2%
Puerto Rico	3,285,874	7	2	469,411	102.8%
Rhode Island	1,097,379	2	1	548,690	88.0%
South Carolina	5,118,425	11	3	465,311	103.7%
South Dakota	886,667	2	1	443,334	108.9%
Tennessee	6,910,840	14	3	493,631	97.8%
Texas	29,145,505	60	15	485,758	99.4%
Utah	3,271,616	7	2	467,374	103.3%
Vermont	643,077	1	1	643,077	75.0%
Virginia	8,631,393	18	4	479,522	100.6%
Washington	7,705,281	16	4	481,580	100.2%
West Virginia	1,793,716	4	1	448,429	107.6%
Wisconsin	5,893,718	12	3	491,143	98.3%
Wyoming	576,851	1	1	576,851	83.7%

districts, a three-member district would have a baseline population of 1.4 million people (Table 7.5). A four member district would have a baseline population of 1.9 million people, and a five member district would have a baseline population of 2.4 million people. The exact size of the districts varies state to state, depending on the voting power of each state. For example, Alabama would be

Members	Population
1	482,621
2	965,242
3	1,447,863
4	1,930,484
5	2,413,105
6	2,895,726
7	3,378,347

Table 7.5: Average District Size

assigned 10 seats in a 695-member Congress, which would be drawn into 2 five-member districts. The 502,428 people per representative in Alabama would have 96.1% voting power, slightly less than average. Each of the five-member districts in Alabama contains just over 2.5 million people. Within each state, the number of people represented by the same size of district should be the same. In practice, my districts are not perfectly proportional; they are almost all within 1,000 people of the population which they are supposed to be. If multimember districts were implemented, they would be drawn to perfection; my purpose here is to provide a close enough estimate to make the point. All the data for the size of each district is shown in each state's section in Chapter 8.

Once I determined how many districts each state would be divided into, and how many members each district would have, I started drawing the lines. I used **Dave's Redistricting**[58] platform to draw all the new maps; Dave's Redistricting has precinct level population data for every precinct in every county in every state. All maps described here are publicly available to view on **Dave's Redistricting website**[59] (search "polemic" to find my maps).

I redistricted each state independently of all others. I discuss the particulars of each state's redistricting in the relevant section in Chapter 8. In general, I used a state's existing legislative district lines as a guide for where to divide communities that I know little about other than their population and location on the map. State legislative lines are to some extent gerrymandered, which is why I only used them as guidelines. I usually started in one corner of a state and then moved across it. For example, in drawing New York's lines, I started at the eastern edge of Long Island, then moved through New York City, then moved into upstate New York; for Florida, I started in the panhandle and moved south to Miami. Each state presented unique challenges, which I discuss on a state-by-state basis in Chapter 8. I also tried to make districts as compact as possible to avoid creating the bizarrely shaped districts that exist in our current system. Ultimately, drawing the districts came down to dozens of judgment calls. Which precinct should be in this district as opposed to a different district? It was a puzzle that came down to trying to balance the population of the different districts.

My districts are not meant to be perfect. They are far from perfect. But they are a clear improvement on the gerrymandered mess of our current system. Since most districts have four or five members, there are around 1.9 million or 2.4 million people in each district. A higher population combined with a lower electoral threshold make it practically impossible to draw districts in such a way as to deny political power to one of the two major parties. The only places this is possible is in the very most liberal parts of New York and San Francisco, and even in those places, conservative voters would have a greater chance of electoral success, as well as alternative parties on the left having the potential to disrupt the dominant Democratic Party.

B. Analytic Methodology For Projecting Electoral Outcomes

In the first part of this chapter, I projected that 133 of the 164 newly drawn districts would be competitive. I also projected that Democrats would safely win 221 seats and Republicans would safely win 192 seats, while a competitor from the left (Progressives) would win 36 seats and compete in 79 more, and a competitor from the right (Libertarians) would win 19 seats and compete in 89 more. For projecting the outcome of the current maps, I used the projections from the September 2023 *Cooks Report,* which rates the competitiveness of each Congressional race.

These estimates for the new maps are for the first election in such a system and are likely an undercount of the number of competitive districts and competitive seats that would emerge as the multiparty system develops and voters and political parties adapt to the new voting rules. I anticipate that more parties would quickly become electorally viable and that within two decades every single Congressional district would be competitive.

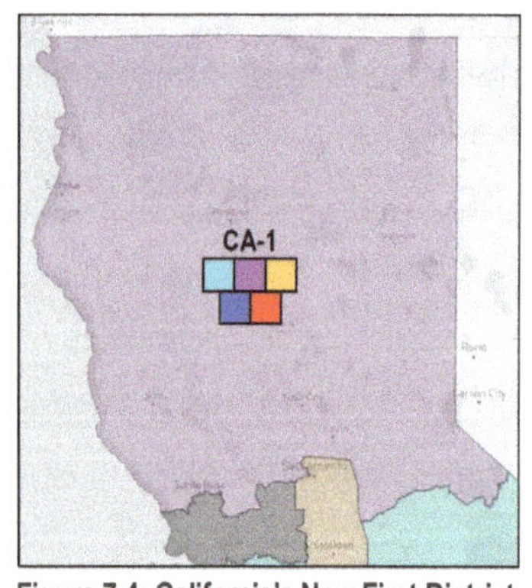

Figure 7.4: California's New First District

For this analysis, I first looked at each district's expected share of Democratic and Republican voters. **Dave's Redistricting**[60] helpfully aggregates statewide election results from 2016–2020 and uses that data to provide an estimated number of Democratic and Republican voters in each precinct. For example, the new California First District, a geographically sprawling five-member district next to Oregon and Nevada, is expected to have 50.4% Democrats and 47.4% Republicans (Figure 7.4 and Table 7.7).

Second, I assume that roughly 40% of each party's voters would be willing to vote for an alternative party. This assumption is based off **Gallup's 2022 research**[61] showing that 56% of Americans believe a third-party is needed, and **Pew Research Center's 2022 research**[62] showing that nearly 40% of Americans wish there were more political parties to choose from.

The 40% assumption is a more of a rule of thumb than a strict demarcation. In politics, you must expect the unexpected; you must keep your mind open to low-probability events. All of the data analyzed here is from 2016 through 2020, yet in some ways it already feels out of date because politics changes so quickly. Further, every state and region has idiosyncratic politics. In districts with similar partisan projections, alternative parties may be more popular in one part of the country than another part of the country. People that vote for Democrats in New York could have a very different collective preference for a Progressive Party than people that vote for Democrats in Texas; people that vote for Republicans in Washington State could have a very different collective preference for a Libertarian Party than people that vote for Republicans in Florida.

State and regional idiosyncrasies aside, in general, the more members in a district, the more likely an alternative party could be competitive to win one or more seats. For example, in a five-member district, I would expect alternative parties to be competitive for one seat when a major party reaches about 40% of the vote and to win one seat when a major party reaches about 42% of the vote (Table 7.6). In a four-member district, alternative parties could be competitive when the major party reaches about 45% of the vote and could win one seat when the major party reaches about 50% of the vote. In this way, alternative parties are viable not just in the most liberal cities or most conservative exurbs, but in more evenly divided districts across every part of the country.

Even if someone wanted to gerrymander these districts, there are too many competitive thresholds to consider. Imagine trying to gerrymander a four-member district to ensure one party will win 3 seats. In a two-party system, you could draw a district so that your party was projected to win 63% of the vote, a comfortable margin above the 60% electoral threshold to win 3 seats in a four-member district. In doing so, you would guarantee one seat to the opposing major party. But you would also be practically ensuring an alternative party or independent candidate will compete for one of your seats! An alternative party would need to win just one third of your party's voters to win 20% of the vote. The electoral outcome would be 2 seats for your party, 1 seat for

Table 7.6: Alternative Party Electoral Threshold Rule of Thumb

Major Party Projected Vote	Alt. Party Projected	Projected Alternative Party Seats By District Size						
		1-Member	2-Member	3-Member	4-Member	5-Member	6-Member	7-Member
36%	14%	0	0	0	0	0	1	1
42%	17%	0	0	0	0	1	1	1
50%	20%	0	0	0	1	1	1	1
63%	25%	0	0	1	1	1	1	2
85%	34%	0	1	1	1	2	2	2
100%	40%	0	1	1	2	2	2	3

the opposition, and 1 seat for an alternative party. To ensure 3 seats, you would have to draw the district so that more than 80% of voters are projected to vote for your party. This is practically impossible; there are very few parts of the country in which it is possible to draw such a large district with such a large partisan majority. Gerrymandering only works in our current system because we use single-member districts, which are far easier to gerrymander than multimember districts.

For example, consider three new districts, the California First, the Texas Second, and the Illinois Sixth.

Table 7.7: Example District Analysis, CA-1, IL-6, TX-2

District	Population	Dem %	Rep %	Seats	P Safe	P or D	D Safe	D or R	R Safe	R or L	L Safe
CA-1	2,409,997	50.4%	47.4%	5	0	1	1	1	1	1	0
TX-2	2,426,250	24.8%	73.3%	5	0	0	1	0	2	1	1
IL-6	1,971,217	75.4%	19.7%	4	1	0	2	1	0	0	0

I project CA-1 would elect 1 Democrat and 1 Republican, with a third seat competitive between the 2 parties. Additionally, 1 seat would be competitive between the Democrats and a Progressive Party, and 1 seat would be competitive between the Republicans and a Libertarian Party. With just 17% of the vote necessary to win 1 seat, each of the major parties would have to contend with a challenge. In the existing two-party system, Democrats are projected to win 50.4% of the vote in CA-1. Similarly, Republicans are projected to win 47.4% of the vote. Is it plausible that 40% of Democratic voters would support a Progressive candidate? Is it plausible that 40% of Republican voters would support a Libertarian Party, or some other conservative leaning political party? Absolutely! Both alternative parties could plausibly win 1 seat. Depending on how the ranked choice voting shook out, CA-1 could end up electing a delegation with representatives from four different parties.

I projected "safe" Progressive and Libertarian seats in districts with large Democratic or Republican majorities. For example, because Democratic voters make up 75.4% of Illinois' four-member Sixth District (Chicago), it is highly likely that a Progressive or independent left-wing candidate would win 20% of the vote. Similarly, because

Republican voters make up 73.3% of Texas' five-member Second District, (Lubbock, North Texas), it is highly likely that a Libertarian or independent right-wing candidate would win 17% of the vote, and plausible for a Libertarian Party to challenge the Republicans for 34% of the vote and a second seat.

Again, this analysis is likely an undercount because it is based on election data from our current single-member district, two-party system! This proposal's method of lowering the electoral threshold and reversing gerrymandering would certainly have unknown consequences. I use Progressive and Libertarian parties in this analysis because these ideas already exist in our politics today. But new ideas and new coalitions would emerge in a system like this, designed to foster competition among parties. The tired, old, sclerotic Democratic and Republican parties might be eclipsed by successor parties, just as the Whigs faded in the years leading up to the Civil War.

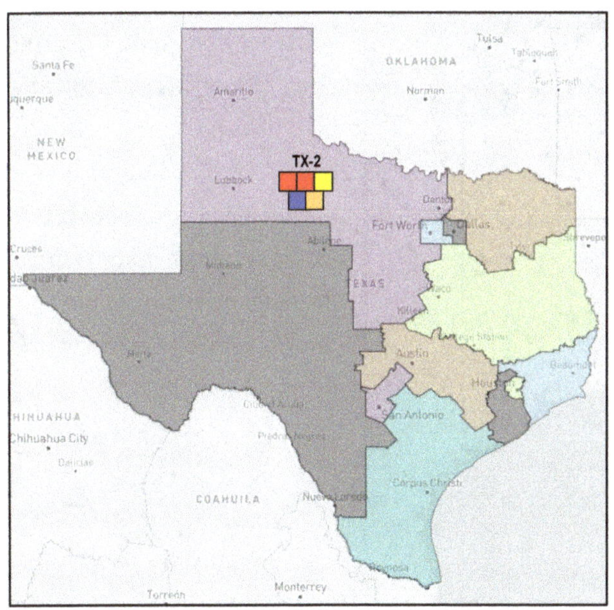

Figure 7.5: Texas' New Second District

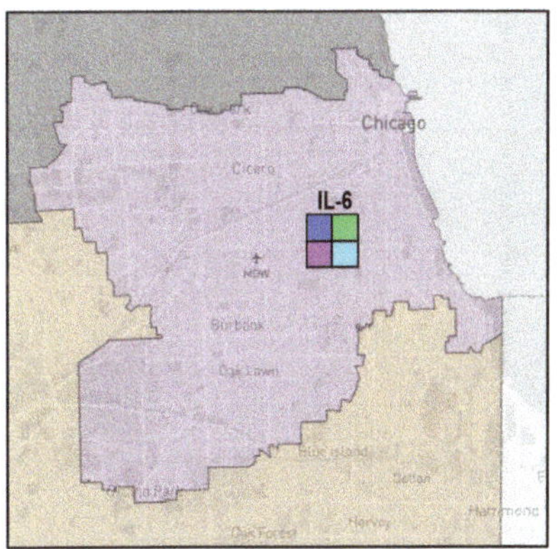

Figure 7.6: Illinois' New Sixth District

C. A Note on Data

All population data used in creating and analyzing these maps is from Dave's Redistricting, based on the 2020 U.S. Census. These population figures are slightly different compared to the 2020 Census figures used for apportionment in the Chapter 5, on average 0.11% lower (Table 7.8).

Table 7.8: Minor Population Data Differences Between 2020
U.S. Census and Dave's Redistricting

State	2020 US Census	Dave's Redistricting	Absolute Difference	Percent Difference
USA	335,421,874	335,047,628	374,246	0.11%
California	39,576,757	39,523,437	53,320	0.13%
Texas	29,183,290	29,145,505	37,785	0.13%
Florida	21,570,527	21,538,187	32,340	0.15%
New York	20,215,751	20,201,249	14,502	0.07%
Pennsylvania	13,011,844	13,002,700	9,144	0.07%
Illinois	12,822,739	12,809,545	13,194	0.10%
Ohio	11,808,848	11,799,448	9,400	0.08%
Georgia	10,725,274	10,711,908	13,366	0.12%
North Carolina	10,453,948	10,439,388	14,560	0.14%
Michigan	10,084,442	10,077,331	7,111	0.07%
New Jersey	9,294,493	9,283,016	11,477	0.12%
Virginia	8,654,542	8,631,393	23,149	0.27%
Washington	7,715,946	7,705,281	10,665	0.14%
Arizona	7,158,923	7,151,502	7,421	0.10%
Massachusetts	7,033,469	7,029,917	3,552	0.05%
Tennessee	6,916,897	6,910,840	6,057	0.09%
Indiana	6,790,280	6,785,528	4,752	0.07%
Maryland	6,185,278	6,175,403	9,875	0.16%
Missouri	6,160,281	6,154,913	5,368	0.09%
Wisconsin	5,897,473	5,893,718	3,755	0.06%
Colorado	5,782,171	5,773,714	8,457	0.15%
Minnesota	5,709,752	5,706,494	3,258	0.06%
South Carolina	5,124,712	5,118,425	6,287	0.12%
Alabama	5,030,053	5,024,279	5,774	0.11%
Louisiana	4,661,468	4,657,757	3,711	0.08%
Kentucky	4,509,342	4,505,836	3,506	0.08%
Oregon	4,241,500	4,237,256	4,244	0.10%
Oklahoma	3,963,516	3,959,353	4,163	0.11%
Connecticut	3,608,298	3,605,944	2,354	0.07%
Puerto Rico	3,285,874	3,285,874	-	0.00%
Utah	3,275,252	3,271,616	3,636	0.11%
Iowa	3,192,406	3,190,369	2,037	0.06%
Nevada	3,108,462	3,104,614	3,848	0.12%
Arkansas	3,013,756	3,011,524	2,232	0.07%
Mississippi	2,963,914	2,961,279	2,635	0.09%
Kansas	2,940,865	2,937,880	2,985	0.10%
New Mexico	2,120,220	2,117,522	2,698	0.13%
Nebraska	1,963,333	1,961,504	1,829	0.09%
Idaho	1,841,377	1,839,106	2,271	0.12%
West Virginia	1,795,045	1,793,716	1,329	0.07%
Hawaii	1,460,137	1,455,271	4,866	0.33%
New Hampshire	1,379,089	1,377,529	1,560	0.11%
Maine	1,363,582	1,362,359	1,223	0.09%
Rhode Island	1,098,163	1,097,379	784	0.07%
Montana	1,085,407	1,084,225	1,182	0.11%
Delaware	990,837	989,948	889	0.09%
South Dakota	887,770	886,667	1,103	0.12%
North Dakota	779,702	779,094	608	0.08%
Alaska	736,081	733,391	2,690	0.37%
District of Columbia	689,545	689,545	-	0.00%
Vermont	643,503	643,077	426	0.07%
Wyoming	577,719	576,851	868	0.15%
Four Territories	338,021	338,021	-	0.00%

The difference is so slight that it does not impact my purpose here, which is to show what a Cube Root Congress elected by ranked choice voting in multimember districts might look like. These maps are not intended to be perfect; if we implemented multimember districts, new maps would be drawn and approved by the people of each state.

Chapter 8

THE NEW MAPS: STATE-BY-STATE ANALYSIS

This chapter is designed for you to be able to flip through quickly to view all the new district maps in all the states. Written analysis for every state is available for any state that you wish to explore more deeply.

I encourage you to judge these maps based on three criteria:

1. *Competitiveness:* Would more people in each state vote in competitive elections with the new map than the current map?

2. *Proportionality:* Would the expected electoral outcome be more proportionally representative with the new map than the current map?

3. *Vibe Check:* Do the districts look like a reasonable division of each state's population? Does the map look biased toward either major party?

Across the 53 states, there are 17 one-district states, 13 two-district states, 10 three-district states, 3 four-district states, 4 five-district states, 2 six-district states, 2 nine-district states, 1 twelve-district state, and 1 seventeen-district state.

In this analysis, every state is divided into districts of 3, 4, or 5 seats, except for the smallest states apportioned only 1 or 2 seats. However, multimember districts of 6 of 7 seats could also be used. The benefit of 6- or 7-member districts is that it is easier for alternative parties and independents to win representation. The drawback is that the population of the district might become so large that smaller regional idiosyncrasies might be ignored.

The options are straightforward with the smaller states: 7-seat Iowa can be divided into 1 three-member district and 1 four-member district or be drawn as 1 seven-member district; 11-seat South Carolina can be drawn as 1 three-member district and 2 four-member districts or as 1 five-member district and 1 six-member district. The options increase as the states get larger. New York is the fourth-largest state and would be represented by 42 members in a 695-seat Congress. In this analysis, I divided New York into 3 four-member districts and 6 five-member districts. What if, instead, New York were divided into 7 equal six-member districts? With the lower electoral threshold of larger districts, every district would have more opportunities for political competition. Or, to get creative, New York could be divided into 2 four-member districts, 2 five-member districts, and 3 six-member districts. Such a diversity in district size would allow for regional communities to remain distinct from other parts of the state in terms of electing their representatives. These decisions should be made by the people of each state through their legislatures, their state courts, or an independent commission.

To be clear, this analysis only considers 4 parties: the 2 main parties and 1 splinter party to the left and to the right. Eventually, I expect multiple and new parties to form and win representation, as explored in the previous chapter. But projecting, with any reasonable amount of confidence, electoral outcomes of multiple parties with overlapping constituencies and policy goals is practically impossible with data from our two-party system. Even so, I make an attempt at modeling a six-party system in Washington State in Chapter 11.

Without further ado, here is each state's new congressional map if we expanded Congress to 695 members and implemented P-RCV, from smallest to largest.

A. One-District States

One-district states are those in which all the state's representatives are elected in the same district. Their maps are as simple as can be, the entire state as one district.

Table 8.1: One-District States - Current Map

State	Population	Partisan Lean		Projected Seats (Sept. 2023 Cooks Report)			
		Democratic	Republican	Total	Democratic	Republican	Competitive
Total	19,725,205	x	x	26	11	11	4
New Mexico	2,117,522	54.1%	42.3%	3	2	0	1
Nebraska	1,961,504	36.6%	60.9%	3	0	2	1
Idaho	1,839,106	32.4%	63.2%	2	0	2	0
West Virginia	1,793,716	32.6%	64.7%	2	0	2	0
Hawaii	1,455,271	65.9%	30.6%	2	2	0	0
New Hampshire	1,377,529	45.2%	52.0%	2	2	0	0
Maine	1,362,359	47.8%	46.6%	2	1	0	1
Rhode Island	1,097,379	60.6%	37.3%	2	2	0	0
Montana	1,084,225	42.7%	55.1%	2	0	2	0
Delaware	989,948	58.7%	39.2%	1	1	0	0
South Dakota	886,667	36.7%	62.2%	1	0	1	0
North Dakota	779,094	29.1%	66.9%	1	0	1	0
Alaska	733,391	41.8%	52.8%	1	0	0	1
District of Columbia	689,545	91.6%	4.8%	x	x	x	x
Vermont	643,077	58.1%	37.0%	1	1	0	0
Wyoming	576,851	26.4%	69.5%	1	0	1	0
Four Territories	338,021	x	x	x	x	x	x

The 19.7 million Americans (5.89% of the total population) living in these 17 states would be represented in Congress by 42 members (6.04% of Congress), an increase from the 26 members they currently have and within 15/100[ths] of a percent of perfect collective proportionality.

I project that 12 seats across 8 states would be competitive. There are more competitive seats than competitive states because some states have multiple competitive seats. For example, I project Nebraska would have two competitive seats. One would be competitive between the Democrats and Republicans, and a second would be competitive between the Republicans and Libertarians.

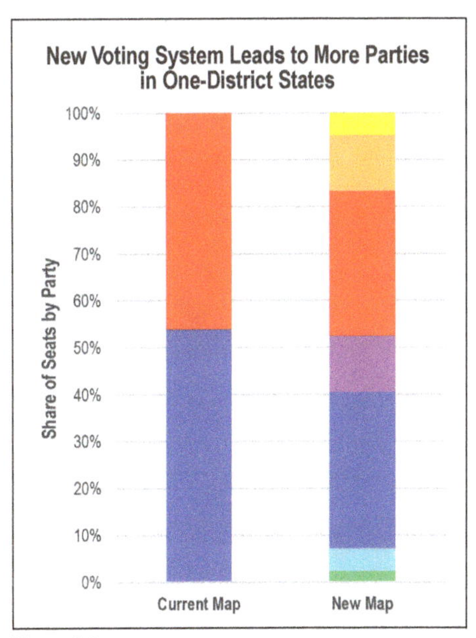

Figure 8.1

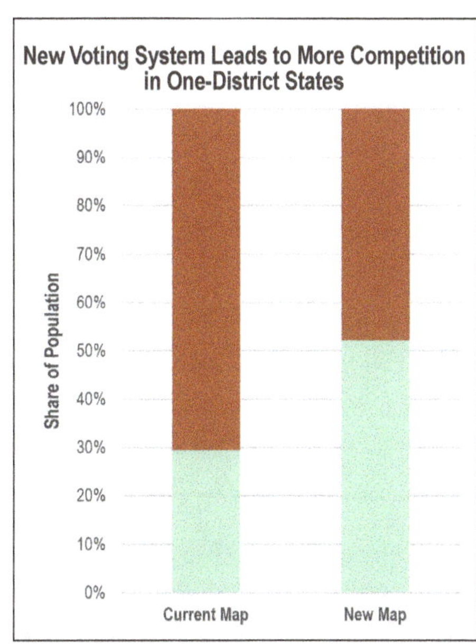

Figure 8.2

The competitiveness projection in Figure 8.2 is likely understated because for that graph I do not count it as competitive if an alternative party is projected to safely win a seat. For example, Idaho and West Virginia are not counted as competitive states because I project that the Republicans would safely win two seats, the Democrats would safely win one seat, and the Libertarians would safely win one seat. The prospect of a third-party winning representation makes Idaho and West Virginia more competitive, despite this competition not being captured in Figure 8.2.

i. Three, Four, and Five Seats: New Mexico, Nebraska, Idaho, West Virginia, Hawaii, New Hampshire, Maine

States comprising a single 3-, 4-, or 5-member district would become more proportionally representative compared to existing maps. There would be zero states with 5 seats in a 695-seat Congress based on 2020's census, though that could change as populations change.

Currently, all 7 three- and four-seat states are represented in the House by only one party. By switching to a multimember district, the minority party would win at least one seat in each state. For example, New Hampshire and Maine are each currently represented in Congress by Democrats. In an expanded Congress, New Hampshire and Maine would each have three seats. Due to multimember districts, 1 Democrat and 1 Republican would be elected in each state, and then the third seat in each state would be competitive between the two parties.

Alternative parties, such as a Progressive Party from the left or a Libertarian Party from the right, could challenge the majority party in states with supermajorities. For example, the Republican Party currently dominates with a projected more than 60% of the vote in West Virginia, Idaho, and Nebraska. In each of these four-member district states, the Republicans could face a challenge from a Libertarian party that needs just 20% of the total vote to win a seat. The result of this could be that West Virginia and Idaho each elect a delegation of 2 Republicans, 1 Democrat, and 1 Libertarian. Nebraska, with a slightly smaller Republican supermajority, could result in the Republicans facing competition from both the Democrats and the Libertarians. Similarly, because the Democratic Party in Hawaii is projected to have a supermajority of 65% of the vote, it could face a challenge from a Progressive Party. If a Progressive Party won 25% of the vote in Hawaii's three-member district, Hawaii could elect a delegation of 1 Democrat, 1 Republican, and 1 Progressive. In more evenly split New Mexico, both major parties could face challenges from alternative parties because only 20% of the vote would be needed to win one seat.

Table 8.2: One-District States - 3, 4, or 5 Seats

State	Population	Dem %	Rep %	Seats	P Safe	P or D	D Safe	D or R	R Safe	R or L	L Safe
New Mexico	2,117,522	54.1%	42.3%	4	0	1	1	0	1	1	0
Nebraska	1,961,504	36.6%	60.9%	4	0	0	1	1	1	1	0
Idaho	1,839,106	32.4%	63.2%	4	0	0	1	0	2	0	1
West Virginia	1,793,716	32.6%	64.7%	4	0	0	1	0	2	0	1
Hawaii	1,455,271	65.9%	30.6%	3	0	1	1	0	1	0	0
New Hampshire	1,377,529	45.2%	52.0%	3	0	0	1	1	0	1	0
Maine	1,362,359	47.8%	46.6%	3	0	0	1	1	1	0	0

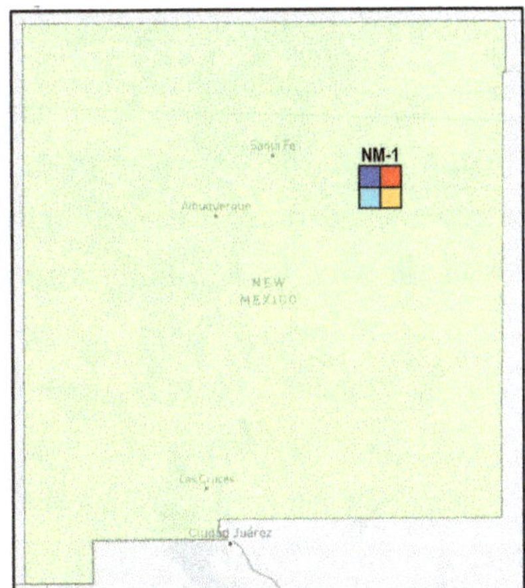

Figure 8.3: New Mexico

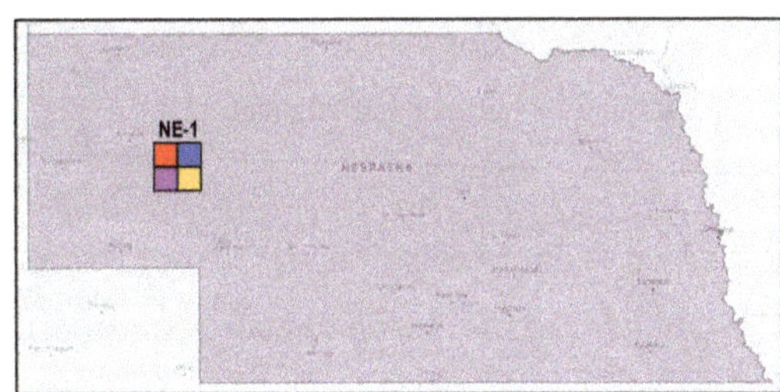

Figure 8.4: Nebraska

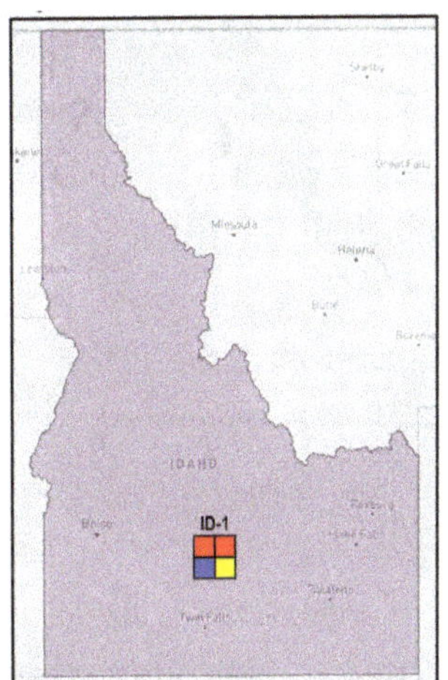

Figure 8.5: Idaho

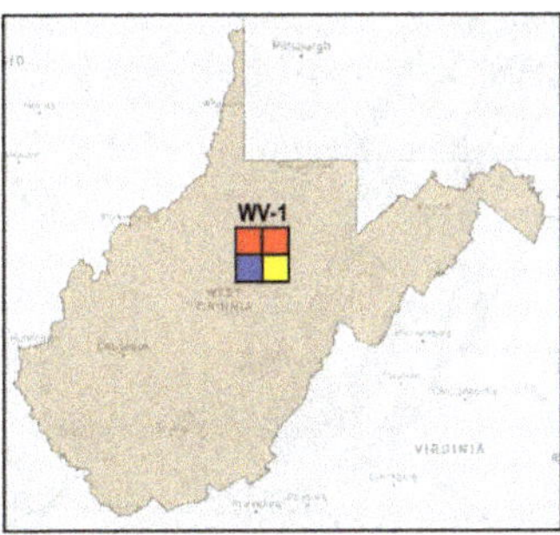

Figure 8.6: West Virginia

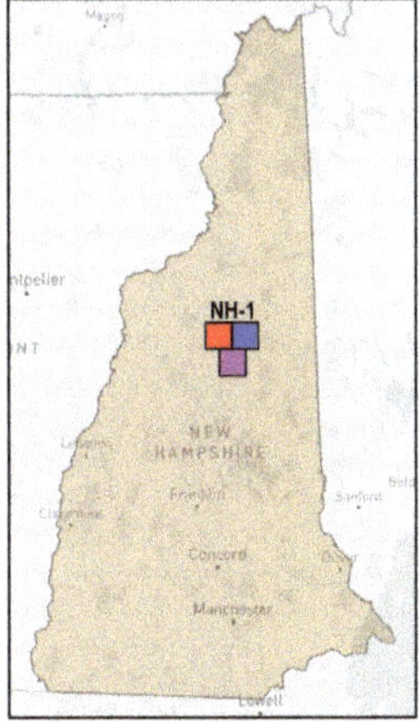

Figure 8.7: New Hampshire

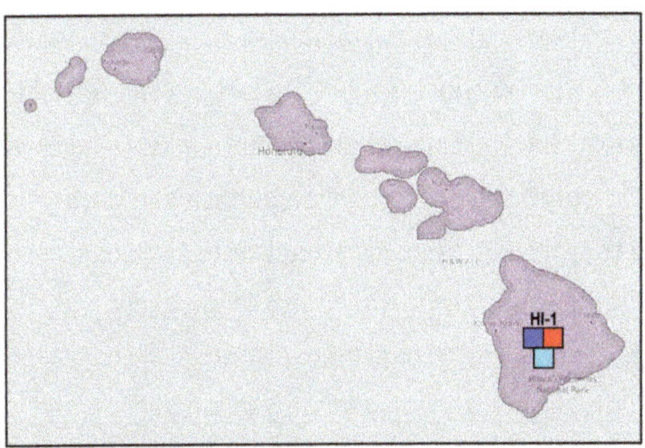

Figure 8.8: Hawaii

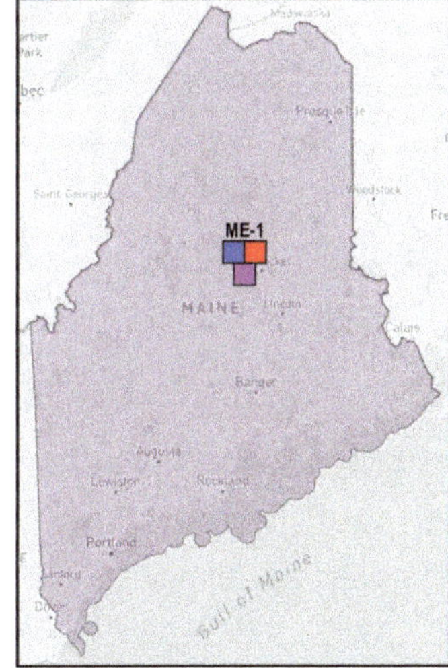

Figure 8.9: Maine

ii. Two Seats: Rhode Island, Montana, Delaware, South Dakota, North Dakota, Alaska, District of Columbia

All 7 two-seat states are currently represented in the House by only one party. With two-member districts, most states would be represented by 1 Democrat and 1 Republican. One party would need to win 67% of the vote to win both seats. For example, the minority Republican Party in Democratic-leaning Rhode Island and Delaware and the minority Democratic Party in Republican-leaning South

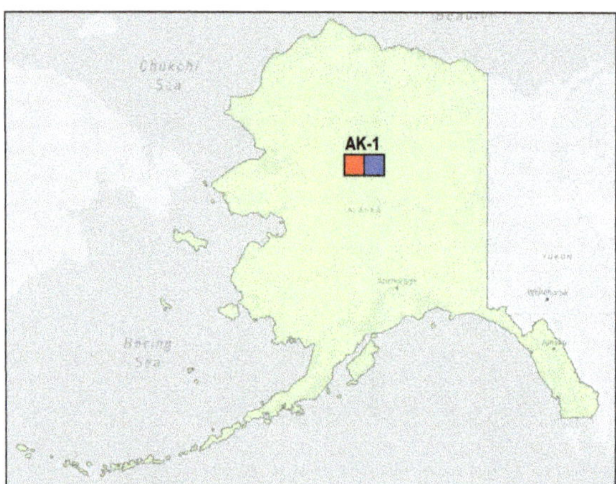

Figure 8.10: Alaska

Dakota, would win 1 seat in each state, the same as the majority party. A 60% majority has the same outcome as a 51% majority.

While I project that both Montana and Alaska would each elect 1 Democrat and 1 Republican, the idiosyncratic politics of these two states could result in an alternative party or an independent candidate winning a seat. For example, as discussed in Chapter 6, a Democrat beat 2 Republicans in a ranked choice election for Congress in Alaska in 2022.

Large majorities could be vulnerable to a challenge from an alternative party. Alternative parties would need to win 33% of the vote to win one seat in each of these states. In a strictly two-party system, North Dakota's 67% Republican majority could win both seats. However, the more likely scenario in a multiparty system is for some portion of the Republican majority to

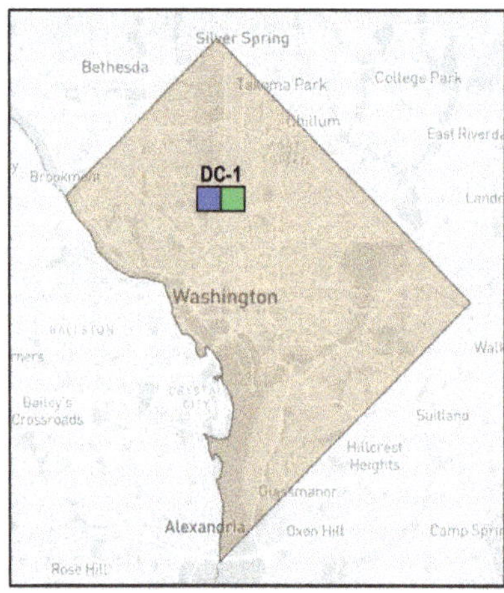

Figure 8.11: District of Columbia

split off and attempt to steal enough voters from the Republican majority to take a seat. Perhaps a Libertarian Party in North Dakota could appeal to some Democrats, too, to win sufficient support to win a seat. The District of Columbia is another example of this. With a 92% majority in the two-party system, even just 35% of Democrats in D.C. splitting off into a Progressive Party would be enough to win one seat.

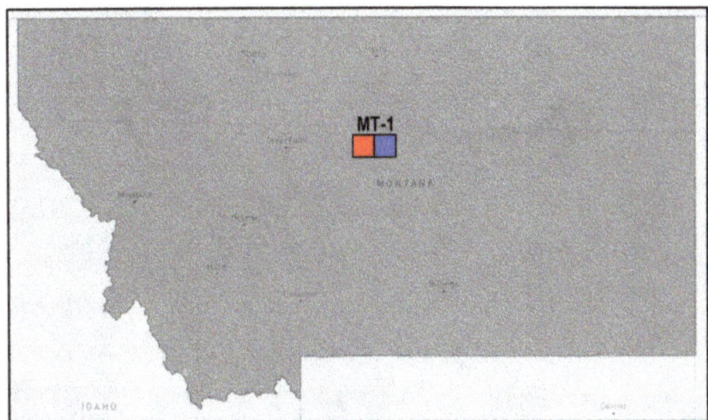

Figure 8.12: Montana

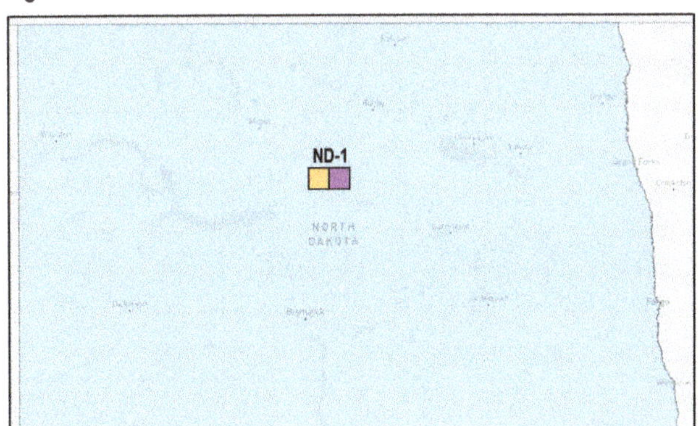

Figure 8.13: North Dakota

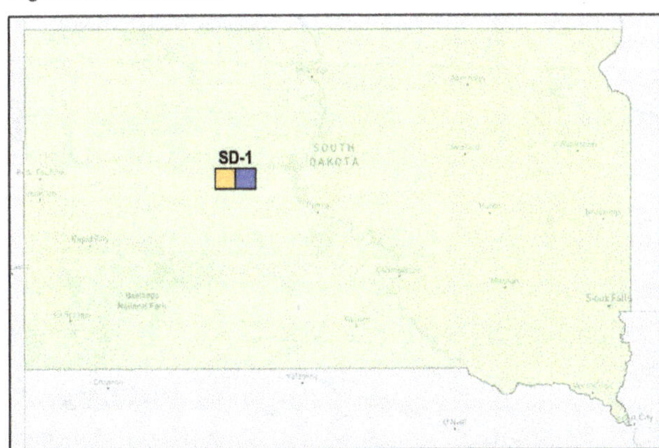

Figure 8.14: South Dakota

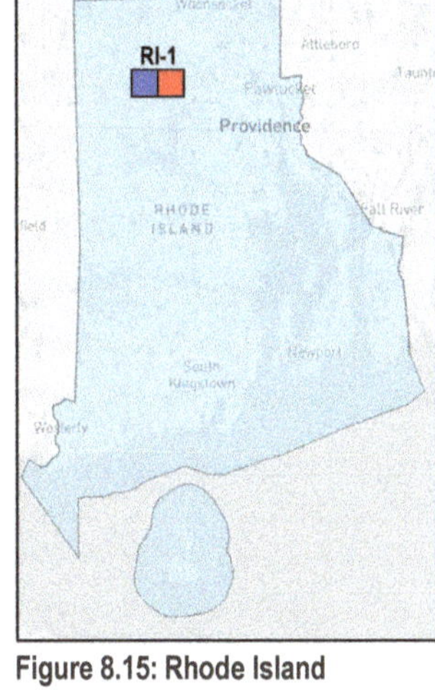

Figure 8.15: Rhode Island

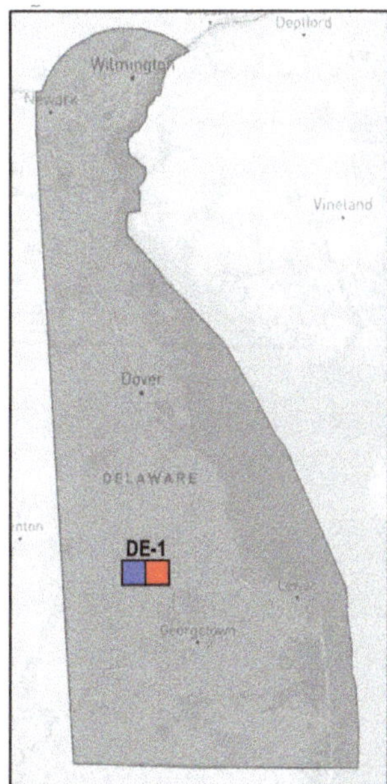

Figure 8.16: Delaware

Table 8.3: One-District States - 2 Seats

State	Population	Dem %	Rep %	Seats	P Safe	P or D	D Safe	D or R	R Safe	R or L	L Safe
Rhode Island	1,097,379	60.6%	37.3%	2	0	0	1	0	1	0	0
Montana	1,084,225	42.7%	55.1%	2	0	0	1	0	1	0	0
Delaware	989,948	58.7%	39.2%	2	0	0	1	0	1	0	0
South Dakota	886,667	36.7%	62.2%	2	0	0	1	0	0	1	0
North Dakota	779,094	29.1%	66.9%	2	0	0	0	1	0	1	0
Alaska	733,391	41.8%	52.8%	2	0	0	1	0	1	0	0
District of Columb	689,545	91.6%	4.8%	2	1	0	1	0	0	0	0

iii. One Seat: Vermont, Wyoming, Four Territories

Three states are so small that even in a 695-member Congress they would only receive 1 seat: Vermont, Wyoming, and the Four Territories. These three states operate just like existing single-member states, with the majority party winning 1 seat. The minority party is out of luck. Democrats, or Independents, would win in Vermont, and Republicans would win in Wyoming. I labeled the Four Territories' seat as competitive between the two major parties because no relevant data exists.

Figure 8.17: Wyoming

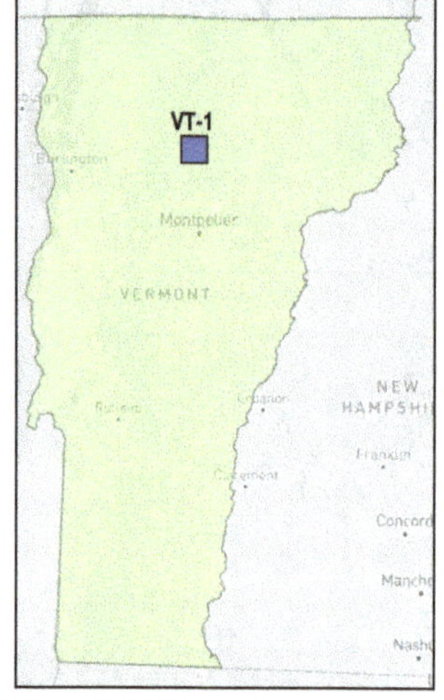

Figure 8.18: Vermont

Table 8.4: One-District States - 1 Seat

State	Population	Dem %	Rep %	Seats	P Safe	P or D	D Safe	D or R	R Safe	R or L	L Safe
Vermont	643,077	58.1%	37.0%	1	0	0	1	0	0	0	0
Wyoming	576,851	26.4%	69.5%	1	0	0	0	0	1	0	0
Four Territories	338,021	x	x	1	0	0	0	1	0	0	0

iv. Thought Experiment: Minimum Three Seats Per State

One way to accommodate the people of small states for losing their representation in the Senate would be to institute a 3-seat minimum for all states. A 3-seat minimum mirrors the current total representation for the smallest states (2 Senators and 1 Representative). The people of these 10 states would be overrepresented compared to all other Americans (Table 8.5). They would have a minimum voting power of 132%. Wyoming, Vermont, and the District of Columbia would have voting power greater than 200%, and the Four Territories would have voting power of over 400%.

The 13 seats assigned to the small states to meet the 3-seat minimum would come out of the seats apportioned for all the other states, further reducing overall representation equality for people in the affected states. As determined by the Priority Value formula, Florida, Massachusetts, California (twice), North Carolina, Nevada, South Carolina, Texas, Pennsylvania, Louisiana, Michigan, Iowa, and Missouri would lose seats. Nevada would become the most underrepresented state, and all 12 states affected would have less than 100% voting power, though the larger states would be less negatively impacted.

Table 8.5: States Affected by Additional Voting Power for Smallest States

State	2020 Population	Proposed Congress			Minimum 3 Seats Congress		
		Seats	Pop. Per Rep.	Voting Power	Seats	Pop. Per Rep.	Voting Power
United States	*335,421,874*	*695*	*482,621*	*100.0%*	*695*	*482,621*	*100.0%*
Four Territories	338,021	1	338,021	142.8%	3	112,674	428.3%
Wyoming	577,719	1	577,719	83.5%	3	192,573	250.6%
Vermont	643,503	1	643,503	75.0%	3	214,501	225.0%
District of Columbia	689,545	2	344,773	140.0%	3	229,848	210.0%
Alaska	736,081	2	368,041	131.1%	3	245,360	196.7%
North Dakota	779,702	2	389,851	123.8%	3	259,901	185.7%
South Dakota	887,770	2	443,885	108.7%	3	295,923	163.1%
Delaware	990,837	2	495,419	97.4%	3	330,279	146.1%
Montana	1,085,407	2	542,704	88.9%	3	361,802	133.4%
Rhode Island	1,098,163	2	549,082	87.9%	3	366,054	131.8%
Nevada	3,108,462	6	518,077	93.2%	5	621,692	77.6%
Iowa	3,192,406	7	456,058	105.8%	6	532,068	90.7%
Louisiana	4,661,468	10	466,147	103.5%	9	517,941	93.2%
South Carolina	5,124,712	11	465,883	103.6%	10	512,471	94.2%
Missouri	6,160,281	13	473,868	101.8%	12	513,357	94.0%
Massachusetts	7,033,469	15	468,898	102.9%	14	502,391	96.1%
Michigan	10,084,442	21	480,212	100.5%	20	504,222	95.7%
North Carolina	10,453,948	22	475,179	101.6%	21	497,807	96.9%
Pennsylvania	13,011,844	27	481,920	100.1%	26	500,456	96.4%
Florida	21,570,527	45	479,345	100.7%	44	490,239	98.4%
Texas	29,183,290	60	486,388	99.2%	59	494,632	97.6%
California	39,576,757	82	482,643	100.0%	80	494,709	97.6%

If that is the price for abolishing the Senate, so be it.

With 3 seats, the minority party in each of these small states would only need to win 25% of the vote to win 1 seat. The majority party would either win 2 seats or be challenged by an alternative party for the third and final seat (Table 8.6). A Libertarian Party would be favored to win a seat in South Dakota, North Dakota, and Wyoming, and compete for a seat in Montana, Alaska, and the Four Territories. A Progressive Party could compete in Rhode Island, Delaware, Vermont, and the Four Territories. The District of Columbia would likely elect 1 Progressive and 1 Democrat, with the third seat competitive between them.

Table 8.6: Hypothetical 3 Seat Outcome

State	Population	Dem %	Rep %	Seats	P Safe	P or D	D Safe	D or R	R Safe	R or L	L Safe
Rhode Island	1,097,379	60.6%	37.3%	3	0	1	1	0	1	0	0
Montana	1,084,225	42.7%	55.1%	3	0	0	1	0	1	1	0
Delaware	989,948	58.7%	39.2%	3	0	1	1	0	1	0	0
South Dakota	886,667	36.7%	62.2%	3	0	0	1	0	1	0	1
North Dakota	779,094	29.1%	66.9%	3	0	0	1	0	1	0	1
Alaska	733,391	41.8%	52.8%	3	0	0	1	0	1	1	0
District of Columbia	689,545	91.6%	4.8%	3	1	1	1	0	0	0	0
Vermont	643,077	58.1%	37.0%	3	0	1	1	0	1	0	0
Wyoming	576,851	26.4%	69.5%	3	0	0	1	0	1	0	1
Four Territories	338,021	x	x	3	0	1	0	1	0	1	0

Further, alternative parties are much more likely to win the 25% of the vote necessary for a seat in a three-member district than the 33% of the vote necessary for a seat in a two-member district.

v. Thought Experiment: Two States, One Federal District?

Another way of improving representation among the smallest states would be for two states to join together into a single multimember district for the purposes of federal representation.

To be clear: the state governments would remain separate and continue functioning as normal! The only change would be to how the states chose their federal representatives.

For example, Montana (2 seats) and Wyoming (1 seat) could pool their allotted representatives to become a three-member district. The benefit of this, aside from giving representation to minority parties and making it easier for alternative parties to win, would be to increase the total number of representatives accountable to the people of each state while avoiding the overrepresentation issue of the 3-seat per-state minimum thought experiment. The obvious counterargument, which may prove insurmountable, is that the people of each state would prefer complete control over their representatives. That is why this remains a thought experiment—the choice should be up to the people of each state!

B. Two-District States (6–10 Seats)

In a 695-seat Congress, 13 states would be allotted between 6 and 10 seats and be drawn into 2 multimember districts. Each district would have between three and five members. As discussed previously, larger districts provide for more accurate representation overall, ensure representation for the primary minority party except in the most extreme circumstances, and provide legitimate opportunities for alternative parties.

The 47.8 million Americans (14.3%) who live in these 13 states would be represented by 98 representatives (14.1%) in the new Congress, almost exactly proportional representation. About 1/3 of seats (34 of 98) would be competitive, an increase from the current 10% (6 of 59 seats). Of the 13 two-district states, 10 would have 2 competitive districts. In the remaining 3 states (Kentucky, Oregon, Connecticut), 1 district would be competitive. Collectively, the population of these 13 states living in a competitive district would increase from 4.5 million (9% of their combined population) to 42.3 million (89%). Alternative parties would be competitive in all 13 states (Figures 8.19 and 8.20).

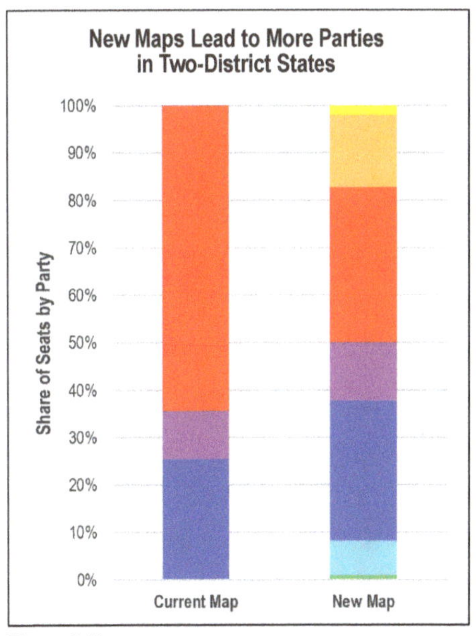

Figure 8.19

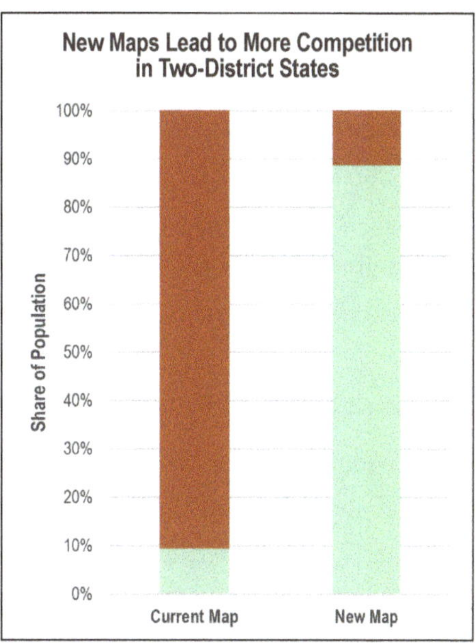

Figure 8.20

Currently, most of these states are overwhelmingly represented by a majority party despite that party rarely possessing overwhelming voting majorities (Table 8.7). For example, nearly 40% of voters in Alabama are Democratic, but Democrats only represent 1 seat of 7. Further, because gerrymandering in Alabama ensures there are no seats rated competitive heading into 2024, this gross partisan imbalance will continue. In Oklahoma, Connecticut, Utah, and Iowa, gerrymandering combined with a geographically evenly distributed majority allow the majority party to control all the state's seats despite the minority party making up as much as 40% of voters. Excluding Puerto Rico due to lack of representation, 7 of these states have zero districts rated competitive heading into 2024.

Table 8.7: Two-District States Current Representation

State	Population	Partisan Lean		Projected Seats (Sept. 2023 Cooks Report)			
		Democratic	Republican	Total	Democratic	Republican	Competitive
Total	47,753,581	x	x	59	15	39	5
Alabama	5,024,279	39.6%	59.4%	7	2	5	0
Louisiana	4,657,757	38.3%	59.7%	6	1	4	1
Kentucky	4,505,836	39.7%	58.4%	6	1	5	0
Oregon	4,237,256	54.8%	40.5%	6	3	2	1
Oklahoma	3,959,353	32.3%	63.8%	5	0	5	0
Connecticut	3,605,944	56.7%	41.0%	5	4	0	1
Puerto Rico	3,285,874	x	x	x	x	x	x
Utah	3,271,616	31.3%	63.6%	4	0	4	0
Iowa	3,190,369	43.9%	53.3%	4	0	3	1
Nevada	3,104,614	48.8%	46.0%	4	2	1	1
Arkansas	3,011,524	34.2%	63.0%	4	0	4	0
Mississippi	2,961,279	42.7%	56.2%	4	1	3	0
Kansas	2,937,880	40.0%	55.5%	4	1	3	0

Multimember district maps make gerrymandering practically impossible. The districts are simply too large to draw around specific populations. In two-district states with 6, 8, or 10 seats, each district contains half of the state's population. In states with 7 or 9 seats, the districts will be uneven. States with 7 seats will have 1 three-member district and 1 four-member district; states with 9 seats will have 1 four-member district and 1 five-member district. While states with 9 seats could be drawn into 3 three-member districts, I decided to prioritize larger districts so as to make it easier for alternative parties to compete.

i. Southern States: Alabama, Louisiana, Kentucky, Arkansas, Mississippi

These 5 southern states have similar partisan demographics. In all 5, Republicans make up about 60% of voters, while Democrats make up between 34% and 42% of voters. But gerrymandering and single-member districts allow Republican majorities to win supermajority representation in Congress. Republicans control 23 of the 27 seats across these 5 states; only one district is rated competitive heading into 2024.

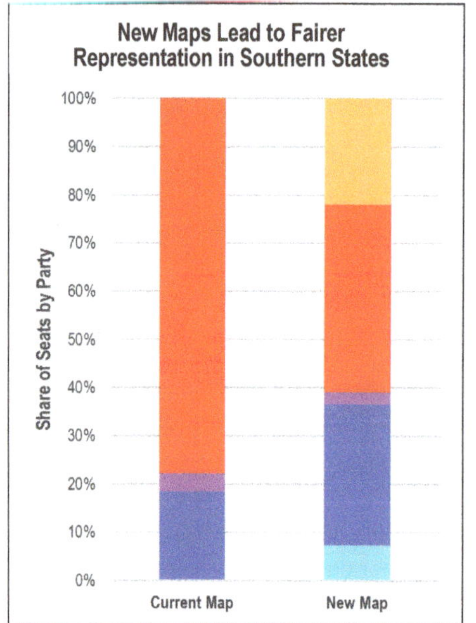

Figure 8.21

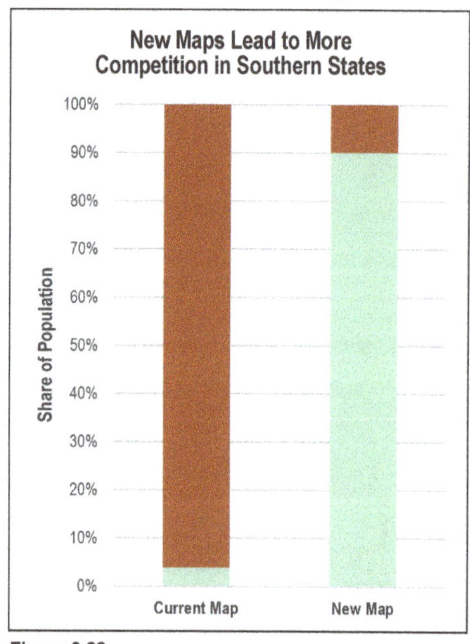

Figure 8.22

Implementing multimember districts in these states would send a more proportional number of each party to Congress and would open the door for alternative parties to win representation (Table 8.8).

Partisan identity is **closely correlated with race**[63] across the South. For example, in 2014[64], 90% of Alabama Republicans were white and 56% of Democrats were Black. Partisan gerrymandering in effect acts as racial gerrymandering. Because of this correlation, fair partisan representation is doubly important as fair racial representation. Further, the fact that partisan identity is associated with racial identity may hinder the emergence of alternative parties in the South.

Table 8.8: Two-District States - Southern States Summary

State	Population	Dem %	Rep %	Seats	P Safe	P or D	D Safe	D or R	R Safe	R or L	L Safe
Alabama	5,024,279	39.6%	59.4%	10	0	2	2	0	4	2	0
Louisiana	4,657,757	38.3%	59.7%	10	0	1	2	1	4	2	0
Kentucky	4,505,836	39.7%	58.4%	9	0	0	4	0	4	1	0
Arkansas	3,011,524	34.2%	63.0%	6	0	0	2	0	2	2	0
Mississippi	2,961,279	42.7%	56.2%	6	0	0	2	0	2	2	0

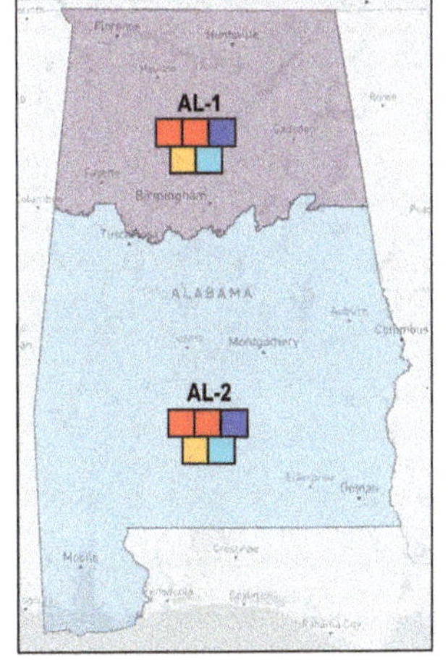

Figure 8.23: Alabama

Both of Alabama's districts have similar partisan breakdowns. I project that each of Alabama's five-member districts would elect 2 Republicans and 1 Democrat. Both parties would face competition to win an additional seat. The Republicans could face competition against a Libertarian Party to win a third seat while the Democrats could face competition from a Progressive Party to win a second seat (Table 8.9).

If the major two parties won all the seats, Alabama would send a delegation of 6 Republicans and 4 Democrats, almost exactly proportional to the number of each party's current voters. If the alternative parties won the 17% of the vote needed for a seat, Alabama's delegation could end up as 4 Republicans, 2 Democrats, 2 Libertarians, and 2 Progressives.

Louisiana's five-member First District (Shreveport, Lafayette) has a 66% Republican supermajority. Democrats would be able to safely win 1 seat but would face competition from the Republicans to win a second seat. Republicans would safely win 2 seats but could see competition from a Libertarian Party peeling

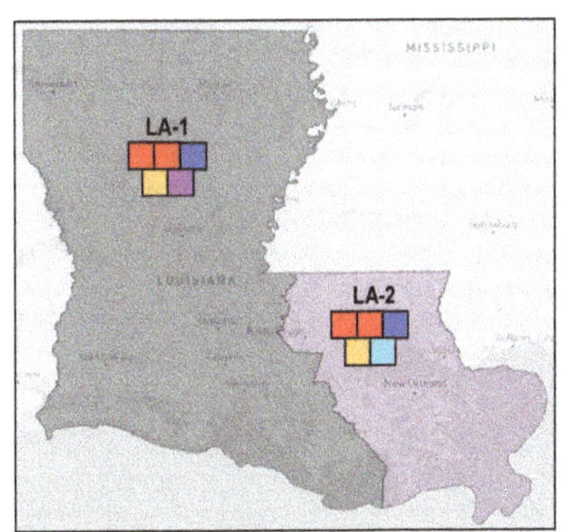

Figure 8.24: Louisiana

voters away from the right. Depending on the strength of their competitors, Republicans could win between 2 and 4 seats.

Louisiana's five-member Second District (Baton Rouge, New Orleans) is more evenly split than the First. Democrats would safely win 1 seat and could face competition from a Progressive Party for a second seat. Republicans would safely win

2 seats and could face competition from a Libertarian Party for a third seat. Both Louisiana districts would be competitive and together would send a proportional delegation to Congress.

Kentucky's First District (western Kentucky, Louisville) is a relatively evenly split district. Republicans have a 54% majority, but would need a landslide victory to

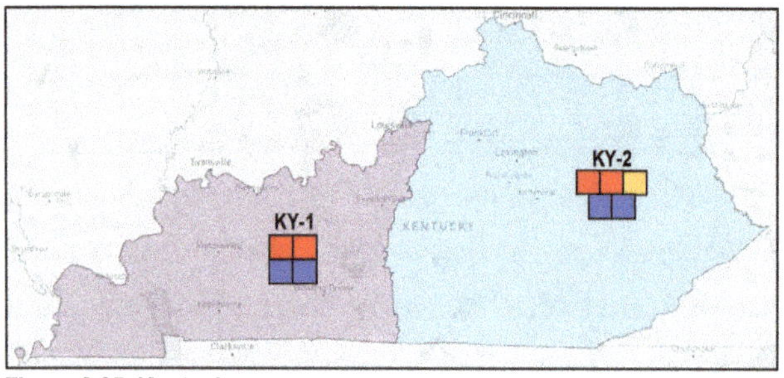

Figure 8.25: Kentucky

win the 60% of the vote necessary for a third seat in the four district. Democrats are projected to have a comfortable 44% minority, enough to safely win 2 seats. Alternative parties would need to win 20% to win 1 seat, which may be difficult in an evenly split district in which both major parties are incentivized to get out the vote to win 2 seats each.

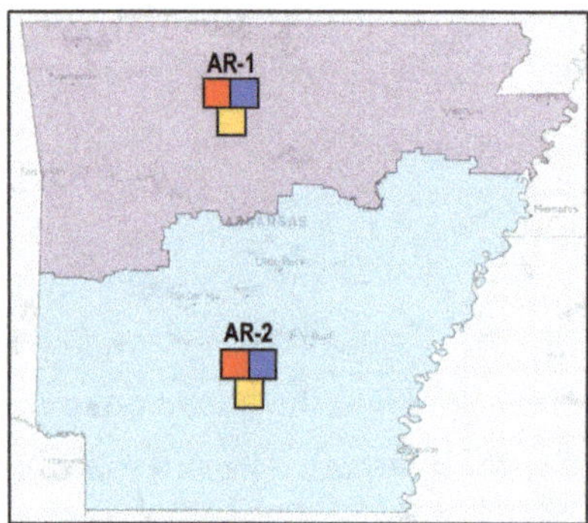

Figure 8.26: Arkansas

Kentucky's five-member Second District (Lexington, Cincinnati suburbs) is projected to have a 62% Republican majority. Republicans would safely win 2 seats and could face competi-tion from a Libertarian Party for a third seat. Democrats would likely have enough support to win 2 seats, but not so much support that a Progressive Party could mount a challenge for 1 seat. In total, Kentucky could send a proportional delegation of 5 Republicans and 4 Democrats, or 4 Republicans, 4 Democrats, and 1 Libertarian to Congress.

Arkansas's population is split evenly into 2 three-member districts. Both districts would have Republican majorities. Still, the Democratic minority in each district would be able to win 1 seat. The Republicans in both districts could face competition from a Libertarian Party that needs just 25% of the vote to win 1 seat. In total,

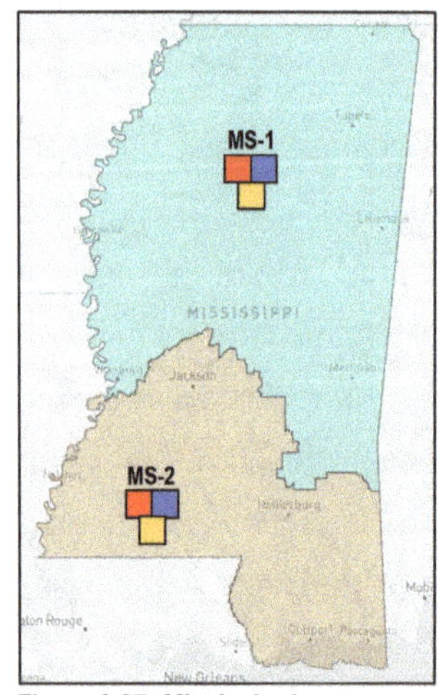

Figure 8.27: Mississippi

depending on the success of the Libertarians, Arkansas would send a delegation of 2–4 Republicans, 2 Democrats, and 0–2 Libertarians.

Mississippi would send a similar overall delegation as Arkansas. Republican majorities in each of Mississippi's three-member districts would win either 2 seats or 1 seat while a Libertarian Party claimed the last seat. Democrats would safely win one seat in both districts. In total, Mississippi would likely elect 2–4 Republicans, 2 Democrats, and 0–2 Libertarians.

Table 8.9: Two-District States - Southern States Districts

District	Population	Dem %	Rep %	Seats	P Safe	P or D	D Safe	D or R	R Safe	R or L	L Safe
AL-1	2,511,984	37.5%	61.3%	5	0	1	1	0	2	1	0
AL-2	2,512,295	41.8%	57.4%	5	0	1	1	0	2	1	0
LA-1	2,329,038	32.1%	66.0%	5	0	0	1	1	2	1	0
LA-2	2,328,719	44.4%	53.4%	5	0	1	1	0	2	1	0
KY-1	2,002,395	44.2%	53.9%	4	0	0	2	0	2	0	0
KY-2	2,503,441	36.0%	62.1%	5	0	0	2	0	2	1	0
AR-1	1,505,626	28.7%	68.2%	3	0	0	1	0	1	1	0
AR-2	1,505,898	39.4%	58.1%	3	0	0	1	0	1	1	0
MS-1	1,480,810	43.5%	55.5%	3	0	0	1	0	1	1	0
MS-2	1,480,469	41.9%	57.0%	3	0	0	1	0	1	1	0

ii. Majority Republican States: Oklahoma, Utah, Iowa, Kansas

Gerrymandering and single-member districts make it so that Republicans currently hold 16 of 17 seats in these 4 states despite Democrats making up between 30 and 40% of the voting population. Further, only 1 seat is rated competitive heading into 2024.

Under the new multimember district maps, all voters in these 4 states would live in a competitive district. Republicans would maintain their majority while Democrats

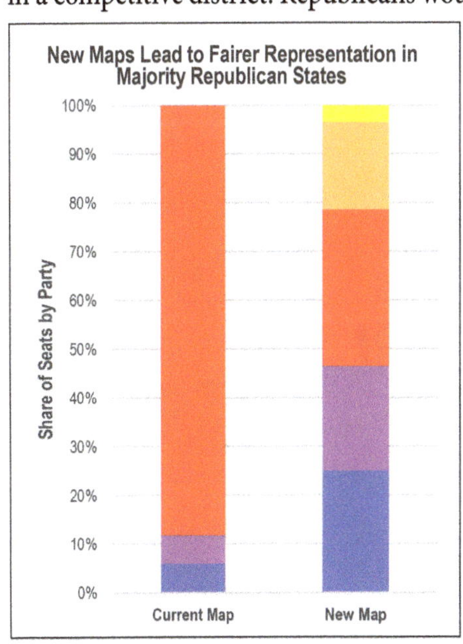

Figure 8.28

Figure 8.29

would win proportional representation. A Libertarian Party could challenge the Republicans for at least 5 seats across the 4 states.

Table 8.10: Two-District States - Republican Majority States Summary

State	Population	Dem %	Rep %	Seats	P Safe	P or D	D Safe	D or R	R Safe	R or L	L Safe
Oklahoma	3,959,353	32.3%	63.8%	8	0	0	2	1	3	2	0
Utah	3,271,616	31.3%	63.6%	7	0	0	1	2	2	1	1
Iowa	3,190,369	43.9%	53.3%	7	0	0	2	2	2	1	0
Kansas	2,937,880	40.0%	55.5%	6	0	0	2	1	2	1	0

Oklahoma's two districts each have four members, meaning the electoral threshold is 20% of the vote to win 1 seat. Democrats are projected to win between 30 and 35%

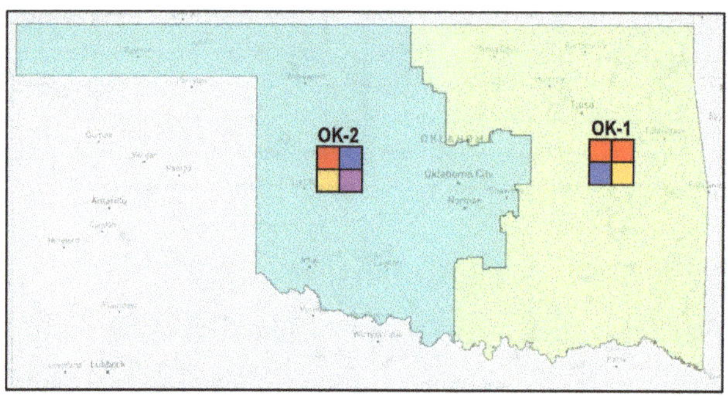

Figure 8.30: Oklahoma

of the vote in each district, providing them with 1 safe seat. While Democrats could contend for a second seat in OK-2 (Oklahoma City, western Oklahoma), Republicans would be favored. In a two-party system, Republicans would likely win 3 of the 4 seats in each district. However, Libertarians would need to peel off only about 1/3 of the Republican vote to win 1 seat, which is plausible in both districts. In total, Oklahoma could elect a delegation of 4 Republicans, 2 Democrats, and 2 Libertarians.

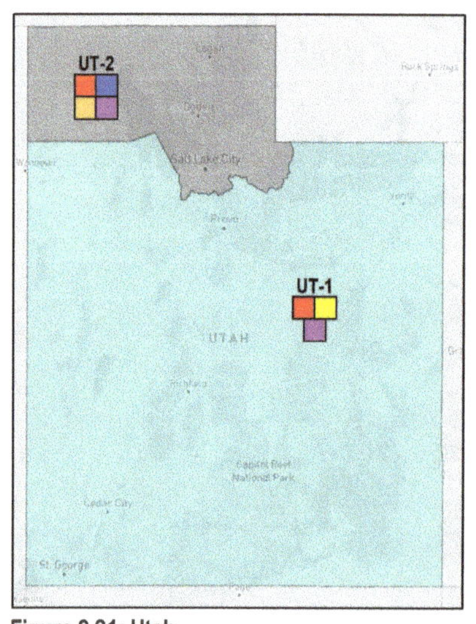

Figure 8.31: Utah

Utah's First District (Provo, southern Utah) is one of the most conservative districts in the entire country. Republicans are projected to win an overwhelming 74% of the vote while Democrats are projected at just 21%. UT-1 is a three-member district, making the electoral threshold 25%. The Democratic Party could plausibly win 1 seat, though Republicans would be favored. I project that a Libertarian Party could safely win 1 seat in UT-1, needing only 1/3 of the existing Republican vote to win.

Utah's Second District (Salt Lake City) is a four-member district with a smaller Republican majority. I project Democrats would safely win 1 seat and contend for a second, while Republicans would safely win 1 seat and compete against both the Democrats and the Libertarians for an additional 2 seats. In total, Utah could plausibly send a delegation of 3 Republicans, 2 Democrats, and 2 Libertarians.

Iowa's Republican majority is narrow in both districts. Similar to UT-2, IA-1 (Des Moines, western Iowa) would safely elect 1 Democrat and 1 Republican, with competition between the Democrats and Republicans for the third seat and competition between the Republicans and Libertarians for the fourth seat. Three-member IA-2 (Cedar Rapids, eastern Iowa) is almost evenly split between the 2 major parties. IA-2 would likely safely elect 1 Democrat and 1 Republican, with the 3rd seat competitive between the 2 parties.

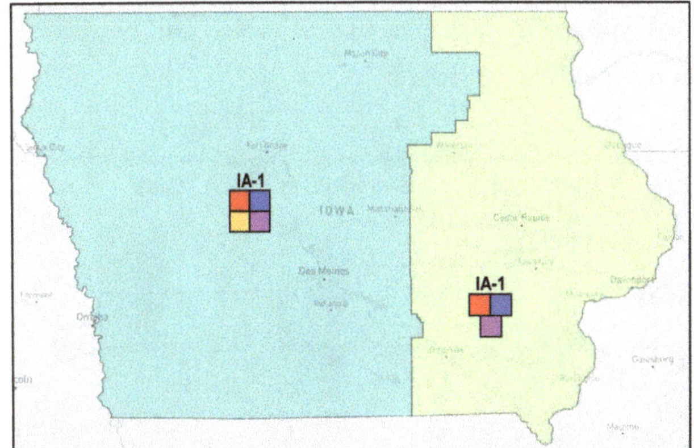

Figure 8.32: Iowa

Kansas is divided into 2 equally populous three-member districts. Both major parties would safely win one seat in each district. In the evenly split KS-1 (Kansas City, Topeka), Democrats and Republicans would compete for the third seat, while in the more conservative KS-2 (Manhattan, Wichita), Republicans would compete against the Libertarians for the 3rd seat.

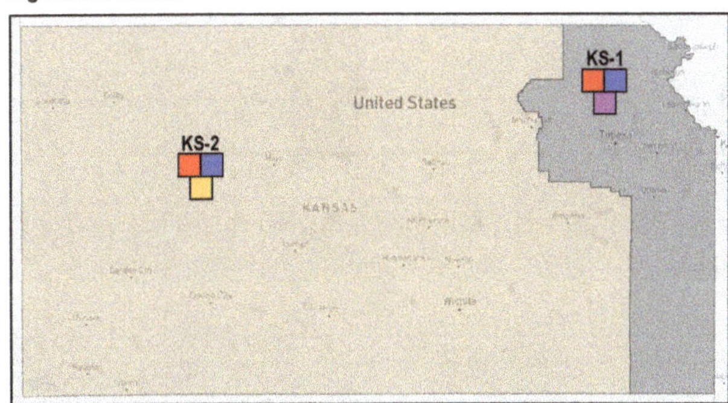

Figure 8.33: Kansas

Table 8.11: Two-District States - Majority Republican States Districts

District	Population	Dem %	Rep %	Seats	P Safe	P or D	D Safe	D or R	R Safe	R or L	L Safe
OK-1	1,979,629	30.5%	65.9%	4	0	0	1	0	2	1	0
OK-2	1,979,724	34.3%	61.6%	4	0	0	1	1	1	1	0
UT-1	1,402,239	20.6%	73.8%	3	0	0	0	1	1	0	1
UT-2	1,869,377	38.9%	56.2%	4	0	0	1	1	1	1	0
IA-1	1,823,076	40.9%	56.4%	4	0	0	1	1	1	1	0
IA-2	1,367,293	47.8%	49.2%	3	0	0	1	1	1	0	0
KS-1	1,469,575	46.9%	48.6%	3	0	0	1	1	1	0	0
KS-2	1,468,305	31.9%	63.6%	3	0	0	1	0	1	1	0

iii. Majority Democratic States: Oregon, Connecticut, Puerto Rico, Nevada

Similar to the majority-Republican states, these majority-Democratic states convert slight voting majorities into large electoral majorities thanks to a combination of gerrymandering and single-member districts. Conservative voters would gain proportional representation in all 4 states if these multimember maps were implemented. Each state with existing partisan data (Puerto Rico is a special case, discussed below) has at least 1 competitive district heading into 2024. However, these multimember districts are more competitive, ensuring that at least 1/2 of the voters living in each state will vote in a competitive district.

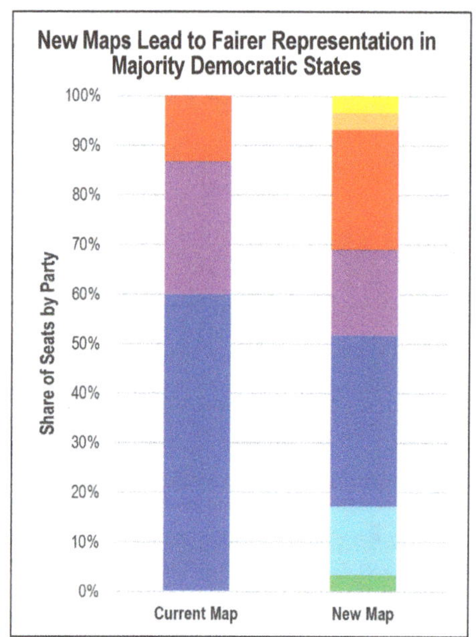

Figure 8.34

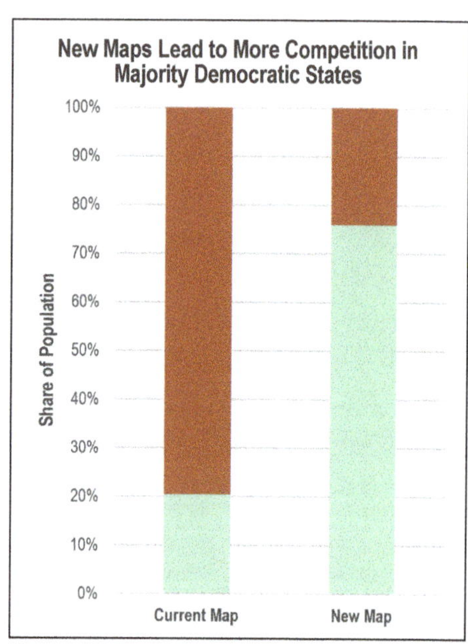

Figure 8.35

Table 8.12: Two-District States - Democratic Majority States Summary

State	Population	Dem %	Rep %	Seats	P Safe	P or D	D Safe	D or R	R Safe	R or L	L Safe
Oregon	4,237,256	54.8%	40.5%	9	1	1	3	1	2	0	1
Connecticu	3,605,944	56.7%	41.0%	7	0	1	3	1	2	0	0
Puerto Ric	3,285,874	x	x	7	0	1	2	2	2	0	0
Nevada	3,104,614	48.8%	46.0%	6	0	1	2	1	1	1	0

Oregon's statewide Democratic majority is based upon the party's large majority in the populous Portland metro area. The five-member OR-2 (Portland) would likely elect 1 Democrat, 1 Republican, and 1 Progressive. The Democratic Party would face competition from the Progressives from the left and the Republicans from the right for the final 2 seats. In most other five-member districts with around a 62% Democratic majority, I would not project the Progressives to be competitive for a second seat. However,

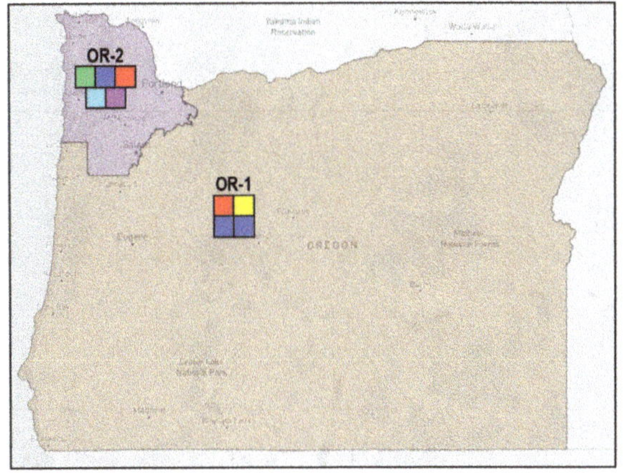

Figure 8.36: Oregon

Portland is an exception. In 2023, voters in Portland approved a ranked choice multimember district system to elect their city council, which would give alternative parties and independents the chance to build up grassroots support, which in turn would help them prepare to run in congressional elections. Similarly idiosyncratic, the majority conservative OR-1 (eastern Oregon, Eugene) would likely elect 2 Democrats, 1 Republican, and 1 Libertarian. Oregon's population is so heavily concentrated around Portland that OR-1 has a smaller population than OR-2. If OR-1 had 5 members, the Libertarians could likely contend for a second seat. In total, Oregon could elect a delegation of 4 Democrats, 3 Republicans, 1 Progressive, and 1 Libertarian.

Connecticut's Democratic majority is relatively evenly distributed across the state. Republicans in Connecticut have zero representation in Congress under the current

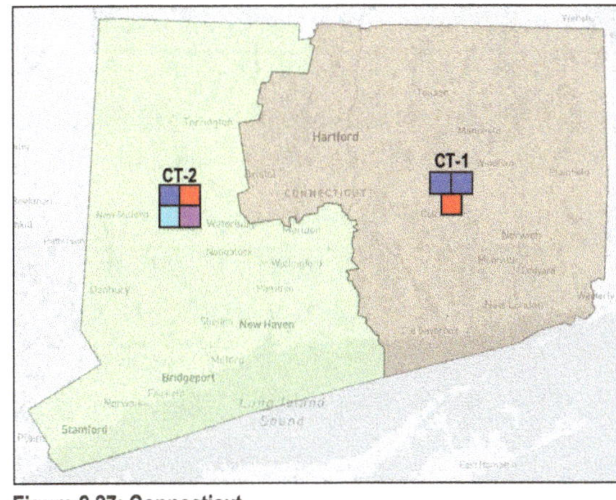

Figure 8.37: Connecticut

map. In the new map, both districts have Democratic majorities of 57% and Republican minorities of 41%. I project the three-member CT-1 (Hartford, eastern Connecticut) would elect 2 Democrats and 1 Republican. The four-member CT-2 (New Haven, western Connecticut) would elect at least 1 Democrat and 1 Republican. A Progressive Party could challenge the Democrats for 1 seat, and the final seat would be competitive between the Democrats and Republicans. In total, Connecticut could elect a delegation of 3 Democrats, 3 Republicans, and 1 Progressive.

Puerto Rico is difficult to project because the Democratic and Republican parties are not the dominant parties in Puerto Rico's politics. Puerto Rico's politics are multiparty due to its existing multimember proportional voting system. The 2 largest parties are the New Progressive Party and the Popular Democratic Party, though these

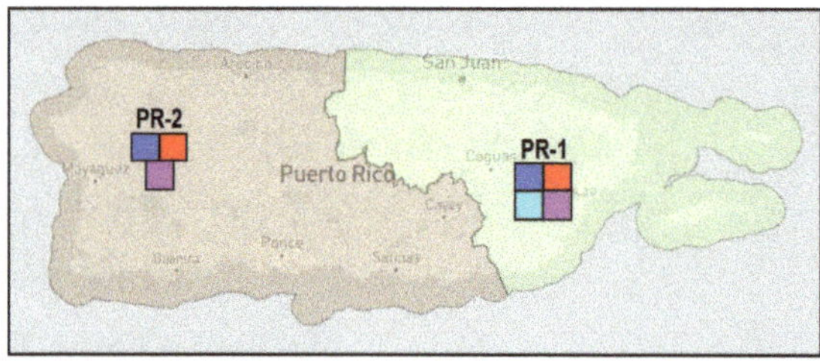

Figure 8.38: Puerto Rico

parties do not correspond to the Progressive or Democratic parties as on the mainland. There is no useful data upon which to project the outcome of Puerto Rico's new map.

Lacking data, I projected the outcome of the 2 districts based on reasonable assumptions. I assume that Puerto Rican representatives would caucus with the existing national parties or with a national alternative party. I assume that Puerto Rican voters will vote similarly to Hispanic voters across the mainland U.S., with somewhere between 55% and 70% voting for Democrats. Under this assumption, I project that the more urban PR-1 (San Juan) would elect 1 Democrat and 1 Republican, with the Democratic Party competing against the Progressives for the third seat and against the Republicans for the fourth seat. For three-member district PR-2 (Ponce, western PR), winning 2 seats requires 50% of the vote and winning 3 seats requires 75% of the vote. As the more rural district, I project PR-2 will favor Republicans more than PR-1, perhaps around a 50/50 partisan split. I project PR-2 would elect 1 Democrat and 1 Republican, with the third seat competitive between the 2 parties. In total, Puerto Rico could elect a delegation of 3 Democrats, 3 Republicans, and 1 Progressive.

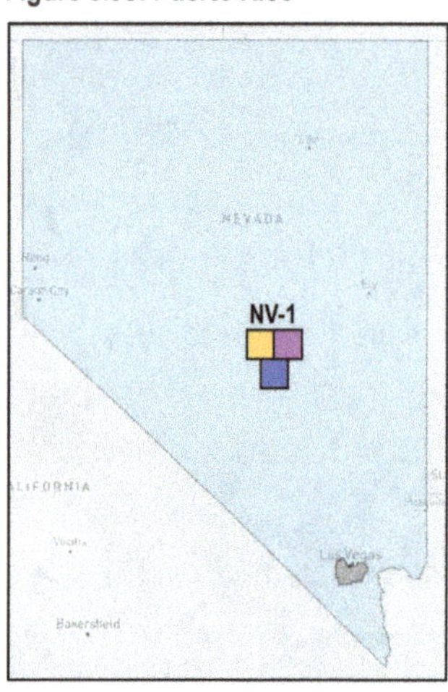

Figure 8.39: Nevada

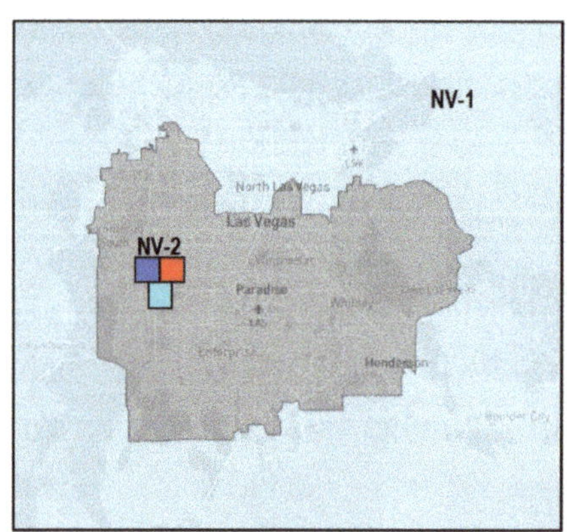

Figure 8.40: Las Vegas Metro

The Las Vegas metro area accounts for more than half of Nevada's population. To equalize the population of the 2 three-member districts, NV-1 (Reno, North Las Vegas) had to include part of the Las Vegas metro. I project the Republican Party would be favored to win 2 seats in NV-1, though each seat would be competitive against either the

Democrats or the Libertarians. Democrats would safely win 1 seat. In NV-2 (Las Vegas), Republicans would safely win 1 seat, Democrats would safely win 1 seat, and a Progressive Party could challenge the Democrats for the third and final seat. In total, Nevada could elect a delegation of 2 Democrats, 2 Republicans, 1 Progressive, and 1 Libertarian.

Table 8.13: Two-District States - Major Democratic State Districts

District	Population	Dem %	Rep %	Seats	P Safe	P or D	D Safe	D or R	R Safe	R or L	L Safe
OR-1	1,883,379	44.8%	50.4%	4	0	0	2	0	1	0	1
OR-2	2,353,877	62.9%	32.4%	5	1	1	1	1	1	0	0
CT-1	1,545,565	56.7%	40.5%	3	0	0	2	0	1	0	0
CT-2	2,060,379	56.8%	41.3%	4	0	1	1	1	1	0	0
PR-1	1,877,121	x	x	4	0	1	1	1	1	0	0
PR-2	1,408,753	x	x	3	0	0	1	1	1	0	0
NV-1	1,552,153	44.1%	50.5%	3	0	0	1	1	0	1	0
NV-2	1,552,461	54.4%	40.7%	3	0	1	1	0	1	0	0

iv. Thought Experiment: Six- or Seven-Member Districts?

I have limited the size of multimember districts in this analysis to a maximum of 5 per district. But this limit is arbitrary; there is no reason districts could not elect 6, 7, or more representatives. Each additional representative would further lower the electoral threshold, making it easier for alternative parties or independent candidates to win. However, I believe it is also important to not make the electoral threshold too low. A threshold of just 9% in a 10-member district would make it possible for extreme candidates to win office that they otherwise would not have enough support to win.

Table 8.14: Electoral Threshold for Large Districts

District Size	1 Winner
3 Members	25.1%
4 Members	20.1%
5 Members	16.7%
6 Members	14.4%
7 Members	12.6%
8 Members	11.2%
9 Members	10.1%
10 Members	9.2%

How should states with 6 or 7 seats draw their districts? Here, I split them into 2 districts of three- or four-members. As shown above, three-member districts have a high enough electoral threshold to make alternative parties viable primarily in districts with lopsided partisan majorities. Changing states with 6 or 7 seats into a single six- or seven-member district would make it easier for alternative parties to win representation. For example, Kansas's three-member districts would each elect 1 Democrat but would likely not be competitive for a Progressive candidate. If Kansas were a single six-member district, Democrats could face legitimate competition from a Progressive for that 2nd seat.

Six-member districts could theoretically be drawn in larger states, such as South Carolina with its 11 seats. In the next section, I draw South Carolina into 2 four-member districts and 1 three-member district. It could be redrawn into 1 six-member district and 1 five-member district, which would make it much easier for alternative parties to win representation. If and when multimember districts become a reality, six-member districts should be considered. For the sake of not making this analysis even longer than it already is, I do not analyze with rigor alternative ways of drawing each state's districts.

C. Three-District States (11–15 Seats)

In a 695-seat Congress, 10 states would be allotted between 11 and 15 seats and be drawn into three multimember districts. Each district would have between 3 and 5 members. The 62.7 million Americans (20.2%) of these states would be represented by 131 members of Congress (18.8%); 45 of the 131 seats would be competitive (34%).

Currently, 7 of the 10 states have zero competitive districts; less than 10% of the people living in these states live in a competitive district. With the new maps, every state would have either 2 or 3 competitive districts, and over 80% of people living in these states would live in a competitive district. Every state would be more competitive than under the current system.

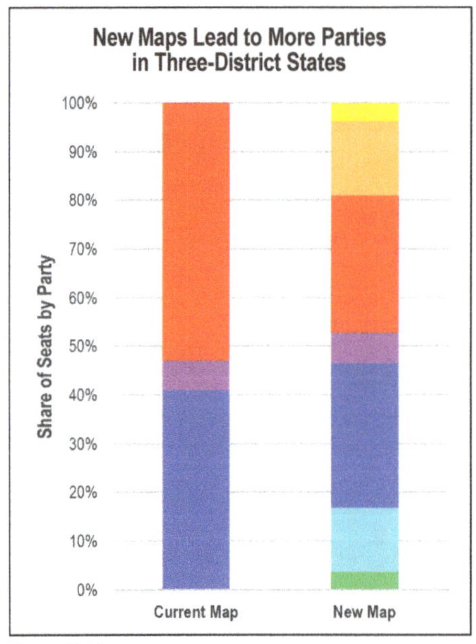

Figure 8.41

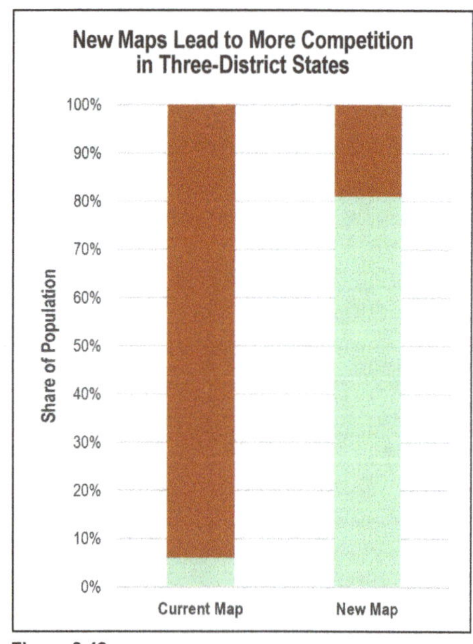

Figure 8.42

These 10 states span the gamut of American political diversity (Table 8.15). Arizona and Wisconsin are purple presidential battleground states. Massachusetts, Maryland, Colorado, and Minnesota are varying shades of blue, while Tennessee, Indiana, Missouri, and South Carolina are varying shades of red. But even the "blue" and "red" states contain political multitudes. Neither party has more than a 60% majority in any of these states, and the smallest minority party is projected at 37% of the vote.

Table 8.15: Three-District States - Current Representation

State	Population	Partisan Lean		Projected Seats (Sept. 2023 Cooks Report)			
		Democratic	Republican	Total	Democratic	Republican	Competitive
Total	62,700,454	x	x	83	34	44	5
Arizona	7,151,502	47.9%	50.1%	9	3	4	2
Massachusetts	7,029,917	60.0%	37.7%	9	9	0	0
Tennessee	6,910,840	37.9%	60.0%	9	1	8	0
Indiana	6,785,528	42.1%	54.7%	9	1	7	1
Maryland	6,175,403	60.3%	36.8%	8	7	1	0
Missouri	6,154,913	41.5%	55.5%	8	2	6	0
Wisconsin	5,893,718	49.5%	48.2%	8	2	6	0
Colorado	5,773,714	52.2%	43.6%	8	4	2	2
Minnesota	5,706,494	51.7%	43.2%	8	4	4	0
South Carolina	5,118,425	42.4%	55.8%	7	1	6	0

Single-member districts make it possible for states with a mere 60% voting majority to elect a congressional delegation composed entirely of one party. Massachusetts is projected to have a 60% Democratic majority statewide, and all 9 of its seats are rated as safe for Democrats heading into 2024. Similarly, Tennessee, Maryland, and South Carolina are projected to elect just 1 member of the minority party. New multimember maps would improve proportionality in all 10 states.

Instead of organizing these states by partisanship, I analyze them by similarities in their population distribution (Tables 8.16 and 8.17). Five of the states (Arizona, Missouri, Wisconsin, Colorado, Minnesota) have one disproportionately large city compared to the rest of the state, making it possible to divide the state into 1 geographically small urban district and 2 larger suburban or rural districts. I intend for this to allow residents of rural areas and of urban areas to pick a full range of representatives according to their regional idiosyncrasies.

Table 8.16: Three-District States - One Urban District

State	Population	Dem %	Rep %	Seats	P Safe	P or D	D Safe	D or R	R Safe	R or L	L Safe
Arizona	7,151,502	47.9%	50.1%	15	0	2	5	1	4	2	1
Missouri	6,154,913	41.5%	55.5%	13	0	2	3	1	4	2	1
Wisconsin	5,893,718	49.5%	48.2%	12	0	3	3	0	3	3	0
Colorado	5,773,714	52.2%	43.6%	12	1	1	4	1	3	2	0
Minnesota	5,706,494	51.7%	43.2%	12	1	1	4	1	3	2	0

The other 5 states (Massachusetts, Tennessee, Indiana, Maryland, South Carolina) also have large cities, but the geographic area of their districts is comparatively even. While I generally followed the existing state legislative lines when deciding district lines, many times I was forced to arbitrarily choose this precinct or that precinct to get the districts to the appropriate population. There are myriad ways that each state's districts could be drawn. But however the lines are drawn, the multimember system makes it difficult to gerrymander in favor of 1 party or another.

Table 8.17: Three-District States - Relatively Equal Area Districts

State	Population	Dem %	Rep %	Seats	P Safe	P or D	D Safe	D or R	R Safe	R or L	L Safe
Massachusetts	7,029,917	60.0%	37.7%	15	1	2	6	1	3	2	0
Tennessee	6,910,840	37.9%	60.0%	14	0	2	3	0	6	2	1
Indiana	6,785,528	42.1%	54.7%	14	0	2	3	2	4	2	1
Maryland	6,175,403	60.3%	36.8%	13	2	1	5	1	3	1	0
South Carolina	5,118,425	42.4%	55.8%	11	0	1	3	0	4	2	1

The states apportioned between 11 and 14 members (South Carolina, Minnesota, Colorado, Wisconsin, Missouri, Maryland, Indiana, Tennessee) could also be divided into 2 districts of between 5 and 7 members each. Generally, I think it makes more sense to divide these states into 3 districts because three relatively smaller districts would allow for regional idiosyncrasies to be better represented than with 2 relatively larger districts. As long as the districts have at least 4 members, alternative parties will be viable. One exception is South Carolina, which with 11 members is small enough that 1 of its 3 districts must have just 3 members. Dividing South Carolina into 2 districts of 5 and 6 members would better allow for alternative parties to win representation.

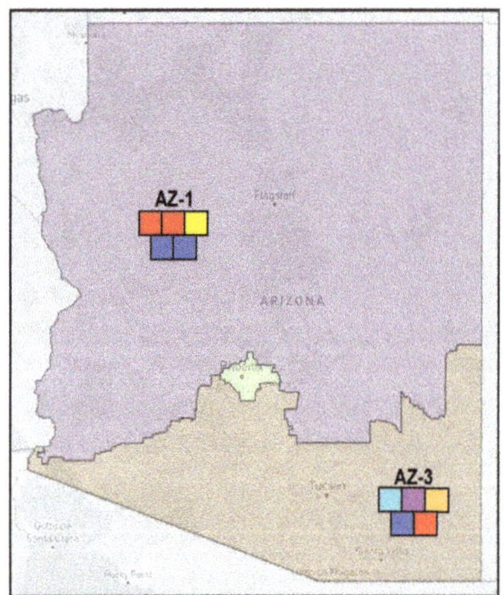

Figure 8.43: Arizona

i. One Urban District: Arizona, Missouri, Wisconsin, Colorado, Minnesota

Arizona would see its 15 members divided into 3 five-member districts of 2.4 million people. The core of the Phoenix metro would be its own district, the majority Democratic AZ-2. Democrats would likely win 2 seats and face competition from the Progressives for a 3rd seat. Republicans would win 1 seat and could face competition from a Libertarian Party for a 2nd seat.

AZ-1 (northern Arizona) has a greater Republican majority than AZ-2 has a Democratic majority. I project AZ-1 would elect 2 Democrats, 2 Republicans,

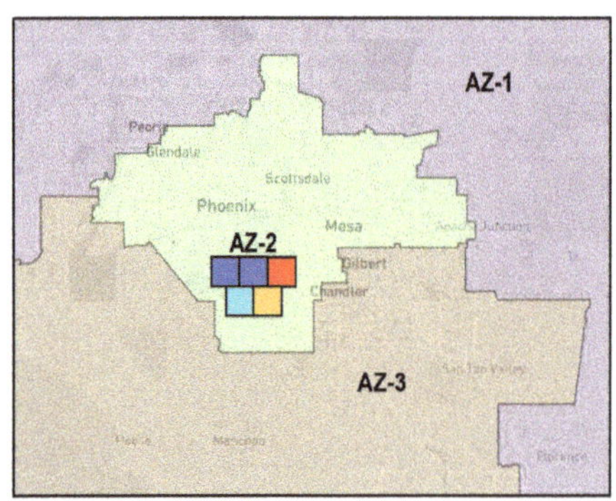

Figure 8.44: Phoenix Metro Area

and 1 Libertarian. With less than 40% Democrats in the district, there may not be enough support on the left for a Progressive Party challenge.

AZ-3 (southern Arizona) is evenly split between Republicans and Democrats. I project Democrats and Republicans would each safely win 1 seat. Progressives could challenge Democrats for the 3rd seat, Libertarians could challenge Republicans for the 4th seat, and the 5th seat would be competitive between the 2 major parties. AZ-3 could plausibly elect representatives from 4 different parties.

In total, Arizona could elect a delegation of 6 Democrats, 6 Republicans, 2 Libertarians, and 1 Progressive.

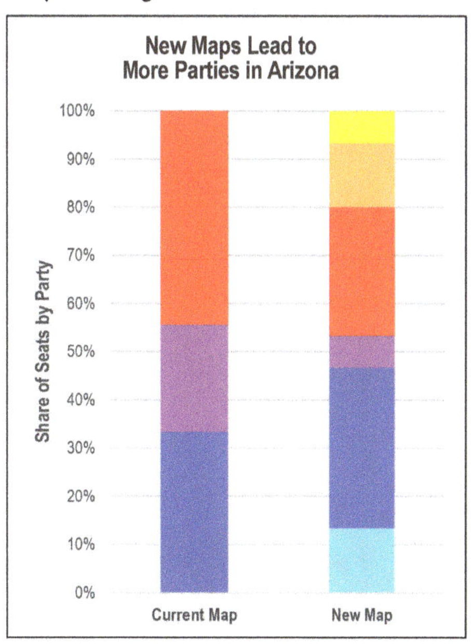

Figure 8.45

Table 8.18: Arizona

	Population	Dem %	Rep %	Seats	P Safe	P or D	D Safe	D or R	R Safe	R or L	L Safe
Statewide	8,631,393	52.8%	45.6%	15	0	2	5	1	4	2	1
AZ-1	2,383,398	39.5%	58.7%	5	0	0	2	0	2	0	1
AZ-2	2,384,204	56.7%	41.1%	5	0	1	2	0	1	1	0
AZ-3	2,383,900	49.4%	48.6%	5	0	1	1	1	1	1	0

Missouri's 13 seats can be divided into 2 four-member districts and 1 five-member district. By drawing MO-3 (St. Louis) as a four-member district, the St. Louis metro remains a majority Democratic district. Conversely, MO-2 (southern Missouri) remains one of the most conservative districts in the country, with a 71% Republican majority. Switching the size of the districts by redrawing the lines to move 500,000 people from MO-2 to MO-3 would dilute both majorities, without the guarantee of increasing competition. As drawn, both districts would be competitive. I project that the urban MO-3 would elect one Democrat and one Republican. Two seats would be competitive, one between the Progressives and the Democrats and the other

Table 8.19: Missouri

	Population	Dem %	Rep %	Seats	P Safe	P or D	D Safe	D or R	R Safe	R or L	L Safe
Statewide	6,154,913	41.5%	55.5%	13	0	2	3	1	4	2	1
MO-1	1,894,263	45.7%	51.1%	4	0	1	1	0	1	1	0
MO-2	2,366,909	25.7%	71.4%	5	0	0	1	0	2	1	1
MO-3	1,893,741	55.7%	41.6%	4	0	1	1	1	1	0	0

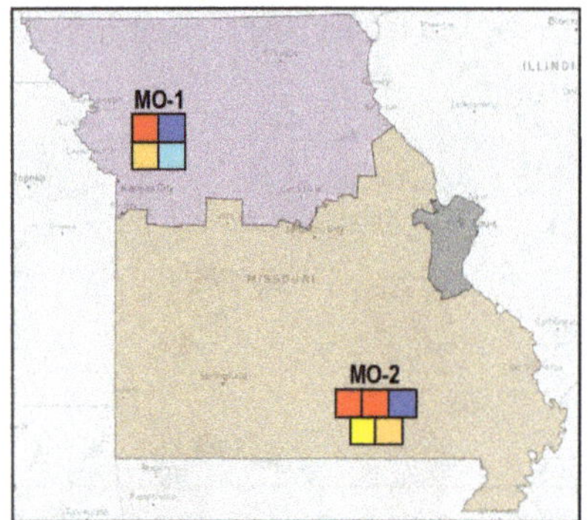

Figure 8.46: Missouri

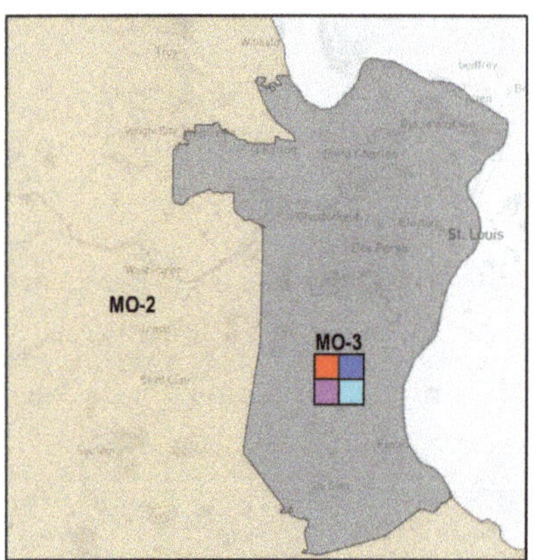

Figure 8.47: St. Louis Metro

between the Democrats and Republicans. The rural MO-2 would likely elect one Democrat, two Republicans, one Libertarian. The 5th seat would likely be competitive between the Libertarians and the Republicans.

MO-1 (Kansas City) is relatively evenly split between Democrats and Republicans. I project MO-1 would elect one Democrat and one Republican, with Progressives challenging Democrats for the 3rd seat and Libertarians challenging Republicans for the 4th seat.

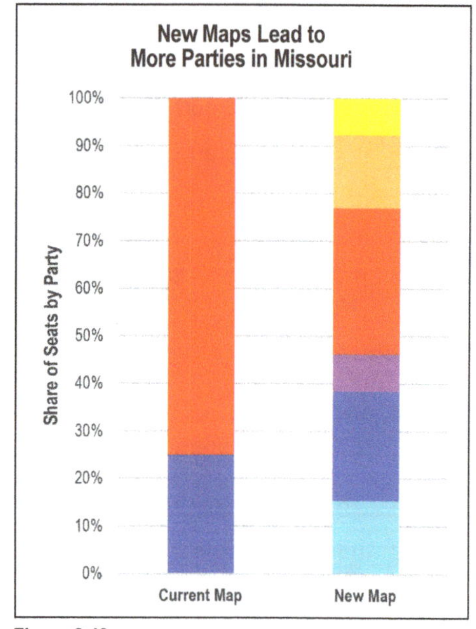

Figure 8.48

In total, Missouri could elect a proportional delegation of 6 Republicans, 4 Democrats, 2 Libertarians, and 1 Progressive. With this map, Missouri's three districts would be competitive instead of the zero competitive districts under the current system.

Wisconsin is a battleground state's battleground state. Unfortunately, gerrymandering in the current system means that Wisconsin has zero competitive districts heading into 2024.

Wisconsin's 12 seats are divided into three equal population four-member districts. All three districts are fairly evenly divided. Rural WI-1 (northern Wisconsin) is projected to have a larger Republican majority (54%), while WI-2 (Madison) and WI-3 (Milwaukee) are projected to have slim Democratic majorities (Table 8.20).

Each district would likely elect one Democrat and one Republican, with the Progressives challenging the Democrats for the 3rd seat and the Libertarians challenging the Republicans for the 4th seat. Wisconsin could plausibly elect a delegation of four Democrats, 4 Republicans, 2 Progressives, and 2 Libertarians.

Wisconsin could also be divided into 2 six-member districts. Each district would elect at

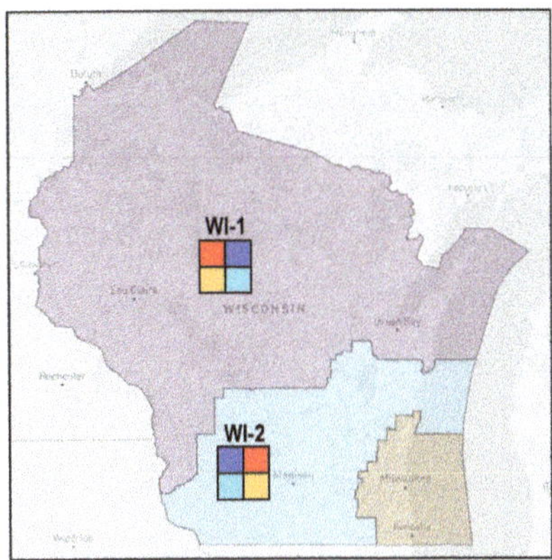

Figure 8.49: Wisconsin

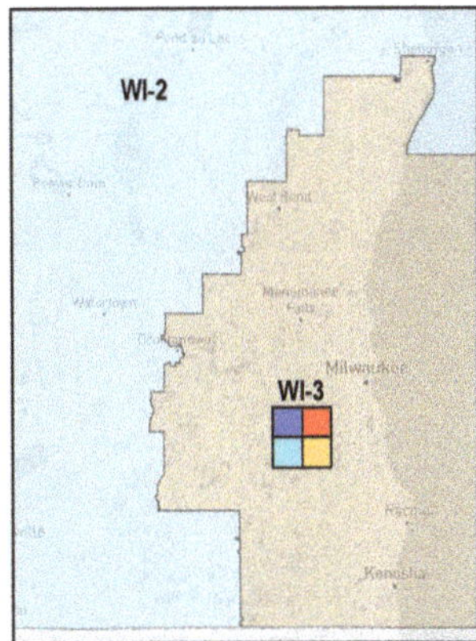

Figure 8.50: Milwaukee Metro Area

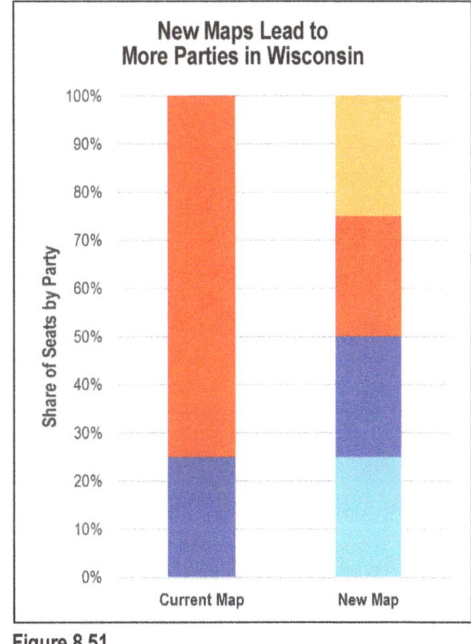

Figure 8.51

least one Libertarian and one Progressive, with both parties potentially competitive for a 2nd seat depending on how the lines were drawn.

Table 8.20: Wisconsin

	Population	Dem %	Rep %	Seats	P Safe	P or D	D Safe	D or R	R Safe	R or L	L Safe
Statewide	5,893,718	49.5%	48.2%	12	0	3	3	0	3	3	0
WI-1	1,964,782	43.5%	54.1%	4	0	1	1	0	1	1	0
WI-2	1,964,406	53.9%	43.9%	4	0	1	1	0	1	1	0
WI-3	1,964,530	51.0%	46.8%	4	0	1	1	0	1	1	0

Colorado would be represented by 12 members across 3 four-member districts. Colorado's population is primarily distributed in the Denver metro, north and south of the city. This unique population distribution makes it difficult to draw compact districts. In this map, CO-3 (Denver) is the core of the Denver metro. CO-1 (Colorado

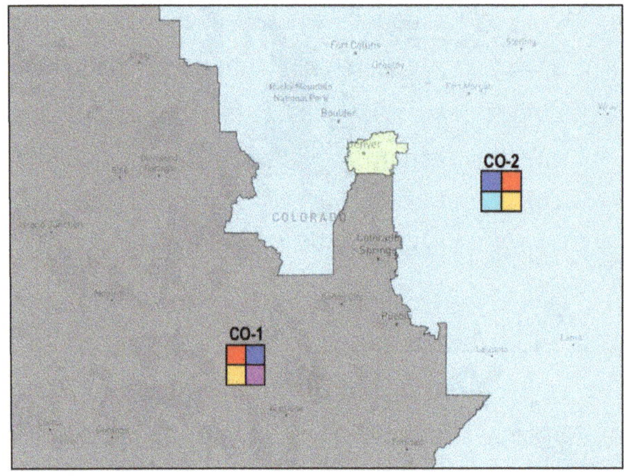

Figure 8.52: Colorado

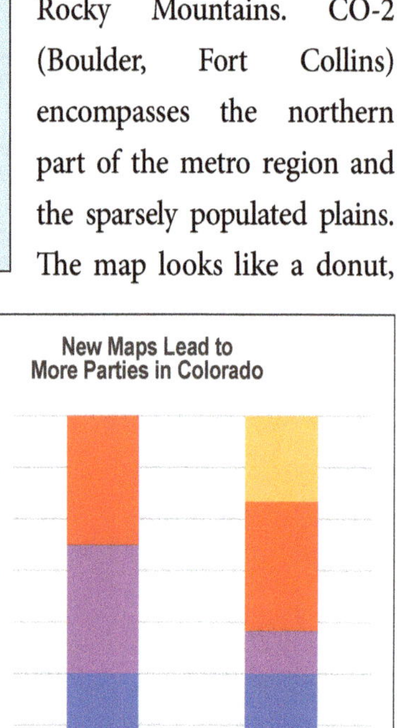

Figure 8.54

Springs, Grand Junction) encompasses the populous region south of Denver and the sparsely populated Rocky Mountains. CO-2 (Boulder, Fort Collins) encompasses the northern part of the metro region and the sparsely populated plains. The map looks like a donut,

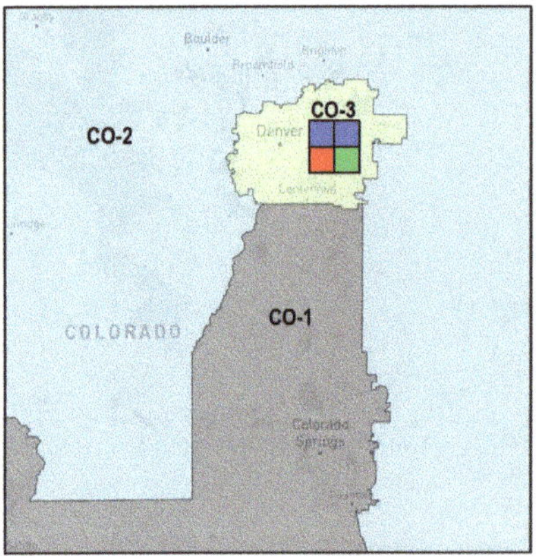

Figure 8.53: Denver Metro Area

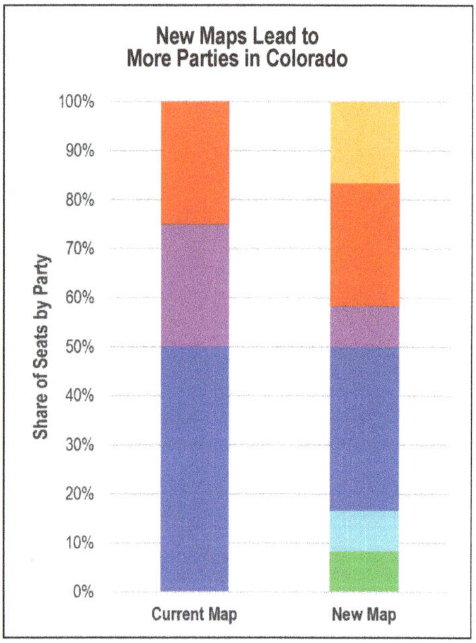

with CO-3 as the donut hole. I made a judgment to make the core metro area its own district. Around CO-3, the boundary between CO-1 and CO-2 could be drawn any number of ways. I used existing state legislative districts to determine which communities should stay in the same district or where it might be appropriate to place a district boundary. If this system were implemented, the Colorado legislature should redraw the lines as it deems appropriate.

Table 8.21: Colorado

	Population	Dem %	Rep %	Seats	P Safe	P or D	D Safe	D or R	R Safe	R or L	L Safe
Statewide	*5,773,714*	*52.2%*	*43.6%*	*12*	*1*	*1*	*4*	*1*	*3*	*2*	*0*
CO-1	1,925,121	41.4%	54.2%	4	0	0	1	1	1	1	0
CO-2	1,924,349	51.3%	44.5%	4	0	1	1	0	1	1	0
CO-3	1,924,244	64.4%	31.5%	4	1	0	2	0	1	0	0

In total, Colorado could elect a delegation of 5 Democrats, 4 Republicans, 2 Progressives, and 1 Libertarian. Libertarians could compete for one seat in each rural district. Progressives would likely win one seat in urban CO-3 and could compete for one seat in CO-1.

Minnesota is a Democratic-leaning state overall. However, its 3 four-member districts have different partisan profiles. Rural MN-1 (northern Minnesota) has a conservative majority. I project that MN-1 would elect one

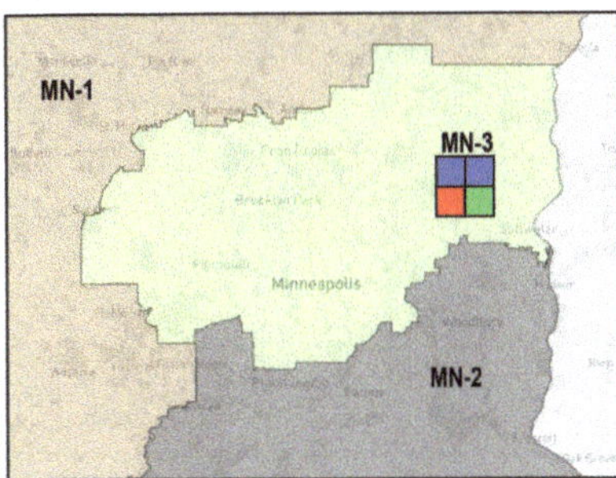

Figure 8.55: Minnesota

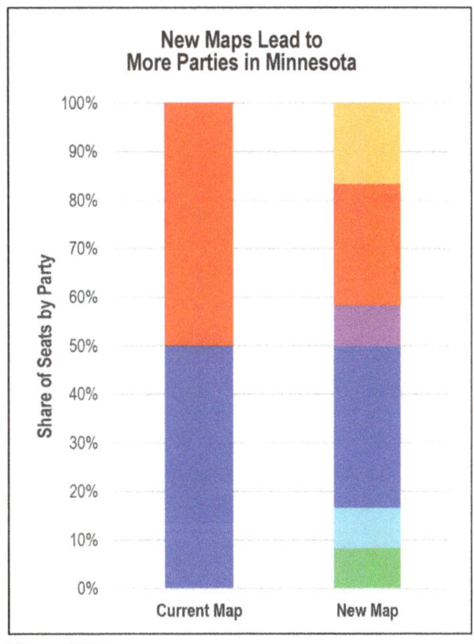

Figure 8.57

Figure 8.56: Minneapolis Metro

Democrat and one Republican, and that the Republican Party would compete against the Democrats for the 3rd seat and against the Libertarians for the 4th seat. MN-2 (southern Minnesota) is evenly split. I project the Democrats and Republicans would each win one seat. The Progressives could challenge the Democrats for the 3rd seat, while the Libertarians could challenge the Republicans for the 4th seat. Urban MN-3 has a sizable Democratic majority. I project MN-3 would elect 2

Table 8.22: Minnesota

	Population	Dem %	Rep %	Seats	P Safe	P or D	D Safe	D or R	R Safe	R or L	L Safe
Statewide	*5,706,494*	*51.7%*	*43.2%*	*12*	*1*	*1*	*4*	*1*	*3*	*2*	*0*
MN-1	1,902,415	39.8%	55.4%	4	0	0	1	1	1	1	0
MN-2	1,901,901	49.3%	45.5%	4	0	1	1	0	1	1	0
MN-3	1,902,178	65.4%	29.3%	4	1	0	2	0	1	0	0

Democrats, 1 Republican, and 1 Progressive. In total, Minnesota could elect a delegation of 5 Democrats, 4 Republicans, 2 Progressives, and 1 Libertarian.

ii. Three Relatively Equal Area Districts: Massachusetts, Tennessee, Indiana, Maryland, South Carolina

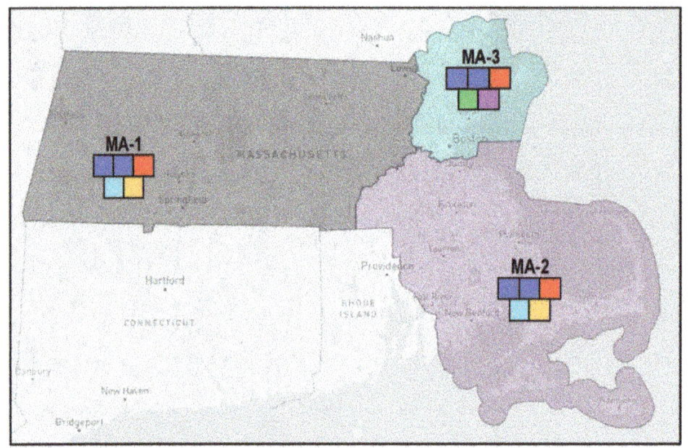

All five of these states are controlled by a majority party with supermajority representation. The minority party in all five states is severely underrepresented. These multi-member maps improve partisan proportionality in all five states.

Figure 8.58: Massachusetts

Massachusetts is the most populous state represented entirely by one party in Congress; Massachusetts Democrats are relatively evenly distributed across the states. All nine of its current representatives are Democrats, and none of the districts are rated competitive heading into 2024. This despite the fact that Republicans make up more than 1/3 of Massachusetts voters. This multimember map would result in proportional representation for Republicans. All 3 five-member districts would be competitive. In total, Massachusetts could elect a delegation of 8 Democrats, 4 Republicans, 2 Progressives, and 1 Libertarian.

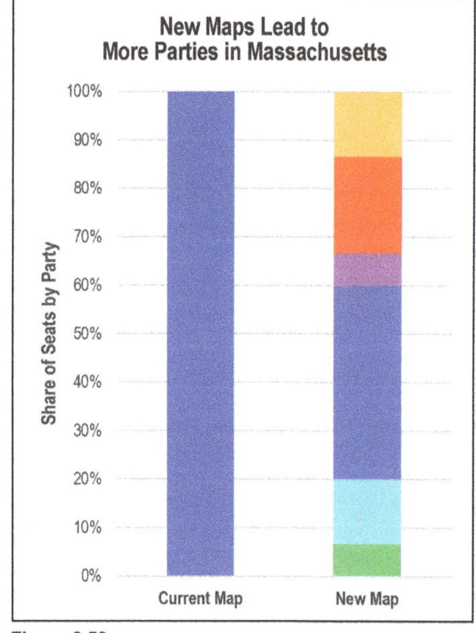

Figure 8.59

Table 8.23: Massachusetts

	Population	Dem %	Rep %	Seats	P Safe	P or D	D Safe	D or R	R Safe	R or L	L Safe
Statewide	7,029,917	60.0%	37.7%	15	1	2	6	1	3	2	0
MA-1	2,342,999	57.4%	40.1%	5	0	1	2	0	1	1	0
MA-2	2,343,559	56.2%	41.7%	5	0	1	2	0	1	1	0
MA-3	2,343,359	66.9%	31.0%	5	1	0	2	1	1	0	0

The majority democratic districts MA-1 (western Massachusetts) and MA-2 (Plymouth, south Boston metro) each would likely elect 2 Democrats and 1 Republican. The Progressives could challenge the Democrats for the 4th seat, while the Libertarians could challenge the Republicans for the 5th seat. The more urban MA-3 (Boston) would likely safely elect 2 Democrats, 1 Republican, and 1 Progressive. The 5th seat would be competitive between the Democrats and Republicans.

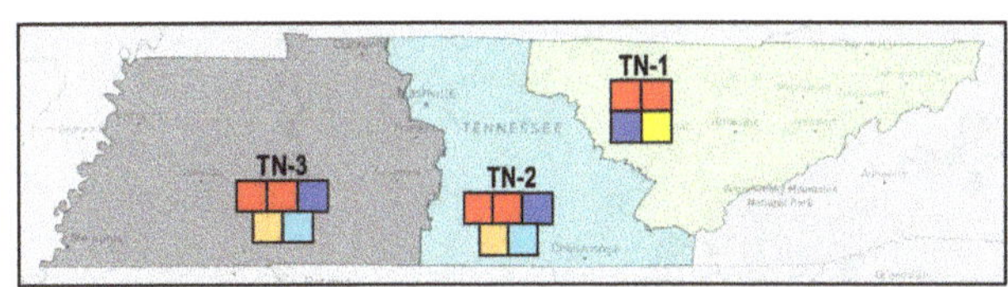

Figure 8.60: Tennessee

In an almost exact partisan reversal compared to Massachusetts, Tennessee is a majority-Republican state represented by a disproportionately Republican super-majority. Democrats make up more than 1/3 of the voters yet only control 1 of 9 seats. Zero districts are rated competitive heading into 2024. With this multimember map, two of Tennessee's three districts would be competitive, and the third would likely elect a representative from a third party. In total, Tennessee could elect a delegation of 7 Republicans, 3 Democrats, 2 Libertarians, and 2 Progressives.

Each of the five-member majority-Republican districts TN-2 (Nashville, Chattanooga) and TN-3 (Memphis) would likely elect 2 Republicans and 1 Democrat. Large urban populations in Memphis and Nashville would allow a Progressive Party to compete against the Democrats for the 4th seat, while the rural parts of each state would allow a Libertarian Party to compete against the Republicans for the 5th seat. The overwhelmingly Republican four-member TN-1 (Knoxville) would likely elect 2 Republicans, 1 Democrat, and 1 Libertarian.

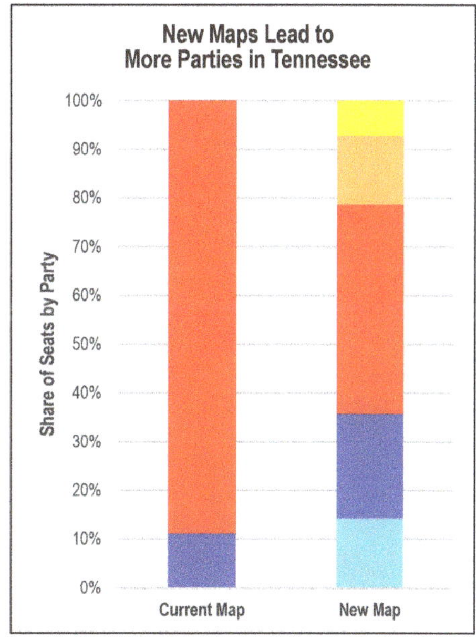

Figure 8.61

Table 8.24: Tennessee

	Population	Dem %	Rep %	Seats	P Safe	P or D	D Safe	D or R	R Safe	R or L	L Safe
Statewide	*6,910,840*	*37.9%*	*60.0%*	*14*	*0*	*2*	*3*	*0*	*6*	*2*	*1*
TN-1	1,974,705	27.6%	70.6%	4	0	0	1	0	2	0	1
TN-2	2,467,906	41.4%	56.2%	5	0	1	1	0	2	1	0
TN-3	2,468,229	42.9%	55.1%	5	0	1	1	0	2	1	0

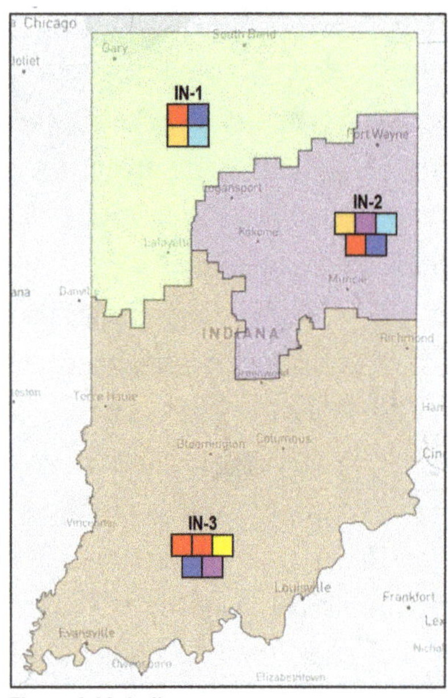

Figure 8.62: Indiana

Indiana is a majority-Republican state, though Democrats make up more than 40% of voters. With the current single-member district system, Indiana has just one competitive district and will likely elect a majority-Republican delegation of 7–2 or 8–1. With this multimember map, all three districts would be competitive. In total, Indiana could elect a proportional 6 Republicans, 5 Democrats, 2 Libertarians, and 1 Progressive.

Two districts are closely split between Republicans and Democrats, the four-member IN-1 (Gary, Lafayette) and 5-member IN-2 (Indianapolis, Fort Wayne). IN-1 would likely safely elect 1 Democrat and 1 Republican, with Progressives challenging Democrats for the 3rd seat and Libertarians challenging Republicans for the 4th seat. IN-2 is the same as IN-1, with the addition of a 5th seat competitive between the Democrats and Republicans. IN-2 includes all of Indianapolis proper. The majority Republican IN-3 (southern Indiana, Indianapolis suburbs) would likely elect 2 Republicans, 1 Democrat, and 1 Libertarian. Republicans would compete against Democrats for the 5th seat.

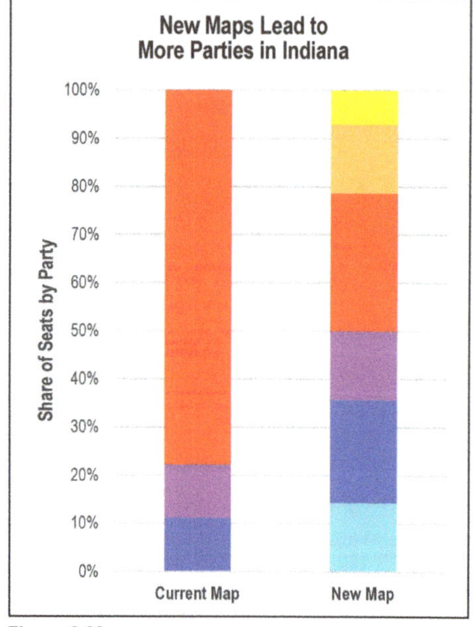

Figure 8.63

Table 8.25: Indiana

	Population	Dem %	Rep %	Seats	P Safe	P or D	D Safe	D or R	R Safe	R or L	L Safe
Statewide	6,785,528	42.1%	54.7%	14	0	2	3	2	4	2	1
IN-1	1,939,210	45.5%	51.4%	4	0	1	1	0	1	1	0
IN-2	2,423,203	46.7%	50.0%	5	0	1	1	1	1	1	0
IN-3	2,423,115	35.2%	61.6%	5	0	0	1	1	2	0	1

Maryland is a heavily gerrymandered majority-Democratic state. The single-member districts are drawn to pack Republican voters into one district and prevent Republicans from winning any other seats. This multimember map would increase Republican representation and provide Democrats with a proportional majority.

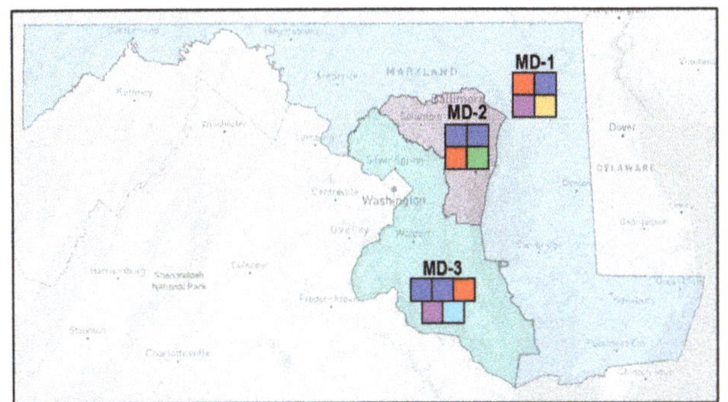

Figure 8.64: Maryland

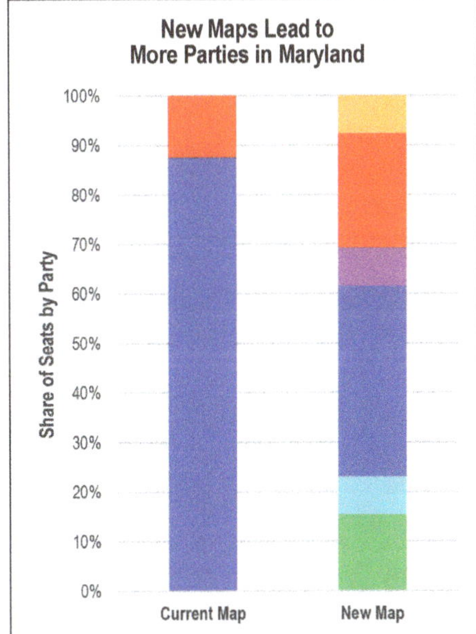

Figure 8.65

In total, Maryland could elect a delegation of 6 Democrats, 3 Republicans, 3 Progressives, and 1 Libertarian. Even the most overwhelmingly Democratic district, MD-3 (DC metro), could safely elect 1 Republican. MD-3 would also likely elect 2 Democrats and 1 Progressive, with the 5th seat competitive between the Progressives and Democrats. The four-member MD-2 (Baltimore) would likely elect 2 Democrats, 1 Republican, and 1 Progressive. I intentionally grouped the rural parts of Maryland into MD-1 (rural Maryland) to create a majority-Republican district in an otherwise majority-Democratic state. MD-1 would elect 1 Democrat and 1 Republican, with the 3rd seat competitive between the Democrats and Republicans and the 4th seat competitive between the Republicans and the Libertarians.

Table 8.26: Maryland

	Population	Dem %	Rep %	Seats	P Safe	P or D	D Safe	D or R	R Safe	R or L	L Safe
Statewide	*6,175,403*	*60.3%*	*36.8%*	*13*	*2*	*1*	*5*	*1*	*3*	*1*	*0*
MD-1	1,899,665	42.0%	54.8%	4	0	0	1	1	1	1	0
MD-2	1,899,425	62.5%	34.3%	4	1	0	2	0	1	0	0
MD-3	2,376,313	74.7%	22.8%	5	1	1	2	0	1	0	0

South Carolina was almost a two-district state; South Carolina's 11th seat was the 689th of 695 seats as determined by the apportionment formula. South Carolina is divided into 2 four-member districts and 1 three-member district. Four-member SC-1 (Greenville, Rock Hill) is majority Republican and would likely elect 2 Republicans, 1 Democrat, and 1 Libertarian. Four-member SC-2 (Columbia) is evenly split, and would likely elect 1 Democrat and 1 Republican, with Progressives contesting Democrats for the 3rd seat and Libertarians contesting Republicans for the 4th seat. Three-member SC-3 (Charleston is majority Republican, and would likely elect 1 Republican and 1 Democrat, with the Libertarians competing with the Republicans for the 3rd seat. In total, South Carolina could elect a delegation of 5 Republicans, 3 Democrats, 2 Libertarians, and 1 Progressive.

Another way to divide the state would be into 1 five-member district and 1 six-member district. Due to the lower electoral threshold of larger districts, there would likely be at least 1 Libertarian and 1 Progressive elected in each of the two districts.

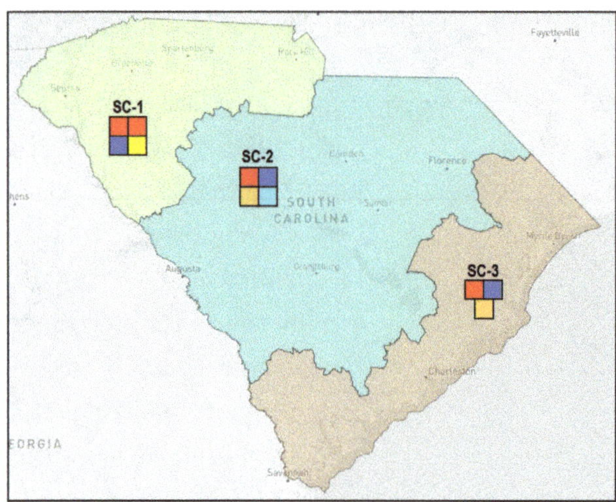

Figure 8.66: South Carolina

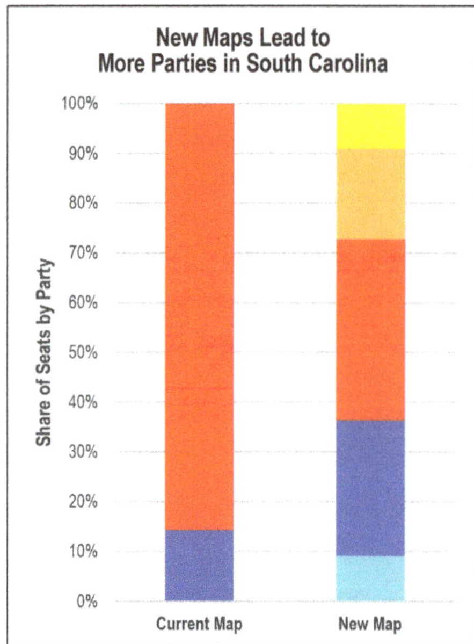

Figure 8.67

Table 8.27: South Carolina

	Population	Dem %	Rep %	Seats	P Safe	P or D	D Safe	D or R	R Safe	R or L	L Safe
Statewide	5,118,425	42.4%	55.8%	11	0	1	3	0	4	2	1
SC-1	1,861,254	34.6%	63.4%	4	0	0	1	0	2	0	1
SC-2	1,861,380	48.3%	50.0%	4	0	1	1	0	1	1	0
SC-3	1,395,791	44.5%	53.7%	3	0	0	1	0	1	1	0

D. Four-District States

New Jersey, Virginia, and Washington—the eleventh, twelfth, and thirteenth most populous states—would be represented by 19, 18, and 16 representatives across 4 districts of four- or five-members each. With the current single-member district maps, each state has just 1 district rated competitive heading into 2024. With these multimember maps, all 4 districts would be competitive in New Jersey and Virginia, and 2 of the 4 districts would be competitive in Washington.

Table 8.28: Four-District States - Current Representation

State	Population	Partisan Lean		Projected Seats (Sept. 2023 Cooks Report)			
		Democratic	Republican	Total	Democratic	Republican	Competitive
New Jersey	9,283,016	55.1%	43.2%	12	9	2	1
Virginia	8,631,393	52.8%	45.6%	11	6	4	1
Washington	7,705,281	57.2%	41.2%	10	7	2	1

i. New Jersey (19 Seats)

New Jersey is a majority-Democratic state which currently sends 9 Democrats and 3 Republicans to Congress. Only 1 of its 12 seats is competitive heading into 2024, and is tenuously held by a Republican, meaning New Jersey's delegation could soon be a lopsided 10–2 in favor of Democrats. This is unfair to New Jersey Republicans.

With this map, New Jersey could elect a multiparty, proportional delegation of 9 Democrats, 6 Republicans, 3 Progressives, and 1 Libertarian. New Jersey's lone four-member district, NJ-1 (south New Jersey), has a slight Democratic majority. NJ-1 would likely elect 1 Democrat and 1 Republican,

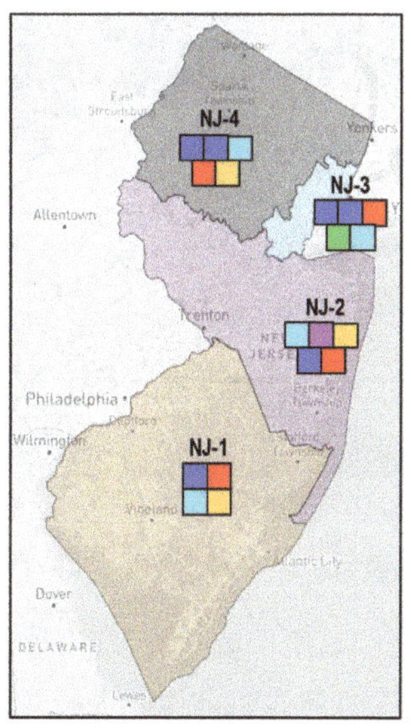

Figure 8.68: New Jersey

with the Progressives and Libertarians each competing for 1 seat. The five-member districts NJ-2 (Trenton, Jersey Shore) and NJ-4 (north New Jersey) would each elect one Republican, with the Libertarians competing for a 2nd seat on the right. NJ-2 is evenly split, meaning Democrats and Republicans would compete for 1 seat, Democrats would safely win 1 seat, and Progressives could compete against the Democrats for the last seat. NJ-4 has a Democratic majority, meaning Democrats would likely safely win 2 seats and compete against the Progressives for the last seat in the district. The urban NJ-3 (Newark) is overwhelmingly Democratic. Even so, Republicans would likely safely win 1 seat. Democrats would likely win 2 seats while Progressives would safely win 1 seat. Progressives and Democrats would compete for the 5th seat.

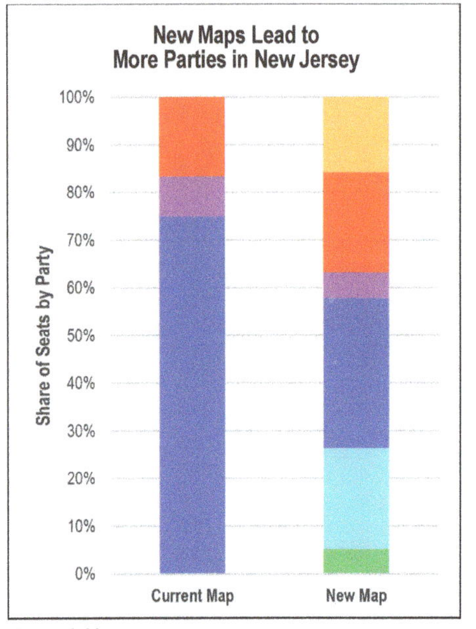

Figure 8.69

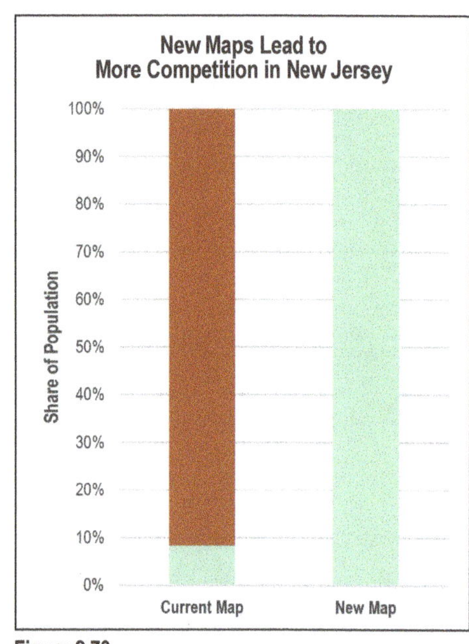

Figure 8.70

Table 8.29: New Jersey

	Population	Dem %	Rep %	Seats	P Safe	P or D	D Safe	D or R	R Safe	R or L	L Safe
Statewide	*9,283,016*	*55.1%*	*43.2%*	*19*	*1*	*4*	*6*	*1*	*4*	*3*	*0*
NJ-1	1,954,656	53.0%	45.2%	4	0	1	1	0	1	1	0
NJ-2	2,442,574	48.4%	49.8%	5	0	1	1	1	1	1	0
NJ-3	2,443,165	71.5%	26.8%	5	1	1	2	0	1	0	0
NJ-4	2,442,621	52.4%	45.9%	5	0	1	2	0	1	1	0

ii. Virginia (18 Seats)

Virginia is a purple state with a slight Democratic majority. Virginia is currently represented by a proportional 6 Democrats and 5 Republicans. However, only one seat is rated as competitive heading into 2024.

This multimember map maintains the current map's proportional representation and would allow all Virginians to vote in a competitive district. In total, Virginia could elect a delegation of 8 Democrats, 7 Republicans, 2 Progressives, and 1 Libertarian.

Virginia's districts are geographically and politically diverse, from the rural, majority-Republican VA-1 (western Virginia) to the densely populated, majority-Democratic VA-4 (Arlington). Four-member VA-1 is projected to have a 61% Republican majority and would elect between 1 and 3 Republicans. The Republicans would face a challenge from a Libertarian Party from the right and the Democratic Party from the left. The

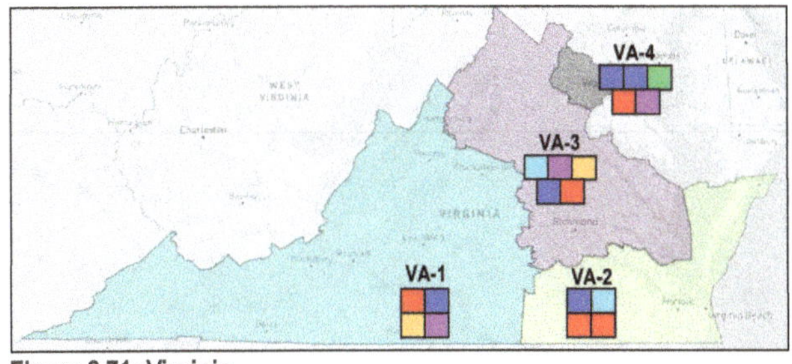

Figure 8.71: Virginia

Democrats would likely win 1 seat in VA-1. Five-member VA-4 is projected to have a 68% Democratic majority, and would likely safely elect 2 Democrats, 1 Republican, and 1 Progressive. The fifth seat would be competitive between the Democrats and Republicans. Five-member VA-3 (Richmond) is an evenly split swing district. Democrats and Republicans would each safely win 1 seat, with the other 3 seats being competitive between the Progressives and Democrats, the Democrats and Republicans, and the Republicans and Libertarians, respectively. Four-member, Democratic-leaning VA-2 would likely elect 2 Republicans and 1 Democrat, with Progressives challenging the Democrats for the 4th seat.

In addition to tinkering around the edges of the districts, the size of Virginia's districts could be swapped. For example, turning VA-1 from a 4-member district to a

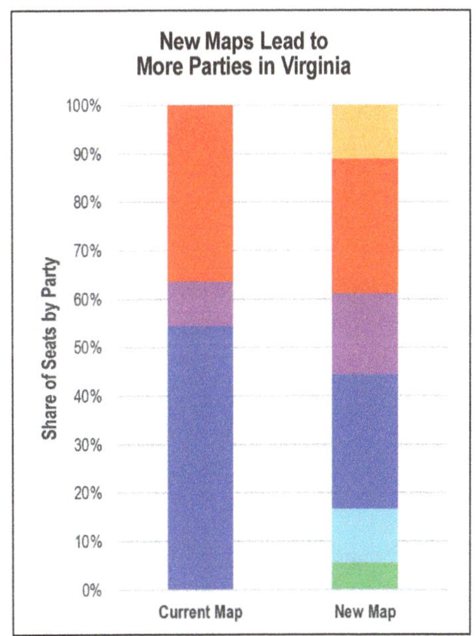

Figure 8.72

Figure 8.73

Table 8.30: Virginia

	Population	Dem %	Rep %	Seats	P Safe	P or D	D Safe	D or R	R Safe	R or L	L Safe
Statewide	*8,631,393*	*52.8%*	*45.6%*	*18*	*1*	*2*	*5*	*3*	*5*	*2*	*0*
VA-1	1,918,165	37.5%	61.1%	4	0	0	1	1	1	1	0
VA-2	1,917,203	55.6%	42.8%	4	0	1	1	0	2	0	0
VA-3	2,398,632	48.4%	50.0%	5	0	1	1	1	1	1	0
VA-4	2,397,393	67.9%	30.1%	5	1	0	2	1	1	0	0

five-member district by annexing parts of VA-2 and VA-3 would increase the likelihood of a Libertarian candidate winning 1 seat. The lower electoral threshold would compensate for the newly five-member VA-1's smaller Republican majority. Another way of redrawing Virginia's districts would be to redraw Virginia into 3 six-member districts. With six-member districts, the electoral threshold for 1 seat is a mere 14.3%. With such a low electoral threshold, both Libertarians and Progressives would likely win at least 1 seat in all 3 districts. Projecting the full outcome is impossible without first redrawing the districts.

iii. Washington (16 Seats)

Washington is a majority-Democratic state. Washington's current congressional delegation is 8 Democrats and 2 Republicans. Only 1 seat is rated as competitive, currently held by a Democrat. For federal representation, Democrats are overrepresented while Republicans are underrepresented. This multimember map would result in reasonably proportional Republican representation.

All 4 districts have have four members, making the electoral threshold 20% for 1 seat and 40% for 2 seats. Every district would elect at least 1 Democrat and 1 Republican, with alternative parties either competitive for or safely winning one seat. Republicans would gain representation in the urban Puget Sound, and Democrats would gain representation in rural eastern Washington, ensuring Washington's congressional delegation spans the gamut of its political diversity. Rural WA-1 (eastern Washington) would likely elect

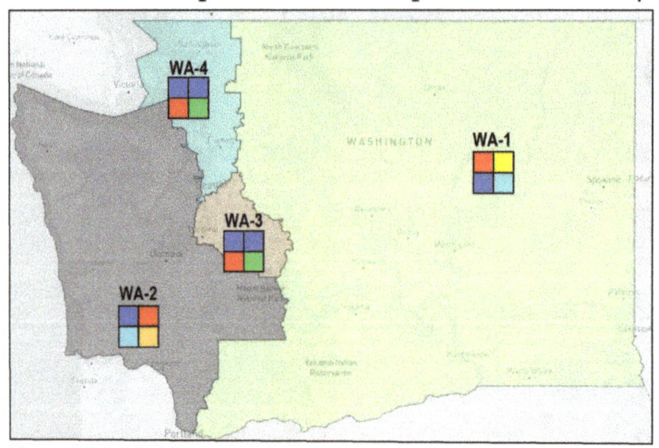

Figure 8.74: Washington

1 Democrat, 1 Republican, and 1 Libertarian. The 4th seat would likely be competitive between the Democrats and Progressives. Because eastern Washington is far less populated than western Washington, it is necessary for WA-1 to cross the Cascade mountains, reaching as far west as Camas and Monroe. WA-2 (Vancouver, Olympia) is an evenly split district and would likely elect 1 Democrat and 1 Republican, with Progressives and Libertarians each competing for 1 seat. The Seattle metro is split into WA-3 (south Puget Sound) and WA-4 (north Puget Sound). Both districts feature large Democratic majorities and would each likely elect 2 Democrats, 1 Republican, and 1 Progressive.

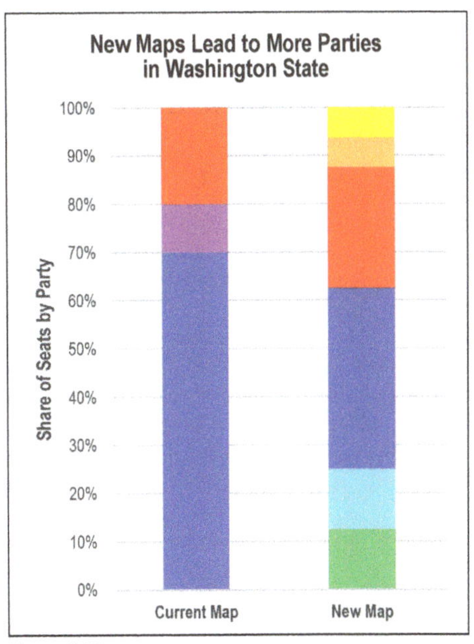

Figure 8.75

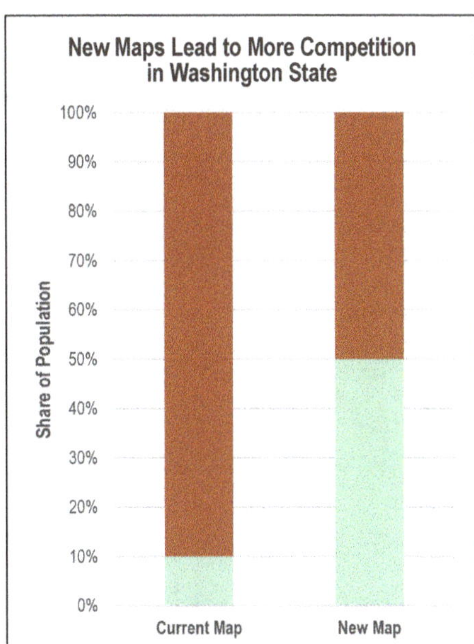

Figure 8.76

Table 8.31: Washington

	Population	Dem %	Rep %	Seats	P Safe	P or D	D Safe	D or R	R Safe	R or L	L Safe
Statewide	7,705,281	57.2%	41.2%	16	2	2	6	0	4	1	1
WA-1	1,926,515	43.1%	55.4%	4	0	1	1	0	1	0	1
WA-2	1,926,236	50.9%	47.4%	4	0	1	1	0	1	1	0
WA-3	1,926,318	66.1%	32.3%	4	1	0	2	0	1	0	0
WA-4	1,926,212	67.5%	30.9%	4	1	0	2	0	1	0	0

There are two alternative ways to divide Washington into multimember districts. First, Washington's four districts do not all have to be equal sized. WA-1 could be reduced to a 1.4 million person, 3-member district located entirely east of the Cascade mountains. This would ensure eastern Washington residents would have their own representatives, though at the expense of increased viability for alternative parties. While all of the other district lines would need to be adjusted, the most impactful change would be changing one of the districts, likely the densely populated WA-3, to be a five-member 2.4-million person district. This would increase the viability of alternative parties in the Seattle metro region.

Second, Washington could be divided into three districts of 2 five-member districts and 1 six-member district. This could look like WA-1 expanding to five-members and extending into the rural parts of the other three districts. The current WA-3 would be eliminated, with the southern part of the district joining the existing WA-2 and the northern part of the district joining the existing WA-4 to form 2 six-member districts.

E. Five-District States

These four large states have all been recent presidential battlegrounds. All four are populated by more than 10 million people in a few large cities and many small towns. And under these new multimember district maps, all four would be more representative and more competitive.

Table 8.32: Five-District States - Current Representation

State	Population	Partisan Lean		Projected Seats (Sept. 2023 Cooks Report)			
		Democratic	Republican	Total	Democratic	Republican	Competitive
Ohio	11,799,448	45.4%	52.4%	15	2	10	3
Georgia	10,711,908	47.2%	51.1%	14	5	9	0
North Carolina	10,439,388	48.3%	49.4%	14	3	7	4
Michigan	10,077,331	50.5%	46.8%	13	6	5	2

i. Ohio (24 Seats)

Ohio is a heavily gerrymandered Republican-leaning state. While Democratic voters make up about 45% of voters, Ohio's current congressional delegation is 10 Republicans and 5 Democrats. Further, only three seats are rated competitive heading into 2024. All three competitive seats are currently held by Democrats, meaning that Republicans will almost certainly control between 10 and 13 of Ohio's 15 seats following the election.

This multimember map would elect a proportionally representative delegation. Four of Ohio's five districts would be represented by five members, while OH-4 (Columbus) would be represented by four members. Each district would elect at least 1 Republican and 1 Democrat. The combination of each party's voters being geographically distributed and at least 1.9 million people living in each district makes gerrymandering practically impossible. Though rated uncompetitive, OH-2 (Toledo, northwest Ohio) and OH-5 (southeast Ohio), would likely elect 1 Libertarian each, still disrupting the two-party establishment. Libertarians could be competitive in two more districts, OH-1 (Cincinnati) and OH-3 (Cleveland). Progressives could be competitive in the three districts anchored by a large city: OH-1, OH-3, and OH-4 (Columbus). Even in OH-2 and OH-5, in which Democrats are projected at only 38% of the vote, a Pro-

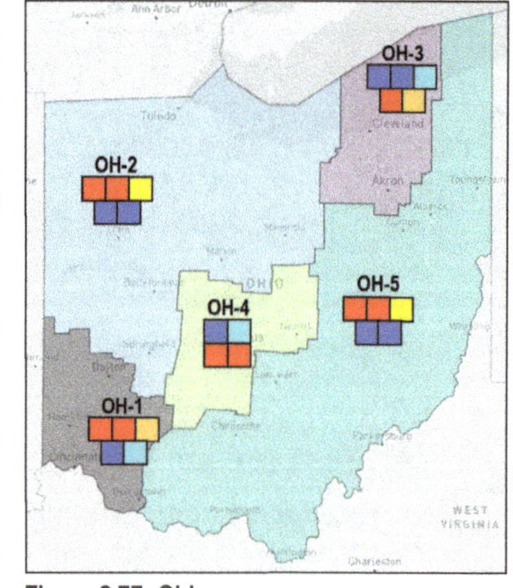

Figure 8.77: Ohio

gressive candidate needing only 17% to win could mount a challenge. Similarly, a Libertarian candidate in four-member OH-4 could plausibly win 20% of the vote given OH-4's current 45% Republican projection. In total, Ohio could plausibly elect a delegation of 10 Republicans, 9 Democrats, 3 Libertarians, and 2 Progressives.

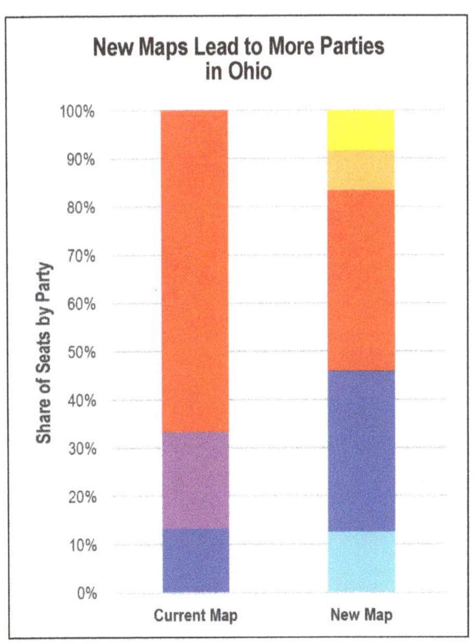

Figure 8.78

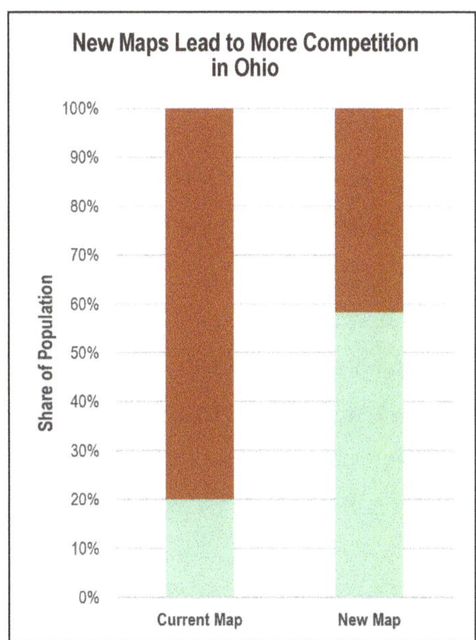

Figure 8.79

Table 8.33: Ohio

	Population	Dem %	Rep %	Seats	P Safe	P or D	D Safe	D or R	R Safe	R or L	L Safe
Statewide	*11,799,448*	*45.4%*	*52.4%*	*24*	*0*	*3*	*8*	*0*	*9*	*2*	*2*
OH-1	2,458,471	42.7%	55.1%	5	0	1	1	0	2	1	0
OH-2	2,457,933	38.0%	59.6%	5	0	0	2	0	2	0	1
OH-3	2,457,977	56.6%	41.3%	5	0	1	2	0	1	1	0
OH-4	1,966,580	52.8%	45.1%	4	0	1	1	0	2	0	0
OH-5	2,458,487	37.6%	60.1%	5	0	0	2	0	2	0	1

Ohio could also divide its 24 members into 4 districts of six-members each. At that size, only 14% of the vote would be needed to win one seat, meaning both Progressives and Libertarians would almost certainly be competitive in all four districts. Voters across every acre of Ohio would be able to vote in a competitive, multiparty district. One way to draw the districts would be to eliminate the current OH-4, dividing the Columbus metro between OH-1, OH-2, and OH-5. OH-3 could be expanded east to Youngstown and south to Canton.

ii. Georgia (22 Seats)

Georgia is projected as a Republican leaning state. However, since the 2020 election Georgia is perhaps the most important and most evenly divided battleground state in the country. Georgia's current congressional delegation is 9 Republicans and 5 Democrats. Zero of Georgia's 14 districts are rated as competitive heading into 2024 due to the combined force of gerrymandering and single-member districts.

This multimember map would ensure partisan competition across Georgia and could plausibly elect a proportional delegation of 9 Republicans, 8 Democrats, 3 Libertarians, and 2 Progressives.

Three of Georgia's districts are four-member. Both GA-4 (southwest Georgia) and GA-5 (southeast Georgia) are majority-Republican and competitive. Each district would likely elect 1 Democrat and 1 Republican.

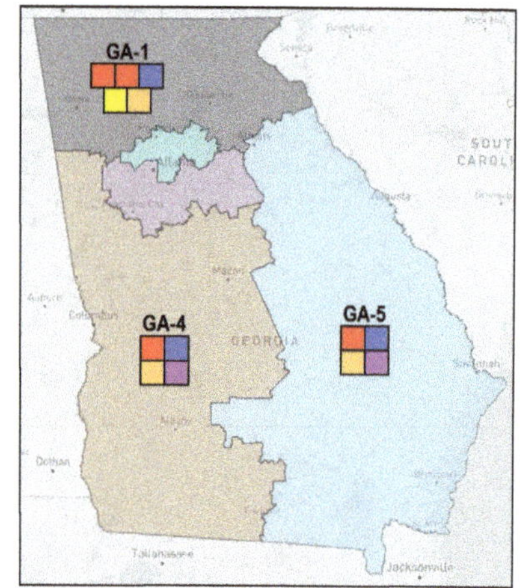

Figure 8.80: Georgia

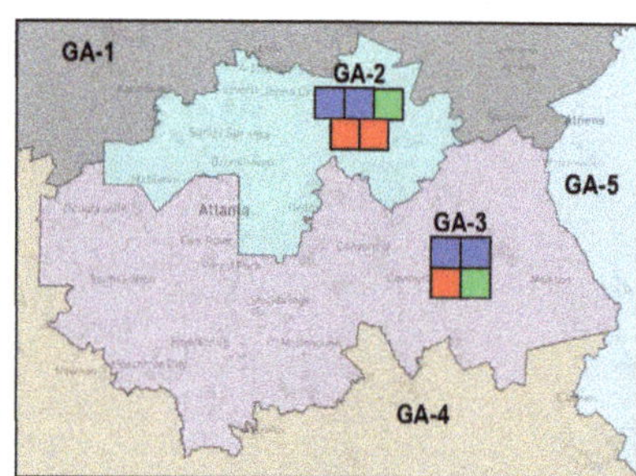

Figure 8.81: Atlanta Metro

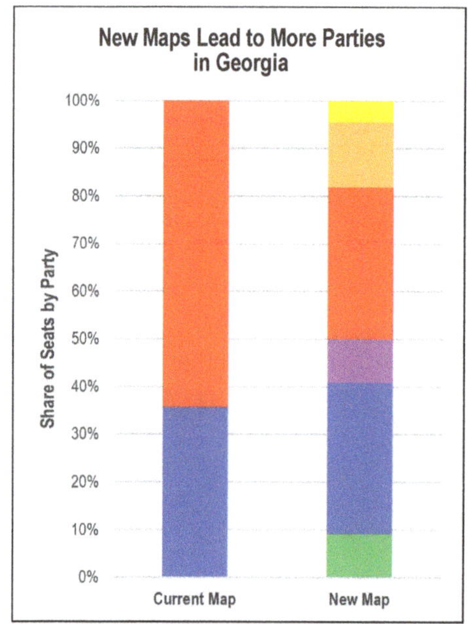

Figure 8.82

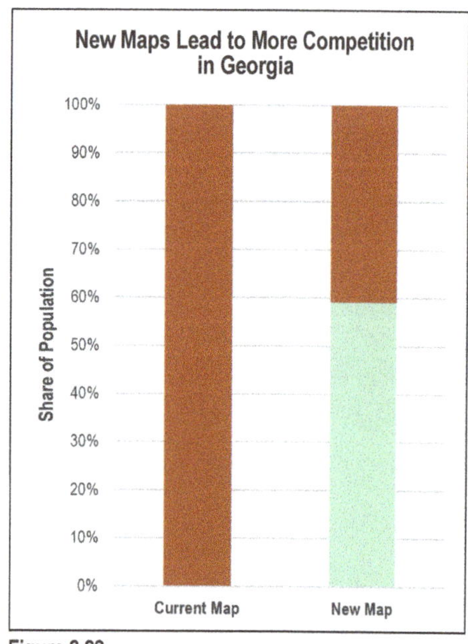

Figure 8.83

The 3rd seat would be competitive between the Democrats and Republicans, and the 4th seat would be competitive between the Republicans and the Libertarians. GA-3 (south Atlanta metro) is a four district with an overwhelmingly Democratic majority. I project GA-3 as uncompetitive yet still subverting the two-party establishment because it would likely elect 2 Democrats, 1 Republican, and 1 Progressive.

Georgia's five-member districts would also likely elect representatives from alternative parties. The very conservative GA-1 (northern Georgia) would likely elect 2 Republicans, 1 Democrat, and 1 Libertarian. The 5th seat would be competitive between the Republicans and the Libertarians. GA-2 (north Atlanta metro) is less liberal than GA-1 is conservative, and would likely elect 2 Democrats, 2 Republicans, and 1 Progressive.

Georgia's 22 allocated representatives could also be divided into 2 six-member districts and 2 five-member districts. One way to draw the districts would be to leave five-member GA-1 and GA-2 as they are. Then, the 3 four-member districts could be combined into 2 six-member districts by shifting the northern part of GA-4 (Columbus, Macon) into GA-3 and shifting the southern part of GA-4 (Albany) into GA-5. Each six-member district would likely elect at least one Progressive and one Libertarian because the electoral threshold to win one seat would be just 14%. Progressives would likely be competitive for a 2nd seat in the expanded yet still majority-Democratic GA-3, while Libertarians would likely be competitive for a second seat in the expanded GA-5.

Table 8.34: Georgia

	Population	Dem %	Rep %	Seats	P Safe	P or D	D Safe	D or R	R Safe	R or L	L Safe
Statewide	10,711,908	47.2%	51.1%	22	2	0	7	2	7	3	1
GA-1	2,434,405	26.6%	71.3%	5	0	0	1	0	2	1	1
GA-2	2,434,100	61.1%	36.8%	5	1	0	2	0	2	0	0
GA-3	1,947,636	67.6%	30.8%	4	1	0	2	0	1	0	0
GA-4	1,947,907	40.2%	58.5%	4	0	0	1	1	1	1	0
GA-5	1,947,860	41.4%	57.1%	4	0	0	1	1	1	1	0

iii. North Carolina (22 Seats)

North Carolina is projected to be almost exactly evenly split between Democrats and Republicans. Each party controls 7 of North Carolina's 14 seats in Congress. Four districts are rated as competitive heading into 2024, though all four competitive districts are currently held by Democrats. North Carolina's current congressional map delivers a proportional outcome only because the North Carolina Supreme Court **struck down**[65] maps gerrymandered by the Republican legislature that would have ensured Republican victory in 10 of 14 districts if Republicans received just 50%

of the vote. However, the dispute is ongoing. After North Carolina's Supreme Court changed from a 4-3 Democratic majority in 2022 to a 5-2 Republican majority in 2023, the new

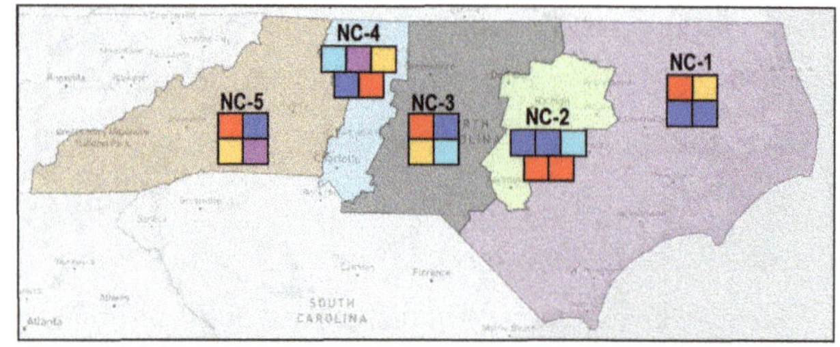

Figure 8.84: North Carolina

Republican majority **reversed**[66] the ruling of the prior court. This brazenly partisan ruling now allows the Republican supermajorities in the North Carolina legislature to **redraw the maps**[67] as they see fit.

If North Carolina were redrawn with multimember districts, this ongoing dispute would be impossible because gerrymandering would be practically impossible. In total, this multimember map could plausibly elect a proportional delegation of 9 Democrats, 9 Republicans, 2 Progressives, and 2 Libertarians. Alternative parties would be competitive in every district, and all North Carolina voters would vote in a competitive district. Every district would elect at least 1 Democrat and 1 Republican.

Four-member NC-3 (Greensboro) and five-member NC-4 (Charlotte) could each plausibly elect representatives from four different parties. NC-3 is evenly split between Republicans and Democrats. Progressives could win 1 seat if they persuade 40% of existing Democratic voters, while Libertarians could win 1 seat if they persuade 40%

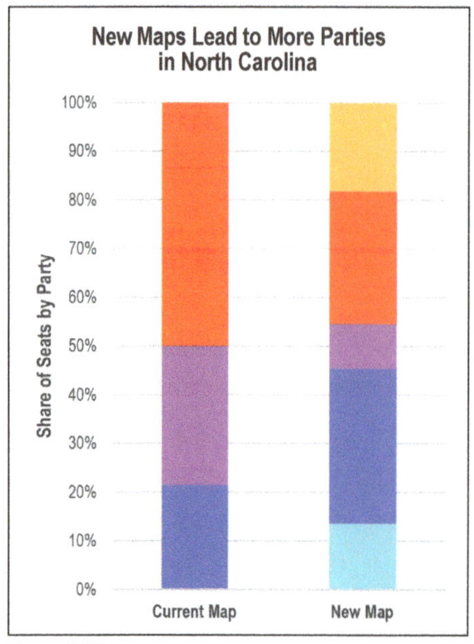

Figure 8.85

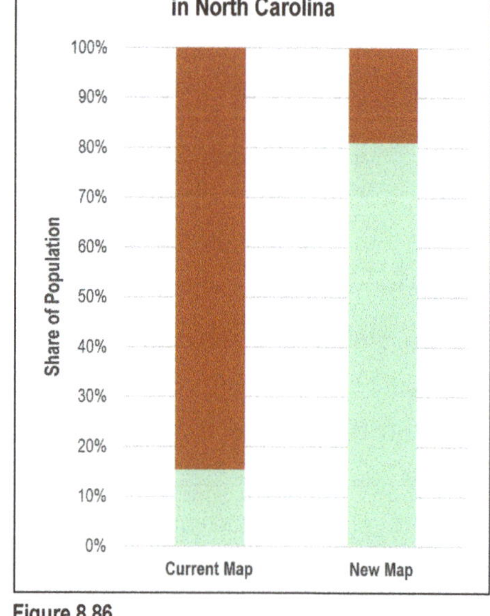

Figure 8.86

of existing Republican voters. The analysis is similar for five-member NC-4, with the alternative parties needing only 17% of the vote to win 1 seat. The 5th seat in NC-4 would be competitive between the Democrats and Republicans, with the Democrats favored.

Libertarians would be competitive for 1 seat in four-member NC-1 (coastal North Carolina), while Progressives would be competitive for 1 seat in five-member NC-2 (Raleigh, Fayetteville). The most conservative district, NC-5 (western North Carolina), would likely elect 1 Democrat and 1 Republican, with the Republicans competing against the Democrats for the 3rd seat and against the Libertarians for the 4th seat.

North Carolina's 22 seats could also be divided into 2 five-member districts and 2 six-member districts. The way I drew this map, alternating from east to west between four-member districts and five-member districts, makes it difficult to quickly redraw the lines. However, larger districts would likely be more evenly divided between the 2 major parties, ensuring that voters across the state would be represented by both Republicans and Democrats. Further, Progressives and Libertarians would likely be competitive in all four districts, needing just 14% to win 1 seat in the six-member districts and 17% to win 1 seat in the five-member districts.

Table 8.35: North Carolina

	Population	Dem %	Rep %	Seats	P Safe	P or D	D Safe	D or R	R Safe	R or L	L Safe
Statewide	*10,439,388*	*48.3%*	*49.4%*	*22*	*0*	*3*	*7*	*2*	*6*	*4*	*0*
NC-1	1,898,080	44.0%	54.0%	4	0	0	2	0	1	1	0
NC-2	2,372,723	58.6%	39.0%	5	0	1	2	0	2	0	0
NC-3	1,898,288	48.6%	49.4%	4	0	1	1	0	1	1	0
NC-4	2,371,918	51.1%	46.4%	5	0	1	1	1	1	1	0
NC-5	1,898,379	36.7%	61.0%	4	0	0	1	1	1	1	0

iv. Michigan (21 Seats)

Michigan is a Democratic leaning battleground state. Michigan currently sends a proportional 7 Democrats and 6 Republicans to Congress. Two of its districts are rated competitive heading into 2024, one each held by the Democrats and the Republicans.

This multimember map would maintain Michigan's proportional congressional delegation and ensure that a majority of Michiganders would vote in a competitive district. In total, Michigan could elect a proportional delegation

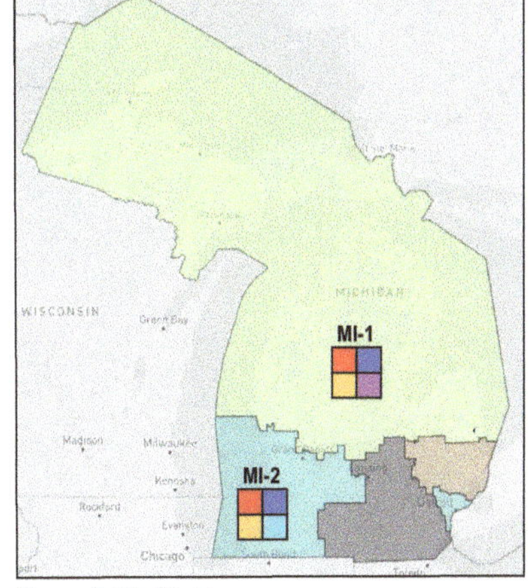

Figure 8.87: Michigan

of 9 Democrats, 8 Republicans, 2 Progressives, and 2 Libertarians.

Michigan's 21 representatives are divided into 4 four-member districts and 1 five-member district. MI-1 (upper peninsula, northern lower peninsula) is majority Republican and would likely elect 1 Democrat and 1 Republican, with the Republicans competing against the Democrats for the 3rd seat and against the Libertarians for the 4th seat. Four-member districts MI-2 (Grand Rapids, Kalamazoo) and MI-5 (Flint, Sterling Heights) are close to evenly split and could elect representatives from four different parties. In both districts, the Progressives would compete against the Democrats for one seat while the Libertarians would compete against the Republicans for one seat.

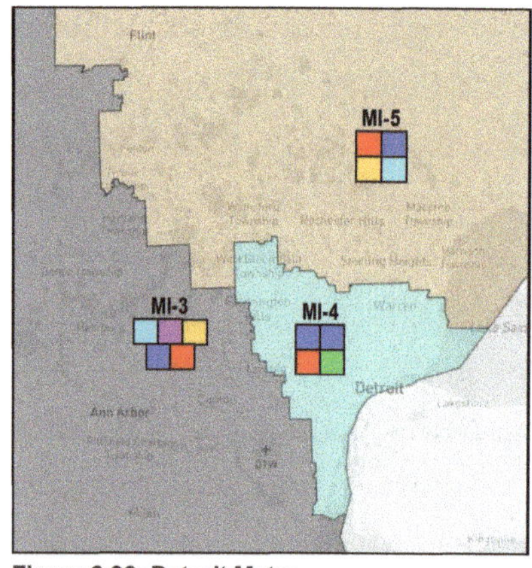

Figure 8.88: Detroit Metro

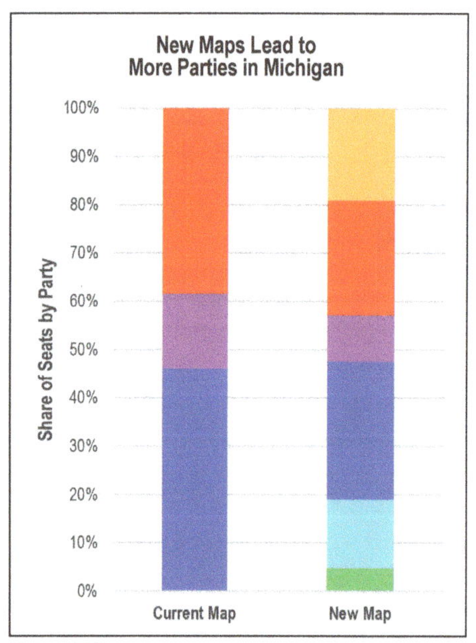

Figure 8.89

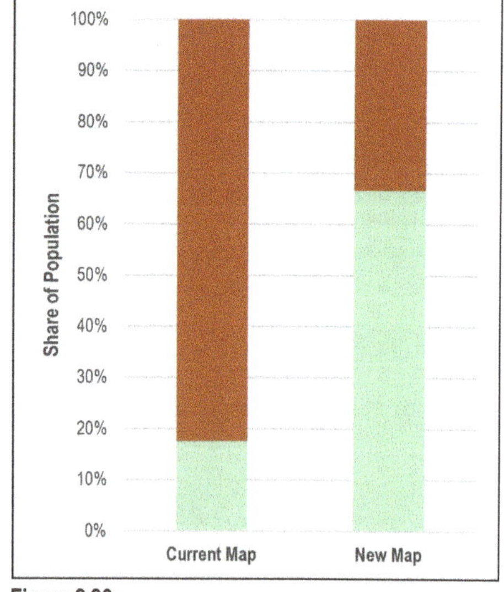

Figure 8.90

Table 8.36: Michigan

	Population	Dem %	Rep %	Seats	P Safe	P or D	D Safe	D or R	R Safe	R or L	L Safe
Statewide	*10,077,331*	*50.5%*	*46.8%*	*21*	*1*	*3*	*6*	*2*	*5*	*4*	*0*
MI-1	1,919,478	39.4%	57.7%	4	0	0	1	1	1	1	0
MI-2	1,919,389	45.7%	51.2%	5	0	1	1	1	1	1	0
MI-3	2,399,747	52.2%	45.1%	4	0	1	1	0	1	1	0
MI-4	1,919,897	70.8%	26.9%	4	1	0	2	0	1	0	0
MI-5	1,918,820	45.7%	51.7%	4	0	1	1	0	1	1	0

In five-member MI-3 (Ann Arbor), the 5th seat would be competitive between the Democrats and Republicans, with the Democrats favored. While MI-4 (Detroit) is the only district projected to be uncompetitive, the two-party establishment would still be threatened. Progressives would likely win one seat due to the projected overwhelming Democratic majority. MI-4 would also likely elect 2 Democrats and 1 Republican.

Michigan could also be redrawn into 3 five-member districts and 1 six-member district. Two important considerations would be to ensure that, however large the districts may be, MI-1 remains a rural district and MI-4 remains an urban district. Five-member districts would increase the likelihood of electoral victory by both the Progressives and the Libertarians, as well as independent candidates.

F. Six-District States

Pennsylvania and Illinois each have about 13 million residents across urban and rural communities. Illinois is dominated by the nearly 10 million people who live in the **Chicago metropolitan area**[68] (some of which spills into Wisconsin and Indiana). Pennsylvania has two primary population centers, the nation's sixth most populous city **Philadelphia**[69] in the east and the 2.3 million people who live in the **Pittsburgh metropolitan area**[70] in the west. In both states, multimember districts would increase the number of people voting in competitive districts.

Table 8.37: Six-District States - Current Representation

State	Population	Partisan Lean		Projected Seats (Sept. 2023 Cooks Report)			
		Democratic	Republican	Total	Democratic	Republican	Competitive
Pennsylvania	13,002,700	51.4%	46.5%	17	6	8	3
Illinois	12,809,545	55.5%	39.9%	17	13	3	1

i. Pennsylvania (27 Seats)

Pennsylvania is a Democratic-leaning battleground state. In 2023, it sent 9 Democrats and 8 Republicans to Congress. Three of its 17 congressional races are rated as competitive heading into 2024, all currently held by Democrats.

This multimember map would increase the number of Pennsylvanians voting in competitive districts from 2.3 million under the current single-member district map to 8.7 million. The two districts I project as uncompetitive, PA-2 (central Pennsylvania) and PA-5 (Allentown, north Philadelphia metro), would each likely elect 1 representative from an alternative party. Republicans would win representation in Philadelphia, and Democrats would win representation in rural central Pennsylvania. In total, with this map Pennsylvania could elect a proportionally representative delegation of 11 Democrats, 10

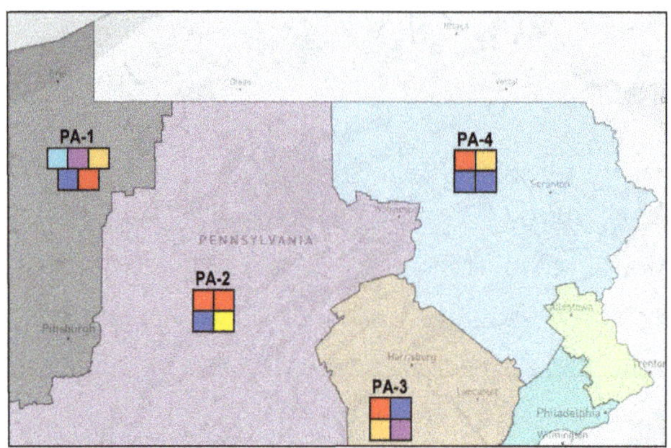

Figure 8.91: Pennsylvania

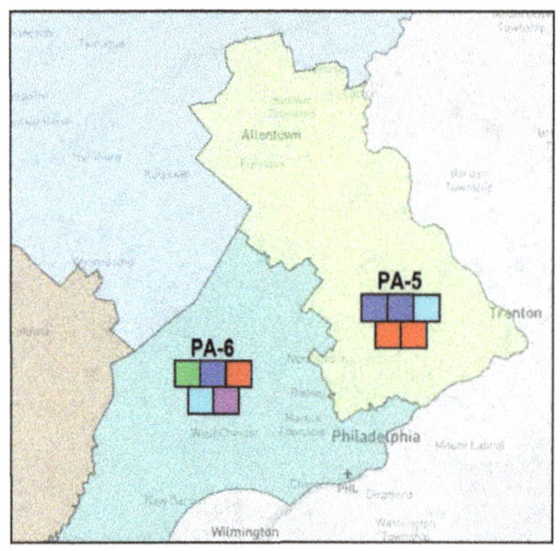

Figure 8.92: Philadelphia Metro

Republicans, 3 Progressives, and 3 Libertarians.

This map would divide Pennsylvania into 3 four-member districts and 3 five-member districts. The four-member districts comprise the geographic majority of the state: PA-2, PA-3 (Lancaster, Harrisburg), and PA-4 (Scranton). All three districts are projected to have Republican majorities. Yet because the four-member district electoral threshold is only 20% to win 1 seat, all three districts would elect at least 1 Democrat. The most conservative, PA-2, would likely elect 2 Republicans, 1 Democrat, and 1 Libertarian. PA-3 would elect 1 Republican and 1 Democrat, with Republicans competing against the Democrats for the 3rd seat and against the Libertarians for the 4th seat. PA-4, with a projected 42% Democratic minority, would likely elect 2 Democrats and 1 Republican, with the Republicans competing against the Libertarians for the 4th seat.

Philadelphia's five-member districts feature its most populous cities. The Philadelphia metro area is divided into PA-5 and PA-6 (south Philadelphia metro). Both Philadelphia districts are projected to have large Democratic majorities. Progressives would likely win 1 seat in both districts and could compete for a 2nd seat in PA-6. Republicans would likely win 2 seats in PA-5 and either 1 or 2 seats in PA-6. PA-1 (Pittsburg, Erie) combines a large city with the rural western edge of Pennsylvania. Both Progressives and Libertarians could be competitive in PA-1, making it plausible for PA-1 to elect representatives from four different parties.

Another way to divide Pennsylvania's 27 representatives would be into 3 five-member districts and 2 six-member districts. This could be accomplished by combining half of PA-3 with PA-2, and the other half of PA-3 with PA-4. Pennsylvania's rural population would be represented by two very large, majority Republican multimember districts. In 6-member districts, despite the Republican majority, Progressives could plausibly compete against Democrats. Libertarians would likely win at least 1 seat in each district, and likely compete against the Republicans for a 2nd seat in each.

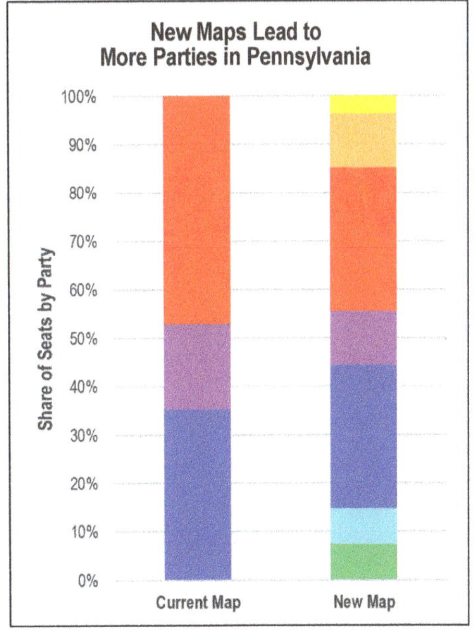

Figure 8.93

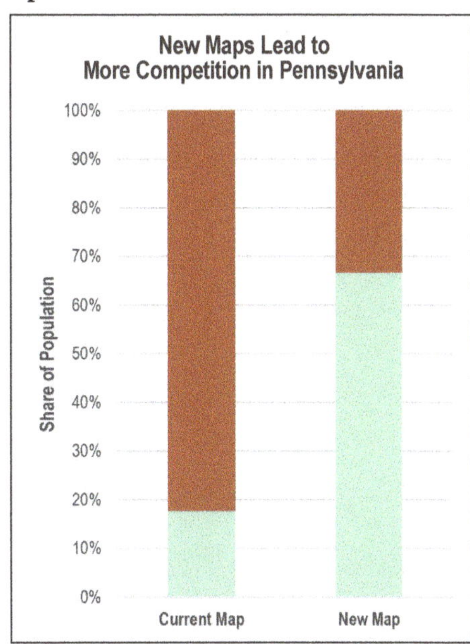

Figure 8.94

Table 8.38: Pennsylvania

	Population	Dem %	Rep %	Seats	P Safe	P or D	D Safe	D or R	R Safe	R or L	L Safe
Statewide	*13,002,700*	*51.4%*	*46.5%*	*27*	*2*	*2*	*8*	*3*	*8*	*3*	*1*
PA-1	2,407,865	51.9%	45.6%	5	0	1	1	1	1	1	0
PA-2	1,926,499	34.0%	63.7%	4	0	0	1	0	2	0	1
PA-3	1,926,358	40.4%	57.0%	4	0	0	1	1	1	1	0
PA-4	1,925,852	42.9%	54.7%	4	0	0	2	0	1	1	0
PA-5	2,407,547	61.2%	37.0%	5	1	0	2	0	2	0	0
PA-6	2,408,579	68.6%	29.7%	5	1	1	1	1	1	0	0

ii. Illinois (26 Seats)

Illinois is a heavily gerrymandered majority-Democratic state. Republicans make up about 40% of Illinois voters yet only won 3 of Illinois' 17 congressional districts in 2022. Further, only 1 district is rated as competitive heading into 2024, meaning Republicans will win no more than 4 seats.

This multimember map ungerrymanders Illinois and could elect a proportionally representative delegation of 11 Democrats, 8 Republicans, 5 Progressives, and 2 Libertarians. All but one of Illinois' six districts would be competitive.

Illinois is divided into 4 four-member districts and 2 five-member districts. Two rural districts, four-member IL-1 (southern Illinois, Springfield) and five-member

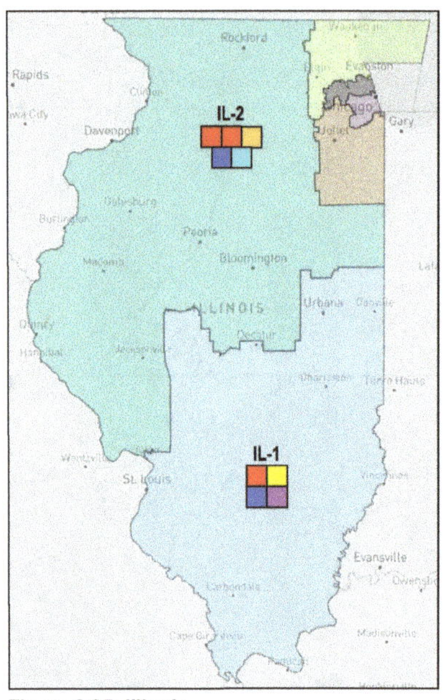

Figure 8.95: Illinois

IL-2 (Bloomington, Rockford), comprise the geographic majority of the state. IL-1 would likely elect 1 Republican, 1 Democrat, and 1 Libertarian, with the 4th seat competitive between the Republicans and Democrats. IL-2 would likely elect 2 Democrats and 1 Republican, with Progressives competing against Democrats for the 4th seat and Libertarians competing against Republicans for the 5th seat.

Illinois' population is concentrated in the Chicago metro area, which is divided into 4 districts. The current gerrymandering is particularly egregious in this part of the state. Because I based this map of existing state legislative districts, some of that gerrymandering filtered into this map, as seen in the oddly shaped boundaries between Aurora and downtown Chicago. If and when Illinois adopts multimember districts, these lines should be redrawn so as to completely ungerrymander them.

All 4 Chicago metro districts would have Democratic majorities. The most moderate of these districts, five-member IL-3 (Waukegan, Aurora), would likely elect 2 Democrats and 1 Republican, with Progressives competing against Democrats for the 4th seat and Libertarians competing against Republicans for the 5th seat. Republicans would also win 1 seat in IL-4 (north Chicago) and 1 seat in IL-5 (Joliet). IL-4 would also elect 2 Democrats and 1 Progressive, while IL-5 would elect 1 Democrat and 1 Progressive, with the 4th seat in IL-5 competitive between the Democrats and Republicans. In the most liberal district, four-member IL-6 (Chicago), Republicans are projected to have 19.7% of the vote, just under the 20% electoral threshold, meaning they would have to compete to win 1 seat. Still, this is a better outcome for Chicago conservatives than the current gerrymandered system. IL-6 would likely elect 1 Democrat and 1 Progressive, with the final seat competitive between the Democrats and Progressives.

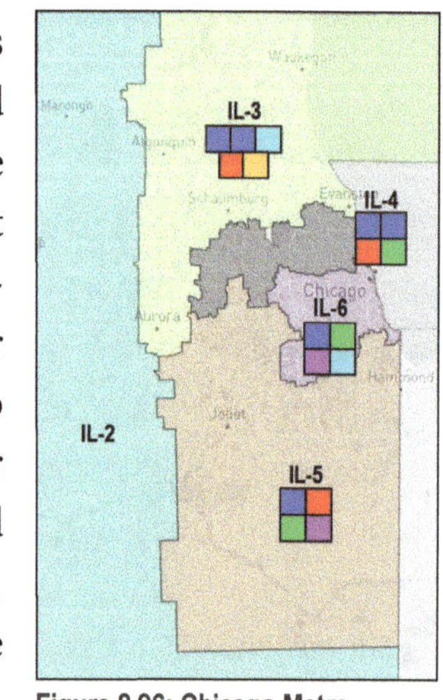

Figure 8.96: Chicago Metro

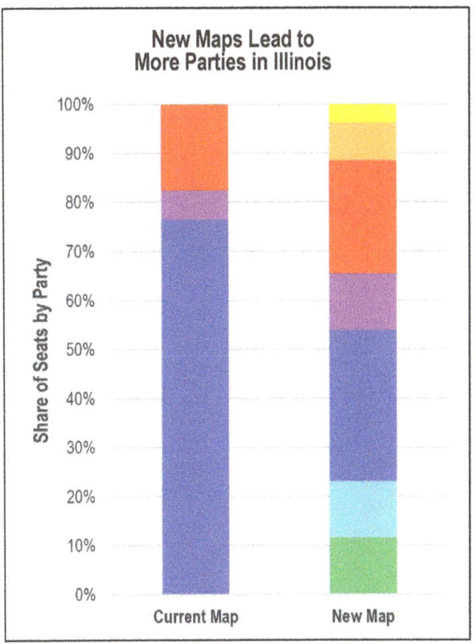

Figure 8.97

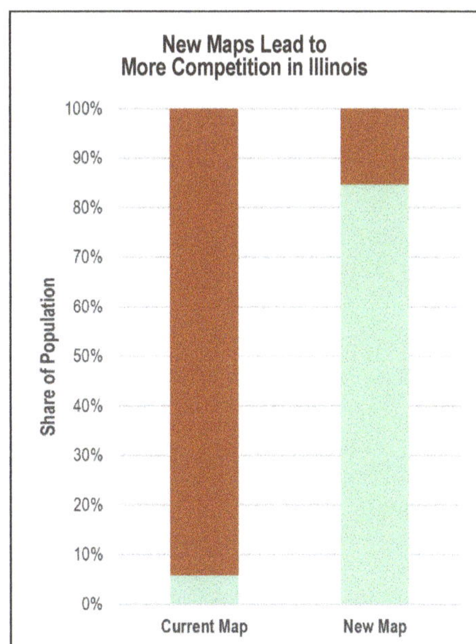

Figure 8.98

Another way to divide Illinois' 26 representatives would be into 1 four-member district, 2 five-member districts, and 2 six-member districts. This could be achieved by combining the Chicago districts IL-4, IL-5, and IL-6 into 2 districts of 6 members each. Republicans would be guaranteed at least 1 seat in both districts due to the low electoral threshold of 14% to win 1 seat. Progressives would win 1 or 2 seats in both districts, or perhaps face competition from another, yet-unknown alternative party. In a diverse metropolis like Chicago, new political factions would almost certainly develop.

Table 8.39: Illinois

	Population	Dem %	Rep %	Seats	P Safe	P or D	D Safe	D or R	R Safe	R or L	L Safe
Statewide	12,809,545	55.5%	39.9%	26	3	3	8	3	6	2	1
IL-1	1,971,207	39.5%	56.1%	4	0	0	1	1	1	0	1
IL-2	2,463,747	40.7%	54.3%	5	0	1	1	0	2	1	0
IL-3	2,463,667	56.2%	39.6%	5	0	1	2	0	1	1	0
IL-4	1,969,555	68.4%	27.1%	4	1	0	2	0	1	0	0
IL-5	1,970,152	61.1%	34.2%	4	1	0	1	1	1	0	0
IL-6	1,971,217	75.4%	19.7%	4	1	1	1	1	0	0	0

G. Nine-District States

For much of American history, New York was the most populous state. Its population growth has stagnated in recent years and it is now the fourth most populous state with about 20 million residents. Conversely, Florida has grown rapidly over the last century and recently surpassed New York to become to third largest state with over 21 million residents.

In both states, multimember district maps would result in a massive increase in the number of voters voting in competitive districts. Additionally, multimember districts would reduce the dominance of the dominant political party, the Republicans in Florida and the Democrats in New York.

Table 8.40: Nine-District States - Current Representation

State	Population	Partisan Lean		Projected Seats (Sept. 2023 Cooks Report)			
		Democratic	Republican	Total	Democratic	Republican	Competitive
Florida	21,538,187	47.5%	50.7%	28	8	19	1
New York	20,201,249	63.3%	34.4%	26	14	6	6

i. Florida (45 Seats)

Florida is a purple state that has trended more Republican in recent years. It currently sends 20 Republicans and just 8 Democrats to Congress. Only 1 of Florida's 28 congressional districts is competitive heading into the 2024 election.

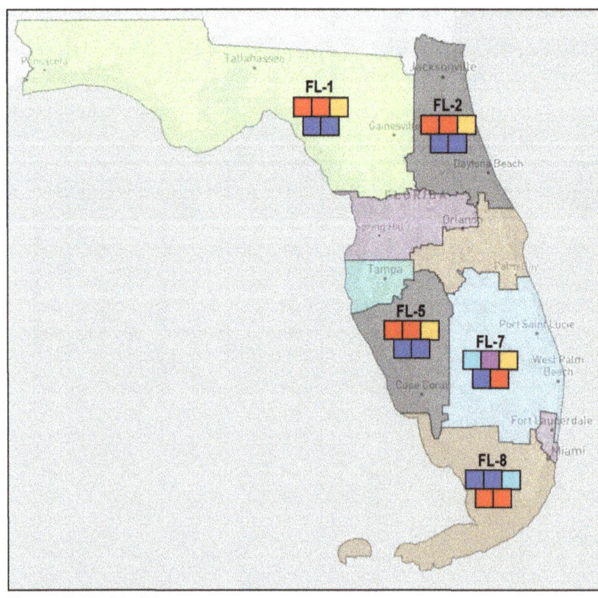

Figure 8.99: Florida

With this multimember district map, all 9 districts would elect five members and all 9 districts would be competitive. Every district would elect at least 1 Republican and 1 Democrat. In total, Florida could elect a delegation of 19 Republicans, 19 Democrats, 4 Libertarians, and 3 Progressives.

In 8 of the 9 districts, the majority party is projected to have less than 60% of the vote. The one exception

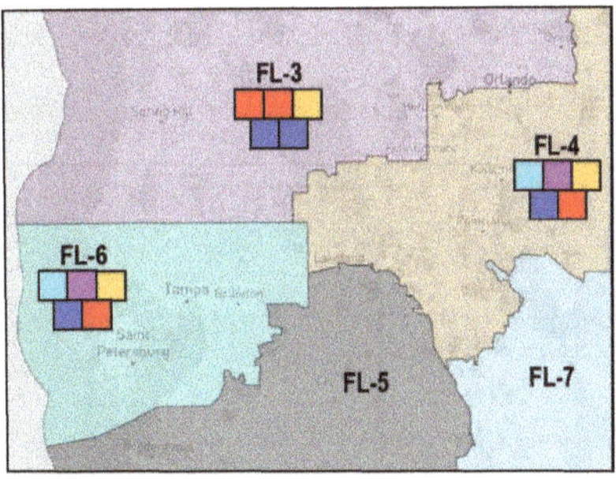

Figure 8.100: Tampa Bay and Orlando

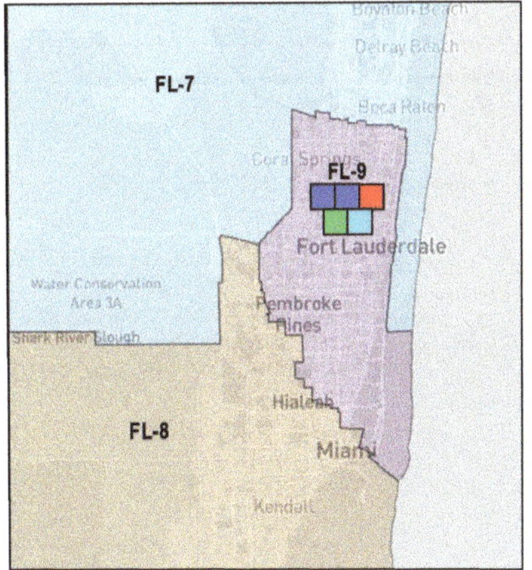

Figure 8.101: Miami Metro

is FL-9 (Miami), where, in a two-party system, the Democratic Party is projected to have a 69% majority. In FL-9, the Progressives would likely win 1 seat safely and could compete for a second seat. Republicans could be competitive for a 2nd seat if a landslide election went in their favor. Republicans could face competition from the Libertarians in 7 districts, especially districts in which they would have at least a 55% majority in a two-party system: FL-1 (Tallahassee), FL-2 (Jacksonville), FL-3 (Spring Hill, north Orlando), and FL-5 (Cape Coral, Bowling Green). In each of these 4 districts, Democrats would likely win 2 seats. The Democratic Party is projected to have a majority in 4 districts, as well, though no majority would be greater than 52%. Progressives could be expected to compete in each of these four districts: FL-4 (south Orlando, Melbourne), FL-6 (Tampa Bay), FL-7 (Port Santa Lucia,

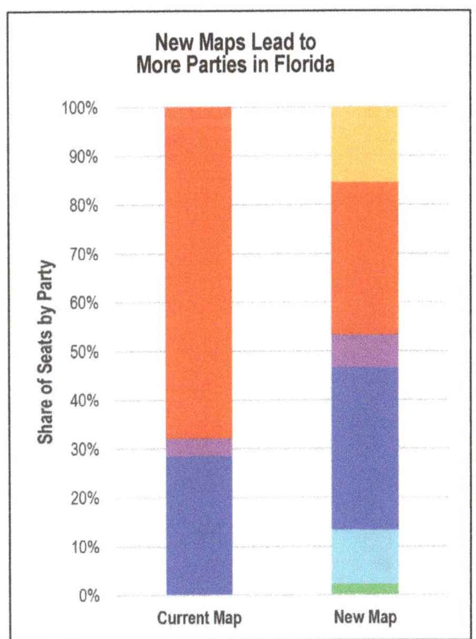

Figure 8.102

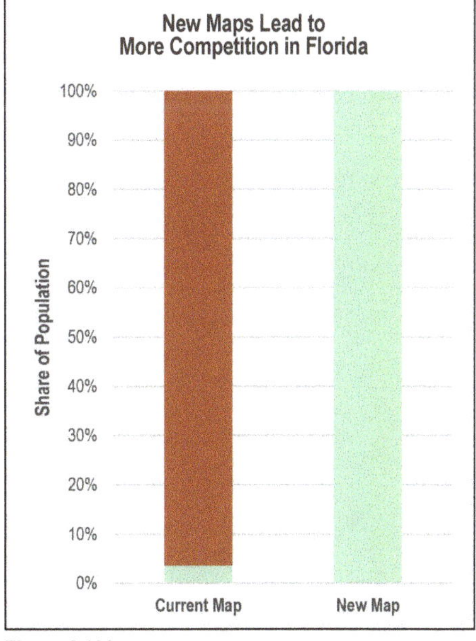

Figure 8.103

West Palm Beach), and FL-8 (Florida Keys, south Miami metro). Further, the Democrats and Republicans would compete against each other in FL-4, FL-6, and FL-7.

Table 8.41: Florida

	Population	Dem %	Rep %	Seats	P Safe	P or D	D Safe	D or R	R Safe	R or L	L Safe
Statewide	*21,538,187*	*47.5%*	*50.7%*	*45*	*1*	*5*	*15*	*3*	*14*	*7*	*0*
FL-1	2,393,099	38.4%	59.8%	5	0	0	2	0	2	1	0
FL-2	2,392,656	40.3%	57.8%	5	0	0	2	0	2	1	0
FL-3	2,392,731	42.8%	55.0%	5	0	0	2	0	2	1	0
FL-4	2,392,960	49.9%	48.0%	5	0	1	1	1	1	1	0
FL-5	2,392,609	38.5%	59.8%	5	0	0	2	0	2	1	0
FL-6	2,394,037	50.2%	47.6%	5	0	1	1	1	1	1	0
FL-7	2,393,622	50.4%	48.4%	5	0	1	1	1	1	1	0
FL-8	2,393,950	52.4%	46.4%	5	0	1	2	0	2	0	0
FL-9	2,392,523	69.2%	29.8%	5	1	1	2	0	1	0	0

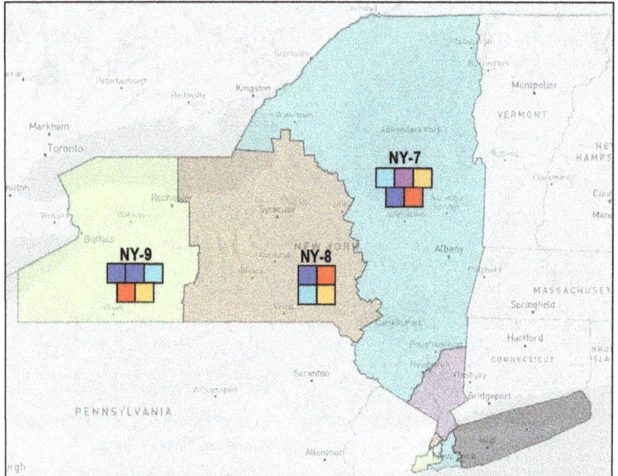

Figure 8.104: New York State

ii. New York (42 Seats)

New York is a mostly Democratic state due to the overwhelming Democratic majority in and around New York City. New York currently sends 15 Democrats and 11 Republicans to Congress, and six districts are rated competitive heading into 2024.

With this multimember map, 90% of New Yorkers would live in a competitive district, and New York could elect a delegation of 8 Progressives, 22 Democrats, 10 Republicans, and 2 Libertarians.

(The data upon which my analysis is based likely overestimates the Democratic vote because it does not consider the 2022

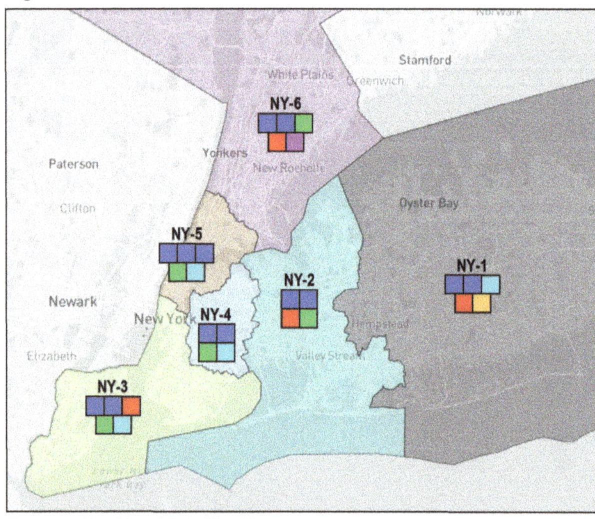

Figure 8.105: New York City Metro

midterms, which in New York were a **red wave relative**[71] to the rest of the country.)

Upstate New York would be divided into three districts with slight Democratic majorities: NY-7 (Albany, northeast upstate), NY-8 (Syracuse, central upstate), and NY-9 (Buffalo, Rochester). Each district would be competitive for the Progressives and the Libertarians, and would elect at least 1 Democrat and 1 Republican. All three districts could plausibly elect representatives from 4 different parties.

The New York City metro area is divided into six districts. New York City would be divided into four districts with overwhelming Democratic majorities ranging from 70% to 88%: NY-2 (Queens), NY-3 (Staten Island, Brooklyn), NY-4 (Brooklyn, Queens), and NY-5 (Manhattan, the Bronx). Republicans would likely only win

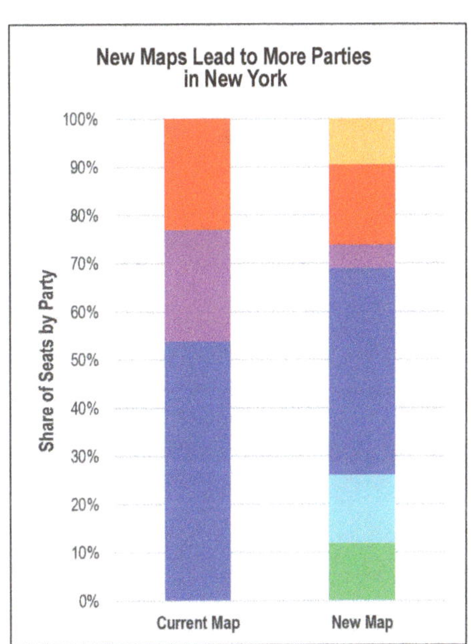

Figure 8.106

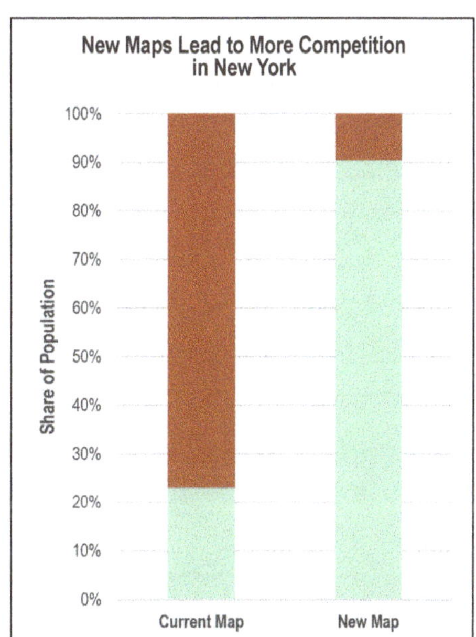

Figure 8.107

Table 8.42: New York

	Population	Dem %	Rep %	Seats	P Safe	P or D	D Safe	D or R	R Safe	R or L	L Safe
Statewide	*20,201,249*	*63.3%*	*34.4%*	*42*	*5*	*7*	*17*	*2*	*7*	*4*	*0*
NY-1	2,405,104	53.1%	45.3%	5	0	1	2	0	1	1	0
NY-2	1,923,911	71.6%	27.0%	4	1	0	2	0	1	0	0
NY-3	2,404,903	70.1%	27.8%	5	1	1	2	0	1	0	0
NY-4	1,923,893	86.6%	11.2%	4	1	1	2	0	0	0	0
NY-5	2,404,981	88.1%	9.8%	5	1	1	3	0	0	0	0
NY-6	2,405,153	66.7%	31.5%	5	1	0	2	1	1	0	0
NY-7	2,404,847	51.5%	45.3%	5	0	1	1	1	1	1	0
NY-8	1,924,183	49.9%	46.6%	4	0	1	1	0	1	1	0
NY-9	2,404,274	52.5%	44.7%	5	0	1	2	0	1	1	0

seats in NY-2 and NY-3. This is similar to the current system in which there is only one elected Republican from New York City, Rep. Malliotakis of Staten Island. Because of multimember districts, New York City would become a battleground between Democrats and Progressives. Progressives would win at least one seat in each of the four districts and could compete for a 2nd seat in NY-3, NY-4, and NY-5.

The NYC metro districts of NY-6 (the Bronx, Yonkers) and NY-1 (Long Island) would also be competitive. Libertarians, or another conservative party, could compete for a seat in NY-1. Progressives would likely win a seat in NY-6 and could be competitive in NY-1.

New York's 42 representatives could also be evenly divided into 7 six-member districts, or a combination of 1 four-member district, 4 five-member districts, and 3 six-member districts.

H. Twelve-District State: Texas (60 Seats)

Table 8.43: Texas Current Representation

State	Population	Partisan Lean		Projected Seats (Sept. 2023 Cooks Report)			
		Democratic	Republican	Total	Democratic	Republican	Competitive
Texas	29,145,505	45.2%	52.6%	38	12	25	1

Texas has 29 million people, four major metropolitan areas, and an economy so large that if it were an independent country it would rank as the 8th largest economy[72] in the world by GDP, larger than Brazil, Canada, or Russia. Its political diversity is masked due

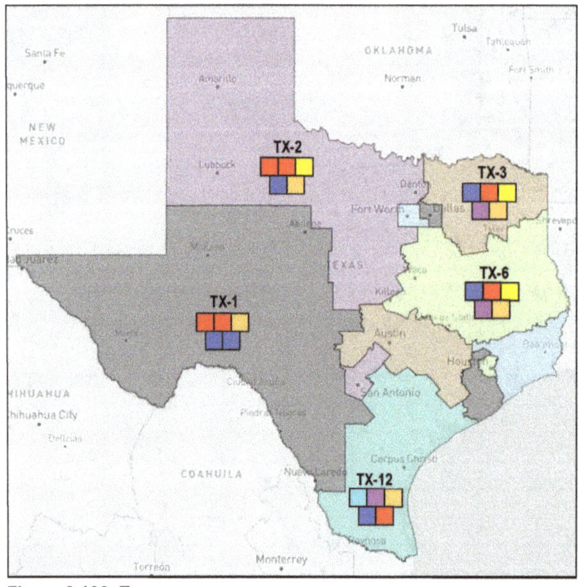

Figure 8.108: Texas

to its status as one of the most gerrymandered states under the current system: only 1 district out of Texas's 38 is competitive heading into 2024. Texas sends 25 Republicans and 13 Democrats to Congress, despite Democrats making up about 45% of voters statewide.

This multimember map ungerrymanders Texas and would seat representatives that span the gamut of Texas's political diversity. Because

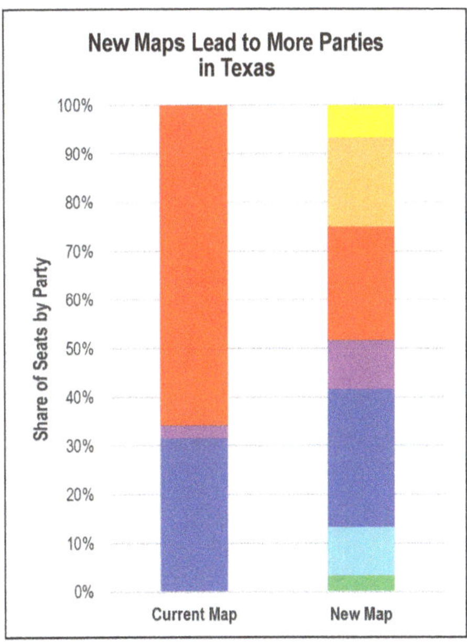

Figure 8.109

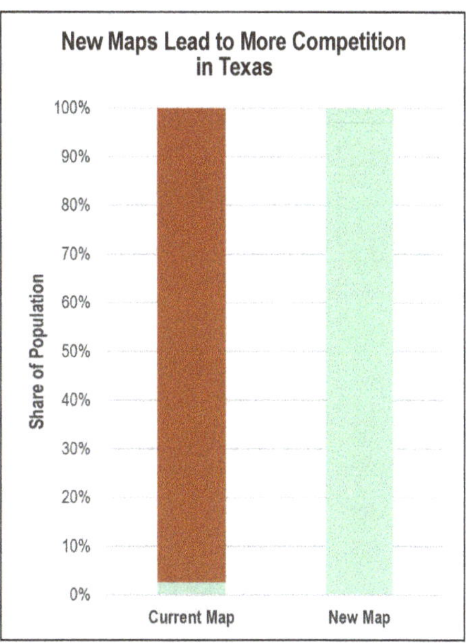

Figure 8.110

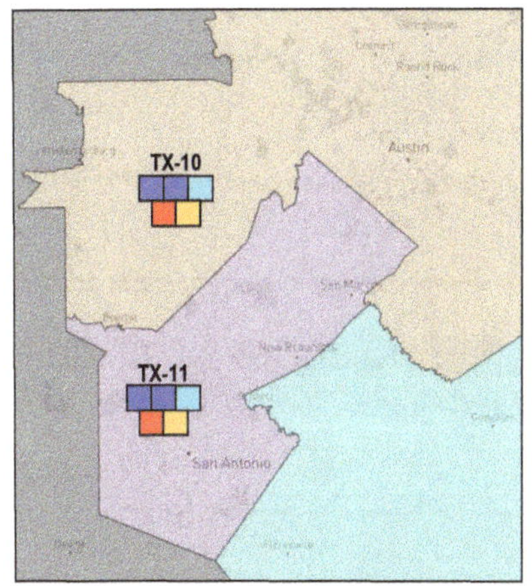

Figure 8.111: San Antonio and Austin

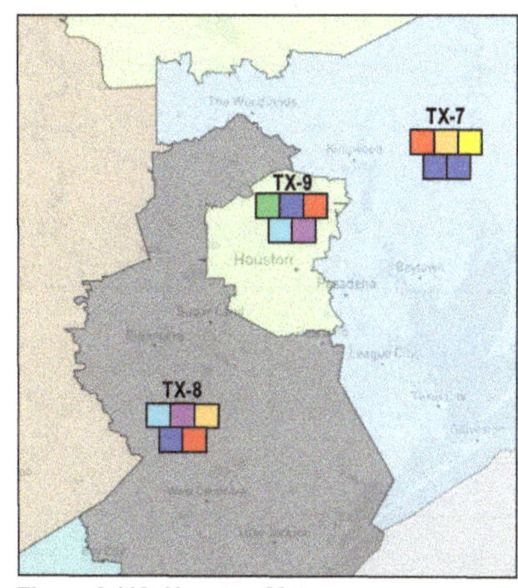

Figure 8.112: Houston Metro

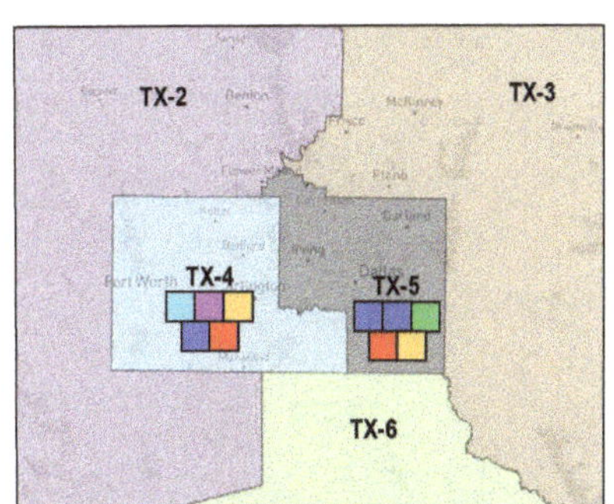

Figure 8.113: Dallas and Fort Worth

all 12 of Texas's districts have 5 seats, I project that all twelve districts would be competitive between parties. Electing rural Texas Democrats and urban Texas Republicans would go far to bridge the ideological divide.

In total, Texas could plausibly elect a congressional delegation of 23 Republicans, 23 Democrats, 9 Libertarians, and 5 Progressives.

Table 8.44: Texas

	Population	Dem %	Rep %	Seats	P Safe	P or D	D Safe	D or R	R Safe	R or L	L Safe
Statewide	*29,145,505*	*45.2%*	*52.6%*	*60*	*2*	*6*	*17*	*6*	*14*	*11*	*4*
TX-1	2,430,525	43.7%	54.1%	5	0	0	2	0	2	1	0
TX-2	2,426,250	24.8%	73.3%	5	0	0	1	0	2	1	1
TX-3	2,428,723	34.2%	63.8%	5	0	0	1	1	1	1	1
TX-4	2,430,224	50.9%	46.9%	5	0	1	1	1	1	1	0
TX-5	2,430,957	60.0%	37.8%	5	1	0	2	0	1	1	0
TX-6	2,428,894	29.7%	68.4%	5	0	0	1	1	1	1	1
TX-7	2,427,775	36.7%	61.4%	5	0	0	2	0	1	1	1
TX-8	2,428,197	46.2%	51.9%	5	0	1	1	1	1	1	0
TX-9	2,428,490	65.8%	32.2%	5	1	1	1	1	1	0	0
TX-10	2,428,317	55.5%	41.7%	5	0	1	2	0	1	1	0
TX-11	2,429,046	52.7%	44.8%	5	0	1	2	0	1	1	0
TX-12	2,428,107	48.1%	50.1%	5	0	1	1	1	1	1	0

The Republican Party could be challenged by a Libertarian Party in 11 of the 12 districts, the only exception being the Democratic stronghold of TX-9 (Houston). But even there, a Libertarian candidate could try their luck and perhaps capture the mere 17% of the vote needed to win one seat. Libertarian candidates would likely safely win one seat and could compete for a 2nd seat in TX-2 (Lubbock, north Texas), TX-3 (northeast Texas), TX-6 (Waco, Longview), and TX-7 (Beaumont, east Houston metro). In total, a Libertarian Party could compete for 15 of Texas' 60 seats and turn Texas into a true three-party state.

From the left, the Democratic Party could be challenged by a Progressive Party in seven districts, mostly centered around Texas's major cities. Progressives could safely win one seat in TX-5 (Dallas) and safely win one and compete for a 2nd seat in TX-9. In three districts, voters could plausibly elect one candidate from four different parties: TX-4 (Fort Worth), TX-8 (west and south Houston metro), and TX-12 (Corpus Christi, Reynosa).

I. Seventeen-District State: California (82 Seats)

California is by far the largest state, with nearly 40 million residents. If it were its own country, it would rank as the 5th largest economy[73] in the world by GDP, ahead of India and the United Kingdom.

Yet despite its large population and diverse economy, in 2023 California is practically a one-party state. California sent 40 Democrats and just 12 Republicans to Congress following the 2022 midterms. Multimember districts would increase Republican

Table 8.45: California Current Representation

State	Population	Partisan Lean		Projected Seats (Sept. 2023 Cooks Report)			
		Democratic	Republican	Total	Democratic	Republican	Competitive
California	39,523,437	63.0%	35.1%	52	39	7	6

representation in California to roughly the equivalent proportion of Republican voters. The Republican Party would become competitive across the state, not just in its current rural strongholds. Additionally, the Democratic Party could be challenged by a Progressive Party for 22 seats, 9 of which are safe for the Progressives. In total, California could plausibly elect a delegation of 40 Democrats, 24 Republicans, 15 Progressives, and 3 Libertarians.

Republicans would safely win at least one seat in fifteen of the seventeen districts. Yet even in the two ultra-liberal districts CA-5 (San Francisco) and CA-15 (Santa Monica), the Republican Party would be competitive

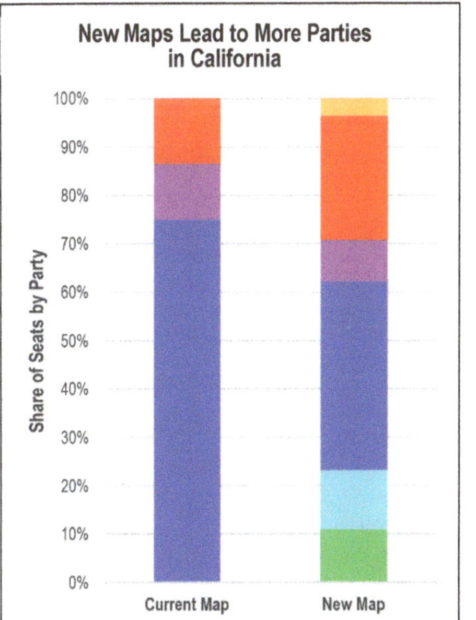

Figure 8.114: California

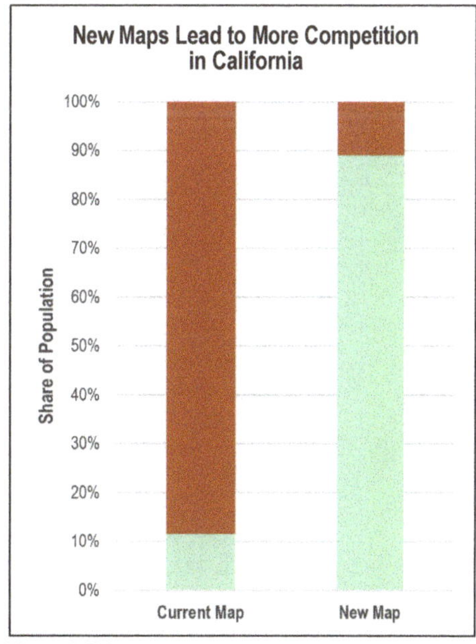

Figure 8.115

Figure 8.116

because they would need only 17% of the vote to win a seat. Republicans are projected at 18.2% of the vote in CA-5 and 17.0% of the vote in CA-15. Having conservative representation across the state, including in these overwhelmingly liberal areas, would add much needed ideological and geographic diversity to Congress.

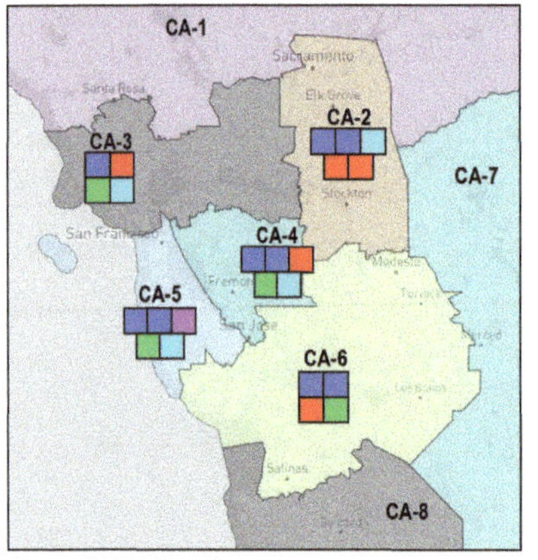

Figure 8.117: Bay Area

The rural districts of CA-1 (Northern California), CA-7 (Fresno), and CA-9 (Rural Southern California) would elect Democrats, Republicans, and possibly Libertarians. Republicans make up between 47% and 53% of each district. In a two-party system, Republicans would either win 2 or 3 seats. However, a Libertarian Party could challenge Republicans from the right in all 3 districts, and the Democratic Party would challenge the Republicans from the left. Progressives could challenge Democrats even in these rural districts. Needing only 17% of the vote to win a seat, all three of these districts could plausibly elect one member from 4 different parties!

A left-wing competitor to the Democratic Party would certainly emerge with five-member districts. A

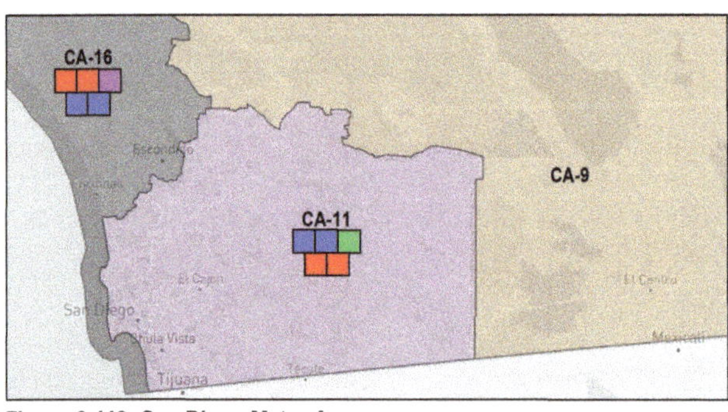

Figure 8.118: Los Angeles Metro

Figure 8.119: San Diego Metro Area

Progressive Party could safely win 17% of the vote to win 1 seat in districts like CA-3 (North Bay), CA-4 (Oakland), CA-5, CA-6 (San Jose metro), CA-10 (Santa Clarita, Burbank), CA-11 (San Diego metro), CA-14 (Los Angeles), CA-15, and CA-17 (Long

Beach). Further, Progressives could plausibly compete for 34% of the vote and a second seat in 7 districts: CA-3, CA-4, CA-5, CA-10, CA-14, CA-15, and CA-17. California could go from a one-party state under the current system to a true three-party state under this new system.

At a minimum, 15 of the 17 districts would be competitive. That means 35.2 million Californians (89%) would live in a competitive district, a massive improvement over the current 4.6 million Californians living in 6 competitive districts heading into 2024. The 2 districts that would not be competitive, CA-6 and CA-11, would still break the two-party system as they would likely safely elect Progressives.

Table 8.46: California

	Population	Dem %	Rep %	Seats	P Safe	P or D	D Safe	D or R	R Safe	R or L	L Safe
Statewide	39,523,437	63.0%	35.1%	82	9	13	29	7	21	3	0
CA-1	2,409,997	50.4%	47.4%	5	0	1	1	1	1	1	0
CA-2	2,409,758	58.8%	39.2%	5	0	1	2	0	2	0	0
CA-3	1,928,211	73.1%	25.0%	4	1	1	1	0	1	0	0
CA-4	2,409,325	76.0%	22.1%	5	1	1	2	0	1	0	0
CA-5	2,409,115	80.0%	18.2%	5	1	1	2	1	0	0	0
CA-6	1,927,987	64.8%	33.2%	4	1	0	2	0	1	0	0
CA-7	2,410,343	45.6%	52.8%	5	0	1	1	0	2	1	0
CA-8	1,928,566	59.3%	38.7%	4	0	0	2	1	1	0	0
CA-9	2,409,819	50.0%	48.3%	5	0	1	1	1	1	1	0
CA-10	2,409,605	66.7%	31.4%	5	1	1	1	1	1	0	0
CA-11	2,410,361	60.6%	37.3%	5	1	0	2	0	2	0	0
CA-12	2,409,038	54.4%	43.6%	5	0	1	2	0	2	0	0
CA-13	2,410,350	58.7%	39.4%	5	0	1	2	0	2	0	0
CA-14	2,410,649	70.9%	27.2%	5	1	1	2	0	1	0	0
CA-15	2,409,682	81.4%	17.0%	5	1	1	2	1	0	0	0
CA-16	2,410,037	47.0%	51.0%	5	0	0	2	1	2	0	0
CA-17	2,410,594	71.2%	26.8%	5	1	1	2	0	1	0	0

Chapter 9

STRENGTHEN THE CHECKS ON EXECUTIVE POWER

The modern Executive Branch has too much power. This is a function of a massive bureaucracy, the celebrity worship nature of our culture, authority the Executive has been assigned by the text of the Constitution and de facto claimed in response to the dysfunction of the Legislative Branch, and a pliant and partisan Supreme Court.

John Dickerson's excellent May 2018 *Atlantic* cover story[74] diagnoses the modern problems and proposes various ideas for reform. Dickerson writes, "If Trump were a less divisive figure, we might . . . consider that what looks like incompetence or impertinence on the part of the officeholder could also be evidence that the office itself is broken."

From my perspective, this issue is far larger than any one President, presidential candidate, or political party. Yet it is also made urgent by the authoritarian danger posed by Donald Trump.

A. Impeach the President with a 60% Majority in Congress

I find it difficult to separate my constitutional arguments in this section from my emotional arguments, fueled by my intense anti-Trump partisanship. Permit me one paragraph of emotional outburst.

For his high crimes and misdemeanors committed as President, in public and in private, Donald Trump should have been impeached, convicted, and removed from office—twice! The evidence was indisputable and overwhelming, and, in the case of his second impeachment, his high crimes took place in full view of the public. His acquittals were a travesty of justice and a mockery of the Constitution.

Yet, he was not impeached. Why? Because the Constitution requires a 2/3 majority in the Senate to convict and remove the President from power. This requirement makes it possible for a hyper-partisan 34 Senator minority, representing as few as 7.5% of Americans, to prevent Congress from checking the power of an out-of-control or criminal President. No President has ever been removed from office through impeachment. (Two Presidents were almost impeached: Andrew Johnson came within one vote of being convicted by the Senate in 1868, and Richard Nixon resigned before impeachment proceedings could begin in 1974 because several key Republican Senators had publicly turned against him.)

A check that is impossible to exercise, practically speaking, is a toothless check. Impeachment under the current rules is a useless check.

We should make impeachment easy enough so it may be a real threat that Congress can use to keep the President in line. That means making the impeachment threshold low enough that a hyperpartisan minority may not keep an obviously criminal President in power.

Yet, at the same time, we must make it hard enough that a single party in Congress might not simply impeach a President of a different party due to a policy disagreement.

We should strive to strike a balance between the Legislative and the Executive Branches. Both branches represent the will of the people.

In *Parliamentary America,* Stearns proposed a 60% threshold for a successful vote of no confidence. While the system proposed here is not a parliamentary system, I agree with Stearns' threshold. A 60% majority is a reasonable threshold for a newly unicameral Congress to impeach, convict, and remove from power the President. This is a middle ground between a 50% threshold, which would give too much power to the Legislative Branch, and a 2/3 threshold, which makes it too difficult for the Legislative to exercise its power. In a 695-member Congress, the 60% threshold would be reached when 417 members had voted in favor of impeachment.

Table 9.1: Impeachment Threshold Comparison

	Current System	Proposed System
Conviction Requirement	67 of 100 Senators	417 of 695 Representatives
Acquittal Requirement	34 of 100 Senators	279 of 695 Representatives
Minimum Pop. Represented by Successful Vote to Convict	101,485,604	197,850,300
Minimum Pop. Represented by Successful Vote to Acquit	24,626,744	131,375,124
Minimum Pop. Successful Conviction Percentage	30.7%	59.1%
Minimum Pop. Successful Acquittal Percentage	7.4%	39.2%

Because the newly unicameral Congress would have nearly equal represesentation for all people, the minimum number of people represented by a successful 60% majority conviction would be 198 million Americans, or 59% of the population. (Calculated by summing the populations of the least populous districts until the threshold of 417 representatives for conviction or 279 representatives for acquittal was reached.)

A 60% majority means the inverse power for the minority: 40% of Congress, elected by and representing at minimum 39.2% of Americans in the newly proportional and representative Congress, would have the power to prevent impeachment. This seems like a reasonable balance between needing to make impeachment easier while ensuring that it remains a high threshold, unlikely to be reached without widespread support across the political spectrum. For a single party to block impeachment of an unpopular and dangerous President, they would need to win more than 40% of the seats in Congress, a very high bar in a multiparty system.

Reasonable people can disagree on what the precise threshold for impeachment should be. But the threshold must be low enough that it can serve as the final stop to prevent an authoritarian President and party from destroying American democracy. At the very least, a 60% threshold in a representative unicameral legislature would be a massive improvement over the current system.

## Chapter 10

ELECT THE PRESIDENT BY RANKED CHOICE POPULAR VOTE

Our government derives its power from the consent of the governed. But twice in the last 25 years has the will of American voters been ignored, usurped, dismissed. It could well happen again in 2024. This is government without the consent of the governed.

Stearns argues that giving the newly elected Congress the power to choose the President will reduce the likelihood of two-party factionalism. I discussed this argument in Chapter 6, and while I am not convined this outweighs the value of allowing the people a direct vote for the highest office in the land, this merits further debate.

Here, I make the argument for electing the President by ranked choice vote.

A. Eliminate the Electoral College

The Electoral College is a morally illegitimate way of choosing the President. A political system in which the person who receives the most votes does not win the election is an illegitimate system. A candidate that wins the Electoral College without the popular vote is only legitimate according to rules that are themselves illegitimate.

The Electoral College produces absurd outcomes. Everyone knows the story of how Al Gore won the popular vote by 500,000 but lost the presidency in 2000 or how Hillary Clinton won the popular vote by 3 million but lost the presidency in 2016 (Table 10.1). Lesser known is how the Electoral College almost proclaimed John Kerry the winner in 2004. In 2004, George W. Bush received 62 million votes (50.7%) while John Kerry received 59 million (48.3%). Bush won the presidency by winning 286 Electoral College votes compared to Kerry's 251 Electoral College votes. But Kerry was just 118,601 votes (2.1%) short of victory in the populous swing state Ohio (Table 10.2). Had the results in Ohio been slightly different, Kerry would have won the Electoral College, and therefore the presidency, despite Bush receiving more than 50% of the popular vote.

Table 10.1: Electoral Results of Coin Flip Elections

Election	Candidate	Electoral College Votes	Popular Votes	Popular Vote Share
2000	George W. Bush	271	50,456,002	47.9%
	Al Gore	266	50,999,897	48.4%
2004	George W. Bush	286	62,040,610	50.7%
	John Kerry	251	59,028,444	48.3%
2016	Donald Trump	304	62,984,828	46.1%
	Hillary Clinton	227	65,853,514	48.2%
2020	Joseph Biden	306	81,283,501	51.3%
	Donald Trump	232	74,223,975	46.8%

What a tragic flip of the coin. Had the Electoral College awarded the presidency to the popular vote runner up in two consecutive elections, first to the Republican nominee and then to the Democratic nominee, perhaps reform could have happened. After all, both parties would have benefitted and suffered from the absurd system. There could have been bipartisan support for reform. But this did not happen. Instead, views on the Electoral College became more partisan as Republicans rhetorically dug into supporting the morally indefensible Electoral College because they perceived it as improving their electoral chances.

The Electoral College almost proclaimed the wrong candidate the winner in 2020. While Joe Biden won the popular vote by 7 million votes, the Electoral College was decided by just a few thousand votes across four states. (Table 10.2). Had 123,473 people across four states had switched their vote from Biden to Trump, Trump would have won the Electoral College and won reelection despite losing the popular vote by 7 million votes. To put that in perspective, that is more votes than the entire population of Tennessee! In this scenario, Biden would have won a clear majority, over 51% of the vote, yet lost to a candidate who received 47% of the vote.

Table 10.2: Popular Votes Necessary to Change Electoral College Outcomes

Election	Key States	Margin of Victory	Electoral College Votes
2000	Florida	537	25
2004	Ohio	118,601	20
2016	Michigan	10,704	16
	Wisconsin	22,748	10
	Pennsylvania	44,292	20
2020	Arizona	10,457	11
	Georgia	11,779	16
	Wisconsin	20,682	10
	Pennsylvania	80,555	20

Due to the arcane rules of the Electoral College and coincidental electoral math, there would have been an Electoral College tie (269 Biden–269 Trump) if just 42,918 votes had instead gone to Trump in Arizona, Georgia, and Wisconsin. In the event of a tie, the presidential election would be decided by the newly elected House of Representatives, with each state's delegation receiving **one vote**.[75] Following the 2020 elections, Republicans held a majority of the seats in 27 states, Democrats held a majority of seats in 20 states, and 3 states were **equally divided**.[76] This means that an Electoral College tie in 2020 would have resulted in a Donald Trump victory.

It is a near certainty that had the House of Representatives chosen chosen Donald Trump as the victor after he lost the popular vote to the Democratic nominee by 7 million, there would have been political chaos.

Table 10.3: Electoral Outcomes are Disconnected from Popular Vote

Election	Electoral College Winner	Popular vote margin of victory	Votes to change Electoral College outcome
2000	George W. Bush	-543,895	537
2004	George W. Bush	3,012,166	118,601
2016	Donald Trump	-2,868,686	77,744
2020	Joseph Biden	7,059,526	123,473

Simply put, the Electoral College increases the likelihood of a disputed Presidency. In 2024, it is plausible for Donald Trump to lose the popular vote a third time but win the Electoral College a second time.

How would people react? How would you react? Would you accept such an outcome as legitimate? Would the governors and legislatures of majority Democratic states accept an outcome that devalues the votes of their constituents?

I can only speak for myself: I would be in the streets protesting such an outcome. I do not consent to the Electoral College. Why should I? Why should any of us? Only a person who wins the popular vote, meaning someone who is preferred by a majority of Americans as determined by their votes, should be considered the legitimately elected President of the United States.

B. How Electing the President by Ranked Choice Popular Vote Would Work

We should elect the President by a ranked choice popular vote. This solution is simple and fair. The entire country would function as a 330 million-person, single-member district. With ranked choice voting, Americans could confidently vote for an alternative party candidate, or an independent, with the knowledge that if and when their candidate lost, their second- or third-choice vote for a major party candidate would still count.

For example, imagine a presidential election with candidates from a Social Democratic Party, a New Democratic Party, a Reform Conservative Party, and an America First Party. Quite a few New Democratic voters might prefer a Reform Conservative to a Social Democrat, while quite a few Reform Conservatives might prefer a New Democrat to an America First candidate. Even if centrist candidates come in third in the first round of the ranked choice instant run-off, they could still win.

Here is one example of how the ranked choice election results could look (Figure 10.1). In the first round, suppose the America First candidate takes first with 30% of the vote, followed by the Social Democratic candidate with 27%, the Reform Conservative candidate with 23%, and the New Democratic candidate with 20%. The New Democratic candidate is eliminated.

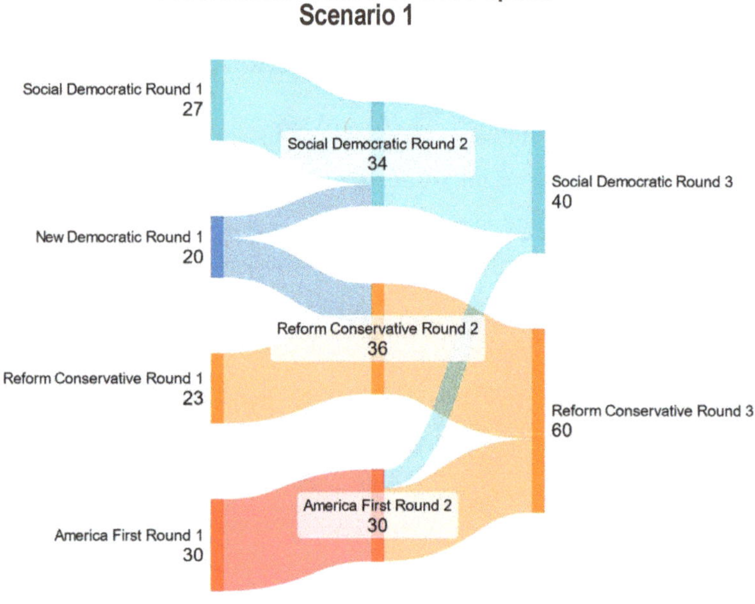

Figure 10.1: Made with **SankeyMATIC**

Suppose in the course of the campaign, the Reform Conservative candidate pledged to appoint a New Democrat as Secretary of State, one of the most powerful cabinet positions, as well as appointing New Democrats to at least two other cabinet positions. With this pledge, most New Democratic voters chose to rank the Reform Conservative second. With 65% of the ND vote going to the Reform Conservative and 35% going to the Social Democrat, the second-round results ended with following the second round, the Reform Conservative candidate jumped into the lead with 36% of the vote, followed by the Social Democrat with 34%. The America First candidate came in third with 30% of the vote and was eliminated.

In the final round, with 80% of America First voters preferring the Reform Conservative to the Social Democrat, the Reform Conservative candidate wins with 60% of the vote.

Yet there are myriad ways the ranked choice vote could unfold, particularly as more parties form, become competitive, and nominate candidates for President. Even with the same proportion of first-round votes, the second-round votes could break differently (Figure 10.2). What if the New Democratic second-choice votes went mostly in favor of the Social Democratic candidate instead? With 30% of New Democrats ranking the Reform Conservative candidate second, the Reform Conservative candidate would come in third with just 29% of the vote. In the third round, the America First candidate

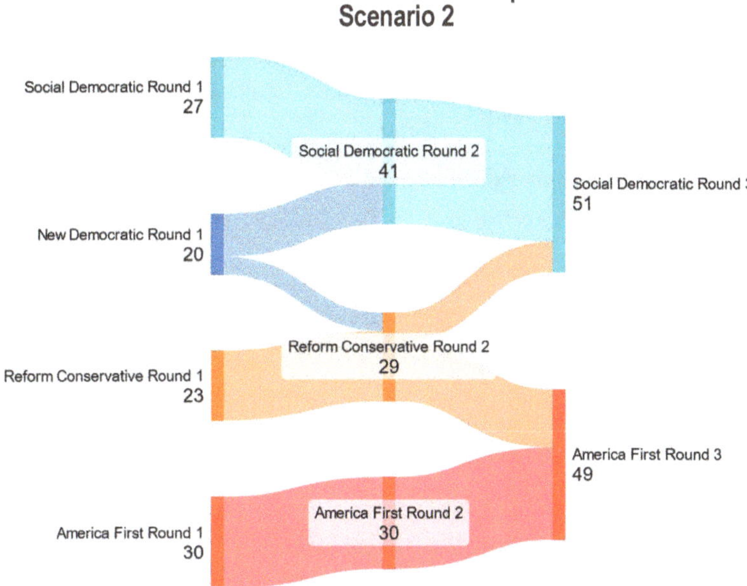

Figure 10.2: Made with **SankeyMATIC**

would need more than 67% of the Reform Conservative vote to win a majority. Such an outcome would be plausible. Equally plausible would be for all first-choice New Democratic second-choice Reform Conservative voters to rank the Social Democrat third. With those third-choice votes locked in for the Social Democrat, the Social Democratic candidate would need just 17% of the first-choice Reform Conservative voters to prefer the Social Democrat to the America First Candidate to win a majority. This is a plausible outcome, because a large number of Reform Conservatives might value the existence of a democratic government more than the policy outcome of an America First presidential victory. Equally plausible is that the Reform Conservative vote tilts the other way, and the America First candidate wins in the final round.

But this is all conjecture! People are complex! Parties might exist on multiple axes, so that the second and third choice of voters is far less predictable than the simple left-right axis scenarios above.

In a ranked choice popular vote, everyone's vote would count equally. Candidates would campaign truly across the entire country, not just the few battleground states that are today the target of billions of dollars of campaign advertising.

Most importantly, electing the President by a ranked choice popular vote reduces the likelihood of there being a disputed election. The popular vote would help safeguard the democratic necessity that is the peaceful transition of power.

Are there any good counterarguments in favor of keeping the Electoral College? The answer is no.

The argument that we should keep the Electoral College out of deference to the Framers is ridiculous. The argument that we should keep the Electoral College to ensure that small states have a say is similarly ridiculous, and I have addressed this same point in Chapter 4 regarding the Senate. Our government represents the people that comprise the states, not the states as separate entities. Electing the President by popular vote is such an obvious constitutional reform that all the arguments have been heard, debated, and analyzed. You can find that discussion elsewhere. Let's move on.

Chapter 11 shows a fully formed multiparty system. Refer to the multiparty color-coded legend to view the projected outcomes in each electoral district, indicated by the boxes below each district number.

For example, in district NY-5, the projection indicates that one representative will be elected from the following parties: New Democratic, Social Democratic, Green, Justice, and America First. And in Washington State's new 4ᵗʰ legislative district, the projection indicates that one representative will be elected from the following parties: Social Democratic, New Democratic, Green, America First, and Libertarian.

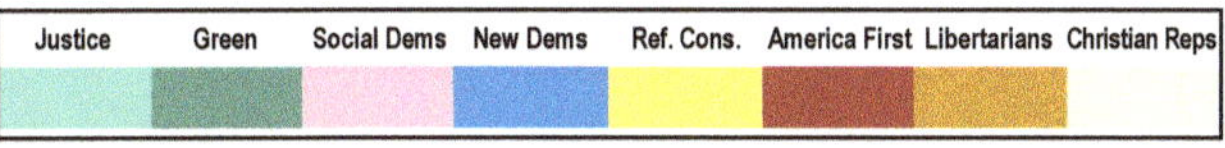

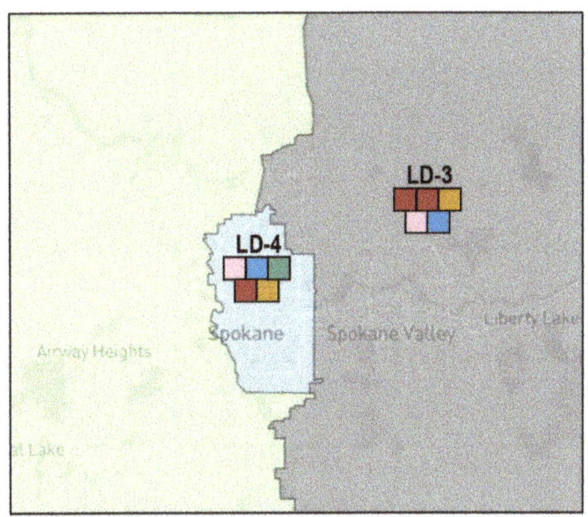

Example - Figure 11.7: Spokane, WA

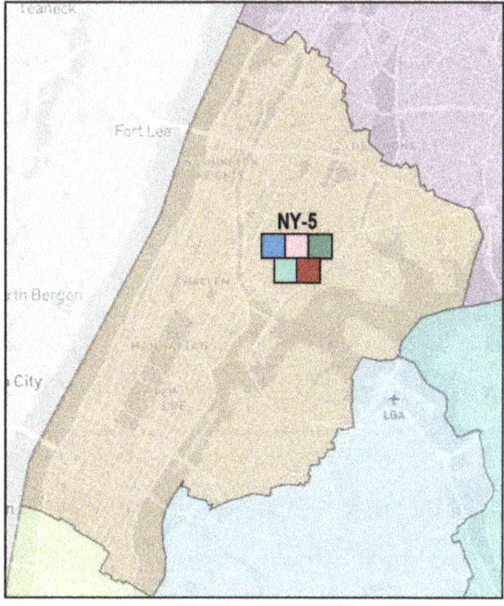

Example - Figure 11.9: New York's New Fifth District

NOTE: *The district's background color is for geographic boundary only. The colored boxes reflect the electoral projections. For example, while the geography of LD-4, Spokane, WA, is light blue, the boxes beneath the LD-4 label show how many seats each party is projected to win.*

Chapter 11

THE NEW POLITICS OF MULTIPARTY AMERICA

In 1860, when Abraham Lincoln became the Republican Party's nominee for President, he was not most Republican's first choice. In the first round of voting at the Republican Convention, Lincoln came in second place, well behind frontrunner (and future Secretary of State) William Seward. But while Seward secured a plurality of support, he failed to win an outright majority. Seward had alienated some of the more conservative members of the party with his (relatively) radical anti-slavery views. Lincoln, with his more moderate views, secured the support of a key delegation (Pennsylvania) as their second choice, and ended the second round of voting in a virtual tie with Seward. With momentum, the anti-Seward vote coalesced around Lincoln, and he comfortably **won the third round of voting.**[77]

Lincoln's victory at the Republican Convention of 1860 is illustrative. In multiparty America, Lincoln's strategy of aiming to be the second choice of the majority could become a dominant campaign strategy. Candidates and parties could find electoral success by seeking not just to be voters' first choice, but also their second or third choice. Negative campaigning, speaking ill of other candidates or parties, works well when there are only two options. But when there are multiple options, demonizing one party could easily result in that party's supporters ranking a different party as their second choice. The result could be electoral punishment for the offending party and electoral success for parties that, like Lincoln, avoid alienating swaths of the electorate.

In this chapter, I look at how an established multiparty system might function at three levels: state government, Congress, and the presidency. For this hypothetical, I use the multiparty system imagined by Lee Drutman and expanded upon by my own analysis. In this hypothetical, there are 8 parties, plus independents:

- **The Social Democrats,** a left-wing party emphasizing an expansive social welfare state;
- **The New Democrats,** a center-left party emphasizing big government investments in transformative environmental technology;

- **The Reform Conservatives,** a center-right party emphasizing growth and investment through tax benefits for families and community-based nonprofit organizations;
- **The Christian Republicans,** a conservative party emphasizing the role of faith and free markets;
- **The America First Party,** emphasizing right-wing culture-war policies;
- **The Libertarian Party,** a party opposed to big government, and emphasizing personal freedoms such as property rights and gun rights;
- **The Justice Party,** a party emphasizing social progress for people of color, and accommodating of differing economic and faith perspectives; and
- **The Greens,** a party emphasizing state takeover of fossil fuel industries to rapidly decarbonize.

What might a Presidential election look like in 2036, ten years after a Constitutional Convention? What about Congressional campaigns? Or campaigns for state and local office? What might be different, and what might stay the same?

A. Theory of Change

One of the first steps as new parties form will be politicians in office defecting from the existing two parties and announcing their new party identification. Experienced politicians, particularly those who are not in established leadership, may sense opportunity. Factions within and across the two parties already exist in Congress: the New Democrat Coalition,[78] the Progressive Caucus,[79] the Freedom Caucus,[80] the Problem Solvers Caucus.[81] Politicians within these factions may decide as a group that they could have more power as leaders of a new party than as mere members in the existing party.

There would also be opportunity for newer politicians, or first time candidates, to join new political parties at the ground level. In new political parties, there would be potential for upcoming politicians to achieve a level of authority which they might otherwise have to wait for years to achieve.

As the new parties form, with both established and new politicians filling their ranks and announcing their candidacies, voters would experience a campaign season both similar and different from anything in living memory.

There would be two primary differences. First, in the current system, primary elections are where voters are exposed to the most diverse candidates and political views. But primary elections have famously lower turnout than general elections, meaning that by the time most voters weigh in, their political options have been narrowed down to the chosen candidates of the two major parties. In a multiparty system, multiple parties would have legitimate electoral viability. Multiple parties would present their candidates to the general electorate. And the general electorate would be able to decide between a diverse slate of political parties and candidates.

Second, in the current system, candidates and parties spend tons of money and time slinging mud at the opposing candidate and party. In a two-party system, such tactics make sense: a vote against your opponent is effectively equivalent to a vote for you. In a multiparty system, this does not hold true. A vote against one of your opponents could well go toward a different opponent! In such a system, it is not enough to merely drag your opponent down. Instead, you must present a positive reason for voters to vote for you, such as a focus on a specific policy that makes your party different than the others.

Perhaps most importantly, you must appeal to your opponents' primary voters for their second- and third-choice votes. Insulting their preferred candidate or party is no way to endear yourself to such voters. In a multiparty system, voters would experience campaigns with less negative advertising and more coalition building.

As voters consider their options, they may engage in "coalition directed voting", or strategic voting. Voters will anticipate that the parties will engage in bargaining to form a governing coalition and vote accordingly. This could lead to more voters voting for candidates outside the two major parties. For example, a moderate conservative voter might rank the moderate conservative party first and the moderate liberal party second as a way to hedge against the influence of both the far left and the far right. Alternatively, a right-wing voter might rank their preferred right wing parties first and second, and the moderate conservative party as a back-up third choice.

Yet, much would be the same. Candidates would still go door to door looking to persuade voters, particularly at the local level. Candidates would still flood television and social media with advertisements. Candidates would still seek endorsements from newspapers and community figures. Candidates would still seek money to fund their campaigns.

Multiparty democracy will not solve all the ills of our current system. But I believe a multiparty system is head and shoulders above the dysfunctional disaster that is our current two-party system.

B. Multiparty Coalition Building

They say all politics is local . . .

Imagine you are at a local town hall. Perhaps it is in a school gymnasium or public park. You are one of several hundred attendees at the town hall to listen to your representatives speak. There are five of them, from five different parties, all with equal claim to represent the people in their district, your district. There are two moderators, both respected local journalists, one local television anchor and one reporter from the largest regional newspaper. There will be one hour of moderated conversation guided by the journalists, and a second hour with questions from the people.

It is three weeks since the end of the Legislative session. Your Representatives are here to listen to what you have to say about their job performance. This being the 21ˢᵗ century, it is also livestreamed and broadcast on television and radio. Moderators may choose to take questions from the live chat.

The first question from the television anchor, "To all of our Representatives, in one minute or less, what was your greatest success in the last legislative session, and what was your greatest frustration?" The town hall begins.

With which five parties do your Representatives caucus? It depends on where you are, specifically. Which part of which state are you in? At the state and local level, politics can be very different than what you see nationally.

State representatives and local politicians—mayors, city councilors, county commissioners—are elected by small, often closely-knit communities. Many local offices are officially nonpartisan. This is politics at its most human level, where people know their elected officials on a first-name basis, where elections are decided by dozens or hundreds of votes, and before the power inherent to national positions begins to corrupt and change even the most altruistic of politicians.

The local level, particularly in state legislatures, is where politicians aspiring for higher office often get their start. It is also the place where new parties can start to build. All the multiparty politicking that might happen on the national level is replicated on the state level: smaller, weirder, more connected to the people.

What kind of novel parties might develop across our idiosyncratic states? The large national parties would likely be present in every state, but what about the smaller parties? Each state's multiparty system could be both independent from and intertwined with the national system.

i. Washington State's Plausible Multiparty Democracy

Let me demonstrate the potential idiosyncrasies of a state-level multiparty system with my home state, Washington. This is the state and these are the people that I know best. I grew up in suburban Pierce County, and now live in Seattle. Yet even though I have lived in Washington my entire life, I have not lived in every county. To other Washingtonians reading this, tell me where I go wrong. And to readers from other states, you know your state and your region better than anyone else! What might be true for party representation in Washington may not be true in your state!

In this hypothetical, Washington will have the same kind of reformed electoral system as the federal reforms: a unicameral legislature elected by Proportional Ranked Choice Voting, with the appropriate number of legislators (198) according to the cube root of its population (7.5 million in 2020). I redrew Washington's 49 single-member districts into 40 multi-member districts. In these new districts, all districts would elect 5 members except for two districts, which would elect 4 members. The five-member districts would have about 194,580 residents and the four-member districts about 155,664 residents, or 38,916 residents per representative. **Assuming**[82] a 75% voting turnout rate, there would be around 114,105 ballots cast in five-member districts and around 91,284 ballots cast in four-member districts. For five-member districts, winning candidates would need to receive 16.7% of the vote, or 19,017 votes; for four-member districts, winning candidates would need to receive 20% of the vote, or 15,214 votes (Table 11.1).

In comparison, a candidate for the Washington State House currently needs to receive an average of 30,546 votes to win a competitive legislative race. There were 57,562 votes cast in the average State House race in 2022,[83] when there was 64% voter turnout. The statewide average hides the fact

Table 11.1: Washington State Legislature Comparison

	Current	Proposed
Total Legislators	147	198
Districts	49	40
Votes needed to win competitive race	30,546	19,017

that more people participate in competitive elections. In the 79 competitive races, defined as a race in which no candidate ran unopposed regardless of the margin of victory, there were an average of 61,090 votes cast. In the 19 races in which a candidate ran unopposed, there were an average of just 42,890 votes cast.

Technically, because Washington's 49 districts elect two Representatives and one Senator each, they are a kind of multi-member district. However, each of the three

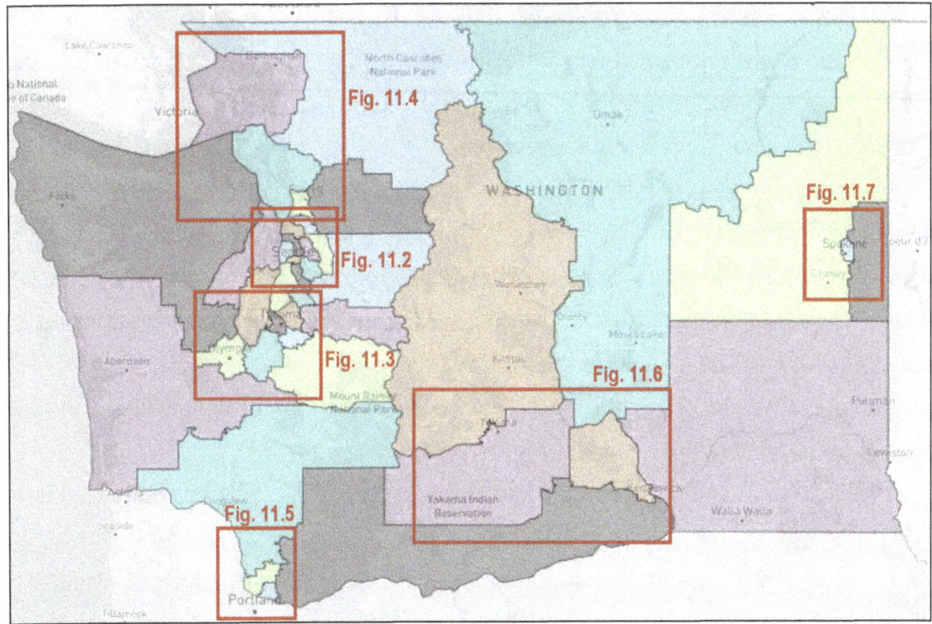

Figure 11.1: **Washington's New Legislative District map, with insets**

elections is voted upon separately, making them single-winner districts occupying the same geographic area, which encourages a two-party system. Washington also uses a "top-two" primary system, in which the top 2 candidates in the primary move on to the general election regardless of their party affiliation.

Washington's primary elections could proceed in one of two ways, both of which would function to provide voters with greater diversity of choice in the general election.

First, each political party could run its own primary, and could choose the number of candidates to nominate for the general. Each party would be able to nominate up to the number of seats in the district. In most Washington districts, this would be up to 5 candidates. For the major parties, it might make sense to nominate multiple candidates. For the smaller parties, it might make sense to nominate just 1 or 2 candidates, which would allow those candidates to consolidate the voters in the smaller party and then have a greater chance of electoral victory.

Second, there could be a "top-ten" or "top-eight" primary, in which the top 10 or 8 candidates regardless of party move on to the general election. For five-member districts, the top 10 candidates; for four-member districts, the top 8 candidates. Either way, there would be a long slate of candidates with diverse political views from which voters could choose in the general election.

Statewide, in a two-party system Washington voters are projected to support a 57% Democratic majority compared to a 41% Republican minority. But there is significant variation across this idiosyncratic state, from one of the most liberal cities in the country, Seattle, to the rural conservative eastern half of the state. There is a strong libertarian streak: Washington was one of the first states to legalize both gay marriage and marijuana. There is a strong environmental focus: Washington's three-term governor Jay Inslee's short-lived 2020 presidential campaign was focused almost entirely on fighting climate change. And though some parts of the state are deeply religious, overall Washington is one of the least-religious states in the country.

Because of Washington's idiosyncrasies, I believe that each of the parties would be slightly different than their national counterparts.

The current Republican Party could fracture into three parties: America First, Libertarian, and Reform Conservative.

In relatively irreligious Washington, the Christian Republican Party could be absorbed by the America First Party, and the America First Party could become the largest of the conservative parties by combining religious and anti-immigrant constituencies. America First could be competitive across the state, and particularly in rural and suburban areas.

The Reform Conservatives would be focused on business friendly policies and would attempt to be neutral regarding social issues. Reform Conservatives would likely be more competitive in urban and suburban Washington than in rural Washington.

Washington has a strong libertarian streak across the state. In Eastern Washington there are many libertarian minded rural communities focused on gun rights and property rights, and in the tech-hub of Seattle there are tech libertarians. A Washington specific Libertarian Party could combine these elements to be competitive not only in rural parts of the state but in the tech-industry hub of Seattle. The Libertarians could challenge the America First Party to be the largest conservative party.

The current Democratic Party would likely fracture into two main parties, the Social Democrats and New Democrats. The Social Democrats in Washington might incorporate the national Justice Party and focus on advancing progressive social and economic policies. The New Democrats could be supportive of progressive social policies, though their main focus could be on advancing moderate-leftist economic policies that promote economic development. The smallest party in environmental conscious Washington could be a Green Party, which could grab support from the existing Democratic Party in larger numbers than at the national level. In Washington, the Green Party could be focused on aggressively reducing statewide carbon emissions and other climate action.

Add all this together, and Washington State's multiparty system could look like Table 11.2. The district by district analysis that supports these figures is found in the next subchapter.

Combined, the Social and New Democrats could fall just 3 votes short of a majority in the State Legislature. Any one of the smaller parties could join the Social and New Democrats to form a majority coalition in return for specific concessions. Perhaps the Reform Conservatives join the majority in return for specific policy related to business regulations? Or the Libertarians in return for policy related to gun ownership, or some moonshot tech idea? Another option could be for the New Democrats to join with the Reform Conservatives and Libertarians to cut the Social Democrats out of the governing coalition altogether! A multiparty system could create political coalitions which seem utterly bizarre to our two-party sensibilities.

Table 11.2: Washington State's Hypothetical Multiparty System

Party	Seats	Legislative Strength
New Democratic	49	24.7%
Social Democratic	48	24.2%
America First	34	17.2%
Libertarian	30	15.2%
Reform Conservative	27	13.6%
Green	10	5.1%

Table 11.3: Six Possible Coalition Governments in Washington State

Coalition	Composite Parties	Hypothetical Party Strength	Hypothetical Coalition Strength
Centrist	Social Democratic	24.2%	62.6%
	New Democratic	24.7%	
	Reform Conservative	13.6%	
Center-Left	Social Democratic	24.2%	54.0%
	New Democratic	24.7%	
	Green	5.1%	
Center-Right	New Democratic	24.7%	53.5%
	Reform Conservative	13.6%	
	Libertarian	15.2%	
Rightwing	America First	17.2%	46.0%
	Libertarian	15.2%	
	Reform Conservative	13.6%	
Environmental Futurism	Green	5.1%	44.4%
	Libertarian	15.2%	
	Social Democratic	24.2%	
Avocado Coalition	America First	17.2%	37.4%
	Green	5.1%	
	Libertarian	15.2%	

Table 11.3 shows 6 potential coalitions and their combined strength in a hypothetical multiparty Washington State.

A Centrist coalition of Social Democrats, New Democrats, and Reform Conservatives could have a combined 62.6% support in the State Legislature.

This coalition would likely govern with socially liberal and economically centrist or conservative policies. Imagine the neoliberal economic policies of the Clinton-era Democratic Party combined with the social policies of the modern Democratic Party.

A center-left coalition of Social Democrats, New Democrats, and Greens could have a combined 54% support. This is essentially the current Democratic Party.

A center-right coalition of New Democrats, Reform Conservatives, and Libertarians could have a combined support of 53.5%. This coalition could focus on personal and economic freedoms, with a particular embrace of technological solutions to policy issues.

The remaining three coalitions would likely not have enough support in Washington State given current politics. However, as politics change over time, the parties could gain enough support to make these coalitions a governing possibility. A right-wing coalition of America First, Libertarians, and Reform Conservatives could be about 5% from forming a governing majority. This coalition is essentially the current Republican Party.

An Environmental Futurist coalition of Greens, Libertarians, and Social Democrats could also be about 5% from forming a governing majority. This coalition may seem strange but could find common ground by focusing on personal and social freedoms, and by addressing climate change using tech-friendly policies. This coalition would oppose the polluting, corporation-friendly policies of the Reform Conservatives, New Democrats, and America First.

Lastly, an Avocado coalition of America First, Greens, and Libertarians could form in opposition to the Centrist coalition. This coalition could work to address climate change with isolationist and xenophobic policies, rhetorically emphasizing some personal freedoms while curtailing others with technological surveillance. Like an avocado, this coalition would be green (environmental) on the outside while brown (fascist) on the inside.

For Washington voters, they could have six viable, legitimate, and serious political parties from which to choose. Candidates from the six parties would make their case directly to voters door-to-door and in local events. In keeping with Washington's existing primary system, in which all candidates compete for votes from all voters, the top 8 or 10 candidates in the primary could move onto the general election. The threshold for making it through the primary would be 11% in an 8-candidate field, or 9% in a 10-candidate field. Smaller parties would need to win just 9% or 11% of the primary vote in order to qualify for the general! With quality candidates and organized campaigning, such a threshold could easily be reached.

In an 8- or 10-candidate general election, there would be at least one party with multiple candidates. These candidates might campaign together asking voters to rank them 1 and 2 on their ballots (or 1, 2, and 3, and so on). The smaller parties might only have one candidate in the general election. In addition to campaigning for first-place votes, smaller parties would actively seek second- or third-place votes from supporters of the other parties. Voters would be able to vote FOR their preferred candidate, not just AGAINST the candidate they do not like, as in our current system.

Smaller parties could be bolstered by convincing an established, well-known, and well-liked local figure to join their party. After all, name recognition is one of the most important markers of a successful campaign. Success begets success: once smaller parties have proven they can win, more voters will believe in the multiparty system, and the power of the entrenched major two parties will be broken.

What an exciting prospect for democratic government!

ii. Washington State's New Legislative Map Analysis

In this section, I break down the analysis on a district-by-district level. For this analysis, I project the expected number of seats for each of the six parties based on the number of seats available in the district, the district's Democratic/Republican projection based on historic 2016–2020 data, and my own understanding of the idiosyncrasies of the people living in each district. When I project some parties as winning 1/2 or 1/4 of a seat, what I mean is that the party would likely be competitive in the district, but that winning a seat is not assured. For example, as much as I would like to project the Greens to win multiple seats, I do not feel such an outcome is likely. However, I project the Greens as winning 1/2 or 1/4 of a seat in many districts in which I believe they would be competitive. In the maps, I project specific winners based on the probabilities in the data tables. Across four or five similar districts, I try to project a representative set of winners.. The outcome really depends on the candidates and their campaigns.

In five Seattle districts shown in Figures 11.2 and Table 11.4, the Democratic Party is projected to win at least 80% of the vote in a two-party system. But as discussed in Chapters 6, 7, and 8, an overwhelmingly dominant party is likely to split in a P-RCV system. In all five districts, I project that the Social Democrats would win 1.75 seats. That means I think that the Social Democrats would certainly win 1 seat and be favored to win a second. After all, Seattle is represented by the leader of the Congressional Progressive Caucus, Pramila Jayapal. With her celebrity and organization, the Social Democrats would be formidable in Seattle. The New Democrats would be similarly popular, almost certainly winning at least 1 seat in all five districts, likely 2 seats in the three most liberal districts. Other parties would be competitive due to the 16.7% electoral threshold to win 1 seat. The Greens would probably win 1 seat in 2 or 3 of the districts, as might the Reform Reform Conservatives or Libertarians parties. Despite Seattle's liberal reputation, conservatives also live

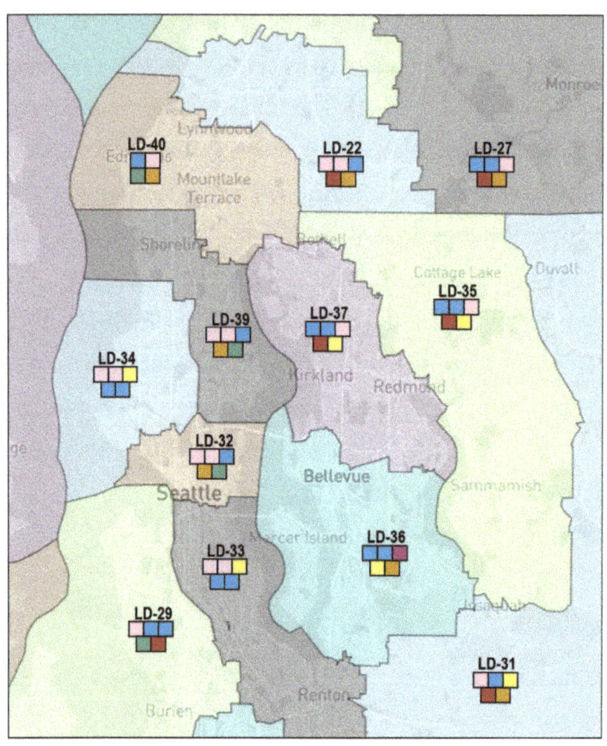

Figure 11.2: Seattle Metro

there. The Reform Conservative party might have success appealing to Seattle's business community, and a tech-infused Libertarian Party could appeal to the tens of thousands of tech workers who drive Seattle's economy, many of whom currently vote for Democratic candidates. Finally, the America First Party might have reactionary success appealing to people upset with Seattle's progressive orthodoxy. There are ten districts projected to have between 60%–70% support for Democrats in a two-party system. Shown in Table 11.5 and Figures 11.2, 11.3, and 11.4, these districts surround Seattle and

Table 11.4: Seattle Districts

District (Seats)	Geography	Dem %	Rep %	Social Democrats	New Democrats	America First	Libertarians	Reform Conservatives	Greens
32 (5)	Downtown Seattle	89.3%	9.4%	1.75	1.75	0	0.5	0.5	0.5
34 (5)	Ballard, Magnolia	87.7%	11.1%	1.75	1.75	0	0.5	0.5	0.5
39 (5)	North Seattle, Shoreline	84.2%	14.5%	1.75	1.5	0.25	0.5	0.5	0.5
33 (5)	South Seattle, Renton	82.1%	16.8%	1.75	1.5	0.25	0.5	0.5	0.5
29 (5)	West Seattle, Vashon Island	80.0%	18.8%	1.75	1.5	0.25	0.5	0.5	0.5

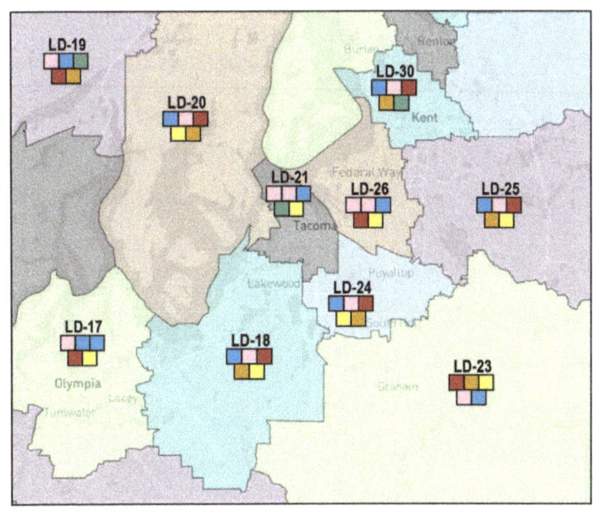

Figure 11.3: South Puget Sound

span much of Puget Sound, from the 17th District in Olympia to the 38th District in Bellingham. In each of these districts, the Social and New Democrats would likely win 1 or 2 seats each, depending on the quality of their candidates and the political moment. Two seats in each district would likely be won by the other 4 parties, all of which would be competitive in these districts. Current Republican party voters make up between 28%–37% of these districts. The 3 conservative parties would likely win 2 seats in the 30th, 22nd, 17th, and 28th districts, and could threaten to win a combined 2 seats in the other six districts. Again, a tech-focused Libertarian Party could also win support from people who currently vote for Democrats. Additionally, the Greens could threaten to win 1 seat in any of these districts.

There are 8 districts projected to have a Democratic majority of between 53%–59% in a two-party system (Table 11.6). These districts come from all over the state, from the 4th District in Spokane (Figure 11.7), to the Nineteeth District in the Olympic peninsula

Table 11.5: Super Majority Democratic Districts

District (Seats)	Geography	Dem %	Rep %	Social Democrats	New Democrats	America First	Libertarians	Reform Conservatives	Greens
37 (5)	Kirkland, Redmond	70.1%	28.1%	1.5	1.5	0.5	0.5	0.5	0.5
40 (4)	Mountlake Terrace, Edmonds	70.0%	28.4%	1	1	0.5	0.5	0.5	0.5
21 (5)	Tacoma	68.7%	29.5%	1.5	1.5	0.5	0.5	0.5	0.5
36 (5)	Bellevue, Mercer Island	68.7%	29.9%	1.5	1.5	0.5	0.5	0.75	0.25
38 (5)	Bellingham, San Juan Islands	68.0%	30.3%	1.5	1.5	0.5	0.5	0.5	0.5
35 (5)	Sammamish, Woodinville	67.0%	31.4%	1.5	1.5	0.5	0.5	0.5	0.5
30 (5)	Kent, Seatac, Des Moines	65.3%	33.3%	1.25	1.25	0.75	0.75	0.5	0.5
22 (5)	Mill Creek	63.8%	34.5%	1.25	1.25	0.75	0.75	0.5	0.5
17 (5)	Olympia	63.3%	34.7%	1.25	1.25	0.75	0.75	0.5	0.5
28 (5)	Everett, Mukilteo	60.6%	37.5%	1.25	1.25	0.75	0.75	0.5	0.5

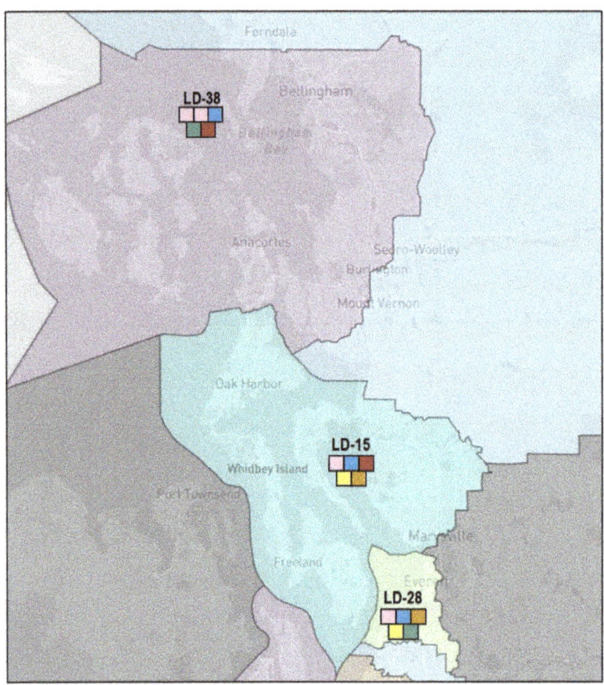

Figure 11.4: North Puget Sound

(Figure 11.3), to the Tenth and Eleventh Districts in Vancouver (Figure 11.5). Current Republican voters make up more than enough of the electorate to win 2 seats in each of these districts. Both the Social and New Democrats would easily win 1 seat in every district, and would compete against each other for the 3rd seat. The Greens and Reform Conservatives might successfully peel voters away from the Social and New Democrats, though it would be dependent on the district and the candidates. The America First and Libertarian parties would be strong in these districts, particularly the more rural districts like the Sixteenth or the Eighteenth.

There are six swing districts, in which neither party would have more than a 52% majority in a two-party system (Table 11.7). Five of the swing districts are in the Puget Sound area (Figures 11.2, 11.3, 11.4), and one is in Yakima (Figure 11.6). There is a decent chance that the five largest parties could each each win 1 seat in each of these districts. The New Democrats might have much more appeal in these swing districts than the Social

Table 11.6: Majority Democratic Districts

District (Seats)	Geography	Dem %	Rep %	Social Democrats	New Democrats	America First	Libertarians	Reform Conservatives	Greens
31 (5)	North Bend, King County	58.2%	39.9%	1.5	1.25	0.75	0.75	0.5	0.25
26 (5)	Federal Way	57.9%	40.5%	1.5	1.25	0.75	0.5	0.75	0.25
4 (5)	Spokane	57.7%	40.8%	1.5	1.25	0.75	0.75	0.5	0.25
19 (5)	Kitsap Peninsula	57.6%	40.3%	1.25	1.25	0.75	0.75	0.5	0.5
16 (4)	Port Angeles, Forks, Shelton	54.0%	44.6%	1	1	1	0.5	0.5	0
10 (5)	Vancouver	53.8%	44.5%	1.25	1.25	1	0.5	0.75	0.25
18 (5)	Lakewood, Yelm, JBLM	53.6%	44.4%	1	1.25	1	0.75	0.75	0.25
11 (5)	Vancouver, Battleground	53.1%	45.3%	1	1.25	1	0.75	0.75	0.25

Democrats and might be able to win a second seat. However, (and perhaps this is wishful thinking on my part), the Greens could play spoiler in one of these districts. Given how evenly split these areas are in the current two-party system, it would be fascinating to see how the parties would campaign in these districts.

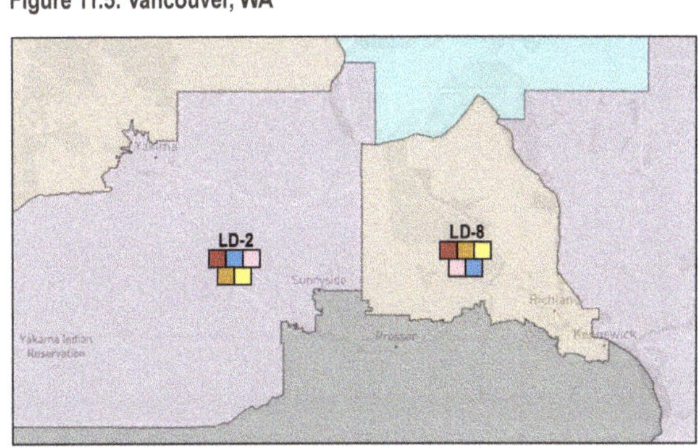

Figure 11.5: Vancouver, WA

Figure 11.6: Yakima, WA and the Tri-Cities

The new Second District, in Yakima (Table 11.6), requires extra discussion. Following the 2020 redistricting cycle, a **judge ruled**[84] that the new map diluted the Latino vote in and around Yakima. The judge required that these districts be redrawn so that 1 district would be majority Latino. With my multimember maps, the Second District is 46% Latino, 44% White, and 8% Native. The point of the judge's ruling to redistrict was to ensure that, if the Latino population voted as a block, they could elect a Latino representative. With multimember districts requiring only 16.7% for a candidate to win, Yakima area Latinos would have no problem winning representation even though they do not comprise an outright majority.

Table 11.7: Swing Districts

District (Seats)	Geography	Dem %	Rep %	Social Democrats	New Democrats	America First	Libertarians	Reform Conservatives	Greens
20 (5)	Port Orchard, Gig Harbor, Tacoma	50.9%	47.0%	1	1.25	1	0.75	0.75	0.25
24 (5)	Puyallup	49.2%	48.9%	1	1.25	1	0.75	0.75	0.25
15 (5)	Whidbey Island, Arlington	49.0%	49.1%	1	1	1	1	0.75	0.25
25 (5)	Auburn, Bonney Lake, Enumclaw	48.9%	49.4%	1	1.25	1	1	0.75	0
2 (5)	Yakima	47.2%	51.7%	1	1	1	1	0.75	0.25
27 (5)	Lake Stevens, Monroe	47.0%	50.9%	1	1.25	1	1	0.75	0

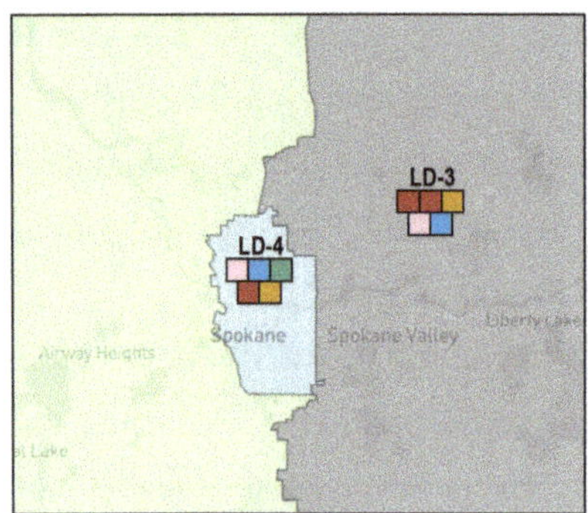

Figure 11.7: Spokane, WA

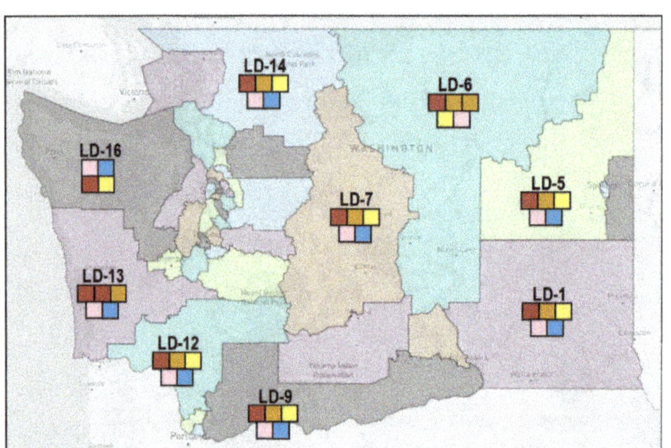

Figure 11.8: Rural Washington

Finally, there are 11 districts projected to have a Republican majority in a two-party system (Table 11.8). Most of these districts are rural (Figure 11.8), though some are in the suburban Puget Sound area (Figure 11.3). With a 65% Republican majority, the most conservative district is the Sixth District. The most conservative districts are less conservative than the most liberal districts are liberal. In all eleven of these districts, each of the three conservative parties would likely win 1 seat. The America First Party might even win a 2nd seat in some districts. Because even in the most conservative districts, Democratic voters would still be at least 34% of the electorate, enough

Table 11.8: Majority Republican Districts

District (Seats)	Geography	Dem %	Rep %	Social Democrats	New Democrats	America First	Libertarians	Reform Conservatives	Greens
1 (5)	Pullman, Walla Walla, Pasco	44.0%	54.5%	1	1	1.25	1	0.75	0
14 (5)	Ferndale, Mt. Vernon	43.1%	55.3%	1	1	1.25	1	0.75	0
13 (5)	Aberdeen, Centralia	42.4%	56.2%	1	1	1.25	1	0.75	0
9 (5)	Goldendale, Camas	42.3%	56.3%	1	1	1.25	1	0.75	0
23 (5)	Graham, Eatonville, Buckley	40.1%	58.1%	1	1	1.25	1	0.75	0
3 (5)	Spokane Valley	39.7%	58.5%	1	1	1.25	1	0.75	0
8 (5)	Richland, Kennewick	39.3%	58.9%	1	1	1.25	1	0.75	0
5 (5)	Cheney, Wilbur, Newport	39.0%	59.5%	1	1	1.25	1	0.75	0
7 (5)	Wenatchee, Ellensburg	39.0%	59.8%	1	1	1.25	1	0.75	0
12 (5)	Longview, Morton	38.1%	60.5%	1	1	1.25	1	0.75	0
6 (5)	Omak, Colville, Moses Lake	33.9%	65.1%	0.75	0.75	1.25	1.25	1	0

to win 2 seats, the Social and New Democrats would likely each win 1 seat in every district. The Greens would probably not be competitive in any of these districts. But, as the multiparty system grows and changes, perhaps the Greens might attempt to expand their party in the rural parts of the state.

C. Multiparty Democracy In Other States

Out of each state's unique multiparty system will come the national multiparty system. Large parties will likely win representation in every state, while small parties may only win representation in the state in which they are strong.

Whichever parties end up winning, nearly every Congressional district will feature competitive campaigns. There would be no more "swing districts," in which 10% of Americans determine the majority in Congress, because in an eight-party system every district would feature some competition between the parties. Every district would become what we now think of as a swing district; every district could determine which parties end up forming the governing majority.

In Chapter 8, my analysis of every state's new Congressional districts was based on the idea of a four-party system: Democrats, Republicans, Progressives, and Libertarians. Here, I analyze ten districts assuming an eight-party system. These ten districts span the breadth of the country's political diversity, from cosmopolitan Manhattan to rugged Utah. There are 4 five-member districts, 4 four-member districts, and 2 three-member districts.

To the people who live in these states and districts, please do correct me where you feel I have misrepresented your state's idiosyncrasies. I do not have the same intimate knowledge of your state as you do.

Each state's unique multiparty system will influence which parties are most likely to win representation in Congress. While the major parties will be competitive in most districts and states, the smaller parties may only be competitive in some regions and not others. For example, even in districts that have the similar amounts of Democrats and Republicans in the two-party system, the Libertarians might be more successful in rural western states than in the Rust Belt or the Deep South. Or, in the Deep South, the Christian Republicans and the Justice Party might be stronger than on the West Coast.

While my analysis is rooted in data collected in our existing two-party system, I have tried to show where parties could compete across today's standard political divisions, and in ways that break our understanding of politics as existing solely along a left-right axis. There could be alliances between odd bedfellows, perhaps between the Libertarians and Social Democrats, or the Christian Republicans and New Democrats.

What this analysis ultimately shows is that in a P-RCV multiparty system, political competition would spread across the country and voters would have more and better options than exist in our current two-party system. What would a multiparty system in your state look like? When the two parties fracture, which new party would emerge strongest in your state?

A different multiparty democracy in every state across America. The dream realized.

i. Ten Districts From Around The Country

I mapped ten districts from various parts of the country, to see what kind of different multiparty systems might develop in different states.

Five-member districts, with their 16.7% electoral threshold, are the districts in which smaller parties are most likely to win representation. Four-member districts have an electoral threshold of 20% to win representation. Three-member districts have an electoral threshold of 25% to win representation.

The most Democratic of the 4 four-member districts is New York's Fifth, spanning Manhattan and the Bronx. The Social and New Democrats could each win 1 seat, and perhaps 2. They both would face competition from the Justice and Greens, which could find passionate constituencies in the densest and arguably most diverse city in the country. In a district with so few Republicans, the Reform Conservatives could be the only competitive conservative party, particularly by appealing to New York business interests.

The California Fifteenth, Santa Monica, is a different flavor of very liberal district. The Social and New Democrats would each win 1 seat, and maybe 2. But with more Republicans than in NY-5, the conservative parties would certainly win 1 seat. The

Table 11.9: Hypothetical National Multiparty System in Ten Congressional Districts

District	Dem %	Rep %	Social Democrat	New Democrat	Reform Conservative	Christian Republican	America First	Libertarian	Justice	Green
NY-5	88.1%	9.8%	1.5	1.25	0.75	0	0	0	0.75	0.75
CA-15	81.4%	17.0%	1.25	1.25	0.75	0.25	0.75	0	0.25	0.5
TX-12	48.1%	50.1%	0.75	0.75	0.75	0.75	0.75	0.5	0.5	0.25
TN-2	41.4%	56.2%	0.75	0.75	0.75	1	0.75	0.5	0.5	0
WA-3	66.1%	32.3%	1	1	0.5	0	0.5	0.5	0	0.5
NM	54.1%	42.3%	0.75	0.75	0.5	0.5	0.5	0.5	0.25	0.25
WI-1	43.5%	54.1%	1	1	0.5	0.5	0.5	0.5	0	0
PA-2	34.0%	63.7%	0.5	0.5	0.75	0.75	1	0.5	0	0
NH	45.2%	52.0%	0.5	0.5	0.5	0	0.75	0.75	0	0
UT-1	20.6%	73.8%	0	0.5	0.5	1	0.5	0.5	0	0

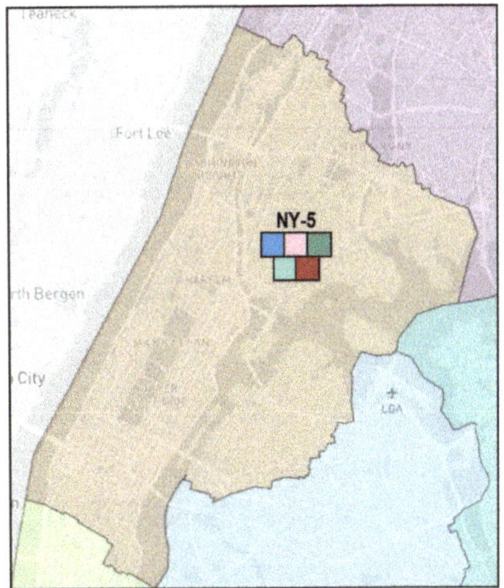

Figure 11.9: New York's New Fifth District

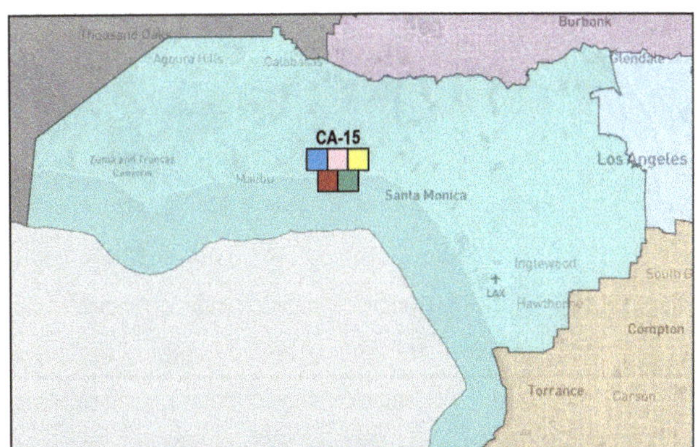

Figure 11.10: California's New Fifteenth District

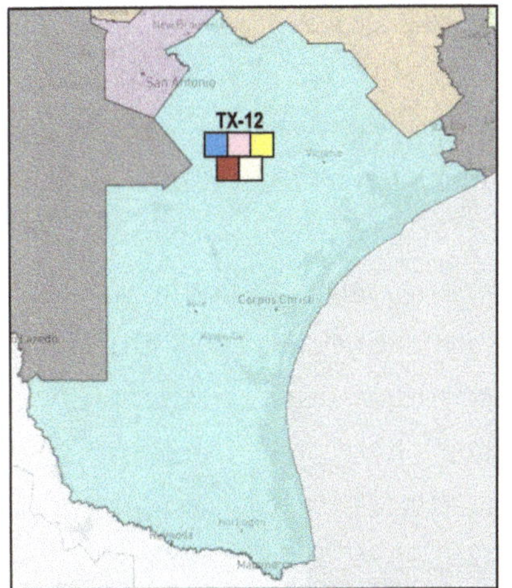

Figure 11.11: Texas's New Twelfth District

Reform Conservatives and America First would compete against each other but also directly against the Social and New Democrats. As old partisan loyalties faded, formerly Democratic voters could find themselves supporting the Reform Conservatives or America First. Smaller parties could also compete. One of the Christian Republicans, Justice, or Greens could win a seat.

The Texas Twelfth, stretching from the suburbs of Houston and San Antonio to the southern border, could feature intense competition between all 8 parties. In a two-party system, this district is almost exactly evenly split between Democrats and Republicans. All five of the major national parties would be favored to win one seat each. However, the Libertarians would be competitive given the rural expanse of the district. And the Justice party could gain traction among voters who wanted to prioritize care for migrants coming across the southern border. Of course, the America First party would take an opposite position. The beauty of P-RCV is that both perspectives could win representation in Congress in the same election. Lastly, the Greens could win in an upset, potentially by connecting the influx of migrants to worsening climate change.

Tennessee's Second District is a majority conservative district that is balanced by the inclusion of liberal Nashville. While all 5 of the major parties would be competitive, in the religious south the Christian Republicans could win the most support. The Libertarian and Justice parties could be competitive, as well. In particular, the Justice Party could gain support and energy from established racial justice advocates and organizers.

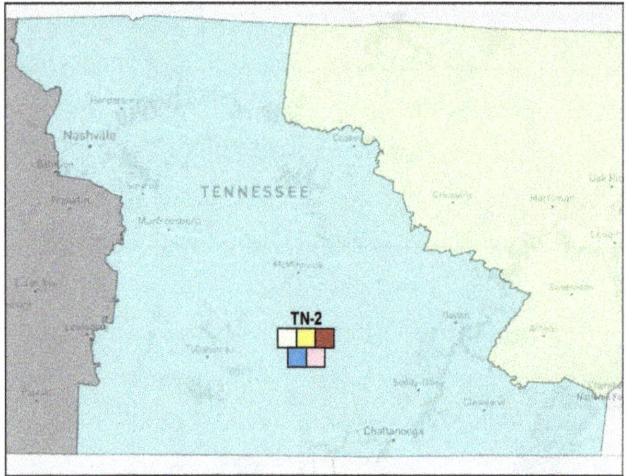

Figure 11.12: Tennessee's New Second District

Washington's Third District (where I was born and raised) spans the urban corridor from Seattle to Tacoma, and also the the more conservative suburbs and exurbs. The Social and New Democrats would likely win 1 seat each. Winning a 2nd seat for your party would require winning 40% of the vote, a fairly high bar in a competitive multiparty system. The competition for the other 2 seats would be between the Reform Conservatives, America First, Libertarians, and Greens. With 32% of the district projected as Republicans in a two-party system, one of the conservative parties would certainly win 1 seat. Depending on the candidates and their campaigns, the remaining seat could go to a second conservative party or to the Greens.

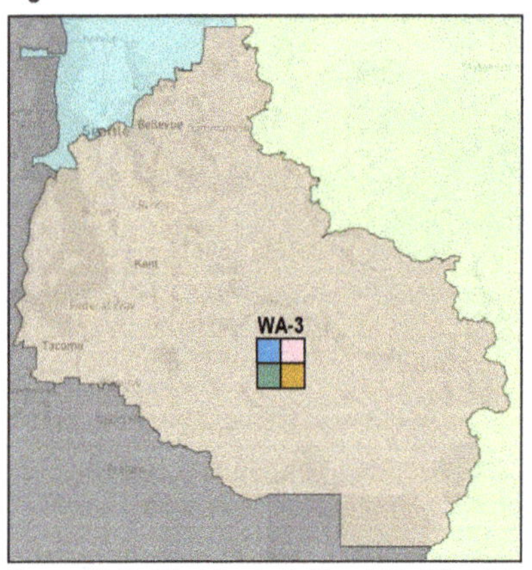

Figure 11.13: Washington's New Third District

New Mexico's single 4-member district would elect representatives across the entire state. All 8 parties could be competitive, depending on how New Mexico's state multiparty system developed New Mexico is a majority Democratic state, but the majority is not overwhelming, at 54%. The Republican

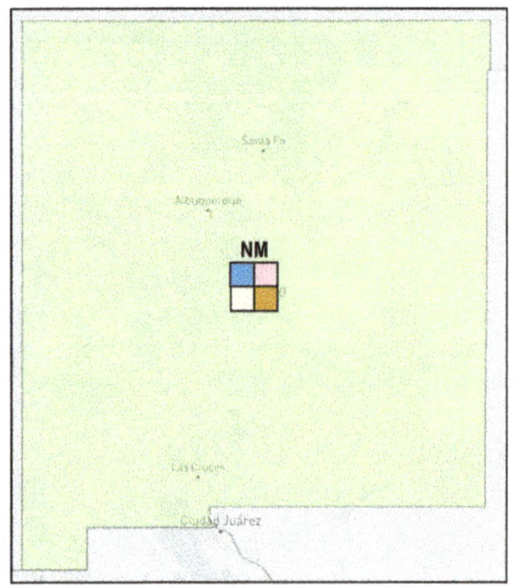

Figure 11.14: New Mexico

minority is projected at 42%, enough to win 2 seats in a two-party system. The Social and New Democrats would likely win 1 seat each, though they might have to fend off challenges from Justice and the Greens. On the conservative side, all four parties could win a seat. I project them all as equally likely to win because I am not sure how New Mexico's conservative politics might develop. For example, an anti-immigration turn could favor America First, while a focus on family could benefit the Christian Republicans.

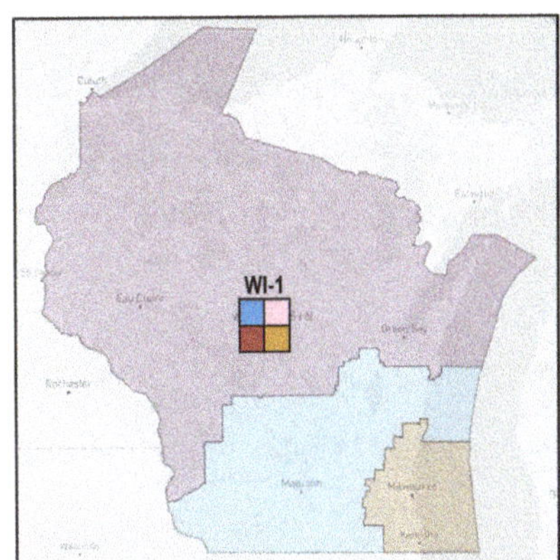

Figure 11.15: Wisconsin's New First District

Wisconsin's rural First District is projected to have a Republican majority of 54% and Democratic minority of 43% in a two-party system, almost exactly the inverse partisanship as New Mexico. On the liberal side, the Social and New Democrats would likely win 1 seat each. With 40% of the vote required to win 2 seats, it is unlikely that a smaller party could challenge the larger parties in this district, even if the smaller parties win representation at the state level in the same areas. On the conservative side, all 4 parties would be competitive. Just as in New Mexico, I'm not sure which would emerge victorious. Would more conservative Wisconsin voters be more persuaded by nativist policies from the America First Party? Or business-friendly policies from the Reform Conservatives? Or community oriented policies from the Christian Republicans? Or personal freedom

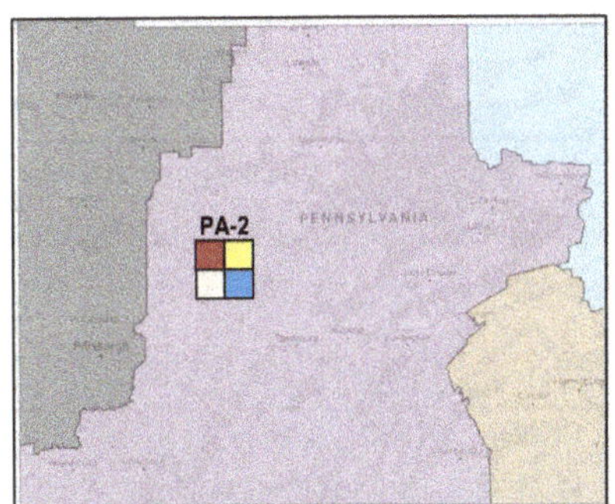

Figure 11.16: Pennsylvania's New Second District

policies from the Libertarians? Whatever the case, these four parties would likely win 2 seats in total.

Pennsylvania's rural Second District is a majority conservative district. Conservative parties would be favored to win 3 of the 4 seats. The America First Party would likely win one seat, and the other 2 seats would be competitive between the Reform Conservatives, Christian Republicans, and the Libertarians. The 4th seat would be competitive between the Social and New Democrats. For these liberal parties to be able to win a 2nd seat, they would need to appeal to voters of the four conservative parties. It could be possible as the multiparty system develops, but is unlikely based on the existing data.

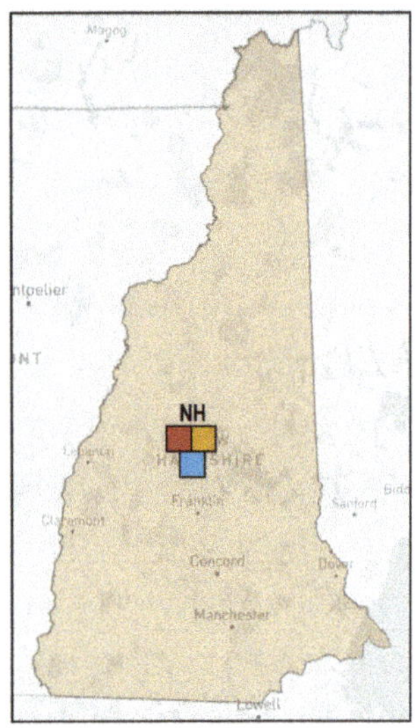

Figure 11.17: New Hampshire

New Hampshire is a moderate Republican leaning state in our two-party system. If its famously large legislature (400 representatives for a state of 1.4 million people, or 1 representative for every 3,444 residents!) had a multiparty system, new parties could readily develop. Even if there were a variety of small parties, the larger national parties would likely win representation to Congress. Of five likely competitive parties, the Libertarian and America First parties could be the largest. Both of them would be favored to win 1 seat each, with the Reform Conservatives also being competitive. New Hampshire's 3rd seat could be competitive between the Social Democrats and the New Democrats. However, the elections could be heavily influenced by the quality of candidates. New Hampshire could elect a congressional delegation of America First, Libertarian, and Social Democrat in one year, and then the two years later elect a delegation of Libertarian, Reform Conservative, and New Democrat.

Utah's Second District, spanning the entire state south of Salt Lake City, would be one of the most conservative districts in the country in a two-party system, with a projected Republican majority

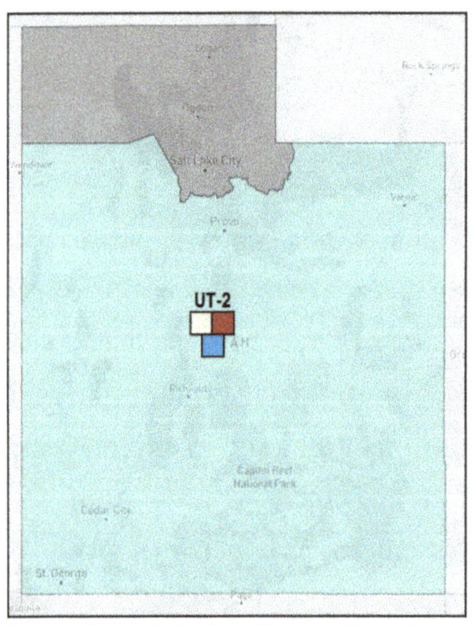

Figure 11.18: Utah's New Second District

of 73%. Utah is one of the most religious states in the country, so the Christian Republicans would likely win 1 seat. A second seat could be competitive between America First and the Libertarians. The last seat could be competitive between the Reform Conservatives and the New Democrats. With so few Democrats in Utah, the Democrats might stay united in order to remain electorally viable.

D. The Presidential Campaign

Imagine, the 2036 Presidential election in a multiparty democracy. In Drutman's hypothetical, a Reform Conservative candidate won the Presidential election in both 2028 and 2032. This means that in 2036, the Reform Conservative candidate would be term limited. There would be no incumbent candidate.

In an open presidential election, cracks would likely emerge in the majority coalition government as each party attempts to best position itself to win the Presidency.

In a ranked choice popular vote election, there would be no such thing as a swing state. Candidates would campaign in every corner of the country, not just in the few swing states and few big cities where they beg for political donations from the financial elite.

Table 11.10: Hypothetical Multiparty Congressional Results, 2026 and 2030 by Drutman, 2034 by me

Party	2026	2030	2034
Social Democrats	24%	26%	24%
America First	22%	10%	15%
Christian Republicans	18%	8%	9%
New Democrats	18%	22%	15%
Reform Conservatives	13%	29%	25%
Centrist-Independents	3%	3%	3%
Libertarians	2%	2%	3%
Justice	0%	0%	3%
Greens	0%	0%	3%

In our current system voters have many choices in the primary election, but then very few choices in the general election.

In 2016, there were **17 Republican candidates**[85] for President. And in 2020, there were **29 declared Democratic candidates**[86] for President. But in both primaries, most candidates dropped out far before most voters had a chance to weigh in. In both the 2016 Republican primary and the 2020 Democratic primary, all but 5 candidates had dropped out before Super Tuesday. And then in the general election, there were functionally only 2 candidates, the nominees of the 2 major parties.

In a multiparty system, voters would have many choices in both the primary and the general.

Each of the 8 parties would have its own nomination process. For the larger parties, the Reform Conservatives, Social Democrats, New Democrats, America First, and the Christian Republicans, the nominating process might look similar to the process which we have today: several candidates might face off against each other in each party. These parties would each have serious ambitions to win the Presidency. Accordingly, they would vet their candidates against each other in the hopes of nominating a candidate most likely to win the most first place votes nationally, as well as appeal to voters from other parties and garner their second- and third-choice votes.

For the smaller parties, the Libertarians, Justice, and Greens, their nominating process might look more like a coronation of the leader of each party. As small parties, they might not have much internal dissent, and might more easily coalesce around a single leader. For these parties, the primary would be more about expanding their electoral reach than actually winning the highest office in the land. The goal for these parties would be to gain enough first-place votes for their endorsement to become electorally meaningful. As discussed in parts A and B of this chapter, smaller parties would be more likely to focus on down ballot races: Congress, State Legislature, local elections.

Additionally, there would likely be a few Independent candidates not attached to any party. These candidates would be wildcards, likely independently wealthy or otherwise famous. Perhaps, erstwhile Independent candidates would join with one of the parties to take advantage of existing party infrastructure.

The calendar of the 2036 Presidential election could look something like this:

- **Summer and Fall 2035:** Candidates announce their candidacy in each of the parties and begin campaigning. For parties with multiple candidates, debates are televised and streamed online.

- **February 2036:** The first state primaries are held. Voters may only vote in one party's primary. Two types of results would be important. First, which candidate won each party's respective primary in each state? And second, the total number of ballots cast in each party's primary. With each state, higher voter turnout for one party or another could foretell the party's strength heading into the general.

- **April—June 2036:** Enough state primaries have happened that the nominee for each party is known.

- **July—August 2036:** Presumptive nominees become formal nominees at each party's national convention. Parties announce their Vice Presidential nominees. Parties would compete for television and streaming ratings. Each party would make its case for why American voters should reward their candidate and party with the Presidency, and why voters from other parties should rank their party second.

- **September—October 2036:** The nominees barnstorm the country in a truly national final stretch of the campaign. Without swing states, political advertisements and campaign appearances are spread across the country, to large cities and small towns alike, depending on internal campaign polling to find those areas with undecided voters, or those areas that are most favorable to a given party.

- **November 4, 2036:** The general election. In a multiparty system, no candidate would likely win 50% of the vote in the first round of voting. As the smaller party candidates are eliminated, their voters' second- and third-choice votes become decisive. Eventually, enough candidates will have been eliminated and their voters' votes redistributed so that one candidate will have received 50% of the vote and be announced the winner.

Throughout the campaign, each party's presidential nominee would likely coordinate with their party's congressional candidates. In addition to winning the Presidency, each party will want to increase their representation in Congress, so that even if they do not win the Presidency, they will have more influence in determining the governing majority coalition in Congress.

Chapter 12
RELEGITIMIZE THE COURT

"[The Chief Justice] has made his decision, now let him enforce it."

While President Andrew Jackson never actually said the **above quote,**[87] it is the pithiest summation of the paradox of the Supreme Court's power. The Constitution, as interpreted in *Marbury v. Madison,* empowers the Supreme Court to be the final arbiter of law and justice. That is how it should be if we are to be a nation of laws. In this way, the Court wields immense power.

Yet, the Court relies entirely upon the other branches of government to carry out and enforce its decisions. The Court has no army. The Court has no police force. The Court's power rests entirely upon the broad acceptance of its authority by the American people, and in the willingness of the other institutions in American government and civil society to accept its decision as final.

We need our Court to be respected and to have broad legitimacy. After all, what is a nation if its law cannot be applied fairly and justly? When faith in the rule is lost, what happens next?

Our Supreme Court today has lost its legitimacy and is unworthy of its power. According to today's Court, corruption is legal and the President is above the law. These combined rulings make the law meaningless. The Court, as Justice Alito put it in the Dobbs decision, has been **"egregiously wrong."**[88] Its error should be rectified by the will of the people, as expressed by the Legislative.

We should reform it so that it might become more insulated from poisonous partisanship, and so that it might regain legitimacy in the eyes of the people whose law it is charged with upholding. Yet as with the other branches, reform can only do so much. Ultimately, the Court must be checked by the Legislative Branch when it oversteps its rulings or when individual members descend to corruption.

Described in detail in section B of this chapter, I propose the following reforms which combined might relegitimize the Court:

- A single, roughly 20-year term for all Justices;
- A set schedule for appointment so that each President has equal opportunity to influence the makeup of the Court; and
- Increasing the size of the Court so that each case would be decided by a panel of Justices.

A. How The Court Lost Its Legitimacy

The Court's illegitimacy has been building for a long time. Now, it is lost.

There are four ways that have combined to cause the Court to lose its legitimacy:

1. The Court's broken, hyperpartisan, and random appointment process;
2. The length of time Justices can spend on the Court;
3. The corruption of individual Justices; and
4. The Court's use of inconsistent logic to gradually claim excessive power over the other branches.

If there is a single moment after which the Court had become illegitimate, I believe it to be in October 2020, when Justice Ruth Bader Ginsburg was replaced by Justice Amy Coney Barrett. The confirmation of Justice Barrett was the end point of the years-long hyper-partisan strategy of the Republican Party. After President Obama nominated Judge Merrick Garland following the death of Justice Antonin Scalia in February 2016, Senate Republicans refused to hold any hearings on the nomination. At the time, they argued that, because it was an election year, the people should choose the President that would nominate the next Justice. If it was not obvious that this was a bad-faith argument in the moment, it became undeniable when Senate Republicans did the exact thing they argued against in 2020 in the nomination and confirmation of Justice Amy Coney Barrett. Except this time, it was even closer to the election.

With Justice Barrett's confirmation, President Trump had appointed three of the nine Justices in a single term, one of which should have been appointed by President Obama. Another two Justices, Chief Justice Roberts and Justice Alito, had been appointed by President George W. Bush, who had first won office thanks to the Electoral College. Five of the six conservative Justices had been appointed by a President who had not won the popular vote. What mockery of popular legitimacy!

This series of hyperpartisan events from 2016 through 2020 demonstrate that the appointment process has become broken. This was the culmination of decades of increasingly bitter confirmation fights, as shown in Figure 12.1.

Supreme Court Confirmations Have Become More Contentious Since WWII
Votes in Favor
Votes Opposed
Number of Senate Votes
100
50
0
Harold Burton
Fred Vinson
Tom Clark
Sherman Minton
Earl Warren
John Marshall Harlan II
William Brennan, Jr.
Charles Wittaker
Potter Stewart
Byron White
Arthur Goldberg
Abe Fortas
Thurgood Marshall
Warren Burger
Harry Blackmun
Lewis F. Powell, Jr.
William H. Rehnquist
John Paul Stevens
Sandra Day O'Conner
William H. Rehnquist
Antonin Scalia
Anthony M. Kennedy
David H. Souter
Clarence Thomas
Ruth Bader Ginsburg
Stephen G. Breyer
John G. Roberts, Jr.
Samuel A. Alito, Jr.
Sonia Sotomayor
Elena Kagan
Neil M. Gorsuch
Brett Kavanaugh
Amy Coney Barrett
Ketanji Brown Jackson
Confirmed Supreme Court Justices, 1946 - 2022

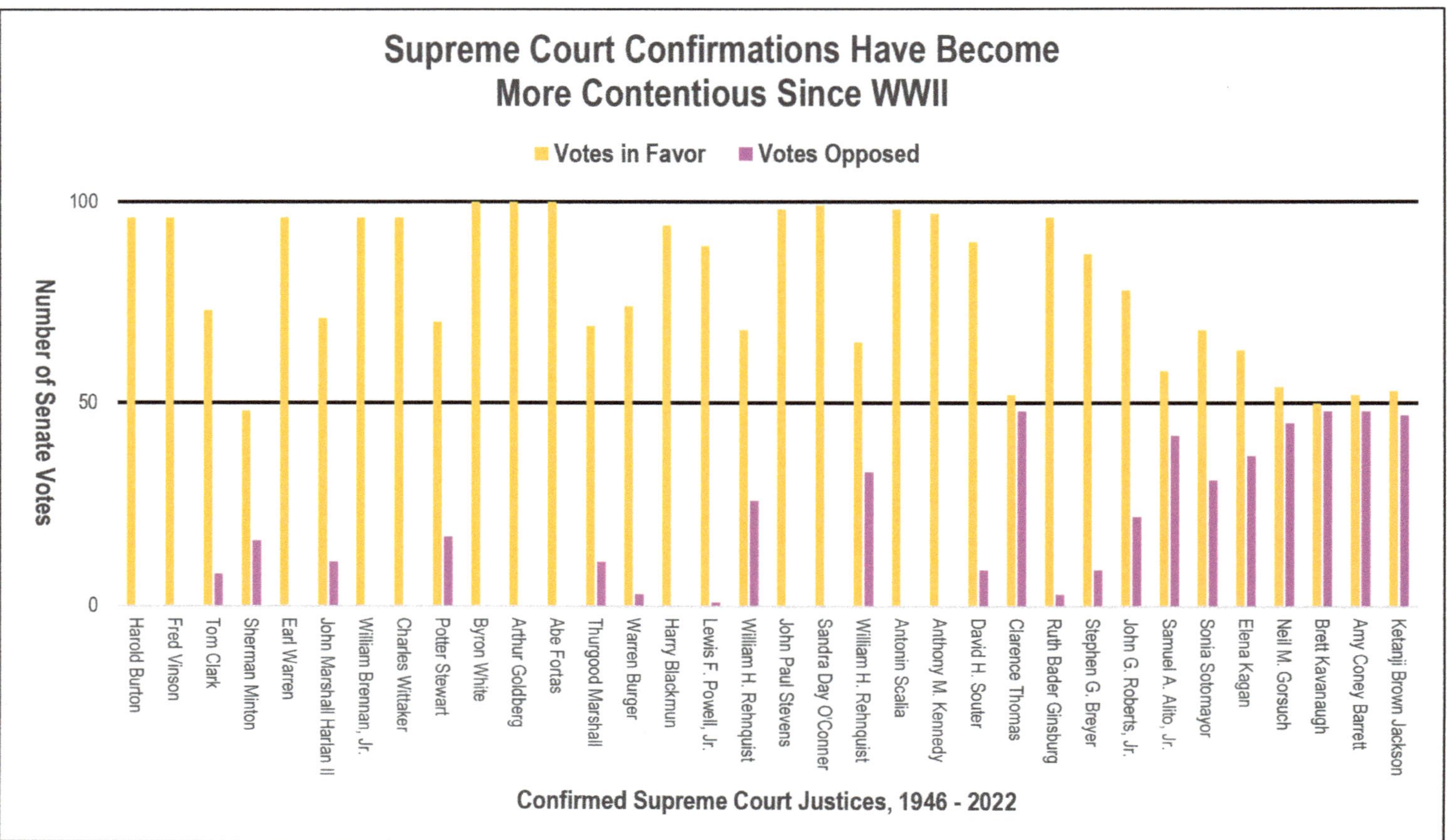

Figure 12.1

From 1946 to 1965 there were 12 Justices (Harold Burton to Abe Fortas) confirmed to the Supreme Court. Eight of those 12 Justices were confirmed by a voice vote, meaning that their nominations were so uncontroversial that the Senate confirmed them unanimously. Of the 14 Justices confirmed from 1967 to 1994 (Thurgood Marshall to Stephen Breyer), five were confirmed without a single vote opposed. The most disputed confirmations were those of William Rehnquist (26 votes opposed for Associate Justice in 1971, and 33 votes opposed for Chief Justice in 1986) and Clarence Thomas (48 votes opposed in 1991). Since 2000, every confirmed Justice (John Roberts to Kentanji Brown Jackson) has received at least 20 votes opposed. The last four confirmed Justices have had between 45 and 48 votes opposed. The current Supreme Court Justices had an average of 41 no votes at their confirmations. The confirmation process has never been as closely divided as it has been in recent years.

The lifetime tenure for justices raises the stakes for each appointment. With longer lifespans thanks to modern medicine, a justice confirmed at age 50 could plausibly be on the Court for 40 years! The 9 justices currently on the Court were confirmed at an average age of 50 and can be expected to serve an average of 33 years if they remain on the bench until death, according to the Social Security Administration's actuarial table.[89]

Table 12.1: Current Supreme Court by Confirmation Outcome and Expected Tenure

Justice	Year Appointed	Expected Replacement Year	Expected Tenure (years)	Votes in Favor	Votes Opposed	Age at Confirmation	Current Age	Expected Lifespan
Average	x	x	32.6	58.7	40.9	50.4	63.4	83.0
Clarence Thomas	1991	2033	42	52	48	43	75	85
John G. Roberts, Jr.	2005	2038	33	78	22	50	69	83
Samuel A. Alito, Jr.	2005	2035	30	58	42	55	74	85
Sonia Sotomayor	2009	2040	31	68	31	55	69	86
Elena Kagan	2010	2045	35	63	37	50	64	85
Neil M. Gorsuch	2017	2047	30	54	45	49	56	79
Brett Kavanaugh	2018	2045	27	50	48	53	59	80
Amy Coney Barrett	2020	2054	34	52	48	48	52	82
Ketanji Brown Jackson	2022	2053	31	53	47	51	53	82

In recent years, justices have chosen to retire when the presidency is occupied by someone they believe will appoint a similar-minded successor. Justice Anthony Kennedy retired in 2018 to allow a Republican president to appoint his replacement, and Justice Stephen Breyer retired in 2022 to allow a Democratic president to appoint his replacement. In this way, only when there is an unexpected death of a justice appointed by one party during the term of a President of the other party does the ideological makeup of the Court change, as it did with the death of liberal Justice Ruth Bader Ginsburg in 2020.

Thanks to longer lifespans, Supreme Court seats are filled less frequently than in the past. Since the end of WWII, there have been 1.7 justices appointed per presidential term. This is lower than the 2.5 justices from 1869 through 1945, or the 2.0 Justices appointed per term from 1789 through 1869 when the Court had fewer than 9 justices.

The randomness of how many appointments a president might make adds unnecessary stress to our system. The more infrequent the appointments, the more important they become, and the more our political parties are willing to risk to gain or deny an appointment.

Since the Carter Administration, there have been six Democratic presidential terms and six Republican presidential terms. Despite an equal time in control of the Executive Branch, the combination of random luck of timely deaths, coordinated retirements, and one partisan theft resulted in Republican Presidents appointing 11 Justices compared to the Democrats five.

For people on the left like myself, what reason do we have to abide by the rulings of such a biased Court as it strips us of our rights, ruling by ruling, year by year?

There is a simple fix for the problems of randomness and lifetime tenure: a regular appointment schedule and a single, roughly 20 year term for Justices.

The issues of corruption and the Court's power consolidation are not so easily fixed.

The conduct of these members of the court, in particular Justices Clarence Thomas and Samuel Alito, is blatantly corrupt and partisan. Justice Alito accepted luxury fishing trips[90]—including flying on a private jet—from a billionaire who later had cases before the Supreme Court. Unsurprisingly, Alito ruled in favor of the billionaire in those cases. In addition to corruption, Justice Alito is blatantly partisan. While the Supreme Court was considering a case related to the 2020 election, an upside-down American flag, at the time a symbol of Trump's Big Lie's "Stop the Steal" movement flew over Justice Alito's front lawn.[91] That is how the New York Times reported the news; note the passive voice in the previous sentence. Justice Alito responded to this revelation with an excuse that no objective observer would find plausible: "I had no involvement whatsoever in the flying of the flag. It was briefly placed by Mrs. Alito in response to a neighbor's use of objectionable and personally insulting language on yard signs." The timing of the events renders this excuse hollow. Justice Alito cannot be trusted to rule impartially. He should be removed from office.

Justice Thomas's behavior is somehow even more egregious. For over 20 years,[92] Justice Thomas accepted gifts from conservative billionaire Harlan Crow, and never disclosed them, in flagrant violation of ethics laws. These gifts included multiple luxury vacations, flights on Crow's private jet and trips on Crow's private yacht, paying for[93] Justice Thomas's grandnephew's private school tuition, and purchasing and renovating[94] Justice Thomas's mother's house. This corruption is laughably obvious! Further, Justice Thomas's conservative activist wife Ginni Thomas spent the weeks following the 2020 election supporting efforts[95] to prevent Joe Biden from assuming office. In a subsequent Supreme Court case which ensured[96] Congress would be allowed to obtain records related to the January 6th insurrection, Justice Thomas was the lone dissent.[97] Justice Thomas is corrupt and cannot be trusted to rule impartially. He should also be removed from office.

Justices Alito and Thomas are merely the most corrupt and partisan examples of a corrupt and partisan institution. In a deeply ironic speech[98] at the McConnell Center for Justice, named for Republican Senate Majority Leader Mitch McConnell, Justice Barrett argued that the Supreme Court "is not comprised of a bunch of partisan hacks." This, after the partisan hackery that allowed

Table 12.2: Randomness of Supreme Court Appointments

#	President	Presidential Terms	Justices Appointed	Justices per Term
	All Presidents	59	121	2.1
	Washington - Johnson	20	39	2.0
	Grant - Roosevelt	19	48	2.5
	Truman - Biden	20	34	1.7
1	Washington	2	10	5.0
2	Adams	1	3	3.0
3	Jefferson	2	3	1.5
4	Madison	2	2	1.0
5	Monroe	2	1	0.5
6	Quincy Adams	1	1	1.0
7	Jackson	2	6	3.0
8	Van Buren	1	2	2.0
9	Henry Harrison	0.02	0	0.0
10	Tyler	0.98	1	1.0
11	Polk	1	2	2.0
12	Taylor	0.3	0	0.0
13	Fillmore	0.7	1	1.5
14	Pierce	1	1	1.0
15	Buchanan	1	1	1.0
16	Lincoln	1	5	4.9
17	Johnson	1	0	0.0
18	Grant	2	5	2.5
19	Hayes	1	2	2.0
20	Garfield	0.1	1	8.0
21	Arthur	0.9	2	2.3
22	Cleveland	1	2	2.0
23	Harrison	1	4	4.0
24	Cleveland	1	2	2.0
25	McKinley	1.1	1	0.9
26	Roosevelt	1.9	3	1.6
27	Taft	1	6	6.0
28	Wilson	2	3	1.5
29	Harding	0.6	4	6.4
30	Coolidge	1.4	1	0.7
31	Hoover	1	3	3.0
32	Roosevelt	3.02	9	3.0
33	Truman	1.98	4	2.0
34	Eisenhower	2	5	2.5
35	Kennedy	0.7	2	2.8
36	Johnson	1.3	2	1.6
37	Nixon	1.4	4	2.9
38	Ford	0.6	1	1.6
39	Carter	1	0	0.0
40	Reagan	2	4	2.0
41	HW Bush	1	2	2.0
42	Clinton	2	2	1.0
43	W Bush	2	2	1.0
44	Obama	2	2	1.0
45	Trump	1	3	3.0
46	Biden	1	1	1.0

Justice Barrett to replace Justice Ruth Bader Ginsburg in the weeks leading up to the 2020 election. The Court has aided partisan Republican causes by acting either quickly (invalidating a Biden Administration vaccination policy) or slowly (taking so long to rule that a contested and Republican favored gerrymandered congressional map in South Carolina had to be used in an upcoming election).[99]

Why should the rulings of an obviously corrupt and partisan Court be respected? Especially when that corrupt and partisan Court issues rulings devoid of consistent logic other than to give itself more power over the other branches of the government?

Such are the questions you might ask after reading Mark A. Lemley's comprehensive November 2022 article in the Harvard Law Review titled "The Imperial Supreme Court."[100] Lemley dives into the opinions issued by the Court in recent years and shows that there is no consistent judicial philosophy behind their rulings, whether that philosophy be "originalism, textualism, dictionary fetishism, stare decisis, or anything else." The only consistency is that the Court's rulings "centralize power in the Supreme Court." In other words, "the Court always wins" at the expense of administrative agencies, Congress, lower federal courts, States, and individual rights.

The Court's June 2024 decision in *Trump v. United States* proves Lemley's argument. In this decision, the Court ruled that the President is effectively above the law. Yet, even here, Adam Serwer of the Atlantic observes that the majority wrote "the decision so as to keep the power to decide which presidential acts would be 'official' and immune to criminal prosecution, and which would be 'unofficial' and therefore not. The president is immune, but only when the justices say he is. The president might seem like a king, but the justices can withhold the crown."[101]

Lemley concludes his article with what will be a familiar observation, that "the Court ultimately exists on the credibility of its judgments, and if it damages that credibility enough, the federal or state governments may decide that they can simply ignore it."

Our current Court is illegitimate, and we could be one poorly received ruling away from the breakdown of law in our country. It could hasten Civil War, as it did in the 1850's with its absurd *Dred Scott* decision.

If the 2024 Election is contested and decided in the Court, as was the 2000 Election, will the losing Presidential candidate accept the result as graciously as did Al Gore? And will the people whose candidate is on the losing side of such a Court decision accept it?

B. How Reform Would Restore Legitimacy

This section makes the case for three proposed reforms:

1. Single term for all Justices, and no Justice may serve more than 1.5 terms (in the event of a Justice being appointed to replace a justice who died, resigned, or was impeached). The term length shall be between 18 and 22 years, depending on the size of the reformed Court.

2. Justices are appointed on a set schedule, so that in each presidential term the President shall appoint the same number of justices. Appointments shall be subject to Legislative approval. Congress shall be required to hold a vote within 60 days of nomination.

3. Increase the size of the Court to 21 Justices. Cases would be decided by a panel of nine randomly selected justices.

Combined, these reforms would reduce the political pressure surrounding each individual appointment. The third reform would amplify the benefits of the first two, though it is more controversial.

First, limiting each justice to a single term of between 18 and 22 years ensures that justices do not hold onto power for 40 years or longer. This lowers the stakes for each judicial appointment because the political parties will know that each new justice will be replaced in roughly 20 years. In a nine-Justice Supreme Court, each Justice would serve a single 18-year term.

Table 12.3: Transition to a Term Limited Nine-Justice Court

Seat	Justices	Year Appointed	Replacement Year	Term Length
1	Associate Thomas	1991	2027	36
2	Chief Roberts	2005	2029	24
3	Associate Alito	2005	2031	26
4	Associate Sotomayor	2009	2033	24
5	Associate Kagan	2010	2035	25
6	Associate Gorsuch	2017	2037	20
7	Associate Kavanaugh	2018	2039	21
8	Associate Barrett	2020	2041	21
9	Associate Jackson	2022	2043	21

Second, by appointing justices on a set schedule, the political parties would know that they would have the chance to influence the makeup of the Court provided they win the Presidency or control enough seats in Congress. Every President would appoint 1 justice in the first year of their term and a second justice in the third year of their term. The benefit of this would be that the President would have to nominate a Justice in response to a changed Legislature following the midterm elections. The set schedule ensures that luck or planned retirements do not make some Presidents more influential than others. Political parties could focus on winning elections instead of partisan gamesmanship around the appointment process.

If the first two reforms went into effect in 2026, the longest tenured Justice would be replaced first. Justice Thomas was appointed in 1991 and will have served for 36 years by the time of his replacement in 2027, double the term length of his successor. Chief Justice Roberts would be replaced next, in 2029, after having served 24 years. Implementing this reform in 2026 would ensure that all sitting justices would serve at least 20 years on the Court, more than the 18-year terms of their successors (Table 12.3).

In the event of an early death, retirement, or impeachment of a Justice, the sitting President would nominate a replacement to serve the rest of the departing Justice's term. Similar to how a Vice President who replaces a President in the middle of their term may run for two additional terms if the replacement term is less than half the length of a normal term, a replacement Justice may serve an additional term if the replacement term is less than half the length of a normal term, in this case 9 years. So, the longest amount of time a Justice could serve on a term limited court is 27 years.

It is important that Congress be required to hold a vote on the President's nominee within 60 days so that a Merrick Garland situation never happens again.

Table 12.4: Transition to a Term Limited 11 Justice Court

Seat	Justices	Year Appointed	Replacement Year	Term Length
1	Associate Thomas	1991	2031	40
2	Chief Roberts	2005	2033	28
3	Associate Alito	2005	2035	30
4	Associate Sotomayor	2009	2037	28
5	Associate Kagan	2010	2039	29
6	Associate Gorsuch	2017	2041	24
7	Associate Kavanaugh	2018	2043	25
8	Associate Barrett	2020	2045	25
9	Associate Jackson	2022	2047	25
10	Associate A	2027	2049	22
11	Associate B	2029	2051	22

The third reform would increase the size of the Court to 21 Justices.

Increasing the size of the Court to 11 would add legitimacy to the Court in the eyes of liberals as a way to make up for the partisan denial of Merrick Garland. Each justice on an 11-Justice Supreme Court would serve for 22 years (Table 12.4). The appointment schedule would remain the same as in the 9-Justice Court, with each President appointing two Justices per term. If implemented in 2026, new Justices would be added to the Court in 2027 and 2029. Starting in 2031, the sitting justices would be phased out as their terms ended. Every sitting Justice would serve at least 22 years, ensuring that no sitting Justice would serve less than the length of the term of their successor. However, increasing the size of the Court to 11 would not make panel decisions possible.

Increasing the Court to 21 Justices in which cases would be decided by a panel of 9 randomly selected justices would further depoliticize the appointment process by reducing the power of each individual justice. A panel of justices would mean that all justices would not issue rulings on all cases. With a 9-justice panel deciding each case, each Justice would rule on a little more than 1/3 of all cases. This would also allow the Supreme Court to take up additional cases, as more Justices would allow for more decisions to be written.

Additionally, the random selection of the justices would make it impossible to predict the ideological makeup of any one case. The interpretation of the law, overtime, would be more just.

Table 12.5: Transition to a Term Limited 21 Justice Court

Seat	Justices	Year Appointed	Replacement Year	Term Length
1	Associate Thomas	1991	2039	48
2	Chief Roberts	2005	2040	35
3	Associate Alito	2005	2041	36
4	Associate Sotomayor	2009	2042	33
5	Associate Kagan	2010	2043	33
6	Associate Gorsuch	2017	2044	27
7	Associate Kavanaugh	2018	2045	27
8	Associate Barrett	2020	2046	26
9	Associate Jackson	2022	2047	25
10	Associate A	2027	2048	21
11	Associate B	2028	2049	21
12	Associate C	2029	2050	21
13	Associate D	2030	2051	21
14	Associate E	2031	2052	21
15	Associate F	2032	2053	21
16	Associate G	2033	2054	21
17	Associate H	2034	2055	21
18	Associate I	2035	2056	21
19	Associate J	2036	2057	21
20	Associate K	2037	2058	21
21	Associate L	2038	2059	21

The transition to a 21-Justice Supreme Court would take over a decade (Table 12.5). Justices would be added one per year starting in 2027 until the Court reached 21 Justices in 2038. Starting with Justice Thomas in 2039, the sitting justices would have their terms end. If any sitting justice died or retired before their term ended, the normal replacement rules would be followed. If there was more than 10 years left in their term, the replacement justice would not be eligible for a full term; if there were 10 years or fewer left in the term, the replacement Justice would be eligible for a full term. Each sitting justice would serve at least 25 years.

In a 21-Justice Supreme Court, each President would appoint four justices per term, one per year. The regular and frequent appointments would make each individual appointment less politically fraught, especially once the full 21-Justice Supreme Court was established.

Adding one justice per year is a better way to increase the size of the Court than adding 12 justices in a single go because adding Justices over time allows for different presidents to change the makeup of the Court instead of a single president making an outsized impact.

These reforms would not solve all the issues contributing to the Court's illegitimacy. Implementing term limits would do nothing to solve the issue of corruption. However, by reducing the power of each individual Justice, Congress may be more inclined to use its power to impeach corrupt Justices. Similarly, these reforms would not address the current Court's repeated interpretation of the law to increase its control over the other branches and institutions of our government. The only clear remedy for this ailment is for presidents to appoint justices who, over the long term, will be more responsible stewards of their power than the current bunch.

The Supreme Court has always been and will always be political. It is inevitable. The best we can do is to create a structure that restrains the power of individuals, and that reduces the political tension surrounding appointments. These reforms accomplish that goal.

## Chapter 13

THE QUARTER MILLENNIUM CONVENTION OF 2026

Imagine the impossible happens: a political window opens and the skeleton political strategy outlined in Chapter 3 is successful. The legislatures of more than 34 states, supported by a supermajority of the American people, have called for a Constitutional Convention.

A Convention in 2026 would be very different from the Convention of 1787. Two hundred thirty-seven years ago, 55 Americans met in Philadelphia to write a new Constitution. The delegates met in closed sessions and they drafted the Constitution in secret.[102] After months of deliberations, they presented the new Constitution to the States and the People for ratification.

Since then, the United States of America expanded across the entirety of North America, its population grew to over 300 million and counting, and it became the preeminent global power.

Technology and society are vastly different. So different, in fact, that despite our relative temporal proximity, the world of 1787 has more in common with the world of ancient Greece and Rome than the world of 2024. Media went from letters and newspapers in 1787 to telephones, radio, television, and the internet today. Traveling in 1787 meant weeks or months of walking, riding horses, or sailing in ships powered by wind and sail; today, you can easily travel from any major city to any other major city, anywhere in the world, in less than 24 hours.

Yet a modern Convention would remain essentially the same as the first: a number of delegates representing every State, meeting in person, working together to draft new Constitution.

The precise rules of the Convention could be agreed to in advance by the State Legislatures. For example, the States could set a deadline of six months for the delegates to agree upon final language. That language would then be subject to approval by the States.

The States would need to agree upon additional rules, such as how many delegates each State would be allowed to send.

States could also agree on rules regarding the amount of administrative support staff for the delegates, as well as how to make subject matter experts like lawyers and academics available to answer questions from the delegates.

Each State would choose how to select its delegates. States could choose delegates through a vote of the people, let the Legislature or Governor appoint delegates, or even select delegates through a **random lottery**.[103]

While it may be better for the delegates to be able to deliberate in secret, the reality of modern media means that the next Convention will be a more transparent affair.

As the movement for a Convention grows, and the State Legislatures begin to seriously pursue this path, the precise rules for the Convention can be determined.

In 2026, we will celebrate the 250th anniversary of American independence. A quarter of a millennium! What better way to celebrate such a milestone than with that same democratic spirit with which our Founders conceived independence?

A. The 28th Amendment

Section 1. The Senate of the United States shall be abolished, including the special status granted to the Senate in Article 5. All legislative powers granted to the Senate in Article 1, Section 3, shall be vested in the House of Representatives, which shall be the sole legislative body of the Congress of the United States. All powers granted to the Senate related to checking the Executive Branch in Article 2 shall be vested in the House of Representatives. All powers granted to the Senate related to checking the Judicial Branch shall be vested in the House of Representatives.

Section 2. The number of Representatives in the House shall be adjusted to 695, and shall be apportioned among the several states according to their respective numbers, as determined by Congress, counting the whole number of persons in each state. After each decennial census, Congress shall adjust its size proportionately to the cube root of the total population of the United States.

Section 3. In States apportioned more than one representative, Members shall be elected by a proportional voting method, decided upon by each State.

Section 4. The Electoral College shall be abolished. The President and Vice President shall be elected by the people of the United States through a national ranked choice popular vote.

Section 5. The President, Vice President, and all civil Officers of the United States, shall be removed from Office on Impeachment for, and Conviction of, Treason, Bribery, or other high Crimes and Misdemeanors, upon a vote of 3/5ths of the Members of Congress.

Section 6. The Judges of the Supreme Court shall hold their Offices for a term of 21 years and shall be ineligible for reappointment thereafter.

Section 7. Appointments to the Supreme Court shall occur once per year so that in each presidential term there are four appointments.

Section 8. The Supreme Court of the United States shall consist of a Chief Justice and 20 Associate Justices. Cases shall be decided by a randomly assigned panel of 9 Justices.

Section 9. Congress shall have the power to enforce this article by appropriate legislation.

B. Caveats

The language of the 28th Amendment in the previous section is a draft, and is intended as a starting point for further conversation.

Setting these specific reforms and this specific language aside, there is a potential danger in drafting new Constitutional language: What if the new Constitution is worse? ("Worse" defined as a government that is less democratic, less accountable, more divisive, and more prone to authoritarian descent.)

This could happen unintentionally, with the purest of motives resulting in the creation of a worse government.

It could also happen intentionally. After all, going back to the Founding Era, there has always been an anti-democratic faction in America.

While drafting and implementing a worse Constitution is a real danger, it is not insurmountable, and should not stop us from trying.

First, as I have argued throughout this book, the existing Constitution is deeply flawed and undemocratic. To create a worse Constitution, the new document would have to be so bad that it is difficult to imagine the delegates agreeing to such a thing.

Second, our knowledge of how parties function in a democracy is much improved from 1787, when there was practically zero knowledge on the subject. With the benefit of over 200 years of history to learn from, the delegates should be able to craft a more functional government.

Third, there are several parts of the Constitution that are worth keeping: the separation of powers, the Bill of Rights, the Civil War Amendments, and others I have not discussed here.

There will be disagreement. While I have made what I believe to be a strong case for this suite of reforms, I know there will be arguments that I have not considered, and that other Americans could, in good faith, favor a different combination of reforms.

In other words, I am open to compromise. As a believer in democracy, how could I not be?

For example, I believe the most controversial reform articulated here is the abolition of the Senate. In Chapter 4, I staked a maximalist position and attempted to address all conceivable counterarguments. And while I believe my arguments are persuasive, some people may not be convinced to abolish the Senate. In this case, a compromise position could be in enacting some kind of reform, such as reducing the power of the Senate so that it functions more as a rubber stamp and only rarely exercises veto power, similar to upper chambers in bicameral legislatures around the world, such as the modern British House of Lords. I leave it to others to make those arguments in favor of the continued existence of the Senate if they so choose.

The point is that these disagreements are what must be worked through at the Convention. This is an alternative path we can choose instead of following the dysfunctional, violent path we appear to be on now.

Chapter 14
AND SO IT GOES

I am writing this conclusion in August 2024. I have put it off for as long as possible, but my editor is annoyed, as she should be, and the deadline for this book to make it to print before the Election has come.

These truly are interesting times! For better or worse, I am glad to be alive in this moment. Today, in America, there is such an opportunity for greatness!

Yet also there is peril.

In the Framework, I called the status quo untenable. No matter November's electoral outcome, I believe there will be change. The specifics are unknowable, but change is a certainty.

I have described democratic action as action by the many. Whatever change comes after November, it will be the result of our collective action and our collective decisions. Mine, yours, and theirs. Together, we shape our future.

In the Proposal, I described what we could do to change our future. If we implement a system such as the one described, or something approximating it, we could see a multiparty system in America in our lifetimes. That path begins with calling for a Convention.

Whether reached through cynicism or hope, it matters little. Action, and action alone, is what counts.

A. My Politics

I must admit to an ulterior motive. I believe that these constitutional reforms would make it more likely for my political views to become law. Or, at least, something closer to my views than what we currently have.

Without going into specific policy detail, my political beliefs are rooted in the values of egalitarianism and environmentalism, plus some good old American distrust of authority. Imagine John Rawls crossed with Octavia Butler crossed with Frank Herbert:

1. All humans have equal moral value, and we should be treated by our government as such.
2. Our home, the Earth, is the only one humanity has; for our own sake, we must take care of it.
3. Power should be only as centralized as necessary to carry out the democratic will of the people as determined by regular, fair elections.

As it exists now, our system is anti-democratic and corrupt. This makes it difficult, if not impossible, to see the values I hold dear implemented by our government.

I believe a multiparty democracy will be better able to enact the democratic will of the people, and I believe that, in general, over the course of a period of time, enacting the democratic will of the people will lead to a more just society

B. Message to America

Finally, to the various factions and forces that together comprise America, a message.

To the Left: I am one of you. Know that I say this with love: we need to get our act together. You drive me crazy with your ever-changing norms around language and your insistence on dismissing good progress as insufficient because it is not perfect. And I realize the irony of the previous sentence considering everything I have said in this book. The problem of organizing the Left is that no one hates a leftist more than another, slightly different leftist. Where is our unified, positive vision? Where is our Project 2025?

To the Right: I recognize there are many facets of your coalition. But I nonetheless address you as a monolith with regard to democracy. When the votes are counted, and the outcome is declared, what are you going to do? Are you going to support that outcome? Or are you going to defy it? In 2020, Donald Trump defied democracy, and, if he loses in November, I fully expect him to do so again. But you don't have to follow him. You have agency. You have choice. Do not give in to that dehumanizing, fearmongering rhetoric! We are all Americans. We are all humans.

To the disaffected Middle: You really have the power to decide this election. You see two parties that you view as getting more and more extreme, and you find the choice between them distasteful. Policy preferences aside, the difference between the Right and the Left is that the Right is organized while the Left is not. If you find the policy goals of the extreme wings of each side equally distasteful, the more organized faction is more likely to be successful in implementing policy goals that you might oppose.

To the non-voters of all persuasions: I say this without judgment: You have chosen to not choose. Your view of our entire political system as corrupt, and flawed, and unworthy of your vote is reasonable. However, our government is worse, I think, for not having had your input. I hope a proportionally representative system, such as described in this book, might earn your choice to cast a ballot. In a multiparty system, you might find a party that earns your support. Or, if you wanted to get real crazy, you could create a new party yourself.

To the Prospective Next Major Party: Start with a single, simple idea. Show the American people you are serious first, before asking them to award you the highest office in the land. The last real new political party in America was the Republican Party, founded in Wisconsin in 1854. It had one core political belief: opposition to slavery. That was the idea that provided unity. What will yours be? Once you have your idea, start local, within your State. And once you are organized, reach out nationally to those who might be like-minded. Don't start just by running a Presidential candidate.

To the Establishment Politicians: Aren't you tired of this system, too? Wouldn't a multiparty system be fun? Do not miss the forest for the trees! In the grand scope of our history, what will your story be?

To the Chattering Class: Ugh. You endlessly annoy me as I consume hours of your content. You treat news items as if they were all equally BREAKING NEWS, damaging your credibility and our discourse. You fritter away our mental energy with your political hobbyism, your breathless, changing-by-the-minute, superficial political arguments. You are exhausting! Do better! Go touch grass!

To the Financial Elites: You guys know that political stability is good for business, right?

To the Bureaucrats: You pride yourself on impartial competence, as you should. But be wary of your impartiality being exploited by malevolent forces. Write down, for yourself, now, the red lines of state power which you cannot abide. Be wary of becoming a cog in a machine sowing banal evil!

To the Military: You are the single institution I trust most in America. I say that not to lick your boots but as a statement of fact. Seemingly, all our other institutions are failing, but you have remained true to your principles. Your honor during the 2020 Presidential Transition will be forever commendable. Yours is the power of the sword, the sharpest, deadliest, and most expensive sword in the history of the world. If the worst comes to pass, and a tyrant orders you to do something you know to be wrong, I hope you will again be honorable. The power is yours.

To the Past: The crimes and triumphs of our land cannot be separated. Together, you have created our present. Now, it is our turn.

To the Present: Our country stands on the edge of an abyss. "We are in the process of a second American revolution, which will remain bloodless if the left allows it to be." That is a frankly very aggressive declaration from **Kevin Roberts,**[104] President of the Heritage Foundation and the author of the Foreword of Project 2025.

Curious and not wanting to let the media determine my views, I read the 17 pages of Robert's Foreword. There is some wild stuff in there, to put it mildly. Although, interestingly, the existential rhetoric of Project 2025, in many ways, mirrors my rhetoric here. In that way, at least, we agree on the stakes of the present.

But the vision described in Project 2025 and the vision I have described here are far apart. My Polemic has at its core a belief in egalitarianism, the idea that all humans are created equal. Project 2025 claims that same American heritage, yet it twists these ideas of human equality so much that they become their opposite. It is also intensely pro-nationalist and pro-religious, specifically pro-Christianity. I find that combination concerning, because "When religion and politics travel in the same cart, the riders believe nothing can **stand in their way.**"[105] Based off my reading of the Foreword, and the events of January 6, 2021, there is ample reason to believe that democracy is not something that the riders of this cart will let stand in their way.

This Polemic has been a scream into the void, a desperate plea to avoid the violence and chaos of a potential civil war. But if such a tragedy comes to pass, I know what side I will be on. I choose the pen, not the sword, and I will forever be on the side of democracy, and truth, and freedom.

To the Future: Let us have that **Great Debate!**[106] For you, I hope we do good.

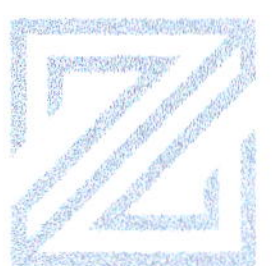

ABOUT THE AUTHOR

Zane Gustafson has dedicated his professional life to researching and writing about some of the most significant challenges facing contemporary America. His political thinking was shaped initially by growing up in Sumner, Washington, a politically diverse suburban community about an hour from Seattle. After feeling inspired to pursue politics as a teenager by President Obama's 2008 campaign, Zane moved to Seattle to study at the University of Washington. He studied Philosophy and Political Science as an undergraduate and then earned a Master's in Public Administration from the UW Evans School of Public Policy with a focus on climate policy.

Professionally, Zane has worked for the Sightline Institute, where he deepened his expertise in policy analysis through contributions to research on voting systems and energy infrastructure. He currently freelances for organizations working in opposition to the fossil fuel industry.

Through his political writing, Zane seeks to provoke serious conversation on politically unconventional solutions to modern problems, particularly regarding the prospect of realistic constitutional reform in the United States. Zane is an avid reader and traveler, and finds inspiration for his work in the stories, cultures, and people he encounters.

APPENDIX

The following tables (pages 200–204) show each state's voting power following the U.S. Census from 1930 to 2020. The voting power columns in each table were combined to create Table 5.18 on page 46.

Table 5.21: Representation in 1930 (48 States)

State	Seats	Population	Pop. Per Rep.	Voting Power
United States	*435*	*122,093,455*	*280,675*	*100.0%*
Nevada	1	86,390	86,390	324.9%
Wyoming	1	223,630	223,630	125.5%
Delaware	1	238,380	238,380	117.7%
Vermont	1	359,611	359,611	78.0%
Arizona	1	389,375	389,375	72.1%
New Mexico	1	395,982	395,982	70.9%
Idaho	2	441,536	220,768	127.1%
New Hampshire	2	465,292	232,646	120.6%
Utah	2	505,741	252,871	111.0%
Montana	2	524,729	262,365	107.0%
South Dakota	2	673,005	336,503	83.4%
North Dakota	2	673,340	336,670	83.4%
Rhode Island	2	687,497	343,749	81.7%
Maine	3	797,418	265,806	105.6%
Oregon	3	950,379	316,793	88.6%
Colorado	4	1,034,849	258,712	108.5%
Nebraska	5	1,375,123	275,025	102.1%
Florida	5	1,468,191	293,638	95.6%
Washington	6	1,552,423	258,737	108.5%
Connecticut	6	1,606,897	267,816	104.8%
Maryland	6	1,631,522	271,920	103.2%
West Virginia	6	1,729,199	288,200	97.4%
South Carolina	6	1,738,760	289,793	96.9%
Arkansas	7	1,854,444	264,921	105.9%
Kansas	7	1,879,498	268,500	104.5%
Mississippi	7	2,008,154	286,879	97.8%
Louisiana	8	2,101,593	262,699	106.8%
Oklahoma	9	2,382,222	264,691	106.0%
Virginia	9	2,421,829	269,092	104.3%
Iowa	9	2,470,420	274,491	102.3%
Minnesota	9	2,551,583	283,509	99.0%
Kentucky	9	2,614,575	290,508	96.6%
Tennessee	9	2,616,497	290,722	96.5%
Alabama	9	2,646,242	294,027	95.5%
Georgia	10	2,908,446	290,845	96.5%
Wisconsin	10	2,931,721	293,172	95.7%
North Carolina	11	3,167,274	287,934	97.5%
Indiana	12	3,238,480	269,873	104.0%
Missouri	13	3,629,110	279,162	100.5%
New Jersey	14	4,041,319	288,666	97.2%
Massachusetts	15	4,249,598	283,307	99.1%
Michigan	17	4,842,052	284,827	98.5%
California	20	5,668,241	283,412	99.0%
Texas	21	5,824,601	277,362	101.2%
Ohio	24	6,646,633	276,943	101.3%
Illinois	27	7,630,388	282,607	99.3%
Pennsylvania	34	9,631,299	283,274	99.1%
New York	45	12,587,967	279,733	100.3%

Table 5.22: Representation in 1940 (48 States)

State	Seats	Population	Pop. Per Rep.	Voting Power
United States	*435*	*131,006,184*	*301,164*	*100.0%*
Nevada	1	110,247	110,247	273.2%
Wyoming	1	250,742	250,742	120.1%
Delaware	1	266,505	266,505	113.0%
Vermont	1	359,231	359,231	83.8%
New Hampshire	2	491,524	245,762	122.5%
Arizona	2	499,261	249,631	120.6%
Idaho	2	524,873	262,437	114.8%
New Mexico	2	531,818	265,909	113.3%
Utah	2	550,310	275,155	109.5%
Montana	2	559,456	279,728	107.7%
North Dakota	2	641,935	320,968	93.8%
South Dakota	2	642,961	321,481	93.7%
Rhode Island	2	713,346	356,673	84.4%
Maine	3	847,226	282,409	106.6%
Oregon	4	1,089,684	272,421	110.6%
Colorado	4	1,123,296	280,824	107.2%
Nebraska	4	1,315,834	328,959	91.6%
Connecticut	6	1,709,242	284,874	105.7%
Washington	6	1,736,191	289,365	104.1%
Kansas	6	1,801,028	300,171	100.3%
Maryland	6	1,821,244	303,541	99.2%
Florida	6	1,897,414	316,236	95.2%
South Carolina	6	1,899,804	316,634	95.1%
West Virginia	6	1,901,974	316,996	95.0%
Arkansas	7	1,949,387	278,484	108.1%
Mississippi	7	2,183,796	311,971	96.5%
Oklahoma	8	2,336,434	292,054	103.1%
Louisiana	8	2,363,880	295,485	101.9%
Iowa	8	2,538,268	317,284	94.9%
Virginia	9	2,677,773	297,530	101.2%
Minnesota	9	2,792,300	310,256	97.1%
Alabama	9	2,832,961	314,773	95.7%
Kentucky	9	2,845,627	316,181	95.3%
Tennessee	10	2,915,841	291,584	103.3%
Georgia	10	3,123,723	312,372	96.4%
Wisconsin	10	3,137,587	313,759	96.0%
Indiana	11	3,427,796	311,618	96.6%
North Carolina	12	3,571,623	297,635	101.2%
Missouri	13	3,784,664	291,128	103.4%
New Jersey	14	4,160,165	297,155	101.3%
Massachusetts	14	4,316,721	308,337	97.7%
Michigan	17	5,256,106	309,183	97.4%
Texas	21	6,414,824	305,468	98.6%
California	23	6,907,387	300,321	100.3%
Ohio	23	6,907,612	300,331	100.3%
Illinois	26	7,897,241	303,740	99.2%
Pennsylvania	33	9,900,180	300,005	100.4%
New York	45	13,479,142	299,536	100.5%

Table 5.23: Representation in 1950 (48 States)

State	Seats	Population	Pop. Per Rep.	Voting Power
United States	*435*	*149,895,183*	*344,587*	*100.0%*
Nevada	1	160,083	160,083	215.3%
Wyoming	1	290,529	290,529	118.6%
Delaware	1	318,085	318,085	108.3%
Vermont	1	377,747	377,747	91.2%
New Hampshire	2	533,242	266,621	129.2%
Idaho	2	588,637	294,319	117.1%
Montana	2	591,024	295,512	116.6%
North Dakota	2	619,636	309,818	111.2%
South Dakota	2	652,740	326,370	105.6%
New Mexico	2	681,187	340,594	101.2%
Utah	2	688,862	344,431	100.0%
Arizona	2	749,587	374,794	91.9%
Rhode Island	2	791,896	395,948	87.0%
Maine	3	913,774	304,591	113.1%
Colorado	4	1,325,089	331,272	104.0%
Nebraska	4	1,325,510	331,378	104.0%
Oregon	4	1,521,341	380,335	90.6%
Kansas	6	1,905,299	317,550	108.5%
Arkansas	6	1,909,511	318,252	108.3%
West Virginia	6	2,005,552	334,259	103.1%
Connecticut	6	2,007,280	334,547	103.0%
South Carolina	6	2,117,027	352,838	97.7%
Mississippi	6	2,178,914	363,152	94.9%
Oklahoma	6	2,233,351	372,225	92.6%
Maryland	7	2,343,001	334,714	102.9%
Washington	7	2,378,963	339,852	101.4%
Iowa	8	2,621,073	327,634	105.2%
Louisiana	8	2,683,516	335,440	102.7%
Florida	8	2,771,305	346,413	99.5%
Kentucky	8	2,944,806	368,101	93.6%
Minnesota	9	2,982,483	331,387	104.0%
Alabama	9	3,061,743	340,194	101.3%
Tennessee	9	3,291,718	365,746	94.2%
Virginia	10	3,318,680	331,868	103.8%
Wisconsin	10	3,434,575	343,458	100.3%
Georgia	10	3,444,578	344,458	100.0%
Indiana	11	3,934,224	357,657	96.3%
Missouri	11	3,954,653	359,514	95.8%
North Carolina	12	4,061,929	338,494	101.8%
Massachusetts	14	4,690,514	335,037	102.9%
New Jersey	14	4,835,329	345,381	99.8%
Michigan	18	6,371,766	353,987	97.3%
Texas	22	7,711,194	350,509	98.3%
Ohio	23	7,946,627	345,506	99.7%
Illinois	25	8,712,176	348,487	98.9%
Pennsylvania	30	10,498,012	349,934	98.5%
California	30	10,586,223	352,874	97.7%
New York	43	14,830,192	344,888	99.9%

Table 5.24: Representation in 1960 (50 States)

State	Seats	Population	Pop. Per Rep.	Voting Power
United States	*435*	*178,559,219*	*410,481*	*100.0%*
Alaska	1	226,167	226,167	181.5%
Nevada	1	285,278	285,278	143.9%
Wyoming	1	330,066	330,066	124.4%
Vermont	1	389,881	389,881	105.3%
Delaware	1	446,292	446,292	92.0%
New Hampshire	2	606,921	303,461	135.3%
North Dakota	2	632,446	316,223	129.8%
Hawaii	2	632,772	316,386	129.7%
Idaho	2	667,191	333,596	123.0%
Montana	2	674,767	337,384	121.7%
South Dakota	2	680,514	340,257	120.6%
Rhode Island	2	859,488	429,744	95.5%
Utah	2	890,627	445,314	92.2%
New Mexico	2	951,023	475,512	86.3%
Maine	2	969,265	484,633	84.7%
Arizona	3	1,302,161	434,054	94.6%
Nebraska	3	1,411,330	470,443	87.3%
Colorado	4	1,753,947	438,487	93.6%
Oregon	4	1,768,687	442,172	92.8%
Arkansas	4	1,786,272	446,568	91.9%
West Virginia	5	1,860,421	372,084	110.3%
Mississippi	5	2,178,141	435,628	94.2%
Kansas	5	2,178,611	435,722	94.2%
Oklahoma	6	2,328,284	388,047	105.8%
South Carolina	6	2,382,594	397,099	103.4%
Connecticut	6	2,535,234	422,539	97.1%
Iowa	7	2,757,537	393,934	104.2%
Washington	7	2,853,214	407,602	100.7%
Kentucky	7	3,038,156	434,022	94.6%
Maryland	8	3,100,689	387,586	105.9%
Louisiana	8	3,257,022	407,128	100.8%
Alabama	8	3,266,740	408,343	100.5%
Minnesota	8	3,413,864	426,733	96.2%
Tennessee	9	3,567,089	396,343	103.6%
Georgia	10	3,943,116	394,312	104.1%
Wisconsin	10	3,951,777	395,178	103.9%
Virginia	10	3,966,949	396,695	103.5%
Missouri	10	4,319,813	431,981	95.0%
North Carolina	11	4,556,155	414,196	99.1%
Indiana	11	4,662,498	423,863	96.8%
Florida	12	4,951,560	412,630	99.5%
Massachusetts	12	5,148,578	429,048	95.7%
New Jersey	15	6,066,782	404,452	101.5%
Michigan	19	7,823,194	411,747	99.7%
Texas	23	9,579,677	416,508	98.6%
Ohio	24	9,706,397	404,433	101.5%
Illinois	24	10,081,158	420,048	97.7%
Pennsylvania	27	11,319,366	419,236	97.9%
California	38	15,717,204	413,611	99.2%
New York	41	16,782,304	409,324	100.3%

Table 5.25: Representation in 1970 (50 States)

State	Seats	Population	Pop. Per Rep.	Voting Power
United States	*435*	*204,053,325*	*469,088*	*100.0%*
Alaska	1	304,067	304,067	154.3%
Wyoming	1	335,719	335,719	139.7%
Vermont	1	448,327	448,327	104.6%
Nevada	1	492,396	492,396	95.3%
Delaware	1	551,928	551,928	85.0%
North Dakota	1	624,181	624,181	75.2%
South Dakota	2	673,247	336,624	139.4%
Montana	2	701,573	350,787	133.7%
Idaho	2	719,921	359,961	130.3%
New Hampshire	2	746,284	373,142	125.7%
Hawaii	2	784,901	392,451	119.5%
Rhode Island	2	957,798	478,899	98.0%
Maine	2	1,006,320	503,160	93.2%
New Mexico	2	1,026,664	513,332	91.4%
Utah	2	1,067,810	533,905	87.9%
Nebraska	3	1,496,820	498,940	94.0%
West Virginia	4	1,763,331	440,833	106.4%
Arizona	4	1,787,620	446,905	105.0%
Arkansas	4	1,942,303	485,576	96.6%
Oregon	4	2,110,810	527,703	88.9%
Colorado	5	2,226,771	445,354	105.3%
Mississippi	5	2,233,848	446,770	105.0%
Kansas	5	2,265,846	453,169	103.5%
Oklahoma	6	2,585,486	430,914	108.9%
South Carolina	6	2,617,320	436,220	107.5%
Iowa	6	2,846,920	474,487	98.9%
Connecticut	6	3,050,693	508,449	92.3%
Kentucky	7	3,246,481	463,783	101.1%
Washington	7	3,443,487	491,927	95.4%
Alabama	7	3,475,885	496,555	94.5%
Louisiana	8	3,672,008	459,001	102.2%
Minnesota	8	3,833,173	479,147	97.9%
Maryland	8	3,953,698	494,212	94.9%
Tennessee	8	3,961,060	495,133	94.7%
Wisconsin	9	4,447,013	494,113	94.9%
Georgia	10	4,627,306	462,731	101.4%
Virginia	10	4,690,742	469,074	100.0%
Missouri	10	4,718,034	471,803	99.4%
North Carolina	11	5,125,230	465,930	100.7%
Indiana	11	5,228,156	475,287	98.7%
Massachusetts	12	5,726,676	477,223	98.3%
Florida	15	6,855,702	457,047	102.6%
New Jersey	15	7,208,035	480,536	97.6%
Michigan	19	8,937,196	470,379	99.7%
Ohio	23	10,730,200	466,530	100.5%
Illinois	24	11,184,320	466,013	100.7%
Texas	24	11,298,787	470,783	99.6%
Pennsylvania	25	11,884,314	475,373	98.7%
New York	39	18,338,055	470,207	99.8%
California	43	20,098,863	467,415	100.4%

Table 5.26: Representation in 1980 (50 States)

State	Seats	Population	Pop. Per Rep.	Voting Power
United States	*435*	*225,867,174*	*519,235*	*100.0%*
Alaska	1	400,481	400,481	129.7%
Wyoming	1	470,816	470,816	110.3%
Vermont	1	511,456	511,456	101.5%
Delaware	1	595,225	595,225	87.2%
North Dakota	1	652,695	652,695	79.6%
South Dakota	1	690,178	690,178	75.2%
Montana	2	786,690	393,345	132.0%
Nevada	2	799,184	399,592	129.9%
New Hampshire	2	920,610	460,305	112.8%
Idaho	2	943,935	471,968	110.0%
Rhode Island	2	947,154	473,577	109.6%
Hawaii	2	965,000	482,500	107.6%
Maine	2	1,124,660	562,330	92.3%
New Mexico	3	1,299,968	433,323	119.8%
Utah	3	1,461,037	487,012	106.6%
Nebraska	3	1,570,006	523,335	99.2%
West Virginia	4	1,949,644	487,411	106.5%
Arkansas	4	2,285,513	571,378	90.9%
Kansas	5	2,363,208	472,642	109.9%
Mississippi	5	2,520,638	504,128	103.0%
Oregon	5	2,632,663	526,533	98.6%
Arizona	5	2,717,866	543,573	95.5%
Colorado	6	2,888,834	481,472	107.8%
Iowa	6	2,913,387	485,565	106.9%
Oklahoma	6	3,025,266	504,211	103.0%
Connecticut	6	3,107,576	517,929	100.3%
South Carolina	6	3,119,208	519,868	99.9%
Kentucky	7	3,661,433	523,062	99.3%
Alabama	7	3,890,061	555,723	93.4%
Minnesota	8	4,077,148	509,644	101.9%
Washington	8	4,130,163	516,270	100.6%
Louisiana	8	4,203,972	525,497	98.8%
Maryland	8	4,216,446	527,056	98.5%
Tennessee	9	4,590,750	510,083	101.8%
Wisconsin	9	4,705,335	522,815	99.3%
Missouri	9	4,917,444	546,383	95.0%
Virginia	10	5,346,279	534,628	97.1%
Georgia	10	5,464,265	546,427	95.0%
Indiana	10	5,490,179	549,018	94.6%
Massachusetts	11	5,737,037	521,549	99.6%
North Carolina	11	5,874,429	534,039	97.2%
New Jersey	14	7,364,158	526,011	98.7%
Michigan	18	9,258,344	514,352	100.9%
Florida	19	9,739,992	512,631	101.3%
Ohio	21	10,797,419	514,163	101.0%
Illinois	22	11,418,461	519,021	100.0%
Pennsylvania	23	11,866,728	515,945	100.6%
Texas	27	14,228,383	526,977	98.5%
New York	34	17,557,288	516,391	100.6%
California	45	23,668,562	525,968	98.7%

Table 5.27: Representation in 1990 (50 States)

State	Seats	Population	Pop. Per Rep.	Voting Power
United States	*435*	*249,022,783*	*572,466*	*100.0%*
Wyoming	1	455,975	455,975	125.5%
Alaska	1	551,947	551,947	103.7%
Vermont	1	564,964	564,964	101.3%
North Dakota	1	641,364	641,364	89.3%
Delaware	1	668,696	668,696	85.6%
South Dakota	1	699,999	699,999	81.8%
Montana	1	803,655	803,655	71.2%
Rhode Island	2	1,005,984	502,992	113.8%
Idaho	2	1,011,986	505,993	113.1%
New Hampshire	2	1,113,915	556,958	102.8%
Hawaii	2	1,115,274	557,637	102.7%
Nevada	2	1,206,152	603,076	94.9%
Maine	2	1,233,223	616,612	92.8%
New Mexico	3	1,521,779	507,260	112.9%
Nebraska	3	1,584,617	528,206	108.4%
Utah	3	1,727,784	575,928	99.4%
West Virginia	3	1,801,625	600,542	95.3%
Arkansas	4	2,362,239	590,560	96.9%
Kansas	4	2,485,600	621,400	92.1%
Mississippi	5	2,586,443	517,289	110.7%
Iowa	5	2,787,424	557,485	102.7%
Oregon	5	2,853,733	570,747	100.3%
Oklahoma	6	3,157,604	526,267	108.8%
Connecticut	6	3,295,669	549,278	104.2%
Colorado	6	3,307,912	551,319	103.8%
South Carolina	6	3,505,707	584,285	98.0%
Arizona	6	3,677,985	612,998	93.4%
Kentucky	6	3,698,969	616,495	92.9%
Alabama	7	4,062,608	580,373	98.6%
Louisiana	7	4,238,216	605,459	94.6%
Minnesota	8	4,387,029	548,379	104.4%
Maryland	8	4,798,622	599,828	95.4%
Washington	9	4,887,941	543,105	105.4%
Tennessee	9	4,896,641	544,071	105.2%
Wisconsin	9	4,906,745	545,194	105.0%
Missouri	9	5,137,804	570,867	100.3%
Indiana	10	5,564,228	556,423	102.9%
Massachusetts	10	6,029,051	602,905	95.0%
Virginia	11	6,216,568	565,143	101.3%
Georgia	11	6,508,419	591,674	96.8%
North Carolina	12	6,657,630	554,803	103.2%
New Jersey	13	7,748,634	596,049	96.0%
Michigan	16	9,328,784	583,049	98.2%
Ohio	19	10,887,325	573,017	99.9%
Illinois	20	11,466,682	573,334	99.8%
Pennsylvania	21	11,924,710	567,843	100.8%
Florida	23	13,003,362	565,364	101.3%
Texas	30	17,059,805	568,660	100.7%
New York	31	18,044,505	582,081	98.3%
California	52	29,839,250	573,832	99.8%

Table 5.28: Representation in 2000 (50 States)

State	Seats	Population	Pop. Per Rep.	Voting Power
United States	*435*	*281,424,177*	*646,952*	*100.0%*
Wyoming	1	495,304	495,304	130.6%
Vermont	1	609,890	609,890	106.1%
Alaska	1	628,933	628,933	102.9%
North Dakota	1	643,756	643,756	100.5%
South Dakota	1	756,874	756,874	85.5%
Delaware	1	785,068	785,068	82.4%
Montana	1	905,316	905,316	71.5%
Rhode Island	2	1,049,662	524,831	123.3%
Hawaii	2	1,216,642	608,321	106.4%
New Hampshire	2	1,238,415	619,208	104.5%
Maine	2	1,277,731	638,866	101.3%
Idaho	2	1,297,274	648,637	99.7%
Nebraska	3	1,715,369	571,790	113.1%
West Virginia	3	1,813,077	604,359	107.0%
New Mexico	3	1,823,821	607,940	106.4%
Nevada	3	2,002,032	667,344	96.9%
Utah	3	2,236,714	745,571	86.8%
Arkansas	4	2,679,733	669,933	96.6%
Kansas	4	2,693,824	673,456	96.1%
Mississippi	4	2,852,927	713,232	90.7%
Iowa	5	2,931,923	586,385	110.3%
Connecticut	5	3,409,535	681,907	94.9%
Oregon	5	3,428,543	685,709	94.3%
Oklahoma	5	3,458,819	691,764	93.5%
South Carolina	6	4,025,061	670,844	96.4%
Kentucky	6	4,049,431	674,905	95.9%
Colorado	7	4,311,882	615,983	105.0%
Alabama	7	4,461,130	637,304	101.5%
Louisiana	7	4,480,271	640,039	101.1%
Minnesota	8	4,925,670	615,709	105.1%
Arizona	8	5,140,683	642,585	100.7%
Maryland	8	5,307,886	663,486	97.5%
Wisconsin	8	5,371,210	671,401	96.4%
Missouri	9	5,606,260	622,918	103.9%
Tennessee	9	5,700,037	633,337	102.1%
Washington	9	5,908,684	656,520	98.5%
Indiana	9	6,090,782	676,754	95.6%
Massachusetts	10	6,355,568	635,557	101.8%
Virginia	11	7,100,702	645,518	100.2%
North Carolina	13	8,067,673	620,590	104.2%
Georgia	13	8,206,975	631,306	102.5%
New Jersey	13	8,424,354	648,027	99.8%
Michigan	15	9,955,829	663,722	97.5%
Ohio	18	11,374,540	631,919	102.4%
Pennsylvania	19	12,300,670	647,404	99.9%
Illinois	19	12,439,042	654,686	98.8%
Florida	25	16,028,890	641,156	100.9%
New York	29	19,004,973	655,344	98.7%
Texas	32	20,903,994	653,250	99.0%
California	53	33,930,798	640,204	101.1%

Table 5.29: Representation in 2010 (50 States)

State	Seats	Population	Pop. Per Rep.	Voting Power
United States	435	309,183,463	710,767	100.0%
Wyoming	1	568,300	568,300	125.1%
Vermont	1	630,337	630,337	112.8%
North Dakota	1	675,905	675,905	105.2%
Alaska	1	721,523	721,523	98.5%
South Dakota	1	819,761	819,761	86.7%
Delaware	1	900,877	900,877	78.9%
Montana	1	994,416	994,416	71.5%
Rhode Island	2	1,055,247	527,624	134.7%
New Hampshire	2	1,321,445	660,723	107.6%
Maine	2	1,333,074	666,537	106.6%
Hawaii	2	1,366,862	683,431	104.0%
Idaho	2	1,573,499	786,750	90.3%
Nebraska	3	1,831,825	610,608	116.4%
West Virginia	3	1,859,815	619,938	114.7%
New Mexico	3	2,067,273	689,091	103.1%
Nevada	4	2,709,432	677,358	104.9%
Utah	4	2,770,765	692,691	102.6%
Kansas	4	2,863,813	715,953	99.3%
Arkansas	4	2,926,229	731,557	97.2%
Mississippi	4	2,978,240	744,560	95.5%
Iowa	4	3,053,787	763,447	93.1%
Connecticut	5	3,581,628	716,326	99.2%
Oklahoma	5	3,764,882	752,976	94.4%
Oregon	5	3,848,606	769,721	92.3%
Kentucky	6	4,350,606	725,101	98.0%
Louisiana	6	4,553,962	758,994	93.6%
South Carolina	7	4,645,975	663,711	107.1%
Alabama	7	4,802,982	686,140	103.6%
Colorado	7	5,044,930	720,704	98.6%
Minnesota	8	5,314,879	664,360	107.0%
Wisconsin	8	5,698,230	712,279	99.8%
Maryland	8	5,789,929	723,741	98.2%
Missouri	8	6,011,478	751,435	94.6%
Tennessee	9	6,375,431	708,381	100.3%
Arizona	9	6,412,700	712,522	99.8%
Indiana	9	6,501,582	722,398	98.4%
Massachusetts	9	6,559,644	728,849	97.5%
Washington	10	6,753,369	675,337	105.2%
Virginia	11	8,037,736	730,703	97.3%
New Jersey	12	8,807,501	733,958	96.8%
North Carolina	13	9,565,781	735,829	96.6%
Georgia	14	9,727,566	694,826	102.3%
Michigan	14	9,911,626	707,973	100.4%
Ohio	16	11,568,495	723,031	98.3%
Pennsylvania	18	12,734,905	707,495	100.5%
Illinois	18	12,864,380	714,688	99.5%
Florida	27	18,900,773	700,029	101.5%
New York	27	19,421,055	719,298	98.8%
Texas	36	25,268,418	701,901	101.3%
California	53	37,341,989	704,566	100.9%

Table 5.30: Representation in 2020 (50 States)

State	Seats	Population	Pop. Per Rep.	Voting Power
United States	435	331,108,434	761,169	100.0%
Wyoming	1	577,719	577,719	131.8%
Vermont	1	643,503	643,503	118.3%
Alaska	1	736,081	736,081	103.4%
North Dakota	1	779,702	779,702	97.6%
South Dakota	1	887,770	887,770	85.7%
Delaware	1	990,837	990,837	76.8%
Montana	2	1,085,407	542,704	140.3%
Rhode Island	2	1,098,163	549,082	138.6%
Maine	2	1,363,582	681,791	111.6%
New Hampshire	2	1,379,089	689,545	110.4%
Hawaii	2	1,460,137	730,069	104.3%
West Virginia	2	1,795,045	897,523	84.8%
Idaho	2	1,841,377	920,689	82.7%
Nebraska	3	1,963,333	654,444	116.3%
New Mexico	3	2,120,220	706,740	107.7%
Kansas	4	2,940,865	735,216	103.5%
Mississippi	4	2,963,914	740,979	102.7%
Arkansas	4	3,013,756	753,439	101.0%
Nevada	4	3,108,462	777,116	97.9%
Iowa	4	3,192,406	798,102	95.4%
Utah	4	3,275,252	818,813	93.0%
Connecticut	5	3,608,298	721,660	105.5%
Oklahoma	5	3,963,516	792,703	96.0%
Oregon	6	4,241,500	706,917	107.7%
Kentucky	6	4,509,342	751,557	101.3%
Louisiana	6	4,661,468	776,911	98.0%
Alabama	7	5,030,053	718,579	105.9%
South Carolina	7	5,124,712	732,102	104.0%
Minnesota	8	5,709,752	713,719	106.6%
Colorado	8	5,782,171	722,771	105.3%
Wisconsin	8	5,897,473	737,184	103.3%
Missouri	8	6,160,281	770,035	98.8%
Maryland	8	6,185,278	773,160	98.4%
Indiana	9	6,790,280	754,476	100.9%
Tennessee	9	6,916,897	768,544	99.0%
Massachusetts	9	7,033,469	781,497	97.4%
Arizona	9	7,158,923	795,436	95.7%
Washington	10	7,715,946	771,595	98.6%
Virginia	11	8,654,542	786,777	96.7%
New Jersey	12	9,294,493	774,541	98.3%
Michigan	13	10,084,442	775,726	98.1%
North Carolina	14	10,453,948	746,711	101.9%
Georgia	14	10,725,274	766,091	99.4%
Ohio	15	11,808,848	787,257	96.7%
Illinois	17	12,822,739	754,279	100.9%
Pennsylvania	17	13,011,844	765,403	99.4%
New York	26	20,215,751	777,529	97.9%
Florida	28	21,570,527	770,376	98.8%
Texas	38	29,183,290	767,981	99.1%
California	52	39,576,757	761,091	100.0%

GLOSSARY

Article 1 of the Basic Law for the Federal Republic of Germany: This establishes that the duty to respect and protect inviolable and inalienable human rights is the duty of state authority.

Article 5 of the United States Constitution: This describes the method for amending the Constitution and for calling a Convention, which requires two-thirds of the House and Senate or two-thirds of the State Legislatures. Amendments to the Constitution become valid after the ratification by three-quarters of the States.

Article 20 of the Basic Law for the Federal Republic of Germany: This establishes Germany as a democratic state, with all authority being derived from the people.

Article 21 of the Basic Law for the Federal Republic of Germany: This establishes that political parties may be freely established, except for political parties that seek to undermine or abolish the democratic basic order.

Article 79 of the Basic Law for the Federal Republic of Germany: This describes the method of amending the Basic Law, which requires two-thirds of the Bundestag and 2/3 of the Bundesrat. The principles established in Article 1 and Article 20 may not be amended.

Battleground States: In presidential elections decided by the Electoral College, these are the competitive states which determine the winner. In 2024, the battleground states are Arizona, Georgia, Michigan, Nevada, North Carolina, Pennsylvania, and Wisconsin.

Bicameral Legislature: A legislature with two chambers. In the U.S., the Congress is comprised of the House of Representatives and the Senate. In the UK, Parliament is comprised of the House of Commons and the House of Lords.

Constitutional Republic: A state in which the chief executive and representatives are elected, and the rules are established in a written document.

Civil War Amendments: The 13th, 14th, and 15th Amendments to the Constitution were ratified between 1865 and 1870. Collectively, these amendments abolished slavery (except for convicted criminals), established birthright citizenship and equal protection under the law for all citizens, and prohibited discrimination in voting rights on the basis of race.

Droop Quota: A method of determining the electoral threshold in multimember districts using ranked choice voting, also known as single transferable vote. The Droop Quota is calculated by dividing 100% by the number of available seats plus 1. For example, in a 4 seat district, the electoral threshold is calculated as 100% / (4+1) = 20%. See Single Transferable Vote.

Electoral College: The historic method of electing the President. Each state is allocated a number of electors equal to the combined total of its Representatives and Senators. States determine how to choose their electors, with most states using a winner-take-all method. Two states, Nebraska and Maine, award two electors to the statewide winner and one elector for each congressional district won by each presidential candidate.

Entrenched Clause: A clause in a constitution that is more difficult or impossible to amend.

Federalism: A system of government with power divided between a federal government and several regional governments. In the United States, the federal government, based in Washington, D.C., is paramount to the fifty state governments.

Filibuster: A legislative procedure used to delay or prevent a vote from taking place on a given issue.

Four Territories: Guam, the Northern Mariana Islands, the U.S. Virgin Islands, and American Samoa are island territories with a combined population of about 338,000. As of 2024, they have no representation in Congress.

Gerrymandering: The practice of drawing voting districts to favor one political party at the expense of the other political party, effectively allowing politicians to pick their constituents, instead of the other way around.

Jim Crow Laws: State and local laws passed between about 1880 and 1910 which enforced racial segregation and disenfranchised African Americans in many Southern states until the passage of the Civil Rights Act of 1964 and the Voting Rights Act of 1965.

Let the good of the people be the supreme law: English translation of the Latin phrase "Salus populi suprema lex esto." This phrase was used in 1942 by the White Rose, an anti-Nazi resistance group, in their Third Pamphlet, which called for the people of Germany to resist and disrupt the Nazi government in any way they could.

Method of Equal Proportions: The formula used by the Census Bureau to determine the number of representatives each state will have following each decennial census. The formula is: $PVn = State\ Population\ /\ \sqrt{(n(n\text{-}1))}$, where n is the number of seats the state would have if it received another seat.

Multimember District: A voting district in which multiple candidates can win office in the same election.

Random Lottery: A method of choosing delegates or representatives that is truly random. All citizens would be eligible and a select number would be chosen at random to represent the body politic.

Ranked Choice Voting: A voting system in which voters rank candidates in order of their preference. If a candidate receives a majority of first choice votes, they are declared the winner. If no candidate receives a majority of first choice votes, the last place candidate is eliminated. All first choice ballots cast for the last place candidate are counted instead for their next choice. Ballots that ranked only a candidate who has been eliminated are exhausted and removed from subsequent rounds of tabulation. This process is repeated until a candidate receives a majority of non-exhausted ballots.

Single-Member District: A voting district in which only one candidate may win office in a given election.

Single Transferable Vote: A proportional voting system that combines ranked choice voting with multimember districts. Ballots cast for winning candidates in surplus of the electoral threshold, or ballots cast for losing candidates, are transferred according to the preferences of each voter until the number of candidates equal to the number of seats exceed the electoral threshold. See Droop Quota.

Unicameral Legislature: A legislature with a single chamber. For example, Nebraska's legislature has only a Senate.

Urban-Rural Divide: The idea, both real and imagined, that there are different interests and political beliefs between Americans who live in urban areas and Americans who live in rural areas. This sentiment has existed throughout the entire history of the United States.

Winner Take All: The practice of awarding all of a state's electoral votes to the winner of the state's popular vote, instead of awarding electoral votes on the basis of proportionality. See Electoral College.

NOTES

CHAPTER 1: Justification

1 Thomas Jefferson, et al., "Declaration of Independence," National Archives, July 4, 1776, https://www.archives.gov/founding-docs/declaration-transcript.

2 "Constitution of the United States of America," National Archives, 1787, https://www.archives.gov/founding-docs/constitution-transcript.

3 Thomas Jefferson, "Thomas Jefferson to James Madison, 6 September 1789", National Archives, 1789, https://founders.archives.gov/?q=Ancestor%3ATSJN-01-15-02-0375&s=1511311111&r=3.

4 Jeffrey M. Jones, "Record Low in U.S. Satisfied With Way Democracy Is Working", Gallup, January 2024,   https://news.gallup.com/poll/548120/record-low-satisfied-democracy-working.aspx#:~:text=WASHINGTON%2C%20D.C.%20%2D%2D%20A%20new,is%20working%20in%20the%20country.

CHAPTER 2: Cynicism

5 Hannah Hartig, Andrew Daniller, Scott Keeter, and Ted Van Green, "Republican Gains in 2022 Midterms Driven Mostly by Turnout Advantage," Pew Research Center, July 2023, https://www.pewresearch.org/politics/2023/07/12/voter-turnout-2018-2022/.

CHAPTER 3: Let the Good of the People be the Supreme Law

6 Independence National Historical Park, "September 17, 1787: A Republic, If You Can Keep It," National Park Service, September 2023, https://www.nps.gov/articles/000/constitutionalconvention-september17.htm.

7 Winston Churchill, "The Worst Form of Government," WinstonChurchill.org, February 2016, https://winstonchurchill.org/resources/quotes/the-worst-form-of-government/.

8   Carl Boix, Michael Miller, and Sebastian Rosato, "A Complete Data Set of Political Regimes, 1800–2007," Comparative Political Studies, November 2012, https://doi.org/10.1177/0010414012463905.

9   Steven Mintz, "Winning the Vote: A History of Voting Rights," The Gilder Lehrman Institute of American History, https://www.gilderlehrman.org/history-resources/essays/winning-vote-history-voting-rights.

10   "Free and Slave Populations by State (1790)," Teaching American History, https://teachingamericanhistory.org/resource/the-constitutional-convention-free-and-slave-populations-by-state-1790/.

11   "Timeline of voting rights in the United States," Wikipedia, Wikimedia Foundation, July 2024, https://en.wikipedia.org/wiki/Timeline_of_voting_rights_in_the_United_States.

12   Christopher Uggen, Ryan Larson, Sarah Shannon, and Robert Stewart, "Locked Out 2022: Estimates of People Denied Voting Rights," The Sentencing Project, October 25, 2022, https://www.sentencingproject.org/reports/locked-out-2022-estimates-of-people-denied-voting-rights/.

13   Paul G. Kauper, "The Constitutions of West Germany and the United States: A Comparative Study," Michigan Law Review, 1960, https://repository.law.umich.edu/mlr/vol58/iss8/22/.

14   Translated by Christian Tomuschat, David P. Currie, Donald P. Kommers, and Raymond Kerr, "Basic Law for the Federal Republic of Germany," Federal Law Gazette, December 19, 2022, https://www.gesetze-im-internet.de/englisch_gg/englisch_gg.html.

15   "The Federal Republic of Germany (since 1949)," Deutscher Bundestag, https://www.bundestag.de/en/parliament/history/parliamentarism/frg_parliamentarism.

16   "1984 New Zealand general election," Wikipedia, Wikimedia Foundation, July 27, 2024, https://en.wikipedia.org/wiki/1984_New_Zealand_general_election.

17   "What is MMP?" Electoral Commission New Zealand, https://elections.nz/democracy-in-nz/what-is-new-zealands-system-of-government/what-is-mmp/.

18   "1996 and beyond—the road to MMP," Ministry for Culture & Heritage, April 14, 2021, https://nzhistory.govt.nz/politics/fpp-to-mmp/1996-and-beyond.

19   Maxwell L. Stearns, "Parliamentary America: The Least Radical Means of Radically Repairing Our Broken Democracy," John Hopkins University Press, Baltimore, MD, 2024. http://leedrutman.org/breaking-the-two-party-doom-loop.

20 Lee Drutman, "Breaking the Two-Party Doom Loop: The Case for Multiparty Democracy in America," Oxford University Press, New York, NY, 2020. http://leedrutman.org/breaking-the-two-party-doom-loop.

21 Lee Drutman, "How I updated my views on ranked choice voting," Undercurrent Events, September 18, 2023, https://leedrutman.substack.com/p/how-i-updated-my-views-on-ranked.

22 John M. Carey and Simon Hix, "The Electoral Sweet Spot: Low-Magnitude Proportional Electoral Systems," American Journal of Political Science, April 2011, https://onlinelibrary.wiley.com/doi/epdf/10.1111/j.1540-5907.2010.00495.x

23 "Entrenched Clauses," Oxford Constitutional Law, December 2021, https://oxcon.ouplaw.com/display/10.1093/law-mpeccol/law-mpeccol-e31.

24 Translated by Christian Tomuschat, David P. Currie, Donald P. Kommers, and Raymond Kerr, "Basic Law for the Federal Republic of Germany," Federal Law Gazette, December 19, 2022, https://www.gesetze-im-internet.de/englisch_gg/englisch_gg.html.

CHAPTER 4: Sunset the Senate

25 John D. Dingell, "I Served in Congress Longer Than Anyone. Here's How to Fix It." The Atlantic, December 4, 2018, https://www.theatlantic.com/ideas/archive/2018/12/john-dingell-how-restore-faith-government/577222/.

26 Carl Hulse, "Is the End of the Filibuster Near?" The New York Times, March 13, 2024, https://www.nytimes.com/2024/03/13/us/politics/filibuster-senate-manchin-sinema.html.

27 Eric W. Orts, "The Path to Give California 12 Senators, and Vermont Just One," The Atlantic, January 2, 2019, https://www.theatlantic.com/ideas/archive/2019/01/heres-how-fix-senate/579172/.

28 Jamelle Bouie, "There Are 100 People in America With Way Too Much Power," The New York Times, July 23, 2022, https://www.nytimes.com/2022/07/23/opinion/senate-power-amendment.html.

29 "File:Combined—Control of the U.S. House of Representatives – Control of the U.S. Senate.png," Wikimedia Commons, December 20, 2022, https://commons.wikimedia.org/wiki/File:Combined--Control_of_the_U.S._House_of_Representatives_-_Control_of_the_U.S._Senate.png.

CHAPTER 5: Equal and Universal Representation
in an Expanded Congress

30 Steven Manson, Jonathan Schroeder, David van Riper, Katherine Knowles, Tracy Kugler, Finn Roberts, and Steven Ruggles, IPUMS National Historical Geographic Information System: Version 18.0 [dataset]. Minneapolis, MN: IPUMS. 2023. http://doi.org/10.18128/D050.V18.0 U.S. Census Data 1790–1860.

31 "Decennial Census of Population and Housing by Decades," United States Census Bureau, 2024, https://www.census.gov/programs-surveys/decennial-census/decade.html.

32 "Apportionment Legislation 1790–1830," United States Census Bureau, https://www.census.gov/history/www/reference/apportionment/apportionment_legislation_1790_-_1830.html.

33 "Apportionment Legislation 1840–1880," United States Census Bureau, https://www.census.gov/history/www/reference/apportionment/apportionment_legislation_1840_-_1880.html.

34 "Methods of Apportionment," United States Census Bureau, https://www.census.gov/history/www/reference/apportionment/methods_of_apportionment.html#jefferson.

35 "Native American Voting Rights," Library of Congress, https://www.loc.gov/classroom-materials/elections/right-to-vote/voting-rights-for-native-americans/.

36 Steven Levitsky and Daniel Ziblatt, "Tyranny of the Minority," Penguin Books Limited, 2023, page 76. https://www.gov.harvard.edu/2024/02/05/tyranny-of-the-minority/.

37 Steven Levitsky and Daniel Ziblatt, "Tyranny of the Minority," Penguin Books Limited, 2023, pages 76-77. https://www.gov.harvard.edu/2024/02/05/tyranny-of-the-minority/.

38 Steven Levitsky and Daniel Ziblatt, "Tyranny of the Minority," Penguin Books Limited, 2023, page 81. https://www.gov.harvard.edu/2024/02/05/tyranny-of-the-minority/.

39 Steven Levitsky and Daniel Ziblatt, "Tyranny of the Minority," Penguin Books Limited, 2023, page 91. https://www.gov.harvard.edu/2024/02/05/tyranny-of-the-minority/.

40 Walter Reynolds Farley, "100 years ago, Congress threw out results of the census," The Conversation, February 4, 2020, https://theconversation.com/100-years-ago-congress-threw-out-results-of-the-census-129954.

41 "Apportionment Legislation 1890 – Present," United States Census Bureau, https://www.census.gov/history/www/reference/apportionment/apportionment_legislation_1890_-_present.html.

42 "2020 Census Apportionment: Presentation for Public Distribution," United States Census Bureau, https://www2.census.gov/programs-surveys/decennial/2020/data/apportionment/presentation-2020-census-apportionment-results.pdf.

43 "Plebiscito Resultados Isla," Comisión Estatal de Elecciones, November 7, 2020, https://elecciones2020.ceepur.org/Noche_del_Evento_92/index.html#es/default/PLEBISCITO_Resumen.xml.

44 Rebecca Hersher, "D.C. Votes Overwhelmingly To Become 51st State," NPR, November 9, 2016, https://www.npr.org/sections/thetwo-way/2016/11/09/501412360/d-c-votes-overwhelmingly-to-become-51st-state.

45 Eleanor Homes Norton, "Norton responds to incorrect assertion that 23rd Amendment must be repealed before D.D. can be granted statehood," Office of Congresswoman Eleanor Holmes Norton, April 30, 2021, https://norton.house.gov/media-center/press-releases/norton-responds-to-incorrect-assertion-that-23rd-amendment-must-be.

46 "Return the House of Representatives to the People," Thirty-thousand.org, February 1, 2022, https://thirty-thousand.org/overview/.

47 "Decennial Census Historical Facts," United States Census Bureau, October 8, 2021, https://www.census.gov/history/www/through_the_decades/fast_facts/1790_fast_facts.html.

48 Matthew S. Shugart, "Economix: Expand the U.S. House," Fruits and Votes, July 1, 2014, https://fruitsandvotes.wordpress.com/2014/01/07/economix-expand-the-us-house/.

49. "2023 National Population Projections Datasets," United States Census Bureau, November 9, 2023, https://www.census.gov/data/datasets/2023/demo/popproj/2023-popproj.html.

CHAPTER 6: End of the Two-Party SystemThrough
Proportional Ranked Choice Voting

50 "Americans' Dismal Views of the Nation's Politics," Pew Research Center, September 19, 2023, https://www.pewresearch.org/politics/2023/09/19/the-republican-and-democratic-parties/.

51 Gabriel Borelli, "Support for more political parties in the U.S. is higher among adults under age 50," Pew Research Center, October 19, 2023, https://www.pewresearch.org/short-reads/2023/10/19/support-for-more-political-parties-in-the-u-s-is-higher-among-adults-under-age-50/.

52 Lee Drutman, "How I updated my views on ranked choice voting," Undercurrent Events, September 18, 2023, https://leedrutman.substack.com/p/how-i-updated-my-views-on-ranked.

53 "Proportional RCV Information," FairVote, 2024, https://fairvote.org/our-reforms/proportional-ranked-choice-voting-information.

54 "Proportional Ranked Choice Voting," FairVote, 2024, https://fairvote.org/our-reforms/proportional-ranked-choice-voting/.

55 "RCV Detailed Report," State of Alaska Division of Elections, November 30, 2022, https://www.elections.alaska.gov/results/22GENR/US%20REP.pdf.

56 Arend Peter Castelein, "Alaska mobilized the nation around Ranked Choice Voting – for better or worse:" Equal Vote, https://rcvchangedalaska.com/.

CHAPTER 7: The New Maps: National Analysis

57 "Published Maps," Dave's Redistricting, 2024, https://davesredistricting.org/maps#list::Published-Maps,filter::polemic.

58 "Welcome to Dave's Redistricting," Dave's Redistricting, 2024, https://davesredistricting.org/maps#home.

59 "Published Maps," Dave's Redistricting, 2024, https://davesredistricting.org/maps#list::Published-Maps,filter::polemic.

60 "Welcome to Dave's Redistricting," Dave's Redistricting, 2024, https://davesredistricting.org/maps#home.

61 Lydia Saad, "Public Interest in having a Third Major Party Dips to 56%," Gallup, October 6, 2022, https://news.gallup.com/poll/402515/public-interest-having-third-major-party-dips.aspx.

62 "As Partisan Hostility Grow, Signs of Frustration with the Two-Party System," Pew Research Center, August 9, 2022, https://www.pewresearch.org/politics/2022/08/09/the-two-party-system-and-views-of-differences-between-the-republican-and-democratic-parties.

CHAPTER 8. The New Maps: State-by-State Analysis

63 "Party affiliation among adults in the South by race/ethnicity," Pew Research Center, 2014, https://www.pewresearch.org/religious-landscape-study/database/compare/party-affiliation/by/racial-and-ethnic-composition/among/region/south/.

64 "Party affiliation among adults in Alabama," Pew Research Center, 2014, https://www.pewresearch.org/religious-landscape-study/database/state/alabama/party-affiliation/.

65 "Redistricting Litigation Roundup," Brennan Center for Justice, published December 20, 2021, updated August 9, 2024, https://www.brennancenter.org/our-work/research-reports/redistricting-litigation-roundup-0.

66 Michael Li, "Gerrymandering Returns to North Carolina," Brennan Center for Justice, May 2, 2023, https://www.brennancenter.org/our-work/analysis-opinion/gerrymandering-returns-north-carolina.

67 Zach Montellaro, Josh Gerstein, and Ally Mutnick, "North Carolina Supreme Court clears way for partisan gerrymandering," Politico, April 28, 2023, https://www.politico.com/news/2023/04/28/north-carolina-supreme-court-clears-way-for-partisan-gerrymandering-00094433.

68 "Chicago metropolitan area," Wikipedia, Wikimedia Foundation, September 26, 2024, https://en.wikipedia.org/wiki/Chicago_metropolitan_area.

69 "Delaware Valley," Wikipedia, Wikimedia Foundation, September 23, 2024, https://en.wikipedia.org/wiki/Delaware_Valley.

70 "Greater Pittsburgh," Wikipedia, Wikimedia Foundation, August 15, 2024, https://en.wikipedia.org/wiki/Greater_Pittsburgh.

71 Brian Mann, "Republicans won House seats in blue New York. Those wins could help shape Congress," NPR, December 3, 2022, https://www.npr.org/2022/12/03/1139399457/republican-house-wins-new-york.

72 "Economy of Texas," Wikipedia, Wikimedia Foundation, September 10, 2024, https://en.wikipedia.org/wiki/Economy_of_Texas.

73 "California Remains the World's 5th Largest Economy," Office of Governor Gavin Newsom, April 16, 2024, https://www.gov.ca.gov/2024/04/16/california-remains-the-worlds-5th-largest-economy/.

CHAPTER 9. Strengthen the Checks on Executive Power

74 John Dickerson, "The Hardest Job in the World," The Atlantic, May 2018, https://theatlantic.com/magazine//archive/2018/05/a-broken-office/556883/.

CHAPTER 10. Elect the President by Ranked Choice Popular Vote

75 Elaine Kamarck, "What happens If Trump and Biden Tie in the Electoral College?" The Brookings Institute, October 21, 2020, https://www.brookings.edu/articles/what-happens-if-trump-and-biden-tie-in-the-electoral-college/.

76 "117th United States Congress," Wikipedia, Wikimedia Foundation, September 1, 2024, https://en.wikipedia.org/wiki/117th_United_States_Congress#Party_summary.

CHAPTER 11. The New Politics of Multiparty America

77 Doris Kearns Goodwin, "Team of Rivals: The Political Genius of Abraham Lincoln," Simon & Schuster, New York, 2006, pgs, 237–256. https://www.simonandschuster.com/books/Team-of-Rivals/Doris-Kearns-Goodwin/9780743270755.

78 "New Democrat Coalition," Wikipedia, Wikimedia Foundation, August 31, 2024, https://en.wikipedia.org/wiki/New_Democrat_Coalition.

79 "Congressional Progressive Caucus," Wikipedia, Wikimedia Foundation, September 20, 2024, https://en.wikipedia.org/wiki/Congressional_Progressive_Caucus.

80 "Freedom Caucus," Wikipedia, Wikimedia Foundation, September 20, 2024, https://en.wikipedia.org/wiki/Freedom_Caucus.

81 "Problem Solvers Caucus," Wikipedia, Wikimedia Foundation, September 7, 2024, https://en.wikipedia.org/wiki/Problem_Solvers_Caucus.

82 "Voter Turnout by Election," Washington Secretary of State, 2024, https://www.sos.wa.gov/elections/data-research/election-data-and-maps/reports-data-and-statistics/voter-turnout-election.

83 "November 8, 2022 General Election Results," Office of the Secretary of State, November 29, 2022, https://results.vote.wa.gov/results/20221108/legislative-all.html.

84 Daniel Beekman, "New WA district shifts spotlight to Yakima Valley's Latino voters," The Seattle Times, August 4, 2024, https://www.seattletimes.com/seattle-news/politics/new-wa-district-shifts-spotlight-to-yakima-valleys-latino-voters.

85 "2016 Republican Party presidential debates and forums," Wikipedia, Wikimedia Foundation, September 5, 2024, https://en.wikipedia.org/wiki/2016_Republican_Party_presidential_debates_and_forums.

86 "2020 Democratic party presidential primaries," Wikipedia, Wikimedia Foundation, September 20, 2024, https://en.wikipedia.org/wiki/2020_Democratic_Party_presidential_primaries.

CHAPTER 12: Relegitimize the Court

87 Thomas A. Donovan, "'John Marshall Has Made His Decision, Now Let Him Enforce It'—Attributed to President Andrew Jackson, 1832," The Federal Lawyer, September 2012, https://www.fedbar.org/wp-content/uploads/2012/09/sidebar-sep12-pdf-1.pdf.

88 "Dobbs v. Jackson Women's Health Organization," 597 U.S. 2022, page 5, https://www.supremecourt.gov/opinions/21pdf/19-1392_6j37.pdf.

89 "Period Life Table, 2021, as used in the 2024 Trustees Report," Social Security Administration, 2024, https://www.ssa.gov/oact/STATS/table4c6.html.

90 Justin Elliott, Joshua Kaplan, and Alex Mierjeski, "Justice Samuel Alito Took Luxury Fishing Vacation With GOP Billionaire Show Later Had Cases Before the Court," ProPublica, June 20, 2023, https://www.propublica.org/article/samuel-alito-luxury-fishing-trip-paul-singer-scotus-supreme-court.

91 Jodi Kantor, "At Justice Alito's House, a 'Stop the Steal' Symbol on Display," The New York Times, May 16, 2024, https://www.nytimes.com/2024/05/16/us/justice-alito-upside-down-flag.html.

92 Joshua Kaplan, Justin Elliott, and Alex Mierjeski, "Clarence Thomas and the Billionaire," ProPublica, April 6, 2023, https://www.propublica.org/article/clarence-thomas-scotus-undisclosed-luxury-travel-gifts-crow.

93 Joshua Kaplan, Justin Elliott, and Alex Mierjeski, "Clarence Thomas Had a Child in Private School. Harlan Crow Paid the Tuition." ProPublica, May 4, 2023, https://www.propublica.org/article/clarence-thomas-harlan-crow-private-school-tuition-scotus.

94 Justin Elliott, Joshua Kaplan, and Alex Mierjeski, "Billionaire Harlan Crow Bought Property From Clarence Thomas. The Justice Didn't Disclose the Deal." ProPublica, April 13, 2023, https://www.propublica.org/article/clarence-thomas-harlan-crow-real-estate-scotus.

95 Bob Woodward and Robert Costa, "Virginia Thomas urged White House chief to pursue unrelenting efforts to overturn the 2020 election, texts show," The Washington Post, March 23, 2022, https://www.washingtonpost.com/politics/2022/03/24/virginia-thomas-mark-meadows-texts/.

96 Ian Millhiser, "The Supreme Court breaks with Trump on January 6," Vox, January 19, 2022, https://www.vox.com/2022/1/19/22892248/supreme-court-january-6-trump-thompson-commitee-subpoena.

97 Mark Sherman, "The Supreme Court allows Jan. 6 committee to get Trump documents," The Associated Press, January 19, 2022, https://apnews.com/article/us-supreme-court-congress-donald-trump-30d5d01db49f0591d641d9e92d4092a8.

98 Martin Pengelly and Joan E. Greve, "Amy Coney Barrett claims supreme court 'not comprised of partisan hacks,'" The Guardian, September 13, 2021, https://www.theguardian.com/us-news/2021/sep/13/amy-coney-barrett-supreme-court-not-partisan-hacks-abortion.

99 Leah Litman, "Something's Rotten About the Justices Taking So Long on Trump's Immunity Case," The New York Times, June 19, 2024, https://www.nytimes.com/2024/06/19/opinion/supreme-court-trump-immunity.html.

100 Mark A. Lemley, "The Imperial Supreme Court," Harvard Law Review, November 2022, https://harvardlawreview.org/forum/vol-136/the-imperial-supreme-court/.

101 Adam Serwer, "The Supreme Court Fools Itself," The Atlantic, July 24, 2024, https://theatlantic.com/politics/archive/2024/07/roberts-supreme-court-2024-termm/678983/.

CHAPTER 13: The Quarter Millennium Convention of 2026

102 "Constitution of the United States (1787)," National Archives, April 10, 2024, https://www.archives.gov/milestone-documents/constitution.

103 Dylan Matthews, "Can randomly selected citizens govern better than elected officials?" Vox, January 12, 2022, https://www.vox.com/future-perfect/22878118/jury-duty-citizens-assembly-lottocracy-open-democracy.

CHAPTER 14: And So It Goes

104 Associated Press, "Leader of the pro-Trump Project 2025 suggests there will be a new American Revolution," Politico, July 4, 2024, https://www.politico.com/news/2024/07/04/leader-of-the-pro-trump-project-2025-suggests-there-will-be-a-new-american-revolution-00166583.

105 Frank Herbert, "Dune," the Penguin Group, 1965, page 408, https://www.
     penguinrandomhouse.ca/books/352036/dune-by-frank-herbert/9780441013593/
     excerpt.

106 Francis Ford Coppola, director, Megalopolis, Liongate, 2024, https://www.vulture.
     com/article/review-francis-ford-coppolas-megalopolis-is-totally-nuts.html.

RESOURCES

Democracy requires dialogue.

Get in touch with Zane at one of these platforms:

Email:	polemicfordemocracy@gmail.com
Instagram:	impolitiksubstack
X:	zane_gustafson
Substack:	impolitik.substack.com

Other platforms will be added here:

https://linktr.ee/zanegustafson